BISHOPS BY BALLOT

BISHOPS
BY
BALLOT

AN EIGHTEENTH-CENTURY
ECCLESIASTICAL REVOLUTION

THE FRANK S. and ELIZABETH D. BREWER

PRIZE ESSAY FOR 1975

The American Society of Church History

FREDERICK V. MILLS, SR.

NEW YORK · OXFORD UNIVERSITY PRESS · 1978

Copyright © 1978 by Oxford University Press, Inc.
Library of Congress Cataloging in Publication Data

Mills, Frederick V., 1931–
   Bishops by ballot.

   Bibliography: p.
   Includes index.

   1. Church of England in America—Bishops.
2. Bishops—Appointment, call, and election—
History. I. Title.

BX5881.M55   262'.12   78-857
ISBN 0-19-502411-7

Printed in the United States of America

To My Parents
James Henry Mills, Sr.
and
Lillian May Vandever

:aders, to ascertain their reaction to resident bishops both
re and after the war.

careful examination of the American Anglican commu-
in the 1760s and 1780s reveals an extensive, and in places
tensive, internal controversy over episcopacy. Some Angli-
saw the prewar proposal for a bishop as a possible "ecclesi-
l Stamp Act," and others were curious about who would
the candidates and how bishops would be supported
cially. All were concerned about what powers a resident
p might or might not possess. But the most determined
sition came from the colonies where the church was larg-
d legally established. In these areas the major fear gener-
opposition to a bishop, whom many saw as an agent of
and parliament, was that he might interfere with estab-
ecclesiastical practices and customs. Also, the hierarchical
cter of the episcopal office was a major objection in both
rewar and postwar decades among Anglicans as well as
ters. But the idea of a "primitive episcopate" did not
ke anywhere near the hostility that the concept of a tradi-
English-style episcopate produced. After the war and the
ablishment of the church in the southern states, some of
me churchmen who opposed the episcopal scheme in the
participated in the reorganization of the church, which
ed the election of candidates to the office of bishop. But
39 the Protestant Episcopal church had adopted a repub-
ype ecclesiastical constitution which permitted the parish
o elect by democratic process delegates who, in equal
er with the clergy, would vote in convention to elect by
ty ballot the episcopal candidates. Then opposition to
pacy, for whatever reason, virtually disappeared among
imen as well as among the Congregationalists and Pres-
ns. In essence the modification of English-style episco-
o suit republican Americans was an ecclesiastical counter-
the political main event.

inderstand the how and why of this concept of elective
pacy one needs to examine the church's colonial experi-

Preface

The American Revolution was the most productive era for political and constitutional activity in the history of the republic.
Within the quarter-century following the Treaty of Paris in
1763—which terminated the French and Indian War in the
New World as well as the Seven Years' War in Europe—and
ending with the ratification of the Constitution of the United
States in 1789, there occurred the most intense political discussion in American history. Out of this epoch emerged a revolutionary ideology and a succession of events that brought the
separate and individualistic colonies to unite in a confederation, organize respective state governments, and defy successfully the greatest military power of the day. By 1789 the revolutionary character of the era was revealed in the Constitution,
which showed how certain abstract doctrines such as the rights
of man and the sovereignty of the people could be reduced to
practice by assemblages of levelheaded gentlemen exercising
constituent power in the name of the people. Through this
process the power of the Revolution was managed and a foundation provided for the freedom that was the ultimate concern
of the Revolution.

While the political and constitutional phases of the American
Revolution have been studied extensively, the ecclesiastical
phase has received far less attention. It is, therefore, the aim of
this study to focus upon one part of this period's ecclesiastical
history—the Church of England in America—and to demonstrate that at the same time the civil revolution was under way
there was also an ecclesiastical revolution occurring within the
oldest continuous church communion in the English part of the
New World. Like the states, the Anglican church in America

had been related to the mother country, but the war ended that official connection. In many respects American Anglicanism had grown up with the people and in the revolutionary generation shared many similar experiences with the people and the nation. For example, its communicants, like the populace in general, divided over the issue of independence into Patriots, Loyalists, and Neutralists. Then in 1783, those churchmen who supported the founding of the new nation frequently found themselves in positions of leadership in church as well as in their respective states and the nation. Under the leadership of these churchmen the remnants of the Church of England in the United States fashioned the Protestant Episcopal Church.

One issue, episcopacy, symbolizes more than any other the internal conflict through which the Anglican church in America passed to become the Protestant Episcopal Church. The British government and the Church of England had come to consider the thirteen colonies to be within the diocese of the Bishop of London and thus a part of the national religious establishment. In the Church of England, bishops were appointed by the king (or queen), consecrated by their spiritual peers, and served church and state as spiritual "Lords of the Realm." Indeed, the salient feature in the ecclesiastical structure of the national church was episcopacy. However, when efforts were made in the eighteenth century to procure bishops for the colonies, they failed, but not without focusing considerable attention upon the issue in the colonies and England. It was, moreover, an episcopal scheme evolved by a coterie of zealous Anglican clergy in Connecticut, New York, and New Jersey to secure a resident episcopate in the 1760s that triggered a heated dispute over the issue at the very time political tensions were running high over the Stamp Act. Although the religious controversy became intertwined with the political one, it was fought out mainly between its own instigators and spokesmen for the New England Dissenters. But the episcopal controversy had widespread reverberations inside the Anglican communion because many churchmen, both

clergy and laity, from Massachusetts to Ge reservations about the timing of the scheme type of episcopate sought, the threat such pose to established practices, or a combinati Partly to mollify dissident churchmen, but m aroused Dissenters, the idea of a "primitive could only ordain, consecrate, and visit cle by the pro-episcopal committee as the typ desired. But in the late 1760s no one cou person to fill this office should or would be, selected, and whether the church hierarchy in England would seriously consider such a from English-style episcopacy.

Though the schemes to settle bishops in A colonial period have been the subject of tw neither examines the reaction of colonial A copal scheme of the 1760s. One book, Ar *Anglican Episcopate and the American Colonies,* focuses upon pro-episcopal forces in Englar gives only token recognition to Anglican o pacy in Virginia. The position taken by C *Mitre and Sceptre,* published in 1962, is es New England Dissenters who traditionall Bridenbaugh, however, goes far beyond C Anglican-Dissenter conflict, arguing that tl senters interpreted the efforts to procure of a conspiracy to subvert their liberties. I position to episcopacy was a major cause o lution. But it is Cross who notes, though that the episcopal issue was not settled Then American churchmen elected their liament temporarily lifted the oath of all from the consecration ritual for the Ame neither author evaluates the concept of ' or relates it to the postwar ecclesiastical either investigate the mainstay of the Ang

ence. First, the 169-year existence of the church in the relative
freedom and isolation of America encouraged deviations from
traditional English ecclesiastical polity. For example, the absence of a resident diocesan in America made impossible the
direct appointment of clergy to parishes by a bishop or, as in
the case of many parishes in England, by a nobleman who was
patron of a given cure. Further, most vestries and parishes in
the colonies claimed successfully the right to select their rector
or minister, even though more than one royal governor tried to
reclaim the prerogative as agent of the king. Then too, colonial
churchmen in the last years before the war were becoming
increasingly self-sufficient financially and were supplying an
increasing number of their own candidates trained in American colleges for Holy Orders. The investment by churchmen of
their talent, time, money, and men had developed a cumulative
and determinative influence upon their attitudes toward
church matters by the 1760s.

In addition, the development of the church under conditions
of the American environment conformed, though roughly at
times, to republican ideas that in time became part of the
church's life and style. The authority assumed by parishes and
vestries to accept or reject a given clergyman was translated in
some colonies into an annual vote to determine the minister's
retention or dismissal. Moreover, Anglican clergy, especially in
New England and the middle colonies, adopted the use of conventions in the absence of a bishop, much in the way that
Congregationalists and Presbyterians used associations and
presbyteries respectively as forums in which to discuss church
policy. Strictly speaking, this was a clear departure from episcopal polity, in which only a bishop could convene or authorize to
be convened such a meeting. In these conventions the clergy
elected a president and decided issues by majority vote. Thus it
was not without precedent that in the ecclesiastical crisis following the war former constituents of the Church of England in
America turned to colonial experience and practices to help
solve their problems. Many of these earlier practices were then

applied on a diocesan and national scale and defined in written ecclesiastical constitutions.

In short, this study is an inside view of the substitution and canonization of republican concepts and practices in place of hierarchical ones within one religious denomination. In the process the Protestant Episcopal Church was born, achieved its identity, and contributed a significant chapter to the annals of Church history.

The assistance of many kind friends has made possible the writing of this book. Richard S. Dunn of the University of Pennsylvania has been a constant source of encouragement from the dissertation stage to the present. In 1970 the American Philosophical Society provided a research grant that made possible a detailed study of the socioeconomic status of Anglicans in Pennsylvania. A grant from the Colonial Williamsburg Foundation in 1972 assisted greatly in studying the interrelatedness of church-state officeholding in colonial Virginia. During the last phase of the manuscript's development Professors Lefferts A. Loetscher of Princeton Theological Seminary and Horton Davies of Princeton University read and criticized major portions of the study. However, had it not been for James I. McCord, president of Princeton Theological Seminary, who appointed me a Visiting Fellow for 1973–1974, and Waights G. Henry, Jr., president of LaGrange College, who granted me a leave of absence to fill the appointment, the book could not have been completed. The selection of this manuscript by the Brewer Prize Committee of the American Society of Church History for its award in 1975 is gratefully acknowledged. Special appreciation is expressed to Charles A. Green for his meticulous evaluation of the typed manuscript. But for my wife, Antoinette, who remained faithful at every stage, my profoundest gratitude is reserved.

LaGrange College   Frederick V. Mills, Sr.
Georgia
March 1978

Contents

ence. First, the 169-year existence of the church in the relative freedom and isolation of America encouraged deviations from traditional English ecclesiastical polity. For example, the absence of a resident diocesan in America made impossible the direct appointment of clergy to parishes by a bishop or, as in the case of many parishes in England, by a nobleman who was patron of a given cure. Further, most vestries and parishes in the colonies claimed successfully the right to select their rector or minister, even though more than one royal governor tried to reclaim the prerogative as agent of the king. Then too, colonial churchmen in the last years before the war were becoming increasingly self-sufficient financially and were supplying an increasing number of their own candidates trained in American colleges for Holy Orders. The investment by churchmen of their talent, time, money, and men had developed a cumulative and determinative influence upon their attitudes toward church matters by the 1760s.

In addition, the development of the church under conditions of the American environment conformed, though roughly at times, to republican ideas that in time became part of the church's life and style. The authority assumed by parishes and vestries to accept or reject a given clergyman was translated in some colonies into an annual vote to determine the minister's retention or dismissal. Moreover, Anglican clergy, especially in New England and the middle colonies, adopted the use of conventions in the absence of a bishop, much in the way that Congregationalists and Presbyterians used associations and presbyteries respectively as forums in which to discuss church policy. Strictly speaking, this was a clear departure from episcopal polity, in which only a bishop could convene or authorize to be convened such a meeting. In these conventions the clergy elected a president and decided issues by majority vote. Thus it was not without precedent that in the ecclesiastical crisis following the war former constituents of the Church of England in America turned to colonial experience and practices to help solve their problems. Many of these earlier practices were then applied on a diocesan and national scale and defined in written ecclesiastical constitutions.

In short, this study is an inside view of the substitution and canonization of republican concepts and practices in place of hierarchical ones within one religious denomination. In the process the Protestant Episcopal Church was born, achieved its identity, and contributed a significant chapter to the annals of Church history.

The assistance of many kind friends has made possible the writing of this book. Richard S. Dunn of the University of Pennsylvania has been a constant source of encouragement from the dissertation stage to the present. In 1970 the American Philosophical Society provided a research grant that made possible a detailed study of the socioeconomic status of Anglicans in Pennsylvania. A grant from the Colonial Williamsburg Foundation in 1972 assisted greatly in studying the interrelatedness of church-state officeholding in colonial Virginia. During the last phase of the manuscript's development Professors Lefferts A. Loetscher of Princeton Theological Seminary and Horton Davies of Princeton University read and criticized major portions of the study. However, had it not been for James I. McCord, president of Princeton Theological Seminary, who appointed me a Visiting Fellow for 1973–1974, and Waights G. Henry, Jr., president of LaGrange College, who granted me a leave of absence to fill the appointment, the book could not have been completed. The selection of this manuscript by the Brewer Prize Committee of the American Society of Church History for its award in 1975 is gratefully acknowledged. Special appreciation is expressed to Charles A. Green for his meticulous evaluation of the typed manuscript. But for my wife, Antoinette, who remained faithful at every stage, my profoundest gratitude is reserved.

LaGrange College   Frederick V. Mills, Sr.
Georgia
March 1978

Contents

Preface

The American Revolution was the most productive era for political and constitutional activity in the history of the republic. Within the quarter-century following the Treaty of Paris in 1763—which terminated the French and Indian War in the New World as well as the Seven Years' War in Europe—and ending with the ratification of the Constitution of the United States in 1789, there occurred the most intense political discussion in American history. Out of this epoch emerged a revolutionary ideology and a succession of events that brought the separate and individualistic colonies to unite in a confederation, organize respective state governments, and defy successfully the greatest military power of the day. By 1789 the revolutionary character of the era was revealed in the Constitution, which showed how certain abstract doctrines such as the rights of man and the sovereignty of the people could be reduced to practice by assemblages of levelheaded gentlemen exercising constituent power in the name of the people. Through this process the power of the Revolution was managed and a foundation provided for the freedom that was the ultimate concern of the Revolution.

While the political and constitutional phases of the American Revolution have been studied extensively, the ecclesiastical phase has received far less attention. It is, therefore, the aim of this study to focus upon one part of this period's ecclesiastical history—the Church of England in America—and to demonstrate that at the same time the civil revolution was under way there was also an ecclesiastical revolution occurring within the oldest continuous church communion in the English part of the New World. Like the states, the Anglican church in America had been related to the mother country, but the war ended that official connection. In many respects American Anglicanism had grown up with the people and in the revolutionary generation shared many similar experiences with the people and the nation. For example, its communicants, like the populace in general, divided over the issue of independence into Patriots, Loyalists, and Neutralists. Then in 1783, those churchmen who supported the founding of the new nation frequently found themselves in positions of leadership in church as well as in their respective states and the nation. Under the leadership of these churchmen the remnants of the Church of England in the United States fashioned the Protestant Episcopal Church.

One issue, episcopacy, symbolizes more than any other the internal conflict through which the Anglican church in America passed to become the Protestant Episcopal Church. The British government and the Church of England had come to consider the thirteen colonies to be within the diocese of the Bishop of London and thus a part of the national religious establishment. In the Church of England, bishops were appointed by the king (or queen), consecrated by their spiritual peers, and served church and state as spiritual "Lords of the Realm." Indeed, the salient feature in the ecclesiastical structure of the national church was episcopacy. However, when efforts were made in the eighteenth century to procure bishops for the colonies, they failed, but not without focusing considerable attention upon the issue in the colonies and England. It was, moreover, an episcopal scheme evolved by a coterie of zealous Anglican clergy in Connecticut, New York, and New Jersey to secure a resident episcopate in the 1760s that triggered a heated dispute over the issue at the very time political tensions were running high over the Stamp Act. Although the religious controversy became intertwined with the political one, it was fought out mainly between its own instigators and spokesmen for the New England Dissenters. But the episcopal controversy had widespread reverberations inside the Anglican communion because many churchmen, both

clergy and laity, from Massachusetts to Georgia, evidenced
reservations about the timing of the scheme's promoters, the
type of episcopate sought, the threat such an official might
pose to established practices, or a combination of the three.
Partly to mollify dissident churchmen, but more to placate the
aroused Dissenters, the idea of a "primitive bishop" (one who
could only ordain, consecrate, and visit clergy) was set forth
by the pro-episcopal committee as the type of bishop they
desired. But in the late 1760s no one could state who the
person to fill this office should or would be, how he would be
selected, and whether the church hierarchy and government
in England would seriously consider such a drastic departure
from English-style episcopacy.

Though the schemes to settle bishops in America during the
colonial period have been the subject of two significant works,
neither examines the reaction of colonial Anglicans to the episcopal scheme of the 1760s. One book, Arthur L. Cross's *The
Anglican Episcopate and the American Colonies,* published in 1902,
focuses upon pro-episcopal forces in England and America and
gives only token recognition to Anglican opposition to episcopacy in Virginia. The position taken by Carl Bridenbaugh in
Mitre and Sceptre, published in 1962, is essentially that of the
New England Dissenters who traditionally opposed bishops.
Bridenbaugh, however, goes far beyond Cross and stresses the
Anglican-Dissenter conflict, arguing that the New England Dissenters interpreted the efforts to procure bishops as evidence
of a conspiracy to subvert their liberties. Indeed, Dissenter opposition to episcopacy was a major cause of the American Revolution. But it is Cross who notes, though in abbreviated form,
that the episcopal issue was not settled until after the war.
Then American churchmen elected their own bishops and parliament temporarily lifted the oath of allegiance to the crown
from the consecration ritual for the American candidates. But
neither author evaluates the concept of "primitive episcopacy"
or relates it to the postwar ecclesiastical settlement, nor does
either investigate the mainstay of the Anglican communion, the

lay leaders, to ascertain their reaction to resident bishops both before and after the war.

A careful examination of the American Anglican communion in the 1760s and 1780s reveals an extensive, and in places an intensive, internal controversy over episcopacy. Some Anglicans saw the prewar proposal for a bishop as a possible "ecclesiastical Stamp Act," and others were curious about who would select the candidates and how bishops would be supported financially. All were concerned about what powers a resident bishop might or might not possess. But the most determined opposition came from the colonies where the church was largest and legally established. In these areas the major fear generating opposition to a bishop, whom many saw as an agent of king and parliament, was that he might interfere with established ecclesiastical practices and customs. Also, the hierarchical character of the episcopal office was a major objection in both the prewar and postwar decades among Anglicans as well as Dissenters. But the idea of a "primitive episcopate" did not provoke anywhere near the hostility that the concept of a traditional English-style episcopate produced. After the war and the disestablishment of the church in the southern states, some of the same churchmen who opposed the episcopal scheme in the 1760s participated in the reorganization of the church, which included the election of candidates to the office of bishop. But by 1789 the Protestant Episcopal church had adopted a republican-type ecclesiastical constitution which permitted the parish laity to elect by democratic process delegates who, in equal number with the clergy, would vote in convention to elect by majority ballot the episcopal candidates. Then opposition to episcopacy, for whatever reason, virtually disappeared among churchmen as well as among the Congregationalists and Presbyterians. In essence the modification of English-style episcopacy to suit republican Americans was an ecclesiastical counterpart to the political main event.

To understand the how and why of this concept of elective episcopacy one needs to examine the church's colonial experi-

Illustrations

I

THE EPISCOPAL
CONTROVERSY

1763–1775

*That the Bishops to be sent to America, shall have no Authority, but
purely of a Spiritual and Ecclesiastical Nature, such as is derived
altogether from the Church and not from the State—That this Authority
shall operate only upon the clergy of the Church, and not upon the
Laiety nor Dissenters of any Denomination—That the Bishops shall not
interfere with the Property or Privileges, whether civil or religious, of
Churchmen or Dissenters—That, in particular, they shall have no Concern with the Probate of Wills, Letters of Guardianship and Administration, or Marriage-Licenses, nor be Judges of any Cases relating
thereto—But, that they shall only exercise the original Powers of their
Office as before stated, i.e. ordain and govern the Clergy, and administer Confirmation to those who shall desire it.*

An Appeal to the Public
Thomas Bradbury Chandler, 1767

*And indeed, my Friend, if this Scheme had been effected, it would have
overturned all our Acts of Assembly relative to ecclesiastical jurisdiction: most of which acts have received the Royal assent, and have
existed, amongst us, almost from the First establishment of the
Colony . . .*

*I profess my self a sincere Son of the Established Church; but I can
embrace her Doctrines, without approving of her Hierarchy, which I
know to be a Relick of the Papal Incroachment upon the Common Law.*

Col. Richard Bland to Thomas Adams,
August 1, 1771

1

The Anglican Church
in America

"My mission continues to flourish and increase."
                Rev. Mr. Andrews to Secretary
                of S.P.G. Wallingford, Connecticut,
                June 26, 1764

On January 9, 1770, William Tuckey, director of music for Trinity Church, New York City, conducted a benefit concert consisting of selections from George Frederick Handel's *Messiah*. In this first reported performance of Handel's oratorio in the New World Tuckey demonstrated his talent as a musical innovator. As early as the 1750s he had held singing classes two nights a week as part of his duties to Trinity Church and trained a choral group of fifty-six voices. For the dedication of St. Paul's Chapel in 1766 he conducted a program of vocal and instrumental music that received considerable acclaim. In his own right Tuckey was a prolific composer best known for "Psalm XXIV" and a noted organist who made excellent use of Trinity's organ, probably the first built in America, the craftsmanship of John Clemm of Philadelphia, Pennsylvania.[1] Indeed, while the hallelujahs of Handel's *Messiah* were reverberating within the nave of Trinity Church, the echoes could be heard throughout many parts of the Anglican Church's life in mainland America.

WORSHIP

Trinity Church, New York, was by no means the only Anglican Church in America with a penchant for church music. King's

Chapel, Boston, had been given the first pipe organ imported into America after the Brattle Square Church had rejected it from the intended donor, the Honorable Thomas Brattle, as unsuitable for its mode of worship. Christ Church, Boston, possessed a set of eight bells hung in the church tower, the finest in the colonies until they were superseded by the White-chapel bells of St. Michael's Church, Charleston, South Carolina. In Philadelphia, Christ and St. Peter's parish provided a charity choir school, and the press of Benjamin Franklin was prompt in reproducing the latest materials related to psalmody and hymnody. When St. Peter's Church was dedicated in 1761 the ceremony was enriched by the singing of an anthem especially written for the occasion. Thus in a number of churches music was developing beyond the "New Version" of metrical psalms by Tate and Brady, the official songbook of the Church of England. No one aided this development more than Francis Hopkinson—poet, musician, jurist, and future signer of the Declaration of Independence—who in the 1760s resided within Christ and St. Peter's parish. Hopkinson, who perhaps has the best claim to being America's first native composer, was recognized for "A Collection of Psalm Tunes with a Few Anthems and Hymns," printed in 1763.[2] Included within this work were tune settings for five hymns, among which were two of Joseph Addison's hymns: "When All Thy Mercies, O My God" and "The Spacious Firmament on High."

Beyond the larger churches that existed in the urban seaboard centers, there was little musical variation in the order of Anglican worship from the traditional psalm singing. A clerk would usually select and announce the psalm with the formula, "let us sing to the praise and glory of God," and then, perhaps with the aid of a pitch pipe, he would line out the psalm, which the congregation would repeat. The tunes were taken from John Clark's collection, which in 1701 had been printed as Henry Playford's *The Divine Companion, or David's Harp New Tun'd*. A few well-known tunes like "York," "Windsor," "Canterbury," or "Old 100th" were most frequently used. The congregation remained seated, while singing either in unison or in octaves. To assist the worshipers in remembering the words of the psalms, the first edition of the Book of Common Prayer printed in America by William Bradford, a vestryman of Trinity Church, New York, contained the "New Version" by Tate and Brady.

As church music in the colonial churches was largely a version of English models, so the services of worship were conducted in accordance with the Prayer Book of 1662. The two basic types of services of worship were Morning and Evening Prayer and Holy Communion. A typical morning service included Morning Prayer, the Litany and Ante-Communion or "Altar Prayer," and the Prayer for the Church Militant, with the sermon following the Nicene Creed. During the colonial period how often the celebration of Holy Communion took place varied from once a month to three times a year, with the majority of churches falling into the latter category. The Supper of the Lord, or Holy Communion, involved the sacrament in both kinds, with an Exhortation, Invitation, Confession, Absolution, Comfortable Words, and Prayer of Humble Access preceding the administration of the elements. The musical parts of the service were the Kyrie, Gloria in Excelsis, Sanctus, and Agnus Dei, but an Introit, Offertory, and Communion anthem could be added. In most cases, however, the service of Holy Communion, even in its essentially musical parts, was conducted out of necessity in the "parochial mode" or the spoken voice.[3]

Since the service of worship with a sermon was far more common than services including Holy Communion, the sermons of the era are of particular interest. The concept of an ideal sermon was that of a discourse upon some moral topic, clearly presented and correctly argued. In delivery, the minister was expected never to arouse emotion in himself or in the hearers. Because of the influence of rationalism and scientific method, the Scriptures were called into examination before one's natural reason, which was called upon to decide the truth or validity of the proposition presented. The result was a style of preaching that was intentionally quiet and prosaic, and always genteel. The function of religion was, therefore, to provide support and sanction for morality and "to tell people what is their duty, and convince them to do it." In the process of showing how reasonable and beneficial Christianity was, preaching became more dependent on rationalism and produced a latitudinarianism in America as it had done in England. The result of this type of theological thinking brought about a deemphasis of the more orthodox Christian concepts of sin, redemption, and salvation while the subjects of duty, obedience, goodness, and character received greater attention. One prominent clergyman, William Smith, who was also provost of the College of Philadelphia, in a sermon representative of his day, entitled "The Gospel Summons," took for a text Luke 16:2, "Give an Account of Thy Stewardship," and began preaching by admonishing: "Render up your stewardship—give an account of your conduct— . . . Hear it ye rich, and ye poor; ye rulers, and ye subjects; ye pastors, and ye people!"[4]

Though the dominant theme of preaching among American Anglicans was reasonableness, the church was confronted by the challenge of evangelicalism as a result of the Great Awakening. This movement put primary emphasis upon an individual's relationship to God, the problem of sin, and the need for salvation. At the height of the revival George Whitefield, a clergyman in Anglican orders, arrived from England and conducted preaching services in a manner and style that little reflected the temper of his ecclesiastical connection. At first churchmen received him cordially, but his frequent arguments with Anglican leaders and denunciations of its clergy as "unspiritual" eventually closed Anglican pulpits against him. Indeed, American Anglican leaders came to look upon Whitefield as a betrayer of their cause because on many issues—the Scriptures, the Prayer Book, emotionalism, church government—he appeared to side with Dissenters. As a result of the antagonism between the American Anglican leaders and Whitefield, evangelicalism had only limited influence among the clergy, though the laity, particularly in the middle and southern colonies, were often sympathetic. At no time, however, did the Great Revival threaten a schism among Anglicans as it did among Congregationalists and Presbyterians, who divided internally over the issue into New Lights and Old Lights.[5]

CLERGY

A mark of dynamic church life within Anglicanism in the 1760s and 1770s is evident from the increased number of ministers serving churches. Of the number of ministers whose place of birth is identifiable, an increasing proportion were American-born. The register of the bishops of London shows that between 1745 and 1775 there were 409 clergymen licensed for America. Of the total number, 156 were licensed between 1745 and 1760, compared with 253 between 1761 and 1775. The colony with the largest number of Anglican clergymen in 1776, Virginia, had 122, of whom 38 were Virginians and 6 more were from other colonies with but 11 from England and 14 from Scotland and 1 each from Ireland and Wales, while the origin of the remainder is not determinable. But the region that provided and retained the largest number of its clergymen was New England, and in particular Connecticut. In Connecticut between 1702 and 1785, of the ninety-two clergymen who served, seventy were natives of the northern colonies and sixty-five were born and reared in New England, and of this total number about two-thirds, or sixty, had converted to Anglicanism from Congregationalism. Of the other twenty-two ministers originally from Great Britain, five had received most or all of their education in New England.

Though the total number of Anglican clergymen in the

colonies is impressive, there was always a shortage of trained ministers. Because of this condition many vestries employed lay readers or clerks who performed the clerical services, except for the administration of the two sacraments and marriage. From the ranks of the lay readers many parishes recruited pastors. These men were known locally and employed by the vestry, and if recommended to the bishop of London they were known to be acceptable to the parishioners. Even though the practice of employing lay readers came under attack from ministers born and trained in England, the practice remained, and none other than the Reverend Doctor Samuel Johnson, rector of Christ Church, Stratford, Connecticut, and president of King's College from 1753 to 1762, defended them as necessary and meaningful. Indeed, the records indicated that the clergymen who were native-born and educated, and approached Holy Orders through a lay-readership, rarely had difficulty during their career with vestries or parishioners. So successful were New England Anglicans in providing lay readers to the authorities in England for ordination that a rule was made requiring the sponsors to get approval from the bishops in England before sending candidates if they expected cooperation.[6]

During his fifty years of service between 1722 and 1772, Dr. Johnson is credited with instructing most of the forty-two Yale graduates, twenty-nine of whom were converts to Anglicanism who took Holy Orders. Between 1745 and 1775 it is possible to determine that thirty-three more clergymen were educated in the colonies, with the College of Philadelphia training nine, Harvard and Princeton producing eight each, and King's College and William and Mary graduating at least three apiece. For the same 1745 to 1775 period eighteen clergymen who served in America had received their training in the British Isles; of these six were from Oxford, five from Cambridge, one each from Edinburgh, Dublin, and Aberdeen, and one listed as simply Scotland. But interestingly the ratio of prospective

Society for the Propagation of the Gospel in Foreign Parts. On June 23, 1701, King William III granted a charter for the S.P.G. and from that day until 1775 its area of service in America grew. The years between 1763 and 1775 were most significant for the Society in terms of men assisted and aid sent to the mainland colonies. In fact, the Society's aid was a major factor in the development of the Church of England in New England, New York, New Jersey, and North Carolina. Without Society aid many of the new congregations and parishes that had been opened could not have paid a living wage to a minister. In the larger picture, there were ninety-nine missionaries licensed for the thirteen colonies in the thirty years preceding the Revolutionary War. Forty were licensed between 1745 and 1762, but fifty-nine or an increase of almost 50 percent between the years 1763 and 1775 were commissioned.[10] With the S.P.G. commission there was granted to the missionary an annual stipend of £50 per year. In addition, the Society bore the expense of untold numbers of Bibles, Prayer Books, catechisms, manuals, devotionals, and books of sermons. Moreover, similar aid was needed and received by Anglicans in New Jersey and Pennsylvania, where many of the churches and especially the newer ones had not completely developed the ability to support a minister.

A variety of methods were used to raise additional funds in the parishes of the northern and middle colonies beyond those received from the S.P.G. For example, Christ Church, Boston, like many other churches, made the payment of pew rents a prerequisite for voting for vestrymen in the annual church election. By this means the average-sized churches could realize perhaps £100 a year. Then there were subscriptions such as the one conducted by Godfrey Malbone, a layman of Pomfret, Connecticut, for the building of a church in that community. Hugh Neill, an S.P.G. missionary at Oxford, Pennsylvania, conducted a lottery to raise funds, and Christ and St. Peter's churches, Philadelphia, in 1765 raised £3000 in the same way

clergymen taking their training in the colonies after 1[?]
to one.[7]

The clergy who settled in the colonies from Ma[?]
Georgia where the Church of England was legally es[?]
were supported financially by taxation. In these five[?]
the respective governments established parishes, au[?]
special taxes for church construction, and defined wha[?]
the local vestries could exercise. The governors, in the[?]
of a bishop, controlled the probating of wills and is[?]
marriage licenses, and performed the act of induction [?]
tion of a minister into a parish. In Virginia, which [?]
largest Anglican establishment in America, the House [?]
gesses authorized a tobacco tax to be handled by the ve[?]
provide ministerial support. Maryland, which had the[?]
largest Anglican establishment, also supported its clergy[?]
tobacco tax collected by the sheriff and paid directly[?]
minister. By 1767 the average annual salary for a Ma[?]
rector ranged between £250 and £300 and not surp[?]
there was a waiting list of applicants seeking appointme[?]
Maryland parish. In contrast, South Carolina paid its cler[?]
of the general treasury, which allocated funds to a Bo[?]
Commissioners who authorized direct payment. This m[?]
was most satisfactory to the clergy because it was more de[?]
able than a tobacco tax in the hands of a sheriff or vest[?]
1765 the stipend paid the established clergy by South Ca[?]
was £110 per year. Under the prodding of Governor A[?]
Dobbs, North Carolina raised its ministerial support to[?]
per year plus an additional £20 if the parish had no [?]
house. Georgia at the same time jumped its stipend for e[?]
lished clergy from £25 to £50 annually.[8] In general, the [?]
paid the Anglican clergy in America compared most favo[?]
with those in England, where an average stipend for a cu[?]
was £50 and for a vicar or rector £100 to £150 annually.[9]

Many of the clergy serving Anglican churches outside[?]
southern colonies were aided to a considerable degree by[?]

for repairs to the existing churches in Pennsylvania and the construction of new ones. Moreover, burial and marriage fees added to the ministers' support. But many churches were the recipients of significant gifts at one time or another. Colonel Mackintosh gave land and £200 for a church in Bristol, Rhode Island; Samuel Colburn of Dedham, Massachusetts, in his will stipulated that if he did not return alive from the French and Indian War his estate was to be used to build a church, and in 1763 it was so used. Many donations similar to these are recorded, and in Cambridge, Massachusetts, a group of eight families banded together and pledged to raise the funds needed to build a church and contribute to a minister's support if the S.P.G. would send a missionary.

CHURCHES

Another unmistakable sign of Anglican growth along the western perimeter of the British Empire was the rapid pace of new church construction. Between 1750 and 1760 only twenty-one new Anglican churches were built, but in the 1760s ninety new houses of worship were erected. The sharp increase in the number of new churches equalled the rate of Presbyterian expansion and almost paralleled Congregationalist expansion. Besides, Anglicanism was represented in all thirteen colonies with the heaviest concentration in Maryland and Virginia. The Congregationalists were most numerous in New England, but outside that region they were represented in only three colonies. Although there were Presbyterian churches in eleven colonies, the center of their strength was in the middle colonies.[11] This marked advance of Anglicanism ensured its position as a major religious body and enabled its clergy and constituents to extend their influence in spite of the keen competition among all religious bodies.

The colony in which the number of Anglican churches built

CHURCH CONSTRUCTION

	1750	1760	1770
Anglican	289	310	400
Baptist	132	240	350
Congregational	465	575	675
Dutch Reformed	79	105	125
German Reformed	90	135	175
Lutheran	138	190	225
Presbyterian	233	300	390
Roman Catholic	30	47	54
Total	1456	1902	2394

increased fastest was Connecticut. There were thirty Anglican churches reported in Connecticut in 1761, but a survey made in 1774 at the order of the General Court reported forty-seven churches or chapels and twenty congregations which met in court, town, or school house. A few dramatic conversions of Congregationalists to the Church of England in 1722 had sparked and sustained this growth. The most notable converts were Dr. Timothy Cutler, president of Yale; Daniel Brown, formerly tutor at Yale; Samuel Johnson, pastor at West Haven; and James Wetmore, pastor at North Haven. This coterie of divines went to England and were ordained in the episcopal tradition. In time they attracted to their numbers Samuel Seabury, Sr., Jeremiah Leaming, Agur Treadwell, Richard Mansfield, Samuel Andrews, and Thomas B. Chandler. Under their guidance the first Anglican church in Connecticut was opened at Stratford in 1724 with Samuel Johnson as rector. It was these converts who in time provided the strongest and most zealous leadership in the campaign for a resident American episcopate. All these men were of the "High Church" Anglican tradition—which held that bishops in the historic apostolic succession were necessary for the existence of the church—and they insisted upon the faithful execution of all offices and services that made the Church of England distinct from other religious bodies.[12]

The colony with the next largest number of new churches was Maryland, which added ten along with several chapels in parishes that were large enough to warrant them. Virginia built at least nine new churches, and in 1765 North Carolina adopted an ambitious plan to put a church in every one of its twenty-eight parishes. Another six churches were built in New York; Pennsylvania and South Carolina added four each. New Jersey, Massachusetts, and New Hampshire planned or built two each while Georgia authorized one. In this large-scale development of new churches, those located in coastal and urban centers as well as in the northeast almost always bore traditional ecclesiastical names like Christ Church, Trinity, or St. Peter's while those on the frontier and in the interior regions of the southern colonies sometimes had such names as Yeocomico Church, Aquia, Merchant's, Hope, Beaver Dam, Cattail, Turkey Run, and Rattlesnake Church.

The colonial Anglican churches were architecturally designed after English prototypes and were basically of two types, the rectangular and the cruciform.[13] Out of economic necessity they were relatively small, perhaps 30' by 50', and reflected the economic and social status of the constituents in the communities where they were located. Within the edifice, usually built with materials immediately available, a wooden altar was located in the east and behind a railed chancel. Usually the Decalogue, Apostles' Creed, and Lord's Prayer were painted on tablets fastened to the wall on either side of the chancel. Inside the chancel was the communion table, on which a copy of the Scriptures and the Prayer Book were placed in an upright position, and on communion Sunday the table was usually covered with a fair linen cloth on which the chalice, paten, flagon, and alms basin were placed. Centrally located between the chancel and nave stood a high pulpit, under which there was a reading desk; at the bottom the clerk's stall. The pews were the high square type allotted to families according to the well-understood hierarchical social structure of the community, with those of highest rank and greatest wealth pewed at the front or in a position advantageous with regard to the pulpit. Within this type of sparsely ornamented sanctuary, enclosed by four interior white walls gleaming in the light from the clear glass windows, the parishioners assembled. The liturgical portion of the service was conducted from the reading desk by the minister, dressed in a black gown with white bands at the neck, and was followed by the sermon delivered from the pulpit desk. On communion Sunday a white surplice may have been worn by the parson over his gown.

Anglicans in the 1760s were not only successful in building new additional churches and manning them with ministers, but they were also able to fill them with increasing numbers of worshipers. Clergymen from Massachusetts to Georgia, in the turbulent years preceding the Revolutionary War, reported increased church attendance to the S.P.G. and the bishops of London. In 1766, Dr. Johnson, of Stratford, the recognized Anglican leader in the northeastern colonies, stated that in general the churches in his region were growing.[14] Dr. Johnson was also one of the few men in America with whom Thomas Secker, archbishop of Canterbury, corresponded, and therefore his report on the churches in Massachusetts, Connecticut, and New York was at least semiofficial. Behind Dr. Johnson's report covering the larger region were numerous reports by local missionaries giving firsthand accounts. Edward Bass at Newbury, Massachusetts, claimed a large and attentive congregation; J. Wingate Weeks in Marblehead, Massachusetts, boasted the addition of several new families. Samuel Auchmuty, rector of Trinity Church, New York, was convinced of the need for another church because his church and chapel were both consistently filled on Sundays. There was, moreover, a revival of religion in Virginia among some Anglican parishes; according to Devereux Jarratt, rector of Bath Parish, Dinwiddie County, one of the few Anglican clergymen who were openly evangelical, large crowds attended his preaching everywhere he went in Virginia and North Carolina.[15] A remarkable record of accomplishment by an Anglican itinerant was that of Charles Woodmason, of St. Mark's parish in the backcountry of South Carolina, who claimed on March 26, 1771, that he had baptized 2,000, married 100 couples, and preached 500 discourses.[16]

Another source of strength to the Anglican church was the increasing number of governmental officials and prominent families who were communicants—those receiving Holy Communion according to Anglican rites—and constituents—that is, attending but not participating in the sacrament. The governor of Massachusetts from 1760 to 1769, Francis Bernard, was an active layman. William Tryon, who served as governor of North Carolina from 1765 to 1771 and of New York from 1772 to 1775, was an unusually zealous churchman. Sir William Johnson, Indian agent for the Northern Department, joined the S.P.G. Moreover, all the governors from New Jersey to Georgia in the 1760s and 1770s were either churchmen or openly patronized the Church of England in their colonies. Furthermore, the Dulany family in Maryland was active in St. Mary's parish, Annapolis, and Daniel Dulany served as secretary of the province from 1761 to 1774. In Virginia, the Lee family, of which Richard Henry Lee—a future defender of the Church in the 1780s—as well as numerous other families were noted for their devotion to the Anglican church.[17] The Rutledges, Pinckneys and Laurens, of Charleston, South Carolina, were also identified with the established church. Indeed, the talent, time, and service which these families as well as numbers of others contributed to the American Anglican church provided a major portion of its strength and resources.

The status enjoyed by the Church of England in the 1760s and 1770s, especially in the northeast, was a far cry from what it had endured a generation or two earlier. In 1687, the governor of Massachusetts, Edmund Andros, by the use of executive authority, arranged for the conducting of Anglican services in

Old South Meeting House, Boston. Soon King's Chapel, the first Anglican church in Boston, was built, but as a result of the Glorious Revolution in England and the ousting of Andros, the opponents of Anglicanism vented their fury by extensively damaging King's Chapel. A new colonial charter in 1691 recognized the rights of Anglicans to worship without interference and provided the basis whereby churchmen could vote and hold political office. In New York, Anglicans with the aid of the home government were forceful enough to get a Ministry Act passed in 1693, which made possible the establishment of Anglicanism in six parishes. Although Pennsylvania had always been noted for religious diversity, Anglicanism in the 1760s had the privilege of counting the proprietary family among its adherents. Anglicanism had long held the place of social predominance in Maryland and Virginia, and it was not unusual for members of other religious groups to unite with the Church of England in these colonies.[18]

VESTRIES

Basic to the functioning of any parish was the vestry, yet in the Canons of 1604, by which the Church of England ordered its practices, the vestry was not mentioned or defined. In England, the vestry emerged out of the annual meeting of parishioners, authorized in Canon 89, which chose two churchwardens by the consent of the minister and parishioners. By the sixteenth and seventeenth centuries the select vestry, a smaller group of laymen acting for the whole, emerged. These bodies were given approval by the bishops, and usually they were composed of the most substantial and discreet men of the parish. These groups came to appoint their successors, levy the church rates, and present offenders to the courts. In this evolution the churchwardens came to exercise a dual function because they not only represented the parish interest to the government but were authorized by the state to collect money for the poor and present those charged with offenses for prosecution. Though not universal in the seventeenth century, the practice of choosing select vestries was spreading, and its example was copied by the Anglicans in the American colonies.[19]

The vestries in the British mainland colonies were all of the select type, but their powers and status varied considerably depending upon whether they were located in the southern, middle, or New England regions.[20] Virginia alone had favored Anglicanism from its inception and attempted to duplicate the English ecclesiastical establishment. But 3,000 miles' distance and three months' traveling time, the absence of bishops, and pressing demands for effective administration produced modifications. Here the legislature recognized the legality of vestries, limited the membership of each to twelve, and authorized their election by the parish freeholders. From the vestry, two churchwardens were selected to serve as executive officers of the parish. But the Virginia House of Burgesses recognized the right of each vestry to select its minister and provided it with authority to raise a tobacco tax for his support. In addition, vestries hired clerks or lay readers and petitioned the legislature for new churches or chapels. These prerogatives were exercised in Virginia at a time when perhaps not a single vestry in England selected the parson or supervised the collection of a tax for his support. After a Virginia vestry had decided upon a minister, the governor would induct him; after which he was known as rector and possessed life tenure in his post. However, a practice that emerged and grew was the granting of one-year contracts between vestries and clergymen; such contracts might or might not be renewed. Thus the power over ministers and finances which the Virginia vestries acquired forged a new lay-clerical relationship which for many decades suited the interests of churchmen.[21]

In the middle colonies of New York, Pennsylvania, New

Jersey, and Delaware, the vestries had a position midway between their counterparts to the south and north. They did not have the legal status of the establishment, but they were legally authorized by individual charters of incorporation that enabled them, including minister and churchwardens, to represent the parish officially. But these charters did not bestow a position superior to that of any other religious body. The vestries in this region were left with the responsibility of raising funds as they chose, and they were granted explicitly or implicitly the right to choose the parish minister, with authority to bestow or deny life tenure. Because of their position in the eyes of the law, vestries in the middle region were freer than were those in Virginia because the colonial government did not interfere with their local operations in any way. It was up to the vestry, minister, and congregation to make the parish function. If the S.P.G. extended aid to the ministers, it was much appreciated, and it worked well as long as the Church of England did not try for a preferred position.

Vestries in New England were organized in much the same way as those in the middle colonies. When a congregation was first formed, the members would sign the petition requesting a minister and S.P.G. assistance, but before long the names of six to twelve individuals designated vestrymen and churchwardens appeared. Because many Anglicans in early-eighteenth-century Connecticut were former Congregationalists, it was not unusual that in the annual meetings they elected "moderators" to preside over what they called "The Episcopal Society" of the town in which they resided. But in New England the government did not meddle with the vestries by telling them how many members they were to have and what their duties were. Instead, here the vestries played a leading role in the struggle against state-imposed taxation for the support of Congregationalism. In the late colonial period the Connecticut assembly did receive petitions from individual vestries requesting that they be permitted to collect the Church tax for the support of their own clergymen, and in some cases the petitions were granted. A law passed by Massachusetts in 1753 did grant legal status to the Anglican vestries in that colony.[22]

In the process of building up or expanding the Anglican Church in New England the local vestries gained considerable control. Although they were at first dependent on the S.P.G. for men and almost always for financial assistance, they demonstrated a determination to influence church life. Like their Virginia brethren they hired lay readers when clergymen were unavailable, and persuaded many of them to take Holy Orders and return to the parish. Then too, the laity committed themselves to provide a glebe, a parsonage, and an annual stipend for the minister at least equal in value to that supplied by the Society. The degree to which each vestry achieved the objective of self-support seems to have been the degree to which they made known their choice for minister. The interdependence of clergy and laity was so pronounced that Dr. Johnson urged the Society to heed the desires of the lay vestries as they provided the best prospect for the success of the church.

Power, prestige, and position came to be associated with the vestries in all three regions of British America, but not all clergymen were ready to accept this condition. While the clergymen born and trained in America accepted the vestry's role, especially on matters pertaining to ministerial selection and salary, their British colleagues found these departures from English practice harmful and undesirable. Increasingly, the British clergy found out, in some instances the hard way, that there was no future for a clergyman who could not accept or adapt to the concept of lay authority that was generally accepted in the late colonial period. Clergymen properly trained, ordained, and licensed were encouraged and supported by the laity in their functions as ministers and priests, but the laity of the vestries had achieved their own identity as the legal custodians of the parishes, and this role as the local ecclesiastical elite they were unwilling to relinquish.[23]

EDUCATION AND HUMANITARIANISM

Anglicanism manifested its vigor in still another way in the late colonial period when it contributed to the founding of institutions of higher learning as well as expanding educational services in which it had engaged for numbers of years. In 1763 there were six colleges in America: Harvard, Yale, William and Mary, College of New Jersey, King's College, and the College of Philadelphia. In three of these institutions Church of England influence was dominant or pronounced. Indeed, in the 1750s there was a faster rise of Anglican participation in higher education than had taken place in any previous decade. The College of William and Mary had been founded in 1693 largely as the result of efforts by the Reverend James Blair, Anglican clergyman in Virginia. All the presidents of this institution had been ordained ministers, as had most of the faculty. Then in 1754, churchmen in New York were instrumental in the formation of a second college, named King's College. Here churchmen had agitated for a college since 1746, but the donation of a tract of land by Trinity Church to the project ensured its realization. However, a stipulation attached to the grant required that the president should always be a communicant of the Church of England and that the Prayer Book should be used in chapel services. When King's College opened in 1754, the Reverend Dr. Samuel Johnson, who was considered the most learned Anglican minister in the colonies, was president.[24]

The College of Philadelphia was organized in 1755 on a nondenominational basis, but the Church of England influence became pronounced when Dr. William Smith, an Anglican minister, was chosen the first provost. Smith quickly became a leading figure in church circles in and around Philadelphia. His influence was perhaps greater as a teacher because he trained several young men who became leading laymen and ministers. Among his more notable pupils were Francis Hopkinson, Samuel Magaw, and William White, all of whom played major roles in the development of Anglicanism in the colonial and early national periods. However, Smith's personal ambition and authoritarian manner often drew criticism from his ministerial colleagues and sometimes led him into serious controversies. Nevertheless, Smith was a key figure in education and in the Anglican church. In the mid-1760s he was probably the most widely known Church of England divine in the middle colonies.[25]

There were three more colleges established in the 1760s, but Anglicans were not involved with any of them. Rhode Island College was started under Baptist auspices; Queen's College, New Jersey, was backed by the Dutch Reformed; and Congregationalists were instrumental in the founding of Dartmouth College. There was, however, a plan to found a college in the Berkshires under Anglican influence, to be called Queen's, and it had the support of Massachusetts Governor Francis Bernard, but the legislature rejected it. In Charleston, South Carolina, a genuine concern was manifested by several leading citizens about the need for a college, and men like Henry Laurens and Benjamin Elliot discussed the issue. Though a charter was granted in 1770, the institution did not open until 1785 when a second charter established the College of Charleston with Robert Smith, rector of St. Philip's Church, at its head.[26] The persistent interest of churchmen, therefore, contributed substantially to the founding of a college in South Carolina.

The interest of churchmen in education was not limited to participation in founding and influencing institutions of higher learning. One practice which occurred on the parish level was the utilization of lay readers or clerks as teachers. Though this was not a customary or regular duty, it did exist in a sufficient number of cases to merit note. During the last years of the colonial period in Virginia sixteen different ministers taught school or tutored in the homes of planters. Then too, some vestries, particularly in Virginia, made expenditures for the education of poor children, but there was no consistency or relationship among these incidents. By the end of the colonial period, however, seven of ninety Virginia parishes had endowed schools under the control of parish officials and as the result of an Act passed by the Burgesses in 1755 six parishes built workhouses or poorhouses. The Virginia vestries had no duty to assign poor and orphaned children to apprenticeships, beyond a general oversight of the poor, but there is evidence they assumed this responsibility.[27] In spite of these efforts, however, education at the local level was largely without design or plan, and the Church of England in America was not promoting such a comprehensive scheme.

Beyond the educational activities of the Church in Virginia, some parishes in other colonies often initiated and sponsored similar enterprises. Trinity Church, New York, had organized a Charity School early in the eighteenth century, and part of its program was directed to educating Negroes. The S.P.G. early assisted this program, and by the 1760s the Bray Associates (a small band of dedicated churchmen in cooperation with the S.P.G.) also aided Trinity's thriving school. On Sunday evenings perhaps one hundred catechumens received instruction from Lewis's *Exposition* or one of Archbishop Secker's lectures, or in the singing of the Psalms. Another school essentially for the education of Negroes sponsored by the S.P.G. functioned in Charleston, South Carolina, from 1743 to 1763. Other reports about the instruction of Negroes were made by Hugh Neill of Delaware, William Sturgeon of Christ and St. Peter's churches, Philadelphia, and Jonathan Boucher of St. Mary's parish in Virginia. Though the S.P.G. put itself squarely behind such efforts, it was the Bray Associates who produced the more tangible results in the 1760s when they were instrumental in establishing schools in Williamsburg, Fredericksburg, Philadelphia, and Newport, in addition to assisting the one in Trinity Church, New York. The school in Philadelphia was part of Christ and St. Peter's parish and taught reading, sewing, and knitting as well as religion to the fifty-nine Negro children enrolled between November 1764 and March 1768. But because of the Revolutionary War the Bray Associates terminated their services in America in 1777.[28]

While the Church of England demonstrated in several ways its concern about alleviating to some degree the burden of slavery for the black people, it did not lead or sponsor any effort in behalf of manumission. Nor is there evidence that any colonial Anglican minister or congregation of the period spoke out against the institution of slavery. What the church did, little though it was, was done within the generally accepted socioeconomic system of the time. Yet this does not mean that local clergymen simply "played dead." For example, Alexander Garden, who founded the school in Charleston, kept it open in spite of the Slave Code Act of 1740, which forbade the instruction of Negroes either in public or private. The S.P.G. missionaries' and the Bray Associates' efforts encountered slaveholders in the North as well as in the South who feared that a slave's conversion and baptism would free him on the ground that one Christian could not hold another in bondage. It was also believed that conversion would convey other religious rights by virtue of membership in the Christian community. If this situation occurred, it was believed that slaves would become impossible to handle. Perhaps it was an awareness of a combination of these attitudes that prompted the Rt. Reverend William Fleetwood, bishop of St. Asaph, to assert in the annual S.P.G. sermon in 1711 that Negroes were not inferior and would work for wages. The strongest attack upon the institution of slavery by a representative of the Church of England came from William Warburton, bishop of Gloucester, in the 1766 annual S.P.G. sermon when he specified slavery as the reason for the lack of faith and fidelity within the colonies.[29]

The conversion of the Indians was another facet of the church's life in which some churchmen showed remarkable interest. The S.P.G. supported Indian missions, though on a lower priority than the needs of English settlements. The general assumption of Protestant missionaries to Indians in North

America was that the Indians should be brought to adopt Western civilization first and then Christianized. In the middle of the century Sir William Johnson, Indian agent for the Northern Department, solicited the S.P.G.'s interest in spreading Christianity among the Five Nations of the Iroquois, primarily on the claim that it was good policy. It was Sir William Johnson who pointed out that the Indians could not quickly adjust to a farm type of economy, and with the eventual aid of four missionaries he tried to Christianize and protect them in their culture but also use them as "Warlike Christian Men." Perhaps William Johnson was influenced by the success the Jesuits had had among the Indians of New France, which prompted him to break from the traditional English Protestant approach to Indian missions. Though the Mohawks became nominally Christianized and the Five Nations took the side of Britain during the Revolutionary War, the approach of Sir William Johnson in Christianizing the Indians was not generally accepted by the S.P.G. These efforts are hardly adequate to claim anything but the most limited success for their missions. When Provost Smith of Philadelphia proposed a plan for Christianizing the Indians in the 1760s, a plan which was not put into effect, it required their cultural conversion first.[30]

In still other ways Anglicans in the last third of the eighteenth century engaged in activities that were more humanitarian than educational. The Corporation for the Relief of Widows and Children of Clergymen was initiated by Provost Smith, with assistance from Francis Alison, vice provost of the College of Philadelphia and a Presbyterian minister. With aid from Benjamin Franklin and the S.P.G. a corporation charter was issued, and the first meeting was held on October 3, 1769. The corporation met annually, and the sessions were open to those who voluntarily joined and contributed. By 1774 the assets were listed as £2650.1.2¾. In addition to many clergymen, a considerable number of prominent and wealthy laymen supported this enterprise. At an earlier date a purely lay charitable organization, called the Boston Episcopal Charity Society, had been organized in Boston for the purpose of granting relief anonymously to members of the Society, their families, widows, and minor children, and to persons associated with the Episcopal Church in the Commonwealth as well as inhabitants of the City of Boston. Philadelphia had a St. George's Society backed by Anglican laymen which assisted Englishmen in relocating in that city. In 1772, Dr. John Kearsley, a long-time vestryman of Christ and St. Peter's parish, left a large part of his estate to found Christ Church Hospital, where elderly indigent women were provided care.[31]

ENGLISH CONNECTION

In spite of the expansion American Anglicans experienced in the late colonial period, they were unable to enjoy the full benefits of the Church of England. The rite of confirmation was denied them because it could be performed only by a bishop, and there was no bishop in America. Churchmen who journeyed to England had the opportunity to receive the ordinance, but the unavailability of this rite in the colonies did as much as any other factor to limit the number partaking of communion and made it impossible to determine accurately the number of constitutents who could properly be counted within the fold of Anglicanism. Thomas B. Chandler's claim of one million adherents or more in 1768 was inflated to impress the home government of the need for bishops. A more realistic estimate is 350,000 to 400,000 of which Charles Chauncy, a leading Congregationalist clergyman, believed 225,000 were located in the Maryland-Virginia area.[32] The absence of bishops made impossible the act of consecration for each new church. There was not, moreover, an adequate or designated leader in America to supervise the church or its clergy when the need arose. The only alternative in the case of a serious clerical problem was to present it to the bishop of London, in whose diocese

America traditionally belonged, but this practice was cumbersome and seldom proved satisfactory.[33] A problem which all clergymen born and educated in America had was the required journey to England, an expensive and sometimes hazardous voyage, to receive ordination and licensing. In 1766, Samuel Giles and Hugh Wilson were drowned off the New Jersey coast on their return trip, the ninth and tenth fatalities by sea. For these reasons, therefore, it seemed necessary to certain leading Anglican clergymen, especially Drs. Samuel Johnson and Thomas B. Chandler, that a resident American episcopate be obtained from England.

A measure of the bishop of London's authority had been extended to the colonies in the late seventeenth century by Henry Compton (1675–1713), but by the end of the colonial period such efforts were not duplicated. Bishop Compton appointed the first commissary, James Blair (1689–1743), and assigned him to Virginia. Blair by the force of his personality and strength of will made his office an important one. But other commissaries subsequently appointed to Maryland, South Carolina, Pennsylvania, and New England encountered difficulties.[34] First of all, commissaries could not ordain or confirm. They could visit the clergy and make recommendations to the colonial governors and the bishop of London, but any parish minister had the privilege of appealing a commissary's disciplinary decision to the archbishop of Canterbury. The weakness of commissaries was recognized by the clergy themselves, but it was Bishop Sherlock (1748–61) who discontinued appointing them, and subsequent bishops of London did not resume the practice. Though Virginia was first to receive a commissary and last to relinquish the post, the clergymen who filled that position in the 1760s and early 1770s had at best a questionable commission from England, and the authority of the office was a mere shadow of what it had been under James Blair.[35]

The men who expressed high aspirations in behalf of securing bishops in the 1760s failed to take into consideration the complicated and unpredictable relationship between politics and religion in England. The Church of England in the third quarter of the eighteenth century was conditioned by forces, traditional and contemporary, that gave it a distinct character. Royal supremacy in ecclesiastical policy established by the Tudors was evident, but more pronounced was the role of parliament. To ensure the permanence of the Revolutionary Settlement of 1688–89 and the Hanoverian dynasty established in 1715, parliament asserted authority over church as well as state affairs. The purpose of parliament's action was to produce a period of peace and prevent a recurrence of the theological-political controversies of the seventeenth century. But the growing Erastianism of the eighteenth century had a far-reaching impact upon the Church of England because it relegated the church to the status of a department of the state, whose operations were an extension of government policy. Since the time William Laud had been bishop of London, intermittently succeeding bishops had expressed some interest in settling bishops in the colonies, but always without success. When Thomas Sherlock had tried to force a decision that would permit bishops in America, his effort was foiled by two powerful English politicians, the duke of Newcastle and Horatio Walpole.

Horatio Walpole, son of the former prime minister, Sir Robert Walpole, plainly told Bishop Sherlock on May 29, 1750, that he did not believe the American Anglicans wanted a bishop. "They [American churchmen] have never that I have learnt made any formal application or even intimated to the Crown for the residence of bishops with them . . . and I am afraid a stronger inference may be made from thence of their having no inclination to have a bishop, than can be made from other acts in favor of the Church of England that they desire to have one."[36] He also predicted that any effort to secure a bishop for America would arouse the Dissenters in England and America, generate a controversy among Anglicans in the colonies, and produce a division between the Hanoverian supporters and those jealous of ecclesiastical power in parliament. In summary, Walpole foresaw that an attempt to acquire an American episcopate would "work mischievous effects on the government." Newcastle confirmed the opposition of the ministry and advised that the scheme not be renewed. The message was clear that the ministry opposed bishops for America on political grounds, and Sherlock's efforts were frustrated; his rejection illustrates the inability of the bishop of London to act on his own initiative in respect to America. But in the 1760s a coterie of zealous Anglican clergymen believed circumstances had changed sufficiently to permit a new effort for an American episcopate to succeed. To conduct successfully a new campaign for an American episcopate, however, would require the active support of the Church of England and the English government.

The problems of the Church of England in the eighteenth century were typical of that era of English history, but the main problem with the church which the exponents for an Anglican bishop in America encountered was the stultifying influence which the political structure imposed upon the church establishment. Fortune had resolved to give to the Whigs virtual domination of church offices from the accession of George I to the death of George II. An alliance between Bishop Edmund Gibson and Robert Walpole was successful in achieving for the Whigs a monopoly of episcopal preferments.[37] From 1746 to 1766 the Duke of Newcastle acted as "ecclesiastical minister" and retained control of "ecclesiastical appointments." The series of short administrations that plagued George III's reign in the 1760s before the accession to power of Lord North did not alter the government's control over the episcopate, because the tradition had been established that a clergyman or bishop who expected promotion did not deviate from an incumbent minister's policy. A bishop who was too outspoken, as Thomas Secker was considered to be when in the annual S.P.G. sermon in 1741 he advocated an episcopate for the colonies, would be ostracized. Indeed, Secker remained twenty-one long years in

Oxford before he received his next promotion, and even then it took the personal intervention of the duke of Newcastle to secure it.[38] In 1763, Secker as archbishop of Canterbury showed no less enthusiasm for an American episcopate than he did in 1741, but the intervening years had taught him caution and prudence in ecclesiastical matters. Through correspondence, he and his long-time friend and fellow episcopal promoter, Dr. Samuel Johnson, thought the moment had arrived when their dream of a resident episcopate in America would be realized. It seemed that providence through the events of that year was on their side.[39]

The primary event that encouraged both Archbishop Secker and Dr. Johnson was the ending of the Seven Years' War by the Treaty of Paris signed in 1763. By this treaty Great Britain gained French Canada, the Spanish Floridas, all North America to the Mississippi, the best of the West Indies, and India. With the addition of this vast amount of territory the problems of organizing and administering it would be colossal. Thus, in March of 1763 Secker, who knew the procedures of the government, anticipated that the ministers would soon be making plans for imperial administration, for he wrote to Dr. Johnson: "Probably our ministry will be concerting schemes this summer, against the next session of Parliament, for the settlement of His Majesty's American dominions; and then we must try our utmost for bishops."[40]

Beyond the peace bonus which Secker saw clearly, there were other events which had recently taken place both in England and the colonies that gave added encouragement to the two church promoters. For example, the accession of George III to the throne in October of 1760 was an event filled with promise because the new king, unlike his predecessor, had been born, baptized, and reared a churchman, and Archbishop Secker was not only his spiritual adviser but he had also performed the marriage of George III, baptized his children, and officiated at his coronation.[41]

Moreover, from the colonial side there was the expression of apparent unity among the Anglican clergy in Connecticut, Massachusetts, New York, New Jersey, and Pennsylvania to the new king and archbishop by way of petitions requesting a resident bishop. With these facts in mind it is easy to understand that Secker's optimism about the success of the episcopal cause grew until he wrote: "Indeed, I see not how Protestant bishops can decently be refused us, as in all probability a popish one will be allowed, by connivance at least, in Canada."[42] But in the expectant months of 1763 neither Secker nor Johnson paused to note that no petition requesting a bishop had been received from the laity in the American churches nor from the clergy in the colonies from Maryland southward where the church was established and strongest.

In spite of the reasons for optimism there was a period of suspense when the archbishop warned Dr. Johnson not to get his hopes up for a quick favorable decision. He explained a series of unforeseen circumstances in a letter dated September 28, 1763, just six months after his more triumphal one. "What will be done about bishops, I cannot guess. Application for them was made to Lord Egremont, who promised to consult with the other ministers, but died without making any report from them. His successor, Lord Halifax, is a friend to the scheme; but I doubt, whether in the present weak state of the ministry, he will dare to meddle with what will certainly cause opposition."[43] But Dr. Johnson did not accept this explanation completely, for he knew the vast new territory of Canada required attention and organization. If a bishop for the American colonies was too hazardous an experiment, he was prepared to propose and urge that a bishop be located in Canada who could serve the colonies. Recently, Sir William Johnson, Indian agent for the Northern Department, had made a similar proposal to the Lords of Trade. He advocated using the several Jesuit missions in the territory acquired from France and making their land the basis for an endowed episcopate which Sir

William believed would benefit the government and the church.[44] Since a bishop in England at that time performed both political and ecclesiastical functions, there was no reason to believe one would not do so in the New World.

At the very time when Dr. Johnson and Archbishop Secker were doing all in their powers to forward an American episcopate, an unexpected publication by the Reverend East Apthorp, S.P.G. missionary at Cambridge, Massachusetts, threw the issue of a resident bishop into the arena of controversy. Apthorp in his *Considerations on the Institutions and Conduct of the S.P.G.* wrote essentially a vindication of the Society's record of service, but the controversy which it engendered focused upon the subject of an American episcopate.[45] Immediately Jonathan Mayhew, a Congregational minister from Boston, challenged the episcopal proposal and the S.P.G.'s record, in his *Observations on the Charter of the S.P.G.*, which he charged was backed by a group plotting "to root out all New England churches."[46] Mayhew's counterblast was so severe that Apthorp was relieved when Archbishop Secker, writing anonymously, replied to Mayhew in a fiery and forceful rebuttal entitled *An Answer to Dr. Mayhew's Observations on the Character and Conduct of the S.P.G.* Secker divided Mayhew's argument into three parts: the attack on the Church of England, the denunciation of the S.P.G., and the rejection of the idea for a bishop in America. On the last point Secker claimed that a bishop in America would only visit New England and only reside in a colony that invited him. Moreover, there would be no attempt to seek tax support and political influence for him.[47] But the point of this literary conflict was not that the ire of the Dissenters had been aroused, for it had been aroused by churchmen several times in the past; but this time the issue of establishing a bishop or bishops in America became the focal issue of controversy between Dissenters and Anglicans for the first time, and differences between them over liturgy, theology, and patristical interpretations dropped

into the background. Although the initial phase of the controversy lasted more than a year, the results were inconclusive;
but it was demonstrated how explosive the episcopal issue
could be if improperly handled or misunderstood.

In May of 1764 Secker again expressed a guardedly optimistic assessment about the episcopal scheme to Dr. Johnson but
cautioned that its success might well depend on "various circumstances."[48] What the archbishop was referring to was undoubtedly the fact that two ministries had fallen in four years
and there was a likelihood of another ministerial shake-up. On
October 1, 1761, William Pitt had resigned from the ministry
after a quarrel over war policy. His successor into office, Lord
Bute, remained only until April of 1763 and resigned, wearied
by political struggles. In the meantime the Duke of Newcastle,
after a dispute with George Grenville over the conduct of the
treasury, had left office. Then in 1765 the Grenville ministry,
in trouble over the Stamp Act, fell from power even before
repeal of the measure. In the midst of the rapid ministerial
changes the ecclesiastical patronage also changed hands and so
rapidly that the bench of bishops was forced to be cautious, and
even Archbishop Secker came to admonish Dr. Johnson about
his attempts to advance the episcopal cause: "I beg you will
attempt nothing without the advice of the Society, or of the
bishops."[49]

The efforts of Secker and Johnson to win support quietly
from the English government were plagued by other reverses
as well. The unexpected death in 1762 of the bishop of London, Dr. Thomas Hayter, whom Secker had expected would be
a real asset in the episcopal drive, was a serious loss. Bishop
Hayter's successor, Dr. Richard Osbaldistone, did not survive
two years in office. Then in 1764 Richard Terrick was elevated
to the See of London, but he proved to be a keen disappoint-
ment to Secker because he refused to take out a commission
establishing his jurisdiction over the colonial church or to assist
openly in efforts to procure bishops for the colonial church.

However, what Bishop Terrick did publicly and what he attempted privately on the episcopal issue were two very different things. In a letter addressed to the Lords of Trade in 1772 he recounted:

Soon after I was Bishop of London I went to wait upon the King and laid before him the state of religion in the plantations and the necessity there was of having a bishop settled in those parts. His majesty heard me very graciously, upon which I asked him whether I might apply to his Ministers, he consented to it but I never could have an opportunity of meeting with the Ministers. After frequent delays and no hopes of success I waited upon the King again and had his leave to acquaint the Ministers that it was his Majesty's pleasure they should take the affair into their consideration; this produced a meeting at Newcastle House but the meeting produced nothing. The last effort I made was by desiring the King's consent that I might lay what I had to propose to His Majesty in Council, which accordingly was done six or seven years ago and I have heard nothing of it since.[50]

From this firsthand inside account it is clear that the British ministry during the period never seriously considered establishing an American bishop. This insight explains not only why Archbishop Secker and Dr. Johnson were unsuccessful from 1763 to 1765, but also why Drs. Johnson and Thomas B. Chandler, who renewed the episcopal quest in 1766 and 1767, were equally unsuccessful.

The continuing problem of ministerial instability which existed until Lord North's appointment to power in 1770 prohibited the several ministries from considering any issue that would unnecessarily generate tension and controversy, as they knew the settlement of a bishop in America most certainly would do. In the face of changing ministries and governmental indifference to the scheme, only Archbishop Secker remained a consistent champion of an American episcopate, but he died in 1768. His successor at Canterbury was the bishop of Lichfield, Frederick Cornwallis, who presided until 1783 and is remembered chiefly for his affability, courtesy, and hospitality.[51]

There is no indication that he aided the colonial Anglican leaders or even corresponded with them. Cornwallis's ecclesiastical policy blended perfectly with Lord North's expressed position not to force any new policy on Commons and to conciliate as many leaders as possible. It was this approach that in time proved destructive to the British empire and to the Anglican churches in America. Although the colonial Anglican leaders did not see it at the time, the point had been reached and passed when they could look to the English government for help in solving their problems. If solutions were to be found to the ecclesiastical problems of the colonial churches they would be evolved by those who were intimately concerned with the church's future.

2

The American Zealots

"Now must be the time, if ever, to be in earnest for bishops."
Dr. Samuel Johnson to
Archbishop Secker, August 10, 1763

The epicenter of American Anglican agitation for a bishop in the 1760s and 1770s was located in the northeastern colonies, but more precisely in Connecticut, New York, and New Jersey, with limited participation from Massachusetts. Within this geographical region the most outspoken leaders in the drive for a resident episcopate lived and served. First among this group was Dr. Samuel Johnson, president of King's College from 1753 to 1763 and thereafter a resident of Stratford, Connecticut, until his death in 1772. In New Jersey, Thomas B. Chandler, a former student and close associate of Dr. Johnson, was rector of St. John's Church, Elizabeth Town. Chandler's vigorous personality and pamphlet writings in time made him the leader of the proepiscopal cause in the public mind. The Reverend Henry Caner, rector of King's Chapel, Boston, was the acknowledged leader of the Anglicans in Massachusetts, and for a time he brought the clergy under his influence to support the Johnson-Chandler plan for an American episcopate. All three clerical leaders were native born and Yale educated, and they were converts to Anglicanism zealous to advance their religious communion.

CHURCH AND STATE

Anglican church leaders traditionally had had to act vigorously to keep their church vital in the northern colonies not only because they were a minority, but also in Massachusetts, Connecticut, and New Hampshire the Congregationalists enjoyed the status of legal establishment. Furthermore, the shift to an imperial policy on the part of the British government following the French and Indian War, and the parliamentary legislation designed to implement that policy in the colonies, not only heightened tensions between the colonies and the home government, but also increased suspicion toward all institutions in America, including the Church of England, which symbolized British authority. The Royal Proclamation of 1763, which excluded settlers from the trans-Alleghany country and brought into question the western land claims of several colonies, caused resentment; but the Sugar Act and particularly the Stamp Act of 1765 were greeted with outrage. Even the repeal of the Stamp Act produced only a temporary calm because the Townshend Duties in 1767 again inflamed colonists, and not until repeal (except the tea tax) in 1770 was tension reduced. Then the granting of a monopoly on tea to the East India Company in 1773 triggered the Boston tea party, which proved to be the curtain raiser for several years of open rebellion.[1] Thus the period in which the ardent supporters of an American episcopate argued their case was one charged with hostility toward the British government as well as one in which the Congregational majorities keenly resented Anglican efforts to capitalize upon the home government's increased interest in the colonies to advance their demand for a resident bishop.

It is therefore to the credit of Anglican churchmen in the region that they not only maintained their church but even advanced it markedly. In 1700 there had been three Anglican churches in New England, but in 1750 there were seventy-five in the same area plus New York and New Jersey, and in the twelve years following the Peace of Paris at least twenty-four more were added. By 1774 it was estimated that in Connecticut one in every thirteen persons was a constituent of the Church of England. The financial aid of the S.P.G. was still vital to the continuance of the clergy in most churches of the region, but the local parishes were remarkably successful in recruiting men for their pulpits. It is also important to note that the vast majority of churchmen were from the middle class of farming, professional, and commercial status while some were of the "poorer sort" so that the S.P.G. stipends to the clergy were very necessary. Although a few churchmen did acquire status as members of the social and economic elites—e.g., William Samuel Johnson in Connecticut and James Duane and John Jay in New York—the rank and file who rented the box-pews and occupied them on Sunday were outside the circles of privilege in this region.[2]

In addition to the turbulence generated by imperial measures enacted by parliament after 1763, there were local issues in each colony with which Anglicans had to deal if they wished to advance their church. For example, Anglicans in Connecticut and Massachusetts were in the vanguard of dissent, demanding relief from church taxes which supported the Congregational establishments.[3] The English Toleration Act of 1689 had led in both colonies to legislation permitting the existence of churches outside the establishments. By 1727 Anglicans in Connecticut legally could have their church taxes go to support their own religious teachers, and Massachusetts churchmen who lived within five miles of their churches and produced a certificate of attendance were granted the same privilege. In 1735 the five-mile requirement was dropped, but as late as the 1760s there were reports of harassment by the establishments in both colonies. The most common complaints involved delay or refusal in granting Anglicans church building permits and the nongranting of the tax privilege when a church was without a minister.[4] Those of the Anglican way did not have an easy time but in many instances fought fire with fire. In order to best the opposition the clergy did not hesitate to threaten appeals to the British government charging Connecticut and Massachusetts with violating the 1689 Toleration

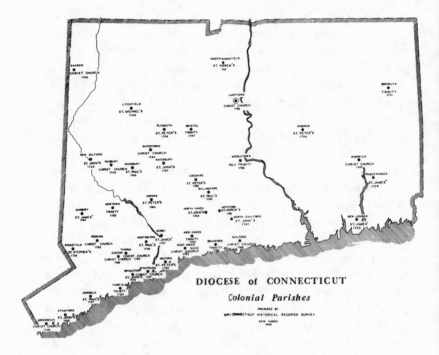

Colonial Parishes in Connecticut. Courtesy of Nelson R. Burr and the Church Missions Publishing Company.

Act. Since both colonies feared charter reviews, which were rumored in the late 1760s, and since they knew the British ministry favored even-handed administration, the authorities were usually amenable to the pressures exerted by the Church of England and other dissenting groups.[5]

An event which in an inverse way proved beneficial to the Church of England in the region and especially in Connecticut was the Great Awakening. Stressing as it did a religion of "the heart," the revival was accompanied by enthusiasm and deviations from traditional practices. Even though the best-known preacher of the movement, George Whitefield, was an Anglican, the leaders of the church came to oppose him and the revival. However, the Congregationalist establishments divided into opponents and proponents of the revival, labeled Old and New Lights. A consequence of this Congregational schism was the strengthening of existing political factions in Connecticut, where religion and politics were inextricably interwoven, and by 1766 the New Light faction had successfully challenged the Old Light domination of the government. In the eye of this religio-political storm the Church of England adhered to its liturgical form of worship and as a result attracted numbers of persons who wanted to escape the turbulence that had engulfed Congregationalism. In two specific instances such large numbers of Congregationalists deserted the established Congregational church for Anglicanism that they were able to carry the churches—one in Stratford and one in Northbury—into the Anglican fold.[6] Thus in Connecticut and to some extent throughout the northeast, the Great Awakening enhanced the image of the Church of England as a dependable, rational representative of Christianity as well as driving new followers into its fold.

In Connecticut, however, the numerical harvest of new adherents was not all clear gain. During the confrontations between Old and New Lights, the Church of England had become associated with the Old Light faction, which drew its support primarily from the traditionally conservative wealthy families. The New Lights who managed to topple the Old faction from power in 1766 were composed largely of freemen and those opposing restrictive legislation against radicals.[7] It was the Stamp Act and the Old Lights' reluctant willingness to uphold it that provided the issue over which the Old Light majority was defeated. Thus the Anglicans who were associated with the defeated faction suffered a loss of political status, but their loss of status was compounded in the public mind when Dr. Johnson, in the midst of the Stamp Act controversy, advised the home government of the loyalty of Anglicans. This action in effect put the Anglican church in Connecticut directly on the road that was marked Loyalism during the Revolutionary War. When the episcopal plan in which Dr. Johnson played a major part became known in the late sixties, it was understandably viewed by many as an attempt to reinstate and enlarge traditional authority, especially that of the British government.

The Church of England in the colony of New York was provided with the legal means for establishment in the city and county of New York, as well as in Richmond, Queens, and Westchester counties, by the Ministry Act of 1693. But the implementation of the legislation depended upon the will of successive royal governors to be made meaningful. Between 1702 and 1776 the church was forcibly planted in the counties, but Dissenters who were an ever-growing majority resisted and even tried to have the act repealed. The Anglican-Dissenter tensions hit a new high over the chartering of King's College in 1754, which for practical purposes became an Anglican institution partially supported by public funds. Chief Justice De Lancey, acting governor, and the council issued a charter for King's without consulting the assembly. Opposition to De Lancey's procedure was led by William Livingston, John Morin Scott, and William Smith, Jr., all Presbyterial laymen. Again in 1766 ecclesiastical and political factionalism erupted when the Presbyterians who petitioned for a church corporate charter were refused on the ground that the king's exclusive obligation was to uphold the rights of the Church of England. By 1770 the acting governor, Cadwallader Colden, was convinced that an attempt to repeal the Ministry Act had merged with the general political attack upon English policies.[8]

By the late 1760s the extent of S.P.G. support to the Anglican ministers in New Jersey was a cause for suspicion by Dissenters. But tensions among churchmen, colonial government, and factional groups did not rise nearly so high in this colony as elsewhere in the northeast. One overt act on the part of the Anglican clergy which did produce temporary resentment was the appeal by that group to the governor and subsequently the bishop of London to deny justices of the peace authority to perform marriages. The action sought was probably intended to improve the financial lot of the Anglican clergy, who could then have expected to perform more marriages and collect fees, but the action failed. The petition did strike many as an attempt to achieve a privileged position by an appeal to authority at a time when colonists were increasingly leery of any outside interference in their affairs. However, the relative calm which Anglicans enjoyed in New Jersey was about to be shattered, for in Elizabeth Town (the largest and one of the most attractive municipalities in the colony) Thomas B. Chandler, after receiving a doctorate from Oxford in 1766, was about to host two intercolonial conventions of Anglican clergy to determine a course of action in the quest for a resident episcopate.[9]

THE PROMOTERS

Although there was a strong commitment to procure an American episcopate, the number of Anglicans who supported the scheme devised at Elizabeth Town were few. If Drs. Johnson and Chandler had not led the episcopal campaign, there would have been little agitation on the part of Anglicans in general for a bishop. The S.P.G. in England, which in earlier years had encouraged its missionaries to seek the appointment of bishops, in the 1760s and 1770s gave no official encouragement to the promoters of the scheme.[10] By the time the S.P.G. became aware of the Johnson-Chandler plan it was well known in England that a succession of ministries had not favored previous suggestions of bishops for America and were not likely to favor a new plan. Thus the controversy that erupted between Anglicans and Congregationalists-Presbyterians was due to the fact that the opponents of the episcopate could not separate politics from polity, or they were fearful that their failure to oppose the newest episcopal scheme might be misinterpreted by the home government, or possibly they were looking for an excuse to fight.[11]

The elevation of Thomas Secker to Canterbury had given renewed emphasis to the idea of bishops for America, for he agreed with Drs. Johnson and Chandler that episcopacy was vital for the life of the American churches. Secret correspondence between Secker and Johnson on the subject reveals that for more than two years after the Treaty of Paris Secker had tried to persuade the ministries to act favorably on an American episcopate but had failed. Dr. Johnson's critical evaluation was:

Had it been done last spring (when the dissenters themselves expected nothing else) and the Stamp Act postponed till the next, it would have been but a nine day wonder, nor do I believe one half of the people of America would have been much if at all uneasy about it. . . . But in truth I am afraid that both the Bible and the episcopate . . . are both sinking in this apostatizing age, both home and abroad. . . . So that unless the poor Church of England in all orders of men soon rouse up and exert a spirit of zeal, courage and activity, I fear there is a greater probability that the episcopate will in not many years be demolished in England than established in America.[12]

There is, moreover, no indication that Dr. Johnson's impassioned plea prompted any action in England, but in the northeastern colonies among Anglican clergymen his word carried considerable weight, and they responded.

The distress evinced by Dr. Johnson over the state of the church was shared by Thomas B. Chandler, who initiated efforts to hold a voluntary convention of Anglican clergy in Elizabeth Town in October 1766. Nineteen clergymen from Connecticut, New York, New Jersey, and Pennsylvania attended. Drs. Johnson and Chandler were present, as were their associates Samuel Seabury, Charles Inglis, Myles Cooper, Jeremiah Leaming, Abraham Jarvis, and Bela Hubbard. Richard Peters, rector of Christ and St. Peter's churches, Philadelphia, and his assistant, William Sturgeon, were the only representatives from Pennsylvania. Only two prominent clergymen, Henry Caner of Massachusetts and Provost William Smith of the College of

Philadelphia, were absent. The most active members of the convention were the native-born converts to Anglicanism— Johnson, Chandler, Leaming, and Robert McKean—and the sons of converts—Seabury and Jarvis. Zeal for their adopted faith was a major motivating force behind the episcopal campaign. Their essentially High Church position was that the episcopacy was essential to the church and there was no substitute or excuse for the Anglican churches not completing their historic and apostolic system of church government. The number of Anglican clergy who attended this intercolonial convention represented about 35 percent of their numbers from the region.[13]

This convention quickly organized itself and began to make policy without consulting the bishop of London, the archbishop of Canterbury, or the S.P.G. The convention provided a way to perpetuate itself by designating nine members a sufficient number to constitute a convention, and for emergency meetings seven would suffice. The group then explained that their resolutions were only advisory and recommendatory and could not bind a clergyman or church. However, these actions did introduce the idea of a regional convention directing and supervising church affairs, and in the postwar years this experience proved valuable. The time would come when a committee of the convention would control the acceptance of elected clerical members and the laity would also be incorporated as an integral part. In fact, the time would come when a national convention would write a republican ecclesiastical constitution that defined episcopacy in a manner acceptable in a new nation; but in 1766 the presumptuous activities of nineteen Anglican clergymen were hardly expected to produce such far-reaching consequences.

The sole purpose of the 1766 convention was forcefully stated "to use their joint influence and endeavors to obtain the happiness of bishops."[14] The minutes do not contain a description of the type or number of bishops desired, but in 1767 when Chandler wrote his *Appeal to the Public* at the urging of Dr. Johnson he described the type of bishops the convention sought. The plan called for a "purely spiritual" episcopate with authority derived from the Church of England and not the British government. Such a bishop could therefore confirm members and ordain and oversee clergy but would have no commission from the government to probate wills, issue marriage licenses, or try morals cases as the ecclesiastical courts in England did. It was emphatically denied that the proposed bishops would have any connection with the colonial or British governments. It was also pointed out that such bishops would have no control over the Anglican laity or the Dissenters. On all these points Chandler was advocating a radical alteration in the type and authority of English episcopacy. Dr. Johnson thought three bishops necessary to meet the colonial needs; Chandler two; but in the light of existing conditions both would have been elated to receive one.

Under the presidency of Chandler the convention undertook to promote the episcopal plan in several ways. First, petitions were sent to the archbishop of Canterbury, the bishop of London, and the bishop of Oxford. Next, agents were selected and letters of authorization prepared to introduce the scheme to the governors and Anglican clergy of Maryland and Virginia. This group of episcopal promoters was well aware of the importance of recruiting the clergy from the colonies where the Church of England was established to support their enterprise. Thus, Myles Cooper, Dr. Johnson's successor in the presidency of King's College, and Robert McKean, S.P.G. missionary to St. Peter's Church, Perth Amboy, and Trinity Church, Woodbridge, were sent "to wait upon and confer with Your Exellency, on an affair we have much at heart, namely an American Episcopate."[15] In addition, each convention member agreed to write to friends, relatives, and other clergymen to persuade them to join the campaign. Charles Inglis, assistant minister at Trinity Church, New York City, sent letters as far south as

North Carolina. Dr. Johnson wrote to Professor John Camm of William and Mary College in Virginia:

And it has been a matter of great wonderment to us that you gentlemen of the most ancient and most respectable province of Virginia and the other southern provinces where the Church is established have never as we know of solicited a bishop. . . . I am, therefore, very apprehensive that our solicitations will fail of gaining the point, unless we could bring it to a general cry, and prevail with the southern provinces to join us. . . . What you suggest with regard to Virginia is of great weight.[16]

Moreover, William Nelson, a future president of the Council of Virginia, reported that a letter soliciting the support of Virginia's clergy was circulated. In Virginia and later in Maryland one colorful and forceful champion of episcopacy to emerge was Jonathan Boucher, who in 1766 was serving St. Mary's Church, Caroline County, Virginia. At the very time Cooper and McKean were executing their southern strategy, Henry Caner informed Drs. Johnson and Chandler that the twelve Anglican clergy in Massachusetts would support the episcopal cause.

As if to reinforce the Johnson-Chandler plan with substantive support, Sir William Johnson, Indian agent for the Northern Department, shortly after the convention advised Chandler and Dr. Johnson of his intentions: "I will not take up more of your time now by enlarging hereon and shall only add that I am so thoroughly persuaded of the importance of bishops in America that you may rely on my continuing to recommend it in strong terms—Albany is most advantageously situated for one to the northward, I should think the united voice of the established clergy here would soon obtain it."[17] Moreover, Sir William Johnson was as good as his word, for on December 3, 1767, he wrote the Earl of Shelburne, secretary for American affairs, and urged the government to give favorable consideration to the request for American bishops. In 1769, he apparently tried to entice the S.P.G. to support vigorously the episcopal scheme by offering 200,000 acres to the Society should it obtain a matching grant.[18]

INTERNAL DISSENT

The members of the Elizabeth Town Convention were well aware of previous plans to settle an episcopate in America. During Henry Compton's tenure as bishop of London (1675–1713) he had advocated a suffragan type of bishop for the colonies who would be appointed as an assistant to one of the bishops in England. This type of bishop could ordain, confirm, and consecrate, but there were no political prerogatives to the office and if the experiment failed a suffragan bishop could easily be withdrawn. This idea came close to realization, but Queen Anne's death in 1715, followed by the accession of George I, ended its prospects for success. In 1748 Bishop Sherlock revived the idea of suffragan bishops and urged the Duke of Newcastle in its behalf, but he too failed. After the close of the French and Indian War, the Dean of Gloucester circulated a pamphlet promoting the idea of sending a bishop, perhaps a suffragan bishop, to Canada. In 1764 Richard Peters, rector of Christ and St. Peter's churches, presented to the archbishops of Canterbury and York a treatise entitled *Thoughts on the Present State of the Church of England in America* in which he favored the appointment of four suffragan bishops by the king, without recourse to parliament, within the archdiocese of Canterbury for service in America.

Based upon this prior experience when the intercolonial convention opened, it was naturally assumed that Richard Peters was one with the group in its desire for an episcopate. Therefore, their consternation was the greater when in convention Peters opposed the action subsequently taken to obtain bishops. What Peters proposed instead was an alternative plan prepared by William Smith, provost of the College of Philadelphia, which called for the appointment of commissaries. One would be assigned to New York and Connecticut; another to Pennsylvania and New Jersey; and the plan could be expanded as required. Within this proposal there was no enlargement of a commissary's traditional functions and the only difference between the proposed commissaries and their predecessors who had served in the colonies was the expansion of the area of jurisdiction from one to two colonies.

The Smith-Peters plan met stiff opposition and was decisively defeated. Beyond this the delegates voted to address the bishop of London and the S.P.G. to express adamant disapproval of this plan.[19] The majority of the convention based their opposition upon the knowledge that a commissary could not perform the ecclesiastical functions they deemed essential. Since a commissary could not ordain, consecrate, or confirm, the most significant services he performed were visitations, convening conventions, and advising governors on the needs of the church. Even an individual clergyman accused of an offense was entitled to appeal over the commissary to the archbishop of Canterbury. For a commissary to operate effectively at all required the solid backing of the bishops of London and since Bishop Sherlock's term such backing had not existed. Then too, the commissaries who had served in the colonies, especially in the southern provinces, had not, in the judgment of the convention, met the needs of the church. Thus the counterproposal of Smith and Peters—though a positive plan that might have been accepted in England because it involved no new features that were likely to cause problems for the government—was totally unacceptable to the Elizabeth Town Convention.

There is, however, in the conduct of Richard Peters between 1764 and 1766 an apparent paradox, for in the first instance he favored resurrecting the suffragan bishop idea and in the second he proposed a much milder form of ecclesiastical supervision in the office of commissary. To Peters the reaction of the colonists to the new imperial policy and especially the Stamp Act served as an early warning incident, demonstrating what might happen if the Elizabeth Town Convention succeeded in procuring bishops. By 1766 both Peters and Smith were very much aware that the Pennsylvania proprietors, Sir Thomas and Richard Penn, were opposed to any possible extension of royal authority in America and particularly in Pennsylvania, where a considerable political faction was trying to have the home government create Pennsylvania a royal colony.[20] The episcopal campaign, no matter how carefully the office of bishop was defined and described, would have the appearance at least of putting the Church of England in the colony in opposition to the proprietors' interest. Since Smith and Peters both were very much wedded to the proprietary cause and because the Penns were the best friends Anglicans had in Pennsylvania, these two leaders took their stand against their zealous brethren and the episcopal plan of the convention.[21] In so doing they demonstrated that churchmen could and would put the local interest of the church before a particular ecclesiastical issue, even episcopacy, to preserve what had already been achieved by the church rather than run the risk of involving the church unnecessarily in controversy.

The resistance of Peters to the proposed American episcopate during the Elizabeth Town Convention should have alerted the others present to possible future difficulties, but there is no evidence that it did. Shortly after adjournment, one of the participants, Samuel Auchmuty, rector of Trinity Church, New York City, had second thoughts about his own participation in the scheme and the actions and procedures which had been taken. He advised Dr. Johnson: "in general we are got too warm and want a cheque. The Jersey clergy are really too importunate, and I fear their late proceeding will hurt the cause rather than do it good. . . . They have fired their whole artillery against commissaries in a letter to the Bishop of London. I doubt whether the bishop will thank them for their remonstrance."[22] Auchmuty's letter was probably not made known to the other clergy who attended the convention, but as rector of one of the most important churches in the region he was in a critical position to promote the scheme vigorously or to try and cool the zeal of his younger colleagues. Auchmuty chose the latter course. Moreover, Samuel Auchmuty realized what Sir William Johnson observed and the zealous clergy knew but refused to admit, simply that "the worst circumstances attending the interests of the Church of England, is the lukewarmness of the great part of its professors."[23] In the opinion of Trinity Church's rector, to push the episcopal scheme too hard would not only increase agitation against the Anglican church in New York, but it would likely produce dissatisfaction among the laity whose support was vital to the church.

CONTROVERSY

In the fall of 1767 New Jersey Anglicans hosted a second intercolonial convention under Chandler's leadership and this time encouraged Chandler to prepare a carefully argued pamphlet setting forth the episcopal cause. It was believed that a rational presentation of their case would allay any fears Dissenters might have and also rally the indifferent and passively resistant Anglicans within the church to the standard. Moreover, Dr. Johnson had previously urged Chandler to prepare such a work in the belief that it would encourage churchmen in the southern colonies from "whose lukewarmness, ignorance, and prejudices it seems we have much to fear."[24] Thus encouraged, Chandler wrote *An Appeal to the Public in behalf of the Church of England* which was published in 1767. It was this overt act of the episcopal campaign that provoked the wrath of Dissenters rather than calmed their fears, and it led to a long and rancorous conflict.

The *Appeal* was divided into four parts: (1) the origin and nature of the episcopal office; (2) reasons for sending bishops to America; (3) a plan by which they were to be sent; and (4) a refutation of objections against the plan. The proposition

Chandler hoped would placate Dissenters was the theory of a "purely spiritual episcopate for America," of bishops who should have no temporal powers, no special relations with the state, no state functions, no exclusive civil privileges. In short, Chandler proposed a bishop with a mitre, but without the support of the sceptre. In other words, this episcopal figure would have the right to ordain, confirm, consecrate, and conduct visitations, but not as an official of the state. But in formulating this proposal Chandler reduced the concept of episcopacy beyond the suffragan idea promoted by Bishops Compton and Sherlock. Though the king would appoint these "spiritual bishops," no suggestion was made that they be a part of the archdiocese of Canterbury or the diocese of London. Nor was the process for selecting the episcopal candidates defined, leaving open the possibility that Chandler was subtly suggesting that an intercolonial convention of Anglican clergy might elect the candidates. There is no hard evidence that this procedure was what Chandler had in mind, but his previous conduct provides circumstantial confirmation. However, there is evidence that Dr. Johnson thought in these terms when he wrote to Myles Cooper, "as long therefore as there is any possibility of yr being a Bp. in America I am not willing you should be one in England."[25]

The calm before the storm lasted six months; then the explosive fury of independent opposition found expression through Charles Chauncy's pen. Chauncy was pastor of First Church, Boston, and at the time of the episcopal controversy the most influential clergyman in New England. His *Appeal Answered* was the initial challenge of a concerted effort in pamphlet and newspaper utterly to refute the position taken by Chandler in the *Appeal*. In time, the contest went through *The Appeal Defended* by Chandler which Chauncy answered in *A Reply to Dr. Chandler's "Appeal Defended." The Appeal Farther Defended* was rebutted by Chauncy's *A Compleat View of Episcopacy* published in 1771.

In his argument, Dr. Chauncy, a long-time opponent of Anglicanism in New England, staunchly denied that bishops even in the Church of England had a divine right to govern the church and were in any sense superior to presbyters. Nor did he admit the claim of episcopal apostolic succession and described extensively how bishops and presbyters in the early church were one and the same. But he also fingered a very sensitive issue when he charged that Anglicans were divided over the necessity of bishops and illustrated it by calling attention to the absence of any lay endorsements. Then the intrepid Chauncy publicized the fact that the clergy who promoted the episcopal scheme had received no authority from the English bishops to do so and had thus violated Canon 73 of their church constitution. Moreover, Chauncy asserted that a secret ballot on the part of churchmen would completely negate the plan.[26] It is surprising that the charges of internal indifference, dissension, and quiet resistance were not directly or fully refuted in the press by a united effort from Anglicans, but they were not. Only Chandler cautiously admitted that a few churchmen might not be in full sympathy with the scheme, but he conspicuously avoided attempting a fuller answer in his pamphlets.

A second part of the controversy exploded with a series of articles entitled "The American Whig" which began in Parker's *New York Gazette* in March of 1768 and ran for fifty-seven issues. The men behind this series were William Livingston, William Smith, Jr., and John Morin Scott, all Presbyterian laymen experienced in New York politics and dedicated to religious freedom. The objective in "The American Whig" series was to explode the idea that Anglicans wanted a primitive bishop. Instead, it was charged that the episcopal plan was really an attempt to secure a benign episcopate and later endow it with full prelatical powers. The claim that an American Anglican bishop would be a "primitive or purely spiritual" bishop was too fantastic for most people to believe.[27] For example, primitive bishops were elected by a free vote of the clergy and could perform only ordination, confirmation, and visitation in the early Christian church. In the third or fourth century it was not unusual that bishops were also local pastors. But after the Edict of Milan issued by Roman Emperor Constantine in A.D. 313 which officially recognized the Christian religion, bishops became associated with the state. The fact that English bishops were appointed by the king, endowed with titles and dignities, and required to engage in secular affairs was evidence of the complete blending of church and state in eighteenth-century England. Livingston, Smith, and Scott asserted it was too much to expect anyone to believe the king or the British government would put aside hundreds of years of ecclesiastical tradition at the request of a few Anglican clergymen in America.

Although Samuel Seabury, Charles Inglis, and Myles Cooper contributed a series of articles that appeared in Gaine's *New York Mercury* entitled a "Whip for the American Whig," they did not have an easy time handling their opponent's arguments. It was generally known among Anglicans and Dissenters alike that English bishops had authority to conduct ecclesiastical courts to determine the legitimacy of births and marriages, probate wills, try morals cases, pronounce excommunication, and compel payment of tithes and stipends. Even though these episcopal prerogatives were more sparingly used in eighteenth-century England than in previous centuries, the civil and canonical statutes permitting such ecclesiastical functions still existed. That this wide range of ecclesiastical authority would be renounced as well as any added tax or tithe to support an American episcopate was more than reasonable men could accept.

A point emphasized over and over by the Dissenter opponents to episcopacy was that many Anglicans did not want bishops for the same reasons Dissenters opposed them. In 1768 a public letter addressed to Chandler, whether from an Anglican or non-Anglican is not apparent, forcibly charged, "it is certain that a great part of your hearers, of your own church, are very far from wishing for any bishop ever to be sent to America."[28] Indeed, "The American Whig" series which also appeared in the *Boston Gazette* and *Pennsylvania Journal* consistently played upon the theme of internal Anglican disunity over the cause for bishops, and no one tried to refute it. It was evident to Chauncy, Livingston, Scott, and Smith that forces within the American Anglican communion were silently and passively resisting the Johnson-Chandler campaign. Then article thirteen of "The American Whig" flatly announced that Anglicans from Maryland to Georgia were unsympathetic to an American bishop. If this charge were true, the promoters could not expect a unified front with which to face the home government in their campaign and thus the cause, barring a miracle, would be lost. But Drs. Johnson and Chandler, aided by their zealous brethren—Inglis, Seabury, Cooper, and Jarvis—refused to recognize publicly the alleged internal resistance to their scheme.

INTROSPECTION

An examination of church records for Connecticut, Massachusetts, New York, and New Jersey reveals no evidence the Anglican laity of the northeastern region supported the clerical proposal for bishops. The overwhelming amount of data shows parish vestries and in some instances congregations exercising increased local authority that in many respects resembled Congregational or Presbyterian polity. A few congregations elected their ministers who were then appointed by the S.P.G. or the bishop of London, but usually the churchwardens acting for the vestry and congregations informed the S.P.G. of their ministerial preference and rarely was such a request denied. It was, moreover, a general practice for Anglicans without a minister to choose a lay-reader to conduct services in spite of the fact that Anglican tradition forbade it. None other than Dr. Johnson came to accept the concept of the lay-reader and he defended it out of practical necessity, but in accepting this measure Anglicans were adopting a practice generally associated with nonconformist religious bodies. All these measures were to some extent contrary to episcopal tradition of clerical appointment, collation, and supervision and in this region many vestries took their prerogatives for granted and evidenced no desire to surrender them.[29] A more direct indication of the laity's attitude toward episcopacy is disclosed in the correspondence of William Samuel Johnson and Godfrey Malbone, two prominent Anglicans from Connecticut.

Godfrey Malbone had been a classmate of the bishop of Bangor in Queen's College, Oxford. In 1769, Malbone moved to Pomfret, Connecticut, to relocate his business and there he helped build an Anglican church and subscribed to its support. He wrote his former classmate, the bishop, to request help in securing a pastor and in the same letter bitterly complained of the ecclesiastical tyranny of the Congregationalists that coerced Anglicans to pay taxes to support their churches. But Malbone never once in this letter or in a series of other letters suggested or even hinted that a bishop would be helpful.[30]

The usual way for churchwardens to seek a pastor was to correspond with Dr. Johnson, whose advice was highly regarded by the church authorities in England, or Dr. Burton, secretary of the S.P.G., and let them know their preference and perhaps the amount of support the local church would provide. If the S.P.G. removed or attempted to remove a missionary who was well liked, the churchwardens did not hesitate to register their disapproval to the Society. When Bela Hubbard, for example, moved from Guilford, Connecticut, in July 1768 at the S.P.G.'s directions, the churchwardens informed the Society of their displeasure. At least six other churches in Connecticut had similar problems during the years of the episcopal campaign and not one of them requested or intimated that a bishop in America would ease their problems or was desired. Every indication suggests the laity preferred to deal with Dr.

Johnson or Dr. Burton on church problems, retaining the local authority they had acquired.

It was, however, the leading Anglican layman of Connecticut, William Samuel Johnson, son of the arch-promoter Dr. Johnson, who dealt the severest blow to the scheme even though he knew intimately the inner workings of the episcopal plan and the campaign strategy. In 1765 when Dr. Johnson and most Anglicans in Connecticut expressed loyal support for the home government following the Stamp Act, William S. Johnson was not among them. Instead he sided with the New Light faction which succeeded in turning out of office numerous Old Lights in the elections of 1766 who had favored compliance with the Stamp Act. As a result, the younger Johnson became the first Anglican to sit on the Connecticut Council. From 1767 to 1771 he was Connecticut's colonial agent in England and in this responsible position managed to maintain the respect of both Anglican and Congregationalist communities. It was he who carried copies of Chandler's *Appeal* to England and about whom the bishop of Oxford, Robert Lowth, wrote, "I sometimes talk over these matters with much freedom with your worthy son . . . ; as I receive of him the best information of everything relating to the affairs in America." Then in the summer of 1769 William S. Johnson advised his father, "I cannot but say I am glad your controversy about American bishops seems to be near its end, since I am afraid it can have no very good effects there, and it produces none at all here."[31]

William S. Johnson's correspondence provides telling evidence of the indifference with which the episcopal scheme was greeted in England. But this evidence is underscored by recordings in his diaries of meetings with the archbishop of Canterbury, the S.P.G., Dr. Burton, and Dr. Berkeley as well as John Wesley and Ben Johnson. In high ministry circles he met with Lord Hillsborough, Mr. Grenville, Lord North, and Mr. Burke. Thus when Governor Trumbull of Connecticut inquired of William S. Johnson in 1771 about the status of the

American episcopal plan, Johnson replied on good authority, "it is not intended at present, to send any Bishops into the American colonies." Then he added, as if to reassure Trumbull of his own loyalty to Connecticut's interest, that the episcopal plan had never sought bishops with the least degree of secular power even over the laity of the Church of England. "If more than this," he stated, "I assure you [it] would be opposed by no Man with more zeal than myself, even as a friend of the Chh of England."[32]

A position similar to the one taken by Connecticut Anglicans existed in Massachusetts where 12 clergymen served the 769 families of the communion. Henry Caner and his clerical associates met separately from the Connecticut, New York, and New Jersey clergy in 1766 and 1767 though they did forward petitions requesting bishops. However, their petitions contained this qualification: "we do however think ourselves happy in this, that the Society will omit no favorable opportunity of representing the advantages that may accrue to the colonies to religion and to the British interest by condescending to this request."[33] It was plain that the Massachusetts Anglican clergy were not trying to force the episcopal issue; when the S.P.G. made no response to their petitions another was not sent before the Revolutionary War. The Anglican clergy of Massachusetts were not carried away with the enthusiasm that motivated their Connecticut, New York, and New Jersey brethren. But the discontinuance of support from Massachusetts in 1768 was keenly felt by Drs. Johnson and Chandler.

Another factor Henry Caner had to consider was his own status as rector of King's Chapel, Boston. He had been selected for the position by a committee of the congregation and elected by the congregation in 1747 before approval was sought from the bishop of London. A similar procedure was followed by Trinity Church, Boston; Trinity Church, New York City; St. John's Church, Providence, Rhode Island; and Christ and St. Peter's churches, Philadelphia.[34] Moreover, the vestries and

congregations of the larger churches showed a definite preference for American-born and educated clergymen who accepted
the vestry's authority more readily than their British cousins.
For a minister in any of these churches or anyone who ever
hoped to be called to one of the larger urban churches to do
anything that might antagonize or undermine the laity was very
unwise. The episcopal campaign itself must have raised questions in the minds of laymen about their role and rights as
elected church officers should an episcopate be procured. Perhaps it was deference to the role of the vestrymen and congregations that explains why no rector of a large church in the
coastal cities of the northeast was a zealous advocate for bishops. Indeed, a degree of Congregational-Presbyterian type polity was already operative in many parishes of the northeast.

The same pattern of local church cooperation with the Society which existed in Connecticut and Massachusetts prevailed
in New York and New Jersey. The vast majority of churches
were directly or indirectly dependent on the S.P.G. subsidies so
they were careful not to offend the Society, but occasionally a
church like Grace Church in Rye, New York, determined to
choose its minister. When James Wetmore died in 1762 the
vestry assumed the authority to invite Ebenezer Punderson of
Connecticut to become its minister without consulting the
S.P.G. In the meantime, Solomon Palmer of New Haven, Connecticut, had requested the Society to assign him to Rye, but
when the vestry learned of Palmer's appeal they replied, "we
did then with one general voice give him Punderson an invitation to be our pastor, and he with our great satisfaction fa-
voured us with his acceptance of it." Then Peter Jay, father of a
future Anglican lay leader, John Jay, the most outspoken member of the vestry, warned Dr. Johnson, who had tried to aid
Palmer, "if there should be another appointment whereof you
entertain some fear, the consequences may prove unfortunate."[35] Though the exact meaning of Jay's implied threat was
not stated, it was obvious a local church could reduce its share

Colonial Parishes in New Jersey. Courtesy of Nelson R. Burr and the Church
Historial Society.

of the minister's support or make conditions so uncomfortable a clergyman could not remain if someone not of their choice was forced upon them. There was, therefore, no support for a bishop among the Anglican laity in Grace Church or for any other ecclesiastical official whose authority might clash with their will.

The internal indifference and passive resistance to the episcopal scheme coupled with the withdrawal of Massachusetts' support depressed Dr. Johnson. Under these conditions Drs. Johnson and Chandler had a serious disagreement over the implementation of their plan. Dr. Johnson had accepted the fact that a bishop in Canada was the best that could be hoped for, but Chandler definitely disagreed. "I am so unfortunate as to differ in opinion from you in some points, but I believe in no [ne] [sic] that are of much consequence, unless the Canadian episcopate may be called so. For the impropriety and uselessness, and was it not that you think otherwise, I would almost venture to say the ridiculousness of such an appointment, are points in which I am at present very clear—but I have not time and room to assign the reasons."[36] This sharp difference in judgment between the two episcopal leaders had marked repercussions. Dr. Johnson, who was in his late sixties, henceforth played a decreasingly minor role, but Chandler in his early forties was a determined person and an energetic writer. It appeared that the ascendency of Chandler if anything intensified the drive for a bishop.

THE BISHOPS' RESPONSE

The bishop of London, Richard Terrick, in 1767 let his displeasure about the Elizabeth Town Convention be known. He advised, "whatever are our sentiments or wishes, we must leave it to the discretion and wisdom of government to choose the time for adopting that measure."[37] In addition, Robert Lowth, bishop of Oxford, wrote, "as to the great and important design of an American episcopate I see no immediate prospect of its being carried into execution." Perhaps the latter response was a partial reply to a letter written in November 1766 by Dr. Johnson to Archbishop Secker. "I humbly beg leave, therefore, . . . to suggest whether it is not incumbent upon the bishops in faithfulness to the church and to their own sacred order, to unite in insisting that bishops be sent into America. . . . If the church must go into a state of open persecution, she must and ought, rather than to let her bishops cease to be, . . . or dwindle into merely worldly political creatures, instead of truly spiritual persons."[38] This most strongly worded plea from the arch-promoter of an American episcopate to the archbishop and indirectly the whole hierarchy was given a silent denial. While Dr. Johnson and his zealous associates were High Church in their view of episcopacy, which meant they considered bishops of the apostolic succession essential to the very existence of the church, the English bishops were bound in the Erastianism of eighteenth-century England and could not act without governmental consent. Although it is certain Archbishop Secker understood Dr. Johnson's plea, he died in 1768 and his successor the bishop of Lichfield, Frederick Cornwallis, showed no interest in the colonial churches.

Moreover, the Standing Committee of the S.P.G.—which normally met four times a year and to whom the American zealots had petitioned for assistance in the episcopal campaign—gave no encouragement or instructions to its missionaries to agitate for resident bishops during the late 1760s and early 1770s. This committee normally received and recorded requests from missionaries and churches and recorded the reply in a space below each itemized entry. In the 1760s and 1770s, for example, Chandler's *Appeal* was received and filed on June 24, 1768 without comment, and Sir William Johnson's petition in favor of the episcopal plan and his offer of land to support an episcopate were also recorded without a word of thanks for his generous offer. It was more than a year before Sir William Johnson was thanked by the Society for his offer, but even then no mention was made of a bishop in the letter of appreciation.

The 1766 and 1767 Elizabeth Town conventions got the Johnson-Chandler plan off to an ambitious start, but it did not gain anywhere near unanimous support among Anglicans. The opposition of New England Congregationalists and New York Presbyterians was not surprising, but the counterproposal of Richard Peters and William Smith, coupled with the inside criticism of the episcopal scheme by Samuel Auchmuty, were causes for serious reflection. Also, the conspicuous absence of lay endorsements from Anglicans was a sign the promoters of a resident episcopate were encountering at least indifference and in some instances resistance to their scheme. The withdrawal of the Massachusetts clergy's support was another unmistakable indication the episcopal plan was not doing well. If it had not been for the indomitable determination of Chandler and a few associates, the episcopal campaign would have folded in 1769, but this contingent continued to press the issue. Not even the negative responses of three English bishops, who had shown great interest in the American churches, was sufficient to dampen the zeal of Chandler and company.

3

Pennsylvania Churchmen

"The Churches are well furnished; the Grave yards in good repair, and the Congregations numerous, orderly, and attentive."

Thomas Barton to the S.P.G.
Lancaster, November 10, 1766

In Pennsylvania Anglicanism existed in an environment much different from that which prevailed in New England, New York, or New Jersey. Pennsylvania was a proprietary colony and the proprietors, Thomas and Richard Penn and the Lieutenant Governor John Penn, had departed the Quaker faith of their father to become communicants of the Church of England. Although the Anglican church was not established in Pennsylvania, it was not discriminated against because there was religious freedom in this colony, permitting a wide variety of religious expression.[1] Nevertheless, the interest of the Penn family in the church was an important feature of its existence in this once predominantly Quaker state. In 1775, there were twenty-two Anglican churches served by nineteen clergymen, but by comparison there were fifty-six Presbyterian churches. Mr. Craig, the S.P.G. missionary in Chester, reported in 1764 that out of a population estimated variously to be between 200,000 and 300,000 there were not more than one-fiftieth who could be counted as adherents of the Church of England.[2] If one accepts these rough figures, there were then but 6,000 or 7,000 Anglicans in the colony in 1764. Without the favor of the proprietors and the leadership of Dr. William Smith and the Reverend Richard Peters, the Anglican church in Pennsylvania would have been of limited significance in the total population. This relationship which bound the church to the proprietors and their representatives was never more evident than in the events of the 1760s.

PROPRIETARY CHURCH INTEREST

Thomas Penn and Lady Juliana frequently expressed their concern for the church in Pennsylvania by entertaining in their home the Anglican clergy newly commissioned for a mission in Pennsylvania as well as those returning to England on business. Of those who journeyed to England for ordination Penn said, "I cannot think it so hard a thing for persons to come over for Orders and an appointment to a mission, as it is but once, and keeps up some sort of dependence on the mother country."[3] Of students trained by Smith in the College of Philadelphia Penn was particularly complimentary. On still other occasions Dr. Smith, Richard Peters, Jacob Duché, and a dozen other Anglican clergymen from Pennsylvania were received by the Penns. In this way, Penn knew personally the ministers who served in his province and quite naturally disfavored any proposals that would interfere or threaten to invade his carefully developed ties with the church. Moreover, the two most prominent Anglican clergymen, Smith and Peters, were faithful in their commitment to the proprietary interest. In return, Smith received a £50 annual pension and Peters, formerly secretary of the land office from 1741 to 1762 before becoming rector of Christ and St. Peter's churches, was also appointed secretary to the Colonial Council.[4]

The personal concern of Thomas Penn in the welfare of an individual minister is disclosed in his correspondence with Thomas Barton. Penn had learned that Barton intended to seek induction into a Maryland parish where the stipend was greater and the appointment more secure. "I am much concerned," Penn wrote, "to find that the missionaries have suffered so much, and that you are so uneasy in your situation as to have asked leave to move into Maryland, the Society either have offered, or intend to offer you an addition to your salary, or some other encouragement if you stay in Pennsylvania, and I have desired Mr. Hamilton who is upon his return to talk to you on this affair . . . and to make you a present from me, if you do not put that design in execution."[5] In this case friendly persuasion coupled with pecuniary consideration convinced Barton to remain in Lancaster. However, Penn was unusual in the personal concern which he showed toward the Anglican clergy and not even the bishops of London in the 1760s or the governors in the royal colonies from Virginia to Georgia where the Church of England was established equalled his example.

In still other ways Thomas Penn expressed good will to the clergy of his province and in so doing enhanced himself in their favor. He made it a point to offer to each man his services as agent to represent the clergy collectively or individually to the bishop of London, archbishop of Canterbury, and the S.P.G.[6] This service he apparently performed with success, for there is a paucity of letters from Pennsylvania Anglican clergymen complaining of conditions in their respective appointments and the few incidents he did detect—e.g., Barton's— were resolved. Moreover, Penn donated his library to the Society along with financial contributions, presumably to aid the work in Pennsylvania.[7] Then too, in the 1760s he made land available for new churches in both Reading and York as well as approving the sale of a considerable tract of city land to Christ and St. Peter's.[8] Understandably, Anglican vestries in Pennsylvania experienced no difficulties or delays in securing charters for their new churches. In no other colony—royal, proprietary, or corporate—was the Church of England treated by the controlling authorities with equal or greater deference.

The dominant personality within the church in Pennsylvania was William Smith, provost of the Academy and College of Philadelphia, who in the controversies that filled the 1760s championed the proprietary cause. Smith assumed the role of a commissary in Pennsylvania though he had no commission to do so, and attempted to direct the clergy. Not surprisingly, Smith's ambition clashed with other clergymen. In 1758, Dr. Robert Jenny, rector of Christ Church, complained to the archbishop of Canterbury about Smith's "officious" manner and his tendency to "misrepresent things." There was, however, no change in Smith's conduct, for in 1767 he prevented Hugh Neill of Oxford from serving St. Paul's Church, Philadelphia, provoking Neill to seek and receive induction into a Maryland parish. On another occasion, in spite of the need for ministers in Pennsylvania, Smith objected to the ordinations of Messrs. Spencer, Dunlap, and Sturgeon because one of their recommenders was Benjamin Franklin, a political enemy of Smith's.[9] Because of his officious manner, Smith was suspected as early as 1756 of being a candidate to become the first Anglican bishop in America. His plan for commissaries introduced through Peters to the Elizabeth Town Convention was probably motivated in part by his desire to exercise authority over his clerical associates.

It is entirely possible that the clergy at the Elizabeth Town Convention of 1766 objected to Smith's proposal for commissaries because they saw a possibility that he might be commissioned one. If that had happened, they knew they could expect the same stern treatment Neill and others had received. Moreover, a commissary would have authority to report directly to the hierarchy in England. This position they did not want re-created and definitely not with a commission for Smith. There was no hint that he might be consecrated a bishop, but if that had become a possibility, it probably would have scuttled the episcopal scheme. Smith's rise to prominence in Pennsylvania after his selection as provost in 1754 had been rapid and his contributions to education, literature, science, and politics were notable, but in 1766 and 1767 the Anglican clergy meeting in Elizabeth Town were not about to promote him for a pair of lawn sleeves or permit him to use their convention and episcopal plan as a launch-pad for his own ambition.[10]

In contrast with Smith, Richard Peters was a benign and steady person who worked effectively within the church and colony with unquestioned loyalty to the proprietors. After twenty-one years in the land office and as secretary of the province, Peters in 1763 became rector of the largest parish in Pennsylvania: Christ and St. Peter's, which he served until his retirement in 1775.[11] During all this time he was favored by the proprietors and after his induction as rector he was able to continue his service to the Penns and retain the uninterrupted good will of his congregation and vestry. Peters requested more than one leave from his vestry in order to serve the proprietors and it was always granted, though concern was expressed that by his double services he was overtaxing his health. When his health did fail in the early 1770s, the vestry insisted on retaining him and the proprietors continued to favor him. As a trustee of the Academy and College of Philadelphia and a member and contributor to numerous societies, Peters in his quiet and serene way served the cause of the church and proprietors.

POLITICS

Politics in Pennsylvania in the 1760s revolved primarily around the issue of proprietary government.[12] One faction, the Quaker party, opposed it and the other, Proprietary party, favored its continuance. On March 24, 1764, the assembly adopted a resolution calling for the substitution of royal government for proprietary privilege in Pennsylvania. Shortly thereafter, Benjamin Franklin left for England where he lobbied for the next ten years in an effort to persuade the British government either to void or buy back Penn's charter. Though Franklin did not succeed in his mission, the very fact that he was in England beseeching the home authorities to act against Penn's interest gave encouragement to the Quaker party. But the opposition of the Proprietary party to Franklin's and the Quaker's plan was sufficient to keep political tensions high for the balance of the decade.[13] Moreover, when other issues were introduced into Pennsylvania politics, they inevitably became intertwined to some degree with this major internal contest.

The proprietors, of whom Thomas Penn was the chief member, had their defenders and among them none were more loyal than the Anglican clerical leaders and most of their constituents. But foremost among the court or Proprietary party were Presbyterians, clergy and laity, because they were convinced that whatever the problems resulting from Penn's proprietorship those that would inevitably come with royal rule would be much worse. The chief proprietary supporter among Presbyterians was the chief justice of the province, William Allen. For a number of years he had been the chief dispenser of proprietary favors and a generous patron of many worthy causes. United with Allen were the Presbyterian clergy of both the Old and New Light factions who in 1758 reunited in an effort to meet the challenge of the Quaker party. Gilbert Tennent, Francis Alison, and John Ewing as the clerical leaders were not enamored with the proprietary interest, but they were convinced the Quakers were out to produce a new oppression which must be resisted.[14] As a result of this Presbyterian position, they developed with the Anglicans a *détente,* though an uneasy one, which considerably strengthened the proprietary cause. However, the Presbyterians were suspicious that the Anglicans might one day seek a resident bishop and to them this was just as objectionable as the Quaker's quest for royal government. Indeed, when the Johnson-Chandler plan became known in Pennsylvania in 1768, the political coalition that had developed between Anglicans and Presbyterians dissolved.[15]

The member of the Proprietary party who put together a political confederation that proved more than a match for the Quaker party in the 1764 elections was William Smith. Smith was anything but a novice in politics and handed the Quakers a stunning defeat when Benjamin Franklin, Joseph Galloway, and three others of their coadjutors were defeated for the assembly. To produce this result, Smith and the Presbyterians worked tirelessly enlisting the aid of German groups, particularly Lutheran and Reformed congregations. In the process many of these congregations were granted church charters. William Allen, who was in England in 1764, persuaded the Quaker leaders there to oppose royal government for Pennsylvania, thus dividing and weakening the Quaker party's position in the eyes of the English authorities. Moreover, Smith and associates in Pennsylvania were able to assemble a petition bearing 15,000 signatures opposing the imposition of royal government. Their opponents responded with one containing 3,500 names. Even though the Quaker party made a comeback in the 1765 elections, the Proprietary party had achieved a vitality it had not possessed before. In 1765, when the Quaker party decided to obey the Stamp Act to assist Franklin in his mission to achieve royal government, the Proprietary party which opposed the act gained further popular acceptance.[16]

There was, however, one defection from the front rank of the Proprietary party after 1765: William Smith. Though Smith opposed the Stamp Act and supported the colonist's rights, the publication of Chandler's *Appeal* ended the era of cooperation between Presbyterians and Anglicans. Moreover, Smith had been endeavoring to bring the Lutheran and Reformed churches into communion with the Anglicans, but the revelation of an episcopal scheme sponsored by the Elizabeth Town conventions contributed to the termination of this early attempt at church union.[17] In 1768 Smith felt compelled to defend the Church of England against the attacks which Chandler's pamphlet had triggered. But in so doing Smith split with the Presbyterians and Germans who opposed the concept of Anglican bishops in America, for both groups considered them dangerous and politically a form of royal government. After this schism within the Proprietary party, Smith never again recaptured the political clout he had acquired as a result of his efforts in the election of 1764, though he continued to be a prominent leader in Philadelphia political and ecclesiastical circles.

CLERICAL RESISTANCE

Due to the political realities which existed in Pennsylvania it is obvious that neither Smith and Peters nor the Anglican clergy in general were in a position to become leaders in the episcopal scheme. The favor which Anglicans received from the proprietors could be easily lost by participation in a controversy which could potentially strengthen the role of the home government in the colonies. It was, therefore, imperative to the interest of Pennsylvania's churchmen that an episcopal controversy not occur in Philadelphia as it had in New York. Even the impression that Pennsylvania's Anglican clergy were supporting a plan that would enhance the British government's authority in Pennsylvania would most certainly weaken Penn's position *vis-à-vis* Franklin. It was the need to defend the proprietor's position that originally brought the Presbyterians and Anglicans to cooperate and it was the need for continued cooperation that kept the traditionally ecclesiastical antagonists from a rancorous debate over the Johnson-Chandler plan. Besides, in Pennsylvania the level of religious freedom tempered the arguments which naturally followed the publication of the *Appeal*. But at no time did the discussion over episcopacy in Pennsylvania acquire the intensity or vindictiveness that characterized the controversy in Boston and New York. Thus in the late 1760s when Chandler and Chauncy, Livingston, Smith, and Morin and Cooper, Seabury, and Inglis were battling for their respective positions, Presbyterians and Anglicans in Pennsylvania, while differing over episcopacy, treated each other with mutual respect.

In the light of conditions in Pennsylvania it was understandable that Richard Peters opposed the plan for episcopacy adopted by the Elizabeth Town Convention. Indeed, Peters and Smith did all that was within their power to deflect the impact of the convention from Pennsylvania and to minimize its appeal to the English hierarchy. Both men promptly alerted the bishop of London, Richard Terrick, about the New Jersey convention and described it as emotional and poorly timed. Smith stated, "Mr. Peters attended now and bore his testimony against these resolves. . . . He was milder, I believe, than I should have been. . . . " Peter's report was more charitable than Smith's, though equally opposed to the convention action, for he added, "they are really good people and some of them very sensible as Dr. Chandler, Mr. Danbury, Mr. McKean, and Mr. Cook. In short, they are all diligent in their cares and have religion at heart, but for all this they cannot observe any temper in the affair of bishops and it is just so with the New York clergy as I hear and have seen a little of it in some of them. . . . They did not take it amiss in me for dissenting from them. . . . My speech tho' well taken did not cool them."[18]

The protest of Smith and Peters to Bishop Terrick was designed to weaken the case of the episcopal promoters. Their description of the irrepressible enthusiasm of the northeastern clergy on behalf of a resident episcopate may also have alerted Terrick to possible problems in dealing with the New World fringe of his diocese and contributed to his decision not to seek a commission authorizing his supervision in America.[19] In any event, it was apparent that with Johnson and Chandler on one side of the episcopal question and Smith and Peters on the other, there was a major problem to be resolved. Moreover, Terrick and the S.P.G., which had also received reports from Smith and Peters, could readily see that each faction had its supporters and was likely to gain added numbers if the issue were allowed to grow. It was, moreover, one thing for Chauncy and the Presbyterians to challenge episcopacy; it was far more serious to promote a cause which might divide the American Anglican community into openly warring camps. If an internal

division over the plan for a resident bishop became widespread, it could easily negate the remarkable gains Anglicans
had achieved and possibly prevent future intercolonial church
cooperation.

While Peters believed that his opposition to the action of the
Elizabeth Town Convention did not produce resentment toward himself, an entirely different reaction was manifested toward Smith. It was Chandler who divulged the hostility which
the convention generated toward Smith in a letter to Dr. Johnson. "Last week I was in Philadelphia, and payed my respects to
the American Colossus. I was treated with politeness by him
and he was very desirous to know the reasons of the general
disaffection of the clergy of our last convention towards him. I
thought it not improper to assign them without disguise or
equivocation. . . . I fear it will not be easy for him to prove that
he has a due degree of affection either for the church or her
clergy or right principles."[20] Although Smith had not attended
the convention, his proposal for commissaries was viewed as a
subversive move to undermine the "high church" concept of
episcopacy and church government which a majority of the
delegates held. Moreover, it appears that Chandler expressed
his personal disapproval of Smith's proposal. Unfortunately
this meeting was the last reported meeting between these able
leaders of the church and their disagreements were not resolved, but carried over into the postwar era.

The expressed displeasure on the part of zealous churchmen
toward Smith did not deter him from again opposing the Johnson-Chandler plan when it became generally known. After the
publication of the *Appeal* in 1767, Smith wrote to Bishop Terrick. "I wrote your lordship that I had much reason to fear the
extraordinary warmth of the Jersey conventions might do hurt.
Their addresses and Dr. Chandler's appeal about bishops for
America, . . . have raised a great flame. There is nothing but
writing in every newspaper. I could not approve of any appeals
to the public here about bishops."[21] Smith explained that he

objected because there had already been too much controversy over episcopacy. He could have added that coming at a time when tensions over the issue of royal government for Pennsylvania were periodically exacerbated by such acts as the Stamp Act and Townshend Duties the subject of a resident bishop only served to accent opposition to the British government.

Richard Peters, in a manner less forceful than Smith's, also opposed the Johnson-Chandler plan by giving aid and comfort to the one prominent clergyman in New York who advised against it. Throughout the controversy over bishops Samuel Auchmuty was rector of Trinity Church, New York. In his private correspondence with Peters, Auchmuty expressed his reservations about the New Jersey convention of 1766. By May of 1767 Auchmuty in preparation for the next convention wrote to Peters to seek his cooperation to cool the zeal of his brethren. "I shall want assistance," he wrote, "at the convention; for I fear that same spirit will prevail that appeared at the last Jersey one: however I shall give myself little trouble about it. Lords all, and Masters all, I find will not do, either in church or state." Unfortunately, the minutes of the 1767 convention do not make it clear that Auchmuty attended or if he did, what part he took in the deliberations. However, in correspondence subsequent to the convention's meeting he disclosed "we are still fighting, and abusing one another. . . . Poor Chandler is mauled from all quarters. I told him before he published his *Appeal* that this would be the consequence, I therefore did not advise the publication, I was not believed, and so the affair went on." The tone of Auchmuty's letter seems to imply that others also felt as he about the publication of the *Appeal,* but there is no hint as to who they were or why they agreed with Trinity's rector. Nevertheless, the known resistance of the rectors of two of the largest parishes in colonial America to the episcopal scheme was significant. In both cases, these clergymen obviously believed that the best interest of the church was served by avoiding controversy. Thus there appears to be a note of relief in Auchmuty's note to Peters in December 1768 when he announced "I have lately received a very affectionate letter from the Bishop of Oxford—No prospect at present of an American bishop."[22]

In still another way the Anglican leaders of Pennsylvania revealed their opposition to the Johnson-Chandler initiative. It was well known in Anglican circles that Sir William Johnson, agent of the Northern Department of Indian Affairs, supported the episcopal campaign and had offered to secure 200,000 acres of land to aid the plan. However, not all the clergy expressed congratulations for Johnson's generous offer. In fact, within the considerable correspondence which circulated among Johnson, Peters, and Smith, all of whom knew each other, the subject of a resident bishop was never mentioned. Although the topics of land, Indians, missionaries, and churches were discussed, the episcopal issue is conspicuously absent.[23] This omission of a topic that was a front-page item in the major newspapers in late 1767 and 1768 was not an oversight, but another form of Smith's and Peter's refusal to encourage a scheme that had serious political implications for Pennsylvania.

THE PUBLIC CONTEST

The newspaper coverage of the episcopal controversy which began in New York and Boston in the spring of 1768 spread to Pennsylvania. "The American Whig" series prepared by Livingston, Smith, and Scott in New York City was reprinted in the *Pennsylvania Journal*. In addition, Francis Alison, John Dickinson, and George Bryan articulated the Presbyterian opposition to the *Appeal* and its proposal and expressed it publicly in a series entitled "Centinel." At the time Alison, a Presbyterian minister, was vice provost of the Academy and College of Philadelphia while Dickinson and Bryan were prominent laymen. In this series there was more light and less heat generated than in the series produced in New York. The purpose of the authors was publicly to ask Dr. Chandler a few questions about resident bishops because his *Appeal* had made it a public issue and it was feared the office of bishop would have political implications for non-Anglicans. It was frankly stated, however, that the establishment of an additional tie with the home government was considered a threat to American liberties. It was also clearly stated that the claim that an English bishop could be sent to America without a court, titles, and tithes was too much for Pennsylvanians to believe.

The main theme of the "Centinel" series was that the establishment of a bishop in America by the English government via an act of parliament would be direct interference in the internal affairs of the colonies.[24] In view of the recent conflict over the Stamp Act an ecclesiastical stamp act was unthinkable. Since Chandler's *Appeal* provided no assurance that the people in America would have a say in the selection or acceptance of the bishop, their interest would in no way be represented. The obvious lack of financial resources to support such a project would mean that a form of legislated income was likely to follow. "Every application therefore, to any other than the legislature of the respective colonies, for laws or regulations relative to our internal policy, I consider as an attack upon the liberty of the colonies. . . . If they may, without the consent of the colonies, establish bishopricks and bishops among us, they may appoint revenues for their support, erect spiritual courts, and enforce obedience." But the creators of the "Centinel" articles were careful to add that they did not "intend any reflection on the laity of that communion [Anglican], nor on all the clergy. The moderation of some is well-known; they have endeavored to bring about a reformation in many things."[25]

The first "Centinel" article appeared in the *Pennsylvania Journal* on March 24, 1768, but there was no response to it for five months, until September 8, 1768. The delay in responding suggests that in Pennsylvania neither the Anglican clergy nor the

laity were anxious to defend Chandler's *Appeal* or the proposed
episcopate. When on September 8th the first installment in a
series called "Anatomist" appeared, its author was Dr. William
Smith. In his responses, Smith neither endorsed nor con-
demned Chandler's work. Professor Cross in his study gave the
impression Smith, in the "Anatomist," supported the episcopal
scheme, but Professor Bridenbaugh correctly argued that Smith
was not writing to defend Chandler or the episcopal plan.[26] The
internal evidence of the "Anatomist" clearly shows Smith was
not concerned with Chandler or the episcopal scheme *per se,* for
he wrote "is Dr. Chandler the Church of England, or the ten
thousandth part of it? or had he any general commission from
that church, or even from his own brethren belonging to it in
America? This is not pretended; and it is certain, that no more
than half a dozen of them ever had an opportunity of seeing his
pamphlet till in print, and of that number, it is confidently said,
not one to the south of Delaware." However, Smith's primary
purpose was forcefully expressed in his determination to defend
the Anglican church and its traditions from the accusations presented in the "Centinel."[27]

To be sure, in issue ten of the "Anatomist" Smith raised the
question of a nonpolitical bishop and argued that it was a theo-
retical possibility. He cited Danish and Moravian bishops as
examples. In these cases, the bishops ordained, confirmed, and
conducted visitation, but did not hold ecclesiastical courts nor
receive titles or tithes. Smith tried to argue that diocesan episcopacy without court, titles, and tithes was possible in America,
but he never once intimated he was advocating such a scheme.
He merely tried to demonstrate that there was historical evidence for the nonpolitical type of bishop Chandler proposed
and Dissenters refused to believe possible. Little did Smith realize he was building a case for the type of episcopacy his church
would adopt within the next twenty years. For the present,
however, his concern was for the welfare of the American Anglican communion and not a particular theory or scheme of

episcopacy. Indeed, Smith's literary effort to deflect hostility and criticism from the Anglican church in Pennsylvania was an apparent success. At the conclusion of his series he urged Anglicans and Presbyterians to live together peacefully. In early 1769 the Johnson-Chandler plan ceased to be publicly debated in Pennsylvania.[28]

THE LAITY

That Smith and Peters enjoyed widespread support from the laity for the position they took toward the Johnson-Chandler plan is evident from the fact that no churchmen in Pennsylvania took issue with them. This relationship is underscored when it is noted that in local parish affairs the laity and especially the elected vestries ruled. The unpublished Vestry Register of Christ and St. Peter's churches, 1760–84, reveals that Peters served both churches with skill and was held in high esteem. In fact, Peters was the vestry's choice for the rectorship when it came open in 1762. After the vestry elected him, it advised the Bishop of London of their choice and requested a license be sent to Peters authorizing him to officiate in America rather than requiring him to travel to England for licensing. To the vestrymen the required journey to England was needless, especially for one already ordained as Peters was, and imposed a hardship.[29] Moreover, their forwardness in requesting the bishop for a variation in ecclesiastical policy to suit their wishes suggests the self-interest with which they conducted parish matters.

After Peters was duly licensed and installed as rector, the same vestry did not hesitate to advise him. For example, in 1763 George Whitefield, the itinerant evangelist, was permitted to preach from Christ Church pulpit for the first time since it was closed to him twenty-three years earlier.[30] The change in attitude toward Whitefield came about primarily because the vestry informed Peters they desired him to preach in Christ

Church and Peters consented. Perhaps a partial explanation
for this action is due to the fact that in 1760 St. Paul's Church
had been opened in Philadelphia and the nucleus of the new
congregation was comprised of former constituents of Christ
and St. Peter's who favored evangelical religion. Their first
minister, William McClenachan, was decidely influenced by
Whitefield. Then too, by 1763 Whitefield had mellowed and his
earlier statements about the unspirituality of the Anglican
clergy were no longer repeated. But more than this was the
influence that the Great Awakening (of which Whitefield was a
major part) had had upon the role of the laity in church affairs.
The Great Revival had encouraged the idea that the laity had a
right to judge a minister's orthodoxy and performance.[31] Unquestionably this idea, though direct proof is impossible,
influenced the Anglican laity as it did those of other denominations, and in 1763 Whitefield was the recipient of an invitation
which indirectly his ministry had helped initiate.

The laity of the Pennsylvania Anglican churches made their
influence felt in a variety of ways. Not only did the vestries levy
and collect annual pew rates, arrange for annual vestry elections, hire school masters or mistresses (Elizabeth Hamilton),
raise funds for the distressed victims of Pontiac's conspiracy in
1763, receive funds in trust as well as handle a plethora of less
important matters, but the laity in Philadelphia had managed
to make all three city churches financially self-sufficient.[32] The
evidence that this gave important status to their position is
found in their practice of selecting and recommending their
own candidates for ordination to the bishop of London without
the concurrence of anyone else. By contrast, in New York, New
Jersey, and Connecticut, the clergy attempted to keep control
of the recommending process and at the very least kept their
hand in it. But the place of the laity in the life of the Pennsylvania churches is further illustrated by the election of a layman,
James Humphreys—printer, as secretary of the colonial convention as early as 1760.[33] In an unforeseen way this relation-

Christ Church in Philadelphia. Here the first General Convention met in 1785, and in 1789 the organization of the Protestant Episcopal Church was completed. Courtesy of Christ Church.

ship between clergy and laity was an omen of what was to come after the Revolution. But this appeared to the clergy of New York and Connecticut as fraternizing with the laity and was taboo among those of "High Church" principles because they stressed the differences rather than the similarities between clergy and laity.[34] In Pennsylvania, however, circumstances had produced and galvanized a working partnership between pulpit and pew that tended to egalitarianism and this was a source of strength.

A closer examination of the lay leaders in Pennsylvania reveals that the vestrymen, by and large, do not fit the generalization that has been made that Anglicans were wealthy aristocrats who loyally supported England. A check of the Philadelphia tax records for 1769 and 1774 disclosed that among the vestrymen of Christ and St. Peter's churches there were men of considerable wealth, some who were well-to-do, but most were men who at best can be described as small merchants, artisans, and in a few cases, skilled laborers. The association of these men in church work across socioeconomic lines suggests the type of cooperation essential for the development of republican concepts.[35] Although sufficiently related data to determine the socioeconomic status of the parish laity outside the city is not available or perhaps does not exist in sufficient quantity to be organizable, the definite impression derived from piecemeal data suggests that the laity were generally within the broad middle class and engaged in farming or small business, but rarely would one qualify as wealthy.

Of the twenty-four vestrymen of Christ and St. Peter's churches in 1769, one was assessed for over £1,000 and was very wealthy, two were assessed in excess of £500 but less than £1000 and were rich; four were listed for between £200 and £499 in taxes; eight were charged more than £50 but less than £199; but the largest number, nine, were taxed less than £50. The lowest tax range is the category that included mostly successful artisans and craftsmen. By 1774 there was a shift in the direction of the lowest tax bracket because thirteen vestrymen were then charged less than £50. The two highest tax brackets lost one vestrymen each and two fell from the fourth category. Through the Philadelphia Wills it is possible to identify the occupations of twenty-one of eighty-nine men who served Christ and St. Peter's parish as vestrymen between 1763 and 1789. Of this group, ten were merchants, three physicians, one silversmith, yeoman, druggist, bricklayer, cordwainer, brush-maker, shipwright, and printer. Typical of those in the lowest tax ranges were Joseph Sims, wine merchant, and James Ham, a "Mathematic and Optical instrument maker."[36]

The fact that Christ and St. Peter's did have its share of wealthy and well-to-do merchants and professional people does not mean they were passive to or subservient to the activities of the English government in American affairs. Indeed, the contrary view is more correct. For example, in response to the Stamp Act of 1765, no fewer than twenty-nine current and future vestrymen before 1775 signed a published Non-Importation Agreement against British goods. The name that headed the list of signers was Thomas Willing, probably the wealthiest man in the parish. Later Jonathan Brown offered Richard Peters £200 profit made from the sale of impounded British goods which the Philadelphia Merchants Association had confiscated. The vestry accepted the money without hesitation and used it to pay for a wall around the burial yard. When the Townshend Duties were passed in 1767 a similar response from churchmen was registered and Willing's name headed the list again. The granting of the tea monopoly to the East India Company in 1773 was equally objectionable.[37]

The data available on the vestrymen of four of the nineteen churches outside Philadelphia—St. John's, Peques; St. Peter's, Great Valley; St. James, Lancaster; and St. James, Perkiomen—are sparse. However, sufficient information on twelve lay leaders at least provides an indication of their socioeconomic status. In the highest order one was a lawyer, another a merchant, and a third left an estate valued at $15,000 in 1816. The rest were more closely grouped and are identified as stonemason, cabinet maker, master rifle-maker, cordwainer, captain in the army, and "recent immigrant." One layman from St. Peter's church, Great Valley, John T. Rowland, probably comes close to representing the typical vestryman and parishioner. An inventory of his estate in 1764 listed 110 acres and buildings, 23 acres of woodland, a grist mill, 5 horses, 6 cattle, 10 sheep, 1 servant, and silver plate.[38] The picture that emerges of the Pennsylvania Anglican laity, imperfect and incomplete though it is, is one which has few wealthy constituents, some well-to-do ones, but the rank-and-file are drawn from the broad middle of eighteenth-century colonial society.

CULTURAL CONTRIBUTORS

A significant feature of Pennsylvania Anglicanism in the 1760s was its cultural creativity, which was increasingly evident to the community at large. The change upward in the status of Anglicans came around 1750 and was aided to a marked degree by the conversion of the proprietors to the Church of England. After this date, churchmen, who were never as numerous as Friends, Presbyterians, or Lutherans, were noted for making several contributions to the cultural life of Philadelphia. In a sense, Anglicanism grew with the city, which by 1776 was second in population only to London within the British empire. Moreover, the tremendous commercial growth which the city experienced in the late colonial period benefited all the divergent social groups of the metropolis, including churchmen. Also, the important political role which Anglicans played in the political arena over the proprietors' interest gave them considerable visibility and greater participation in the colony's life.[39] This newly achieved status was prized highly by churchmen and their desire to retain and enhance it provides a partial reason why they were unwilling to involve themselves in the controversy over the Johnson-Chandler episcopal plan.

The prime mover among Anglicans in the burgeoning cultural life of Philadelphia was Provost Smith. In the Academy and College of Philadelphia Smith, assisted by several laymen, assembled a coterie of able and gifted students. In fact, Smith's indefatigable interest in education had a progressive quality and had he focused consistently on education instead of entering politics, civil and ecclesiastical, his contemporary recognition would probably be greater.[40] To illustrate, Smith adopted a curriculum that was designed to prepare students for good citizenship as well as scholarly pursuits. In a pamphlet published in 1753 entitled *A College of Mirania* Smith elaborated his educational scheme. This publication caught the attention of Benjamin Franklin, who sponsored Smith for the provostship of the Academy and College. Though Smith subsequently showed his preference for classical studies, he nevertheless retained the practical features of his "Mirania plan." Among the students who attended the college were several—Francis Hopkinson, Thomas Godfrey, Nathaniel Evans—who produced literary works of sufficient quality to appear in the *American Magazine and Monthly Quarterly* edited by Smith.

Beyond editing the *American Magazine,* Smith wrote for publication *A Brief State of the Province of Pennsylvania* (1753) and *The Present State of American Affairs* (1764) as well as sermons and addresses which when collected filled two volumes. Moreover, in a day when certain groups disapproved the existence of theatres, Smith unhesitatingly supported the development of the Southwark Theatre in Philadelphia and attended and encouraged his students to do so. One of these students, Francis Hopkinson, organized the Orpheus Club to give musical performances in order to raise money with which to purchase an organ for the college.[41] Smith is also credited with discovering Benjamin West, who became a member of the Royal Academy and historical painter for George III. With the help of Samuel

Powell, a layman from St. Peter's Church, Smith aided Charles Willson Peale, later known as the artist of the American Revolution, in launching his career. No less interested in science than in literature, art, and music, Smith in 1772 arranged a series of twenty-two public lectures at the College on astronomy, electricity, chemistry, and natural philosophy which were crowded to overflowing by interested people.[42]

Beyond promoting education through the Academy and College of Philadelphia which Anglicans controlled by virtue of a majority of members on the Board of Trustees by 1770, Smith, Peters, and a number of laymen sponsored a large-scale plan to establish English schools among the German population. The plan discussed in 1754 called for the establishment of six schools, to be staffed with teachers trained in the College, and a curriculum which included mathematics, geography, history, and ethics to be taught in both English and German. Though most Germans objected to this potential invasion of their customs and communities, the plan did provoke them to found their own schools. Moreover, basic education was also provided in Christ Church Charity School and Evening Singing School. Several churchmen supported both the Library Company and the Union Library Company in Philadelphia. When in 1765, Dr. John Morgan, a communicant and vestryman of Christ and St. Peter's parish, became the prime mover in the establishment of the first medical school in the colonies, a number of his supporters were members of the same parish.

In the 1760s and 1770s Pennsylvania churchmen had cause to rejoice over the expansion, development, and status of their faith. The explosion of the episcopal controversy in Boston and New York was not duplicated because Smith and Peters, who knew well the attitudes and interests of their fellow religionists, opposed the promotion of and deflected the potential thrust of the Johnson-Chandler plan. Though the appearance of the *Appeal* and subsequently "The American Whig" series did produce estrangement between Anglicans and Presbyterians and to

some extent with the Lutherans, the differences over episcopacy in Pennsylvania were slight when compared with what
happened in other colonies. In 1772, the condition of the Anglican church in Pennsylvania is perhaps best reflected in the
performance of "several pieces of solemn church music, and
particularly a Grand Chorus from the celebrated Messiah of
Handel" under the direction of Francis Hopkinson and sung
by the Society of Singers of Christ and St. Peter's churches.[43]

4

The Church Establishments of Maryland and Virginia

"His Lordship by no means wishes to see an episcopal palace rise in America."

Hugh Hamersley, Secretary to
Lord Baltimore, November 11, 1767

"We do not want bishops."

William Nelson,
President Virginia Council,
May 11, 1771

The Elizabeth Town Convention of 1766 commissioned Dr. Myles Cooper, president of King's College, and Robert McKean, S.P.G. missionary in Amboy, New Jersey, to confer with the governors of Maryland and Virginia to solicit their cooperation in promoting the episcopal plan. Dr. Johnson wrote John Camm, professor at William and Mary, "I am, therefore, very apprehensive that our solicitations will fail of gaining the point, unless we could bring it to a general cry, and prevail with the southern provinces to join us."[1] If the Chesapeake region, where the church was established, could be persuaded to join the episcopal cause, its active support would more than compensate for the passive resistance of New England's laity and the opposition of Pennsylvania's senior clergymen. However, in Maryland the final authority in matters ecclesiastical was Frederick Calvert (1731–71), the sixth Lord Baltimore, who jealously guarded his proprietary prerogatives, especially the one of clerical appointments. By contrast, the vestries in Virginia controlled ecclesiastical patronage, but in the 1760s the House of Burgesses and some Anglican clergy were contesting who had ultimate control over ministerial salaries. Thus in both colonies where the Church of England was large and influential there were internal tensions that would largely determine each province's response to the Johnson-Chandler initiative for episcopacy.

CHURCH BY LAW

In 1771 there were 230 Anglican clergymen in America and at least 130 were serving in the two Chesapeake colonies. Maryland had forty-four parishes in 1767 and all were filled, with each incumbent receiving an annual salary between £300 and £500. By 1774 Virginia had ninety-five parishes and ninety of them were filled by parsons whose annual stipend was £150 to £200. The foremost Congregational opponent of the Church of England in America, Charles Chauncy of Boston, estimated there were 270,000 Anglicans in this region. Moreover, the Virginia establishment had as a part of its operation, William and Mary College, the second oldest college in the colonies. Traditionally the presidents of William and Mary and most of the faculty were Anglican clergymen and in the 1760s this remained true. On the basis of size, numbers of adherents, and support the two church establishments of Maryland-Virginia probably equalled or bettered in total strength the rest of the Anglican communion in mainland America.[2]

Though the Church of England was established in both Maryland and Virginia, the church-state relationship differed markedly in each. A charter granted to the Calverts in 1632 made Maryland their proprietary domain, and except for the period from the Glorious Revolution in 1688-89 to 1713 when the crown assumed control, the lords Baltimore were in charge. It was, however, during the period of royal control that acts were passed establishing the church. A law in 1702 provided for a parish system which included vestries of six members each chosen annually by the freeholders. Within the vestry two members retired each year and became ineligible for immediate re-election. Because the post of vestryman was not a popular one, an act in 1730 provided a fine of 1,000 pounds of tobacco for anyone who refused to serve. But the Maryland vestries, unlike those in any other colony, were bound by the wishes of the proprietor in the matter of ministerial selection and appointment because clerical appointments were exclusively a proprietary prerogative. Indeed, the exercise of this privilege by Frederick Calvert in the 1760s, in spite of the known wishes of vestrymen and parishioners, produced an open revolt in 1773.[3]

The duties of the vestries as the corporate body of the parish included building and maintaining churches and associated properties, selecting annually two churchwardens, electing a registrar, conducting spiritual court to try persons accused of moral offenses, raising and receiving the annual tobacco tax to support the ministers, and the imposition of an additional poll tax for church repairs when needed. The Tobacco Act of 1730 directed that each parish be divided into precincts and authorized the vestries to appoint a tobacco counter in each precinct to ensure that the quality of the tobacco paid for ministerial compensation was of standard quality. If a vestry failed to comply with this law, every member, except the minister who was prohibited from being appointed a counter, was subject to a £20 fine in current money. A related law in 1747 required vestries to nominate tobacco inspectors to the governor who then made the appointments. Moreover, because the parish minister was considered the chief vestryman of the six elected members his duties were also spelled out in law.[4] The final authority, however, in all things ecclesiastical for the parishes of Maryland was the lord proprietor, who reviewed all laws passed by the assembly and either allowed or disallowed them.

Virginia, the oldest of the thirteen colonies, within the first twenty-five years of its existence adopted the principal ortho-

dox doctrines of the Church of England, provided a religious
establishment, and authorized the election of twelve vestrymen
for each parish. Vestry duties included the collection of church
levies, account keeping, care of church properties, and after
1642–43 the right to elect the parish minister and present him
to the governor for induction. Though the power to induct,
which if completed meant life tenure to the minister, was
clearly the prerogative of the royal governor by virtue of his
instructions, the Virginia vestries assumed this prerogative and
never relinquished it. In fact, by the early eighteenth century
some vestries adopted the practice of issuing yearly contracts to
their ministers, thus making the clergy more dependent on the
laity. An act in 1748 further specified that a vestry, in the event
of a ministerial vacancy, had a full year to procure a replacement before the governor could offer his candidate. Indeed,
the power of the vestries, which after 1725 tended to become
increasingly self-perpetuating instead of elected, was a prominent feature of Virginia's church.[5] Though they were by law
required to provide a glebe for the minister (usually a tract of
land about 200 acres in size), the vestries assumed the authority
to buy, sell, or lease glebe lands. Fees for marriages, baptisms,
and burials were set by the legislature, but on the parish level
long before 1763 the vestries with the collaboration of the assembly had taken charge of ecclesiastical affairs. The only vestige of influence exercised by the bishop of London on the
Virginia establishment was the license he issued which was required of all Anglican clergymen who served in America. Even
the post of commissary, which under James Blair (1689–1743)
had come the closest to resembling an episcopate in America,
was in the 1760s but a shadow of what it had been. Churchmen
in Virginia knew that since Bishop Edmund Gibson (1723–48)
no bishop of London had taken out a commission authorizing
his jurisdiction in the colonies.[6] Thus the commissaries who
served in Virginia subsequent to 1748 at best had but a letter of
authorization on which to base their office.

The weakened status of the commissariat in Virginia added to the generally recognized problem of the need for clerical supervision. Though the presidents of William and Mary, all Anglican ministers, customarily were designated commissary, thus combining the two positions, a dispute erupted in 1761 between Governor Fauquier and Commissary Robinson that led the governor to oppose successfully Robinson's election to the college presidency. Fauquier was again successful in blocking Robinson's appointment to the Colonial Council, a post commissaries traditionally held.[7] This dispute between the governor and commissary reached the point where Fauquier tried to preempt the commissary's traditional prerogative of recommending candidates to the bishops in England for Holy Orders.[8] Even though James Horrocks, who was elected president of William and Mary in 1764, was designated commissary in 1769 and became a member of the council, the prestige once attached to the office had been lost. William Willie, who succeeded Horrocks in 1771, was also unsuccessful in reviving the status of the office. It was several years after the Revolutionary War before Virginia established any centralized ecclesiastical office to oversee the clergy of the newly organized Protestant Episcopal Church.

PROPRIETARY PREROGATIVE

The task of Dr. Myles Cooper and Robert McKean to win Maryland's governor, Horatio Sharpe (1753–69), and the colony's churchmen to endorse and promote the Johnson-Chandler episcopal plan was opposed both covertly and overtly in Maryland. This colony in the decade before the War for Independence was caught in the turbulence of a major internal conflict between the "court" faction which supported the proprietor and the "country" faction which opposed him. So intense did the controversy become that the two houses of the legislature deadlocked and the normal processes of administration were abandoned. Under these conditions the established church was demoralized by 1773. On every issue involved in this controversy the lower house conceived itself to be a parliamentary body while the proprietary faction considered itself viceregal. The conflict between these two positions was evident at least as early as 1739, but with time and experience the House of Delegates became more articulate and effective. In the 1760s a popular desire to obtain the vote was coupled with the assembly's position. New strength was acquired by the "country" faction that predominated the lower house when it opposed the Stamp Act and Townshend Duties. Under these conditions, therefore, the "court" faction which was defending the proprietary prerogative wanted nothing to do with a resident bishop who might interfere with the proprietor's ecclesiastical rights; and the "country" faction saw the episcopal scheme as another potential avenue for British interference and openly objected to the scheme.

In 1739 the House of Delegates recorded formally their objections to the proprietary system. In a set of resolutions the House declared illegal the tonnage duty for the proprietor and the hogshead tax for the governor; the proclamation fees violations of the charter; buying and selling of clerkships unwarranted; the collection of alienation fines contrary to law; and the collection of naval officers' fees in gold and silver a direct breach of the paper money law. Then the outbreak of King George's War followed by the French and Indian War brought additional crown and parliamentary levies and obligations which the assembly came increasingly to resent and oppose. Within the thirty-five years from 1739 to 1774 the House of Delegates developed the methods and tactics for political combat which led to a victory for internal self-rule over proprietary prerogative in the early seventies. In the process the "country" faction applied these same tactics against Britain's imperial policies in the 1760s and 1770s with marked effect.[9]

The replacement of Governor Sharpe with Robert Eden, a

more personable man, in 1769, did not ease the tension between "court" and "country" factions. During Eden's tenure
the lower house launched a new effort to investigate proprietary revenues, incomes of leading officials, and demanded a
colonial agent to represent them in England as well as control
over the colonial secretary's salary and a hearing of their
grievances by the king. Daniel Dulany, who opposed the
Stamp Act, on the issue of proprietary revenues pled in *The
Right* . . . for Lord Baltimore's claim, but to no avail. The proprietary claim to license fees was waived, but the attempt to
win a hearing in England was unsuccessful. A tobacco law
passed in 1770 specifically omitted giving consent to the proprietor's claim to set fees for the tobacco service. But the area
in which the assembly made most extensive inroads was that
of the church establishment. By 1771–72, the question of the
legality of Maryland's church establishment was raised by
Samuel Chase and William Paca, both of whom were Anglican
laymen. Lawyers offered to plead, gratis, for anyone refusing
to pay clerical taxes. Such a case was tried and won in 1773 in
Charles County. In the same year, the assembly passed a bill
declaring the act of establishment in 1702 unconstitutional,
but the upper house rejected it. But a new church tax act was
passed which reduced the poll levy from forty to thirty
pounds of tobacco and made legal the payment of the poll at
a rate of four shillings per poll. The consequence of this act
was a reduction of clerical salaries by one-fifth to one-half;
efforts to have the act disallowed failed.[10]

The political conditions existing in Maryland in the 1760s
made it virtually impossible for Dr. Cooper and Mr. McKean to
recruit the governor and churchmen in an episcopal campaign.
Proprietary ecclesiastical patronage was under attack and the
governor as proprietary agent in church affairs was constantly
under assault. The continuance of the religious establishment
itself was in doubt after 1773. Neither side in Maryland's internal conflict could conceive of a resident bishop being of value

to his cause. After 1765, the assembly was unalterably opposed to hierarchical-type interference in Maryland's internal affairs by proprietor or king, and a bishop would have been viewed in much the same way. From the viewpoint of the parish clergy there was no advantage to be gained from publicly endorsing the Johnson-Chandler plan and possibly a great deal to be lost. To support the scheme was certain to provoke the disfavor of both governor and assembly. Thus the few clergymen who identified with the episcopal cause risked much, and had it not been for the stand taken by Henry Addison, Bennet Allen, and Jonathan Boucher the episcopal campaign of the late sixties and early seventies would have passed unnoticed in Maryland.

VIRGINIA VESTRYMEN

The cornerstone in the structure of the Church of England in colonial America was the parish vestry. The key to the development and survival of local parishes was this same body because its members, more than the bishop of London, the S.P.G., or an occasional evangelist were the nuclei of Anglicanism. In no colony was the strength and status of the vestry, both within and without the parish, more pronounced than in Virginia. The early establishment of the parish system in 1636 and its subsequent development contributed to this institution. But more than this, the Virginia vestries with their civil as well as church functions had become the first public service training schools for virtually all who subsequently qualified for legislative, executive, judicial, military, and legal positions. In the late colonial period it was usual for a member of the House of Burgesses to be simultaneously a vestryman in his home parish and county. A large proportion of county justices were also vestrymen, as well as the sheriffs, clerks of court, and other local officials. While the wealthier county residents who were vestrymen usually were elected Burgesses, it is also true that other vestrymen, almost all of whom qualified as "gentlemen," held at least one additional post to their vestry seat and in some instances they held three or four offices simultaneously.[11] Thus in Virginia the church and state were intertwined and the political and economical elite were intimately a part of this system.

In the early eighteenth century Governor Alexander Spotswood described the vestrymen of St. Anne's parish as "Twelve Bishops," which is indicative of the power and status they exercised. Long before 1763, Virginia's vestries had become self-perpetuating and subject to election only when the assembly ordered a dissolution. They had successfully defied the royal governor's authority to organize and reorganize parishes and placed that power in the assembly.[12] For decades vestries had exercised the prerogative of ministerial selection and in 1748 the Burgesses passed an act specifying a period of one year in which a vestry could deliberate and decide upon ministerial candidates before the governor could propose his candidate. To keep clergy subject to vestry control one-year contracts were widely used.[13] In addition, the 16,000-pounds tobacco tax for each clergyman's support was collected and paid by the vestry. The two churchwardens chosen by each vestry annually from among its members were officers of the county courts who presented moral offenders, administered relief, established workhouses, supervised land processing, and provided highway maintenance.[14] In governmental terms the vestry was the basic unit in local self-government and in Virginia it functioned effectively for many years.

From 36 vestry records which have survived in whole or in part from the 95 parishes of Virginia in 1774, it is possible to determine that in 1765, 58 of 113 members of the House of Burgesses were vestrymen and in 1775, 61 of 126 were vestrymen. Moreover, 96 of 133 who served as Burgesses and vestrymen between 1757 and 1775 had also served as county justices. It was very common for a vestryman to be county clerk or county surveyor, coroner, tobacco inspector, collector of customs, or a militia officer. One explanation for this type of pluralism is that Virginia law limited an officeholder to one government post of profit. Since vestryman was an uncompensated position, its value was more for in-training and service, so that many members sought an additional post that brought compensation. For example, between 1763 and 1775, all candidates elected to the House of Burgesses from Elizabeth City county and parish—George Wythe, William Wager, Henry King, Worlich Westwood—were vestrymen and three had served as justices and Wager was clerk of court.[15] This interrelatedness of church-state officeholding provided stability but also ensured a continuity of government on both the local and colonial levels.

In the 1760s Virginia's Anglican laymen, whether in the parish or statehouse, had a well-developed sense of self-determination and commitment to their system. To them the wishes of the bishop of London and the royal governors were secondary to their concept of constitutionalism.[16] Even without the imperial acts of parliament in the 1760s to set Virginians in opposition to royal interference, they would have vigorously opposed the Johnson-Chandler plan as a potential means of usurping their prerogatives in ecclesiastical affairs. The very mention of bishop, the description of "purely spiritual" notwithstanding, was a symbolic threat to the powers the vestries exercised over the ministers. Many Virginians knew that their ecclesiastical procedures differed greatly from practices in England. For anyone to suggest or hint at a change in Virginia's ecclesiastical constitution was also taken as a challenge to the Old Dominion's ruling class and such affronts were inhospitably received. Virginia's churchmen who had managed to free themselves from the control of royal governors and commissaries and reduce the bishop of London's influence to a licensing function were not about to relinquish or negotiate any of their long-established ecclesiastical prerogatives.[17] In this largest segment of the Church of England in America, the dominance of the laity was perhaps its most striking feature and the impact of their status had long-range implications.

INTERNAL TENSIONS

Both the Virginia ar⁻¹ Maryland establishments were plagued by serious internal tensions during the third quarter of the eighteenth century. In Virginia, the major issue became known as the Parson's Cause because it involved ministerial salaries and was fought out between a group of clergymen headed by John Camm and the House of Burgesses. The primary dispute in Maryland was between the vestries, who in certain instances insisted on playing a role in ministerial selections, and the governor, who as agent for the proprietor resisted such claims.[18] In Maryland, however, the demands of the vestries for greater participation in ecclesiastical affairs became identified with the "country" faction, but in Virginia the resistance of the assembly to clerical demands for an adjustment in the salary system cast the Burgesses in the role of defending home rule against Camm and company, who appealed to England for a favorable decision. This appeal to England intensified a nascent anticlericalism in Virginia and heightened resentment on the part of many against the church. In both Maryland and Virginia the eventual outcome of the respective disputes was a victory for the assemblies and a loss of status for the Church of England.

Although Virginia's clergymen were among the best paid, a series of events occurred in the 1750s that revolved around clerical support. This conflict between a number of clerics and the assembly was probably inevitable at some point on one issue or another because the clergy had a traditional right to appeal grievances to the bishop of London and the English civil authorities. The clergy were strengthened in the belief that either judicial process in the colony or royal authority in England would sustain their appeals by a case decided in Virginia in 1753 known as *Kay v. Vestry*. In this case the general court decided that the Reverend William Kay, who had been deprived of his living by the vestry of Lunenburg parish, Richmond County, was entitled to £200 damages. Kay also sued for trespass against the vestry and won though Landon Carter, the prime mover in Kay's ouster, appealed the decision unsuccessfully to the Privy Council in an effort to have it overturned. The result of this case was that the clergy came to believe once they were accepted by a vestry, though not inducted, they were entitled to salary and glebe without interference. This obvious check upon the vestries' authority probably contributed to the passage of the 1748 law which gave a vestry a full year to fill a ministerial vacancy. Nevertheless, when the assembly adjusted the salary rates in 1755 and 1758, some of the clergy challenged the assembly's right to do so.

The Virginia Burgesses' claim to vary ministerial rates in 1755 and 1758 to meet existing conditions was not new. In 1753 the assembly passed a bill authorizing Frederick and Augusta parishes beyond the Blue Ridge Mountains to pay their ministers £100 instead of 16,000 pounds of tobacco. This was not an unusual procedure: periodically several counties had been authorized to pay officials in this manner and to accept public dues in money instead of tobacco. However, when in October 1755 the assembly passed enabling legislation to permit the discharge of tobacco debts in money for the present year and set the rate at 16s:8d per 100 pounds the clergy protested and petitioned the bishop of London to seek the law's disallowance. The assembly's reason for the action was the limited tobacco crop for that year. Then too, the demands of the French and Indian War were anticipated. On this occasion the British government allowed the issue to pass and the clergy, like all others affected by this bill, had to accept their loss. When a similar act was passed in 1758 for the same reasons, the clergy were ready. In convention they denounced the "Two Penny Act" and sent John Camm to England to plead for its disallowance; this time their efforts were successful. In fact, not only was the 1758 act disallowed, but the 1755 one as well.

This check to the House of Burgesses' legislative authority opened the door for judicial counter-claims. In 1763, James

Maury, rector of Fredericksville parish, sued in Hanover County Court to recover damages and won. At this point Patrick Henry joined in the vestry's defense and by using emotion and capitalizing upon the clergy's appeal to the king for help persuaded the jury to award one penny in damages.[19] But the issue was not limited to the courtroom, for at the same time Maury's case was being decided a pamphlet war broke out between John Camm for the clergy and Landon Carter and Richard Bland for the assembly. Camm's *A Single and Distinct View of the Act Vulgarly Called the Two Penny Act* was a vain attempt to discredit it. The counter-argument presented in Carter's *The Rector Detected* and Bland's *The Colonel Dismounted, or the Rector Vindicated* played upon the insistence of the clergy for special treatment over and above what ordinary citizens received.[20] But in his pamphlet, Bland touched upon the central issue in the contest with Britain. He argued that Virginians were free, either as Englishmen or as unsubdued natives, and therefore had the right to regulate their internal affairs.[21] At the very time Bland published his treatise, the Virginia Council gave actual meaning to his argument, for it decided that royal disallowance was not a repeal and therefore all claims for compensation were unwarranted. John Camm challenged the council's ruling, sued in general court, but lost. His appeal to England went undecided for some time and was finally dismissed by Lord Northington, president of the council, on a technical error in 1766.

Another source of tension that developed between clergy and laymen in the late 1770s in Virginia involved the acting commissary's claim to be the only person authorized to recommend candidates to the bishops in England for ordination. A particular case involved James Ogilvie, who was sponsored by Thomas Jefferson and the parishioners of Orange parish, but who was objected to by James Horrocks. Ogilvie's request to Horrocks for a recommendation was at first refused, then the commissary agreed not to interfere if Ogilvie sought ordination on his own. But Horrocks apparently reneged on his promise and wrote Bishop Terrick objecting to Ogilvie's ordination, but gave no specific charges. Before Terrick could resolve the problem, Ogilvie appealed to Jefferson for help. Not only Jefferson, but Peyton Randolph, attorney general for Virginia, and Thomas Adams, Virginia's agent in London, interceded for Ogilvie. In the contest Jefferson described Horrocks as a man of "an evil disposition" and "elation of mind."[22] Finally Ogilvie was ordained, but he settled in England instead of returning to Virginia.

In Maryland the internal tensions were expressed primarily by vestrymen in specific parishes toward the governor, who as agent for the proprietor refused to permit the church-tax-paying laity to have a say in the selection of their ministers. Unlike Virginia, the Maryland churchmen had no authorized system through which their desires and views on the ministers of the establishment could be effectively expressed. Moreover, there was no way the clergy collectively could serve the church and alleviate tensions between ministers and parishioners because the proprietor disliked clerical conventions and considered lay petitions a nuisance.[23] Thus, when a vestry objected to a ministerial appointment or requested redress of a grievance, the government's reaction was negative. The virtual refusal to recognize the need for ministerial adjustments within the Maryland establishment and the stolid refusal to honor petitions proved to be counter-productive to the church's best interest. The refusal of the proprietor and his agents to meet the lay request in a positive way heightened resentment against the religious establishment within the church's ranks and contributed to the move to disestablish the Church of England shortly after the Revolutionary War commenced.

Unlike all the other American colonies where the Church of England existed, Maryland churchmen alone had no say in the selection of their ministers. This condition, exacerbated by particular local problems, provoked some parishes and vestries to assert the claim of ministerial selection. For example, Coventry parish in Somerset County suffered for years with a notorious minister and upon his death in 1766 decided to invite on trial a minister of their choice who happened to be Thomas B. Chandler. After hearing him preach and discussing the position with him, the parish petitioned the governor to induct Chandler. Sharpe refused and instead inducted a neighboring minister.[24] The vestry protested to the House of Delegates, claiming to be the true founders of the church in Maryland and professing to be the source of all church powers, but their case was denied. Virginia's example of vestry participation in parish affairs unquestionably influenced the Coventry vestry. But more than this, they were expressing the Lockean concept of compact theory in church government, claiming their natural rights in ecclesiastical matters. In a vivid way the Coventry vestry's petition expressed the essence of the ecclesiastical revolution that was underway within the American Anglican church, though at various stages of development in the several colonies. Insistence upon local ecclesiastical self-government was uniformly evident, and resistance to hierarchical control was everywhere evident. When Coventry's petition failed, the parishioners temporarily revolted, frightening off Sharpe's first appointee and making it so difficult for the second that it took the intervention of the attorney general, court action, and the threatened use of troops to quell the parishioners. In 1769 time was fast running out for those who upheld the proprietor's prerogative of ecclesiastical patronage.

At the same time Coventry parish was in a state of rebellion, another episode occurred, the most public and disgraceful in Maryland's record of proprietary church patronage. Bennet Allen, a friend of Lord Baltimore, arrived in Maryland in 1766 with instructions that he be given a church living. Not satisfied with Sharpe's first offer, he requested St. Anne's in Annapolis, the capital, and St. James's at Herring Bay as well. Pluralism had not been tolerated in Maryland and when word of this possible arrangement got out three powerful laymen who were also governmental officials—Walter Dulany, Brice Worthington, and Thomas Johnson—managed to block Allen's request. So intense did this fracas become that it spilled into the press and commanded more space than the contemporary debate over the Townshend Duties.[25] Finally Sharpe appointed Allen to All Saints' parish, Frederick County, the richest in Maryland, but there Allen provoked controversy. Because of the large size of the parish, the freeholders wanted the parish divided, which would mean another church and minister, but also a division of Allen's salary. Allen blocked the parishioners' desire by taking possession of the appointment before their petition reached the assembly. He then, perhaps to avoid hostility which naturally followed, put a curate in charge while he went to Philadelphia for a year or two enjoying the income from All Saints' parish. Thus in the last years of the colonial era the Maryland church was forced to endure the worst possible consequences of proprietary patronage. Indeed, it seems that no American colony where the Anglican church existed had ministerial problems of the type and frequency that Maryland experienced.[26] The dangers inherent in a patronage or appointment system too tightly controlled from the top were well remembered by churchmen during the postwar reconstruction period.

OPPOSITION TO EPISCOPACY

It was, therefore, in the turbulent political environment of Maryland intensified by the reactions to the Stamp and Townshend Acts that Cooper and McKean attempted to introduce the Johnson-Chandler plan in the fall of 1767. Had it not been for three Maryland clergymen—Henry Addison, Jonathan Boucher, Bennet Allen—the plan would never have been discussed and most certainly not debated in the newspapers. In Virginia, the rising tide of anticlericalism resulting from the clergy's appeal to England during the Parson's Cause was related to the growing resentment toward the British government's new imperial policies.[27] Had not James Horrocks and John Camm decided to champion the episcopal cause in Virginia it probably would have attracted little note. In both provinces, the fact that previously controversial clergymen backed the episcopal cause was certain to produce controversy. Besides, since the realization of such a scheme would inevitably involve an appeal to the king or parliament, both provincial assemblies would automatically oppose it, and in the case of Maryland, Lord Baltimore would view such an appeal as a threat. It is then understandable that the episcopal backers in both Maryland and Virginia at first sought support covertly by calling conventions to consider organizing Societies for the Relief of Ministerial Widows and Orphans. In both instances the cover was blown off by clergymen who did not agree with the scheme or the tactics and fierce public debate ensued in pamphlet and newspaper.

In Maryland the initial opposition to the Johnson-Chandler plan came from Governor Sharpe, who refused Cooper and McKean permission to convene the clergy to discuss the plan. Sharpe's decision was approved by Baltimore and expressed in a letter which stated that the scheme was a potential threat to "his Lordship's charter rights and prerogatives." Neither Sharpe, Secretary Hugh Hamersley, or Lord Baltimore believed an American episcopate possible on the terms stated by Chandler and Johnson, and all three were confident that if a primitive-type bishop were permitted in time other powers would be added to the office.[28] In a subsequent letter Sharpe conjectured that though "the want of some controlling power over the clergy . . . is often much lamented . . . I do not think the people would be so well pleased at a resident bishop being invited therewith as they would to see it lodged with some temporal judges." If Sharpe's assessment was correct, the people of Maryland like the governor and proprietor could not in their thinking separate the office of bishop from the power of the state. In any event, the creation of a new ecclesiastical official was out of the question. This attitude, if correct, plus the proprietor's expressed determination not "to see an episcopal palace rise in America, or to have St. Peter's chair transferred to Maryland," was sufficient reason for the governor to block a potential episcopal campaign in Maryland.[29]

Sharpe, however, was instructed to oppose the plan discreetly or covertly and to "let these schemers lay what they have to offer before the assembly in their own names, which may be better taken than for his Lordship to interfere officiously."[30] In this way the anticipated negative reaction from the public and House of Delegates would become the responsibility of those who provoked it. Thus the difficulties for the promoters would be maximized while those of the governor and council minimized. But the clerical coterie supporting the plan knew how to counter subtlety with subtlety, for during the month of August 1768, when Sharpe was in the process of being replaced by Robert Eden as governor, Addison, Allen, and Boucher on the pretext of organizing a Relief Society called a convention of clergy. While pretending to organize a Society for the Relief of Ministerial Widows and Orphans, petitions for an American episcopate were prepared. Jonathan Boucher, a tutor in St. Anne's parish then and its rector in 1770, seems to have been the leader in enlisting nine clergymen to sign the petition to Governor Eden in behalf of bishops. "We have unanimously resolved that it is highly becoming to make an effort as far as in us lies to introduce if possible episcopacy in America," it read.[31] Also, Eden was advised that petitions had been prepared for sending to the king, bishop of London, and proprietor on the subject.[32]

Governor Eden demonstrated his mastery of the situation when he proposed that the petition signed by the nine clergymen be laid before the assembly. This brought a quick reply—"they were delivered confessedly for your perusal and not intended for the general assembly"—but this letter bore only three signatures.[33] In the face of possible legislative opposition and public denunciation there was little dedicated support for the episcopal scheme in Maryland. Boucher in later years admitted that his efforts in behalf of an episcopate antagonized the Dulanys of St. Anne's parish so that "for some months neither the governor, nor any of the Dulanys, even so much as spoke to me."[34] Perhaps it was this episode that led to his transfer to Prince George County, but there too he got into serious trouble after preaching a sermon entitled "On the American Episcopate." Two vestrymen, Samuel Chase and William Paca, chastised Boucher in the press for his high-handed approach to the vestry. Moreover, they claimed, "the common law shields us against the introduction of episcopacy."[35] It was probably this contest over episcopacy that led Boucher to state "for more than six months I preached, when I did, with a pair of loaded pistols lying on the cushion."[36] So desperate did Boucher's position become that in 1773 he put his parish in the hands of a curate and became himself a curate to Henry Addison, his wife's uncle. In September 1775, Boucher fled to England never to return.

In the printed attack on Boucher and episcopacy, Chase and Paca claimed a majority of Anglican clergy were against the introduction of bishops.[37] Though there is no way to prove or disprove this charge with documentation, it is recorded that John Gordon, rector of St. Michael's, Talbot County, and David Love, rector of All Hallows, Anne Arundel County, wrote to Walter Dulany expressing disgust over "some of our brethren praying establishment of an American episcopate, have judged it necessary to draw up a counter-address; and we propose, if you approve it, to present it signed by as many of our brethren as shall think proper to join us to the governor."[38] Whether or not this measure was taken is not ascertainable and what Dulany thought of it is not recorded. But obviously Gordon and Love were convinced a number of their colleagues were of their persuasion on the subject of a resident bishop. To claim the least is to conclude that the Johnson-Chandler plan received rough treatment in Maryland from members of the second largest Anglican establishment in America. In this colony Boucher correctly observed that churchmen fought the battles of Dissenters.

In Virginia the efforts of James Horrocks and John Camm to muster support for the Johnson-Chandler plan produced an adverse reaction. Though the need for effective clerical supervision was generally conceded, any proposal coming from the clergy in the wake of the Parson's Cause was bound to be suspect. The questionable nature of Horrock's commissarial post also weakened the stature of the office and the one who tried to fill it. It was, however, Horrock's attempt to convene a convention of clergy in 1771 to discuss the plan for resident bishops under the guise of planning to establish a Fund for the Relief of Widows and Orphans, that led some clergy to insist that Horrocks announce the real purpose of the meeting. This action triggered the episcopal controversy in Virginia, which took a variety of forms. But the press coverage alone extended from May 30, 1771 to March 5, 1772 and included some twenty-three letters for and against episcopacy with the anti-side making the most frequent and effective showing.[39] Even within the convention itself when it met on June 4, 1771, only twelve out of more than ninety clergymen in Virginia attended, and of these four staunchly opposed the entire procedure.[40]

Of the four ministers who opposed the convention's action, Thomas Gwatkin and Samuel Henley were professors from William and Mary; Richard Hewitt served Hungar's parish in Northampton County and William Bland the James City parish. Gwatkin and Henley took their protest to the public through the press and became the principal antagonists, though others joined them. Camm and Horrocks assumed the defense. These two teams provided the principal disputants under the title "A Country Gentleman," who opposed the scheme, and "A Country Clergyman," who supported it. Gwatkin and Henley assailed the convention's action because the attendance was small and thus not representative. The charges were made that the convention had no authority to act on an issue affecting other colonies and that the granting of American bishops would inevitably weaken ties with England. Moreover, the failure of the convention leaders to consult the council and assembly on such an important matter was inexcusable and indecent. Indeed, the petition itself implied disrespect for the past services of the bishops of London.[41]

In the midst of the controversy which flooded the newspapers, Horrocks departed for England, giving "poor health" as the reason. William Nelson, president of the council, speculated Horrocks left to seek a mitre.[42] Though John Camm and William Willie tried to keep the episcopal cause alive, opposition mounted both within and without the church. An earlier prediction by Nelson, "I should not wonder if we should hear of the Virginia schism when this matter [episcopacy] comes to be considered and debated," literally came true.[43] Then when the House of Burgesses passed a resolution in July of 1772 thanking the four clergymen who opposed the convention's action for their service, the official seal of disapproval was stamped upon the Johnson-Chandler plan in Virginia. This action of Virginia's assembly was reported in Annapolis, Philadelphia, New York, Boston, and London. An observation by an anonymous author using the name "Martin Luther" was unfortunately true. He pointed out that the controversy over episcopacy was having an adverse effect on Virginia's attitudes toward religion and morals.[44] Certainly by 1771 and 1772 the clerical leaders in Virginia must have realized a struggle over episcopacy at that time would do the church more harm than good. But then the accurate reading of the American political pulse was one thing the episcopal promoters either could not or would not do.

Richard Bland, however, did not hesitate to express vigorously what was probably the consensus view on the subject of episcopacy among Virginia's vestrymen and burgesses. The episcopal scheme as proposed, he argued, if effected, would have overturned the acts of the assembly relative to the church establishment. In his view, the general court had jurisdiction in all cases ecclesiastical and civil and the presence of a bishop would challenge if not change this arrangement. Moreover, the local convention that fostered the episcopal plan had not shown due respect for the assembly, nor had it requested a change in Virginia's laws to accommodate a bishop.[45] In the judgment of Virginia's oligarchy these mistakes were fatal and implied disrespect for the 150-year church-state establishment. Bland then added, "I profess my self a sincere son of the established church; without approving her hierarchy, which I know to be a relic of the papal encroachment upon the common law."[46] Indeed, on practical and historic grounds Bland's view of episcopacy was not noticeably different from that of Congregationalists and Presbyterians. By the early 1770s Virginia Anglicans had formulated their own concept of episcopacy just as they had earlier formulated their practice of vestry prerogative, and their views were "low church." It was hardly likely that years of war with Great Britain to ensure independence for the states and nation could do anything else but confirm and deepen Virginian's commitment to local self-government and further fortify their hostility to hierarchical-type offices.

REFORM EFFORTS

In both Maryland and Virginia the question of clerical supervision had long been an issue, but in the late sixties and early seventies both provincial legislatures took steps to correct this need. Both bills were similar in their approach and were more oriented to Presbyterian-type polity than episcopal. Only the unexpected death of Lord Baltimore prevented the Maryland bill's enactment, and the Virginia bill missed passage only because the burgesses adjourned before final action was taken.[47]

In both colonies tensions were running very high over the question of clerical supervision, but in neither providence was "a bishop" suggested or considered as a possible solution. Instead the respective bills which reflected the thinking of a good number of legislators who were probably churchmen revealed a determination to divide authority in church matters coequally between the clergy and the laity.

As early as 1724–25 an attempt had been made in Maryland to establish legislatively a lay tribunal to supervise the clergy, but the proprietor's prerogative and the governor's action blocked the effort.[48] During Sharpe's administration an attempt had been made to establish a "probationary year" for all new appointees before induction. Another plan would have required a new candidate to sign a bond guaranteeing good behavior before his appointment. Though both methods were tried, neither were applied to Baltimore's favorites, who appear to have been the worst offenders. Then in 1768 the House of Delegates drafted an Ecclesiastical Courts Bill, which authorized the governor to appoint three laymen and three clergymen to a court that could investigate complaints against clergymen, require them to take an oath of loyalty to the government, and swear to make no "simoniacal contract." If a majority of a vestry and the churchwardens of a parish complained in writing to the governor and council about its ministers, the ecclesiastical court would receive the complaint and decide whether to admonish, suspend, or deprive the incumbent of his cure. Moreover, the bill limited a minister's absence from his parish to thirty days consecutively and not more than a total of sixty in any given year. It would seem the Maryland Delegates had Bennet Allen clearly in mind when they framed this legislation.

Although Maryland's Courts Bill did not become law because of Baltimore's death, both the proprietor and the bishop of London had been advised of the measure and there is no record that either objected to it. While the promoters of a resident American episcopate had the tradition of the Church of England on their side, the sponsors of the Courts Bill had the American colonial experience and sentiment on theirs. Though the Courts Bill did not pass in 1773, the determination of the laity to have a greater say was again revealed in the bill declaring the act of establishment of 1702 unconstitutional. Had not the council vetoed the latter measure the governor and proprietor would have been confronted with the most serious challenge to date for control of the church. Instead a compromise measure was passed, reducing the poll tax for the church and authorizing money payment in lieu of tobacco.[49] Thus the dismantlement of Maryland's established church had begun, and many of those who participated were among its constituents who were as determined to have home rule in church as well as in state.

A Virginia legislative committee in 1772 prepared a bill to establish an ecclesiastical commission to supervise the church's ministers. The timing of this measure clearly suggests that it was a retaliatory measure against those who had led the episcopal cause. The proposed commission was to have a president, four clergymen, and a Court of Delegates consisting of an equal number of laymen and ministers. This measure, like the Maryland Courts Bill, was a reflection of how Virginians thought ecclesiastical problems should be handled. Their preference was for a republican- or Presbyterian-type method rather than an episcopal or hierarchial one. Though the measure did not become law, Richard Bland, a burgess and vestryman, argued forcefully for it. "Upon the whole," he declared, "I am clearly of opinion that the governor has no coercive ecclesiastical jurisdiction over the clergy. It has been long ago seen, and ought long ago to have been remedied by the legislature."[50] Bland also excluded the bishop of London from the question of clerical supervision and he was convinced it could not be entrusted solely to the clergy. In Bland's view the bill to provide a commission was the appropriate way to handle the matter.

Charles Inglis, assistant minister of Trinity Church, New

York, and a zealous episcopal advocate, reported the Virginia controversy to Dr. Johnson. His personal anguish over the results is disclosed in his words, "thus you see we have not only open enemies and Dissenters to deal with; but also false brethren, the more pernicious animals of the two."[51] This same information apparently took Chandler by surprise, for he wrote urging the Virginians "if our church is not desirous of bishops, it is not episcopal; . . . But we beg you to consider the natural tendency of such conduct, and to give a candid attention to what we have to offer on the subject; and then we doubt not but you will see your mistake."[52] The only response to Chandler was a letter from Thomas Gwatkin reaffirming the position he and three others had taken previously. In a sense, this was the death knell for the episcopal scheme in Virginia and prerevolutionary America. When John Camm and William Willie tried to assemble a clerical convention in June of 1771, there was no response.[53]

That the Johnson-Chandler plan for an American episcopate encountered the stiffest resistance from within the area where the Church of England was best established and most numerous was the result of several factors. In Maryland the proprietary prerogative dominated the church; in Virginia the vestries, many of whose members were burgesses, controlled the church. In both colonies the legislatures conceived themselves to be "little parliaments" and as such were determined to assert their authority. Then the timing of the episcopal campaign was such that it inevitably became associated with imperial measures and thus symbolized another threat to home rule. But perhaps more important was the fact that these two establishments had existed for many years without bishops and had developed their own methods and procedures for handling ecclesiastical affairs. This had given them a sense of self-reliance that allowed no room for bishops who more than likely suggested royal power and proprietary prerogative to most churchmen in the American heartland of Anglicanism.

5

Carolina and Georgia Anglicans

"It would be as unsafe for an American Bishop (if such should be appointed) to come hither, as it is at present for a distributor of Stamps."

Charles Martyn to the
Bishop of London, October 20, 1765

On April 20, 1770, William Eddis, surveyor of customs at Annapolis, Maryland, wrote to friends in England:

I cannot conceive on what principle the colonists are so strongly prejudiced against the introduction of the episcopal order. . . . Throughout the southern provinces, the members of the established church greatly exceed those of all other denominations; yet I am persuaded any attempt to establish an hierarchy, would be resisted with as much acrimony as during the gloomy prevalence of puritanical zeal. . . . They have, however, conceived such rooted prejudices against the higher orders of the church, that they are positively persuaded the advantages to be acquired, . . . would by no means counter-balance the evils which might arise from it.[1]

Though Eddis did not reveal his source of information, it is probable that in his post he conversed with many merchantmen from the southern colonies on the subject of church government as well as normal business problems. Since Eddis was still new to the region in 1770, he was at a loss to explain the apparent paradox of Virginia and Maryland churchmen opposing episcopacy, nor could he appreciate the growing sentiment for self-determination in North and South Carolina and to a lesser degree in Georgia. Indeed, the quest for local auton-

110

omy in state and church affairs had been developing for many years, but in the decade preceding the American Revolution it dominated the course of events.[2]

THE ESTABLISHMENTS

Anglicanism was the legally recognized religion in North Carolina from the colony's beginning, but it was not until 1765 that the Church of England was established. Under the prodding of Governor Arthur Dobbs the assembly passed a Vestry Act in 1764 and an Orthodox Clergy Act in 1765, which unlike previous legislation of this type was allowed by the authorities in England. Previous legislation had been disallowed in England, though implemented in the colony, because the right of presentation was reserved for the vestries. The acts of 1765 simply did not mention the subject and on this basis was allowed to stand. But it was the absence of precise language on the question of who controlled the ecclesiastical patronage that permitted both the governor, William Tryon, who succeeded Dobbs in 1765, and the vestries to claim the right. It was, therefore, the question of presentation that led many Anglicans to oppose the royal governor and indirectly the crown's policy on church patronage. In the end the vestries won, but in winning they were aided by the long-standing tradition that vestries determined the matter of ministerial employment and the general mood of opposition to any extension of royal authority in North Carolina.[3]

Although the vestry acts prior to 1764 had been disallowed in England, they were to a considerable degree implemented in the colony. Parishes were defined along county lines; in 1765 there were thirty-two. Each vestry was composed of twelve men elected by all freeholders or taxpayers in a parish, and any eligible voter was qualified to be elected vestryman provided he took an oath not to oppose the liturgy of the Church of England.[4] In some parishes, particularly those on the frontier, it was not unusual for non-Anglicans to comprise a majority of the vestry. A minimum ministerial salary was set in 1741 at £50 per year and because of this comparatively low rate the S.P.G. assisted the clergy. It was, however, recognized that ministers could sue in court for back wages in the event the sheriff who collected the annual poll tax of ten shillings was negligent. Moreover, ministerial stipends could become a problem because out of the funds from the annual poll tax the monies for church construction, glebe purchases, and poor relief were also taken.[5]

The two church acts of 1764 and 1765 not only legally established the Church of England in North Carolina, but they also prepared the way for rapid church development. For example, the annual ministerial salaries was raised to £133.6.8. Governor Tryon, who was instrumental in raising the salary scale, also worked to increase the number of clergymen and by 1771 there were eighteen, half of whom were American-born, serving parishes in the colony.[6] An ambitious plan to put a church in every parish except the ten that already had one meant the possible construction of at least twenty new churches. Not only was Tryon's zeal for the church in evidence, but certain members of the laity in New Bern and Edenton set examples of personal stewardship. In each of these communities academies were established by churchmen, but opened to all. Colonel James Innes was the prime mover of the group that succeeded in chartering the New Bern Academy in 1764. Members of the vestry and parish of St. Paul's, Edenton, supported by interested citizens, secured a charter for the Edenton Academy in 1770. Both academies were initiated by locally interested Anglicans, though the S.P.G. did provide an annual stipend for the schoolmasters. Neither institution was dominated by ecclesiastical partisanship.[7]

The number of people served by the religious establishment in North Carolina is difficult to calculate. Information available indicates a white population of 100,000 in 1765 rapidly increasing to 200,000 or 250,000 white and colored inhabitants by 1771. In the years immediately preceding the Revolutionary

War, however, dissenting denominations, especially Baptist and Methodist, were growing rapidly. The late achievement of Anglican establishments belies its strength, because for years numerous congregations had worshiped in chapels or homes under the leadership of lay-readers, receiving the sacraments from visiting Anglican clergymen. It does, however, appear that in 1765 at least a majority of the citizens favored the establishment, though the Vestry Act was never fully effected or enforced in the western counties where Presbyterians and Baptists were most numerous. The opposition directed toward the establishment by Dissenters, and by some Anglicans as well, was primarily the result of the governor's claim to the control of the church as the crown's agent. This policy pursued by Tryon was seen as usurpation of ecclesiastical power and ranked with the Stamp Act as an example of British tyranny.[8]

SOUTH CAROLINA

The Church of England in South Carolina was established by law in 1706 and stood on a much firmer foundation than did its counterpart in North Carolina. Early legislation divided the colony into parishes, required the use of the service of the Church of England, authorized taxation to raise funds for church construction and glebe purchases. Ministers were publicly supported and subject to popular election by those of the Anglican persuasion in the parish which they served. Vestries of seven men were elected annually and the minister was designated a vestry member. Wardens too were elected annually and required to take the oaths of allegiance and supremacy. A commission of twenty-four members appointed by the governor exercised supervision over the secular affairs of the church. This board approved all salary requests by clergymen before payment and reviewed petitions for new parishes and churches.[9]

Guided by these practices, Anglicanism in South Carolina by 1763 had grown to twenty-two parishes, of which twenty had ministers. The development of the church under the commissioners was systematic and free from crisis. The control of ministerial patronage was so firmly in the hands of the parishioners that no one—including the royal governors whose instruction authorized them to control clerical appointments—even bothered to challenge the assumed authority of the parish vestries. Indeed, the commissioners, who apparently played a role in encouraging men to seek Holy Orders and return to South Carolina, did not interfere with the concept of local control of the ecclesiastical patronage. For the governors or commissioners to have attempted to control or influence ministerial selection after the vestries had dominated these procedures for decades would have produced a major internal conflict. Besides, in the period following the French and Indian War the royal governors were fighting a losing battle to uphold the royal prerogative in too many other areas to permit them to challenge the vestry's power.[10]

Evidence of South Carolina's continuing determination and ability to direct its church establishment was demonstrated in several ways. First, the discontinuance of the office of commissary in 1749 after forty-two years' existence in the colony did not disturb the church nor inhibit its growth. When no successor was named for Alexander Garden, who had served as commissary for twenty years, South Carolinians accepted it and did not request a replacement. Second, the growth in financial support for the church was such that by 1766 all S.P.G. assistance to the clergy was discontinued. The ability of the commissioners to assume this responsibility is a sign that the colony was not only prospering, but moving further in the direction of self-determination in church affairs. Third, the number of churchmen in the Commons House, based on St. Michael's vestry record, was such that if a similar proportion belonged to St. Philip's, also in Charleston, churchmen comprised by far the vast majority in the lower house of the legislature and thus could shield the church from outside encroachment. For example, twenty-one of fifty-one names of the members of the Commons House in 1769 were either vestrymen or pewholders in St. Michael's Church.[11] The end result of this local support for the established church was that the hierarchy in England had less and less influence over South Carolina's churchmen. Increasingly the focus of activity and decision-making in church-state matters was in Charleston instead of in Fulham and Lambeth palaces.

GEORGIA

From the beginning of settlement in Georgia the Church of England was favored, but it was 1758, or six years after the proprietary charter passed to the crown, before the church was legally established. The instructions of the royal governors for Georgia were practically identical to those of governors in other royal provinces. As the king's agent, the governor was to uphold the worship of God, foster the reading of the Prayer Book, and see that the sacraments were administered according to the rites of the Church of England. The jurisdiction of the bishop of London was acknowledged and the governor was enjoined not to induct a clergyman unless he had a license from the bishop. But it was an act of 1758 that divided Georgia into eight parishes and designated them the basic election units for the assembly. In each parish a vestry of twelve freeholders was elected by all eligible voters who were charged with the normal duties. But in Savannah the vestrymen of Christ Church were also made superintendents of the watch, required to hire a beadle, and to provide and care for a church cemetery. Indeed, in South Carolina as well as Savannah the vestry was the basic unit in civil government; in this regard both functioned much like the Virginia vestries. But in Georgia special commissions were appointed to perform specified duties.[12]

By 1773, Georgia had twelve parishes inhabited by approximately 33,000 people. Three churches stood—Savannah,

Augusta, Halifax—but not more than three or four Anglican clergy were in the colony at any one time. Christ Church, Savannah, the largest, usually had a catechist on the staff who also provided public instruction. In spite of the annual stipend of £50 for the rector of Christ Church and presumably the ministers of the other two churches, the chief financial support for the Anglican clergy came from the S.P.G. Georgia also had an educational institution, Bethesda Orphan House, founded by the itinerant Methodist evangelist in Anglican Orders, George Whitefield, which reflected many of the features of Georgia Anglicanism. In the 1760s, when Whitefield tried to convert the Orphan House into a college, he received support from Governor James Wright, he council, assembly, and a large segment of the citizenry. It was, however, Archbishop Secker who undid Whitefield's petition by requesting that the president of the new institution be an Anglican clergyman and that daily use of the liturgy of the church be used. Whitefield refused to accept these suggestions and his scheme failed.[13] He believed that the broad base support he had received for the planned college would be betrayed if he consented to the archbishop's request for a more clearly defined Anglican institution. In Georgia, that support was essentially of the "broad" and "low" church varieties.

In 1769, Whitefield preached in Christ Church, one of the Anglican pulpits that had not been closed to him because of his unorthodox views on liturgy and church government, "to a crowded and attentive audience with universal acceptance."[14] Here Anglicans and Dissenters did not display hostility toward each other as was the case in Connecticut and New York. Except for an occasional complaint from the rectors of Christ Church, many of the traditional differences distinguishing Anglicans from Dissenters elsewhere were modified and friction reduced. Indeed, it was common for Dissenters to serve on the vestries, especially in parishes like St. Matthew and St. John, where they outnumbered churchmen.[15] Georgia had never experienced a commissary as had Virginia and South Carolina, and even the bishop of London's authority had been successfully opposed by the proprietors. Georgia Anglicanism was influenced more by local conditions—the need to survive, limited economic resources, fear of attack—than was true in any other mainland colony.[16] Thus, here, church problems, including the episcopal campaign of the sixties, which generated turmoil and conflict elsewhere, scarcely caused a ripple.

INTERNAL ISSUES

Because the Church of England was established in the Carolinas and Georgia it was an integral part of these governments and as such it was influenced by official reactions to the new imperial policies of post-1763. The Stamp Act and Townshend Duties symbolized the attempt to increase the royal prerogative over the colonies, but colonial reaction made it perfectly clear the colonists were not in agreement. The unanimous protest against these measures, though diversified from province to province, made the colonial governments more sensitive to royal encroachments and more quick to respond to similar issues when they appeared. The resulting defensiveness on the part of legislatures in particular led them to scrutinize every issue to determine whether it contained any possible threat to colonial rights. Under these conditions it was natural for parishioners and vestrymen to assume the same attitude as the legislature toward the right of self-determination in parish matters.[17] Had not churchmen in general been in step with the times it is reasonable to assume that the legislatures would have decreased rather than increased official support. In fact, the best evidence that a majority of Anglicans in the three southernmost colonies were in agreement with their assemblies is the continued favor which the religious establishments received until the outbreak of the War for Independence.

In North Carolina it had taken years of maneuvering to establish the Church of England, even though the relationship between assembly, symbolizing home rule, and governor, symbolizing royal prerogative, had been reasonably cordial. After 1762, however, a series of quarrels, usually revolving around money, came to highlight the royal governor-assembly relationship. The main contest between governor and assembly took on the character of "the people" versus "the crown." At issue was the need for defense, the governor's salary, operation expenses, or tax reform that gave the occasion for legislative-executive confrontation. For example, as late as 1764 the lower house still refused to grant Governor Dobbs, who became governor in 1753, a salary or pay rent for the house he used. His successors, William Tryon (1765–71) and Josiah Martin (1771–75) encountered the same problem. So tight was this line being drawn in the contest between governor and assembly that it took the Regulator insurrection (1769–71) to get the assembly to move on matters of tax reform, the currency supply, dishonest sheriffs and judges, unscrupulous lawyers and officials. In other words, it took an armed insurrection to command the attention of governor and legislature, to turn them from their disputes to focus upon the frontier's claim for economic-political justice. Interestingly, the Regulators were not opposed to the church establishment.[18]

The legislative-executive power struggle persisting in North Carolina resembled in many respects the state of political affairs in South Carolina. By the end of the proprietary period in 1719, the popular branch of the legislature or assembly had acquired the right to choose and dismiss the public treasurer, powder receiver, commissioners of fortifications, and all officials paid out of the public treasury. They also held sole authority to initiate legislation and set fees for public officials from the governor on down. Even church patronage, traditionally the prerogative of the governor, had been conferred by the Commons House upon the Anglican inhabitants of the parishes. This same legislative body had managed to deny the council the right to amend or change money bills, control the colonial agent, or interfere in assembly elections. The persistent opposition to the council by the Commons House was based largely upon the latter's resentment of English placemen subservient to the crown who comprised the council. In South Carolina the issue was "home rule" versus rule by a "clique of placemen," who after 1763 were increasingly despised. On most issues after 1763 on which the council agreed with the new imperial policy, the Commons House was able to make them yield by withholding the annual tax bill.[19]

Several matters were disputed by governor and Commons House between 1763 and 1775. The issue of greatest significance, however, was the decision by the assembly in December 1769 to send £1,500 sterling of public money as a contribution to the Friends of Liberty, a defense fund for John Wilkes, and later to forward another £10,500 in currency. News of these gifts outraged George III. Attorney General William deGrey and Lieutenant Governor Bull were ordered to investigate and determine whether or not the assembly had sole authority to appropriate funds. Both reports stated that no warrant existed to authorize such action. Bull was then sent an additional set of instructions, which denied the assembly's claim to be sole dispenser of public funds and instead granted absolute coordinate power to the council in all money bills. The governor, lieutenant governor, and council were expressly forbidden to allow a single farthing to be spent except for specified government services in South Carolina or elsewhere as directed. By forbidding reimbursement to the treasurers, the king hoped to win the constitutional point and eventually sue those officers for thrice the amount involved.

The legislative-executive power struggle stalemated from 1770 to 1775 over Governor Bull's special instructions. Bull refused all tax bills containing amounts to reimburse the treasurers; the assembly refused to enact tax bills without the provision. Commons House demanded the revocation of Bull's

1770 instructions; the crown refused. Between March 20, 1771, and March 4, 1775, not one bill became law in South Carolina.[20] The intransigence of the assembly was intensified in 1773 when Chief Justice Thomas Gordon ruled that the council was an upper house of the legislature, a position the assembly refused to recognize.[21] In South Carolina in the decade preceding the Revolutionary War there was an internal revolution in government underway that was independent of, yet concomitant with the American Revolution. It is natural to assume that many of the vestrymen and pewholders of St. Michael's Church who were in the assembly from 1770 to 1775 were in the forefront of this battle, but unfortunately no records exist by which it can be demonstrated.

The period 1763 to 1775 in Georgia was a time of rapid development, but it also witnessed a break in the normally friendly relations between the royal governors and assembly. Here, however, the power struggle between the executive and legislature was milder and more limited than similar contests in North and South Carolina. In the 1760s, largely due to Georgia's late founding, its status of political development was comparable to that of Virginia's in the early eighteenth century. Besides, royal government, which had arrived as late as 1754, was successful. Especially during the early years of Governor James Wright's administration (1760–82) were relations with the assembly exceptional. For the years 1761 to 1764 the assembly did little more than pass annual tax bills. But the Stamp Act of 1765 shattered this harmony and it was never regained. Beyond the act itself, Wright's success in enforcing it, especially when other royal governors did not, cost him personally in public esteem. Then, when Wright refused to convene the legislature so that it could discuss a circular letter from Massachusetts on the Stamp crises, the House Speaker, Alexander Wylly, did so and thus usurped a governor's prerogative.[22]

It was, moreover, the Stamp Act that in Georgia cast doubt for the first time upon the generally accepted assumption that what was good for the empire was good for Georgia. The result was the emergence of something like an opposition party in the assembly, a faction ready to question and oppose policies of the royal government and compete with the governor for power. Evidence of this development came in 1765 when the assembly temporarily refused to provide supplies for the royal troops in Georgia required by the Quartering Act. By 1768 a Liberty party came to dominate the assembly and its role went virtually unchallenged. Eighteen of twenty-five members in the assembly were avowed members of the Sons of Liberty. By 1774–75 this faction had reduced Georgia politics to a simple contest for control of the government and whether Georgia would join her sister colonies in defying Great Britain. Although the assembly did become more friendly toward Wright after 1772, largely because of fear of Indian attack and the need for British military assistance, the Coercive Acts and finally the military actions at Lexington and Concord forced Georgia to oppose British rule.[23]

VESTRY POWERS

The movement toward legislative dominance in internal affairs by the lower houses in the Carolinas and Georgia was compatible with the determination of local vestries to retain control over ecclesiastical patronage. Though the royal governors had instructions authorizing their control of church appointments, the prerogative was so firmly held by the vestries that only William Tryon tried to obey this instruction and even he succeeded in but a limited number of cases. After his transfer to the governorship of New York, the vestries and assembly undid his claim. In Georgia, Governor Wright was flexible enough to permit a vestry to have its choice when it insisted. In South Carolina there was no doubt about who controlled church livings and no one in the legislature challenged the preeminence of the laity in this sphere in the period preceding the Revolution. As Americans had developed a concept of self-determination in civil affairs, so churchmen had come to the same idea in parish matters and neither royal prerogative nor hierarchial claims impressed them.

In North Carolina, Governor Dobbs informed the S.P.G. in 1764: "[I] could not prevail upon them [Assemblymen] to give up the parsonage to the Crown or Bishop of London, and so have not the nomination nor a right to induct them [clergy] regularly."[24] This time the legislature was unbending as ever in its refusal to agree to or sanction the royal prerogative in cases of clerical induction and collation. The fact that North Carolina had had a decentralized ecclesiastical system before 1765 reinforced assemblymen and vestrymen in their belief that ministerial selection, presentation, and annual renewals were their rights. Later when Tryon tried to assert the letter of his instruction on church appointments, he discovered "some vestries idly imagine the power of presentation is still vested by implication in them."[25] Even after the passage of the Vestry and Orthodox Clergy Acts in 1765 and 1766, neither of which specifically mentioned the question of patronage, Tryon was successful in inducting not more than seven clergymen into parishes while others remained staunchly opposed.

Several clergymen described the controversy generated by Tryon's efforts to exercise the right of induction in their correspondence to the S.P.G. and the bishop of London. John Barnett of Brunswick parish, caught in the cross-fire between governor and vestry, explained to Dr. Burton, secretary of the S.P.G.: "the people of this parish do still violently oppose the presentation of the Crown to the living, that I believe it will be found necessary for me to remove to another part of the province. Permit me sir to assure the Venerable Board that the people are so desirous of my stay with them on the usual terms, of an annual re-election." While Barnett's report is a bit self-serving, it squares with the experience of John Camp, Hobart Briggs, and Alexander Stewart. So incensed did Tryon become

over these outright rejections of his authority that he vowed, "I
purpose to bring this matter on some future occasion to tryal
that they may be convinced of the obstinacy and error of such a
notion, since I find in some parishes, candid argument will not
prevail."[26]

Tryon never took the case for executive prerogative versus
vestry induction to court, but North Carolina churchmen saw
to it that their position was vindicated in the Orthodox Clergy
Act of 1771. The new act clearly gave the right of presentation
to each vestry and permitted a full year in which a vestry could
seek a minister before the governor could interfere. Moreover,
the vestry was specifically authorized to set the time, place, and
frequency of religious services. When this act came before the
bishop of London, Richard Terrick, for review, he exclaimed,
"I rather suspect that they borrow'd the model of their government from the Presbyterians and Independents of New England."[27] It is not clear, however, from the record whether or
not this act was allowed. The transfer of Tryon to New York in
1771 and the succession of Josiah Martin to the governorship
probably meant the act was returned to the assembly for recon-
sideration. Before the measure could be reenacted and returned to England for examination it is likely the Revolutionary War had begun. In any event, the 1771 Act reflected the
sentiment of North Carolina's churchmen. Interestingly, its
provisions were identical with existing practices in Virginia,
which no governor had tried to challenge since Alexander
Spotswood's administration in the first quarter of the century.
But then, in all the mainland colonies the vestries to a greater
or lesser degree exercised more authority over ministerial employment and support than their counterparts in England.[28]

The North Carolina assembly successfully opposed Tryon's
efforts to become head of the ecclesiastical establishment by re-
jecting his claim to executive influence over clerical salaries. The
Orthodox Clergy Act of 1765 set the annual stipend at £133.6.8,
but continued the practice of having the sheriff collect the poll

tax from which salaries were paid. When Tryon supplied an alternative method of paying clergymen directly from the public treasury, it was flatly rejected. This proposal was seen as an obvious attempt to strengthen the governor's prerogative because he also claimed authority to approve governmental expenditures.[29] By keeping clerical payment at the county and parish level and in the sheriff's hands the local vestrymen had a much stronger influence upon the collection and remittance of their ministers' stipends. To the parishioner this method of ministerial compensation, the practice of annual contracts, and vestry selection met their needs, though this type polity was more closely allied to Congregational-Presbyterian polity than to the traditional episcopal concept of church government. Besides, it was in harmony with the rapidly developing and spreading republican concept of representative government.

South Carolina's control of ministerial candidates was very much what North Carolinians wanted their system to become. Though South Carolina had had commissaries from 1706 to 1749, they had not interfered with or diminished the role of vestries. Here all parishioners who were conformists to the Church of England were entitled to vote for the ministerial candidate and a majority was necessary for election. As early as 1731 the Commissioners' Book records the election of Daniel Dwight by the constituents of St. John's parish. But all candidates were not elected, as evidenced in the case of Alexander Leslie, who was recommended by the commissioners but rejected by the ballot; no reason is recorded.[30] Information about an apparent innovation in parish selection practices was reported in 1763 by Charles Martyn of St. Andrew's parish to the bishop of London. "The parish of St. John's in Colleton County . . . has lately wrote to England for a clergyman to be *exported* to them, but at the same time entered into a resolution never to elect him as their rector, let him be ever so deserving, in order to keep him in a state of dependence, and consequently subject = subservience [*sic*] to their humors and caprice."[31] Later Martyn added, "it is growing into a practice with most parishes, to admit no minister among them until he first engages not to sue for election; and then they make an agreement with him in conformity to the mode of dissenting congregations, only from one year to another."[32] Though there is no account of the impact of these developments upon the quality of ministerial services, it is natural to assume that the loss of tenure would discourage men of ability from taking Holy Orders.

Another device the South Carolina vestries possessed to condition ministerial performance was the issuance of a certificate verifying the minister's entitlement to payment from the public treasury. Although the commissioners supervised ministerial payments, each minister was required to submit to the commissioners a signed statement of eligibility for payment. Unless the document was properly executed the salary would be withheld. Moreover, this method of ministerial compensation was further strengthened in 1766 when the colony assumed full responsibility for stipends, thus eliminating any outside gifts from the S.P.G. In practice this system seems to have worked well for clergy and laity; it was more dependable than a poll or tobacco tax and apparently encountered no major problems.[33] Thus, the supervision and control of the Anglican clergy in South Carolina, except for the license from the bishop of London, was completely under the control of the laity.

A symbolic mutation appeared in the ecclesiastical records of South Carolina in the 1760s: the listing of vestrymen ahead of churchwardens, which was the opposite of traditional ecclesiastical protocol. Though a consistent pattern did not develop in all parishes, where it did appear it was interpreted to mean that the popularly elected vestrymen ranked higher in public esteem than the churchwardens who were elected by the smaller body of vestrymen from their ranks. This trend in ecclesiastical affairs simply reinforced and eloquently dramatized the impact republican and congregational concepts of government were having among the people. The introduction of a bishop even of the type Johnson and Chandler advocated into the antihierarchical and prerogative environment of South Carolina would most certainly have been an unwelcome experience. Both Charles Martyn and Charles Woodmason, dedicated as they were to the church and aware of the episcopal scheme, made no move to introduce the subject in South Carolina.[34]

The Church of England establishment in South Carolina was not considered a burden, even by Dissenters, as it was coming to be in Virginia. The absence of any vigorous agitation against it was probably due to the realization by Dissenters that the church was controlled by the laity and in all colonies where the laity were prominent in the church it tended to be more tolerant and flexible toward other religious groups. The strongest piece of evidence that shows how the church was regarded by a significant segment of the population in the 1760s and early 1770s is found among the documents of the Regulator Movement. This group, much like their namesake in North Carolina, was located primarily along the frontier and was convinced that the tidewater region, which dominated the government, was denying them fair representation in the assembly and services. After acquiring a considerable base of support, the Regulators refused to pay taxes until the assembly in Charleston agreed to extend schools, churches, roads, bridges, and protection to the backcountry. In their "Remonstrance" of November 1767 are listed twenty-three demands; three of these focus upon religion. The eleventh point was a demand that the backcountry be laid out in parishes, and churches, chapels, and parsonages built. That ministers be provided was the twelfth item and number thirteen called for the augmentation of country parsons' salaries with provision made for their widows. It was hoped that the enactment of these provisions would encourage "learned and godly men . . . to come over to us."[35] It is very significant that the Regulators, who represented a mixture of religious opinions, did not demand religious freedom and disestablishment. Their concern was partly that the same religious benefits which the tidewater parishes enjoyed be extended equally to them; to achieve this they appealed to Charleston, not Whitehall.

Vestrymen in Georgia were elected by all tax-paying freeholders in a parish without regard to their denominational affiliation. Georgia vestry election practice was, therefore, much broader than South Carolina's, but the power of the vestry over the clergy was less. The governor's instructions authorized him to "collate" ministers into vacant parishes, but in practice these instructions were not always followed. For example, in 1761 the vestrymen of Christ Church, Savannah rejected a Mr. Duncanson whom the governor planned to induct as a replacement for the deceased Mr. Zouberbuhler, but the governor was persuaded to change his mind. In 1771 when Samuel Fink, rector of Christ Church, died, the vestry chose Timothy Lowten of St. John's to be the successor and informed the governor, who concurred. Also, sometime before 1775 it became customary for one planning to seek Holy Orders in England to have a recommendation from a local vestry whether or not he had one from the governor.[36]

In Georgia as in South Carolina the church establishment caused Dissenters little distress, primarily because it was not burdensome. Authority to create new parishes and build churches was vested in a commission established in 1762 comprised of laymen.[37] Taxation for church support fell heaviest upon consumers of liquor. A parish tax was levied on all property owners, but these funds were spent within the parish for repairs and relief. It was, moreover, quite common for Presbyterians and Lutherans to serve as vestrymen and participate in the full range of parish duties. This did not mean non-Anglican vestrymen converted to the Church of England, but that the church in Georgia was in no sense a closed system. In reality, it was flexible, tolerant, and open: quite the opposite of what those with "high-church" views like Chandler, Seabury,

Cooper, and Inglis thought it should be. But in Georgia the survival of the Anglican communion was more dependent upon adaptability than tradition. Although a considerable increase in the number of Dissenters in the decade preceding the War for Independence threatened to overwhelm the established church, hostility between the two major church persuasions did not develop as it did in Virginia.

THE EPISCOPAL CAMPAIGN

There is evidence that news of the Johnson-Chandler plan reached all three of the most southern mainland colonies, yet there is no indication that a controversy over episcopacy broke out in any one of them. Whoever received the news in North Carolina either buried it or handled it so discreetly that no hint of it went into the written records. In South Carolina, Martyn and Woodmason knew of the scheme, but apparently decided to take no action to recruit their clerical colleagues in the cause.[38] By contrast, the *Georgia Gazette* in February 1768 announced the publication of Chandler's *An Appeal,* but only one minister, Samuel Fink of Savannah, showed interest in it.[39] Though the participation of the Carolinas and Georgia establishments was not as important to the episcopal scheme as Virginia and Maryland's, the absence of their concurrence would certainly be noted by the authorities in England. In effect, the grand design of the Elizabeth Town Convention drew a blank from the provinces on the southern tier.

Indifference and potential hostility to the episcopal scheme in North Carolina is understandable when the contemporary internal disputes are considered. The recurring contests between governor and assembly over local issues and new imperial measures became related and viewed as a major struggle between royal prerogative and popular government. On this major issue of the decade Anglican vestrymen and parishioners were by their actions in ecclesiastical affairs on the whole clearly on the side of popular government. Even the able and zealous Governor Tryon was unable to pry most churchmen loose from the concept of parish prerogative in matters of local church government. In this area Anglican practice was more closely related to Congregational-Presbyterian polity and the tenets of republican government than they were to their episcopal and hierarchical tradition as it existed in England. Most churchmen must have believed that taxation for church support necessitated representative vestries and elected ministers. Because of this concept of church government that had evolved in North Carolina, any clergyman who dared to advocate support for the Johnson-Chandler plan had to be unusually courageous or foolhardy.

In South Carolina the ecclesiastical picture between 1763 and 1775 was very much overshadowed by the major internal political controversy. In this province, where the political contest generated a very high social temperature, a dramatic announcement of the Johnson-Chandler plan would have been unwelcome and out-of-place. Reflecting the mood of the period is the *South Carolina Gazette,* which printed the latest news from the colonies and abroad that related to politics and commerce. By contrast, the pro and con series on episcopacy that flooded Boston, New York, and Philadelphia newspapers were not mentioned in the *South Carolina Gazette.* Local religious items were printed and among these the most often repeated was a sale advertisement for John J. Zubly's "A Sermon Upon the Repeal of the Stamp Act" preached by this Independent Presbyterian minister in Savannah on June 25, 1766.[40] But the absence of any reference to the episcopal controversy that raged in New England and New York in the late 1760s strongly suggests that a decision had been made and generally accepted not to import and print any materials that might add fuel to the existing political strife or possibly disturb the religious establishment.

Charles Martyn's evaluation of the political-emotional climate in Charleston leaves little room to wonder what the reaction to an American bishop would have been had one appeared in 1766 or 1767. "If I may form a judgment from that present prevailing turbulent spirit which like an epidemick disorder, seems every where to diffuse itself through this and other colonies, I can venture to affirm that it would be as unsafe for an American bishop (if such should be appointed) to come hither, as it is at present for a distributor of Stamps."[41] In Charleston the stamps had not been distributed and those suspected of cooperating with the British government to land and distribute them were roughly treated. Here, a bishop most certainly would have been identified with the home government's imperial policies and placemen thus jeopardizing his safety and security. Churchmen who worshiped in the classically styled and ornately fashioned St. Philip's Church, the oldest in the province, or in the equally elegant but more modestly fashioned St. Michael's Church, both of which were among Charleston's most impressive architectural accomplishments, were not about to submit to outside ecclesiastical interference any more readily than they had to outside political intrusions.

The attitude of Charleston's churchmen, which was probably representative of the Anglicans in South Carolina, toward clergymen who openly sided with the royal prerogative position is disclosed in the cases of Robert Cooper and John Bullman. Cooper was minister of St. Michael's from 1761 to 1776, but in 1771 noted that he was addressed as "minister" and not "rector." When he requested the vestry designate him "rector," his request was refused and he was retained on an annual reelection basis. In 1776, however, he was dismissed for loyalty to the crown. Cooper's assistant at St. Michael's, John Bullman, was also dismissed from his post after a congregational vote showed that a majority believed a sermon he had recently preached revealed loyalty to the crown.[42] Had Martyn, Woodmason, or any other Anglican in South Carolina publicly espoused the episcopal cause in 1768 or thereafter they most likely would have experienced a fate identical to Cooper's and Bullman's.

Georgia's churchmen were at least as well if not better informed about events emanating from the Elizabeth Town conventions than either North or South Carolina. The February 17, 1768 issue of the *Gazette* reported:

> the church clergy of New York and New Jersey, being assembled together in a voluntary convention, and assisted by some of their brethren from the neighbouring provinces, took into consideration the propriety and expediency of addressing the public, on the subject of an American Episcopate. . . . It was accordingly voted, that something to this purpose would be published, and the Reverend Thomas Bradbury Chandler, D.D. Rector of St. John's Church in Elizabeth Town, New Jersey, was appointed to this service. This work is just published, entitled, *An Appeal to the Publick in behalf of the Church of England in America.*[43]

But in Georgia the notice caused no newspaper controversy nor even a published reaction. Here, in contrast to New England and New York, no deep-seated hostilities existed between churchmen and Dissenters of an ecclesiastical or political nature to which the announcement of Chandler's *Appeal* could add an incendiary touch.

The clearest insight into Georgia Anglicans' attitude toward the establishment and episcopacy was recorded by John Joachim Zubly, pastor of the Independent Presbyterian church in Savannah from 1760 to 1781. Zubly was the most prominent minister in Georgia and a successful businessman in the South Carolina-Georgia area; he had dealings with such business leaders and Anglican laymen as Henry Laurens and John Rutledge of Charleston. On October 10, 1768, Zubly informed Ezra Stiles, "I do not hear that the episcopal clergy in South Carolina or this province have any itch for a Bp. . . . I doubt whether a dozen be in South Carolina who are desirous of being blessed with any such establishment, tho I am acquainted with no inconsiderable number of episcopalians that would rather join against than for it."[44] Zubly went on to add that relationships between Anglican and Dissenters in Georgia had steadily improved and expressed no apprehension that the episcopal controversy raging in the northern colonies would disturb the colony's amicable ecclesiastical status.[45]

The Anglican attitude of opposition to episcopacy detected by William Eddis in his post as surveyor of customs at Annapolis had several contributing causes. Any type of bishop coming from England to reside in America in the late 1760s or 1770s could not escape the image of a royal agent whose purpose overtly or covertly was to strengthen the imperial administration. The fact that all three southern colonies had opposed recent imperial measures meant they most likely would have reacted similarly to a bishop from England. An environment of hostility between Britain and the colonies had developed to the point where even a benign bishop of the primitive type Chandler described would have been viewed by members of the Anglican establishments as well as Dissenters as a mitred placeman armed with full prelatical powers. Moreover, the churchmen who had successfully defended local vestry rights against commissaries, royal governors, and zealous clergymen were not about to condone a plan for an ecclesiastical officer whose claim of authority might well produce the most serious challenge yet to local autonomy in church government.

6

The Anglican Predicament

"The battle for the colonial episcopate was lost."
Samuel Seabury, *Memoirs*

The Church of England in America between 1763 and 1775 found itself increasingly in a paradoxical position. Throughout this period issues that sparked disagreements between the colonies and the British government naturally engendered resentment toward institutions and people who to some degree symbolized British imperial policy. The Proclamation Line, Revenue Act, Sugar Act, Stamp Act, Quartering Act, Declaratory Act, and Townshend duties all served to foster ill will toward the parliament and ministries that sponsored them and the agents who were selected to enforce them. At the very time hostility was building toward Britain and her placemen, the Church of England in America continued to grow and was favored more generously by colonial and English authorities than in previous decades, except in the case of Maryland's establishment. The only instances of serious problems for the church arose when zealous clergymen either initiated or cooperated with the episcopal campaign or got out of step with the will of the colonial legislatures, as happened to a few clergymen in Virginia who were caught up in the Parson's Cause. Otherwise, representatives of the Church of England in the colonies, which was symbolically at least a part of the political-ecclesiastical establishment of England, did not become an object of abuse or opprobrium as did stamp agents, revenue commissioners, admiralty judges, and royal governors until after 1775.

AMERICAN ANGLICANISM

The main reason for the absence of widespread hostility toward the Church of England *per se* in America in spite of its relationship to the British government was due to its being perceived essentially as a local institution. The fact that the basic units of the church or parish vestries were controlled by men who identified with the emerging colonial claims and ideology allayed suspicion. Under these conditions there was little or no fear that an outside agency could command the allegiance of Anglicans and direct their actions. Then, in the colonies where the church was established the assemblies had far more control over the church than the bishop of London or any other official in England. Because the American Anglican churches were so thoroughly dominated by the laity, who for the most part acted consistently with colonial interests, the animosity generated by the imposition of several new imperial measures was not transferred to the church before 1775. Moreover, the increasing number of American-born and -educated clergymen who were known by the vestries prior to their ordination and installation as ministers did much to remove fear that the church represented British rather than local concerns. By 1765 there were only a few Anglican clergymen who openly sided with the British government's Stamp Act and these few were located in Connecticut and New York; they were also those who became leading advocates of a resident episcopate.[1]

It was, however, the system of "select vestries," which existed in all American Anglican parishes, that identified local Anglican churches with the increasingly popular concept of local autonomy. The practice of popular election of vestrymen either by all Anglicans or the freeholders of the parish, except in Virginia where cooption prevailed, made the local administrative body subject to the popular will. The complete control over the ecclesiastical patronage which the parish vestries had achieved, except in Maryland, at a time when perhaps not a single vestry in England had such power, was a major feature of the laity's authority. Then too, the laity controlled ministerial salaries, except the S.P.G. supplements, through taxation in the colonies where the church was established and by their voluntary subscriptions elsewhere. This made the clergy far more sensitive to local suggestions and probably more responsive to them than to the bishop of London. It was, therefore, the reality of local control in Anglican ecclesiastical matters that made the outspoken critics of Britain's imperial measures, many of whom were churchmen, unafraid that the home government would receive anything more than a token response from the Church of England in America.

In the years filled with recurring crises between the forces for home rule versus imperial authority, numerous churchmen in the middle and southern colonies were among the prominent opponents of the British measures. Public evidence for this type action in Pennsylvania was dramatically demonstrated by twenty-nine contemporary and future vestrymen who signed the Non-Importation Agreement of 1765 in response to the Stamp Act. A similar action was repeated in reaction to the Townshend Duties in 1767. Thomas Willing, Joseph Swift, John Gibson, Abraham Usher, John Ross, Richard Bache, Archibald McCall, Joseph Claypoole, and Charles Stedman were all leading citizens with long records of church service to their credit.[2] Provost Smith of the College and Academy of Philadelphia preached a sermon entitled "A Lover of his Country" at the May 1766 commencement, in which he extolled "the patriotic efforts of cool and good men, in the vindication of native and constitutional rights."[3] In Maryland, Daniel Dulany's pamphlet *The Considerations on the Propriety of Imposing Taxes in the British Colonies for the Purpose of Raising a Revenue, by Act of Parliament* was printed soon after the Stamp Act and forwarded to England, where it caught the attention of William Pitt and became an influence toward repeal.[4] Moreover, Virginia's House of Burgesses, the vast majority of whom were churchmen, passed a set of resolves against the Stamp Act which inspired similar protests from the assemblies of eight of the other twelve colonies. Landon Carter and Richard Bland, in addition, made personal contributions to the anti-Stamp Act cause in print, and Bland in his *An Enquiry into the Rights of the British Colonies* came close to claiming that the House of Burgesses had coordinate legislative power with parliament. Moreover, the lower houses of the North and South Carolina and Georgia governments asserted that theirs was the sole right to tax their constituents, and in these three assemblies many members were churchmen.[5] Thus, in the region where the Church of England was largest, there was staunch support for the colonial cause and not the slightest hint the church was leaning toward the British claim. Only in Connecticut and to a lesser degree in New York was there evidence that in 1765 and 1767 the Anglicans followed the leadership of Dr. Johnson and permitted their influence to be registered in favor of compliance with the Stamp and Townshend Acts.

Another characteristic of the major portion of the Church of England in America and one that reduced suspicion of it as a pro-British institution was the prevalence of "Latitudinarian" and "low" church attitudes and practices, particularly in the churches from Pennsylvania southward. These terms "broad" and "low" reflect the type leadership, both clerical and lay, and the nature of the services performed. For example, "broad" churchmen, while retaining their Anglican beliefs, were tolerant toward other religious denominations. Their approach to religion emphasized freedom rather than authority, which meant that while organization in the church was necessary it should not be used to enforce rigidly rules, creeds, and dogma. The term "low" church was similar in meaning to "broad," but also included the elimination of creeds and mystery from worship and little emphasis was placed on the sacraments.[6] In other words, the majority of churchmen were more prone to be tolerant toward those of different religious beliefs than they were to accept their own unique tradition. Some "broad" churchmen even adopted practices from evangelicals—i.e., ex tempore praying and preaching. In these ways differences between Anglicans and Dissenters that stood in sharp relief in New England and New York were minimized throughout the rest of the American communion. If the accounts of Philip Vickers Fithian in Virginia, Josiah Quincy in Charleston, and Charles Woodmason of the South Carolina backcountry are taken as generally applicable, Anglican worship in the early 1770s was usually formal and mannerly rather than distinctive and exciting.[7] There was little in the conduct of the established church's service that would provoke its constituents to be other than responsive to their colonial leaders. Only in New England, New York, and New Jersey does the term "high church" apply, and in this region emphasis upon Catholic truth, patristics, the Prayer Book, and loyalty to England were much in evidence. Here, however, the clerical leaders were more traditionally and theologically oriented and the laity's influence was limited primarily to matters of polity.[8] In New England, where Anglicanism was a minority faith without state support, distinctiveness was a source of strength, but in the area where it was state supported it tended to adjust readily to the source that sustained it.

BRITISH POLICY

The primary aim of the English government in the eighteenth century was to maintain the political equilibrium achieved by the Glorious Revolution in 1688–89 and the accession of the Hanoverian dynasty in 1715. This resulted in domestic and foreign policies designed to further the national interest. In the area of religion within the domestic sphere the accommodation reached between government and nonconformists in the Toleration Act of 1688–89 was maintained. To enhance this arrangement the Occasional Conformity and Schism Acts were repealed in 1718, but the Test and Corporation Acts retained. On the other hand, while the position of the Church of England was maintained, its power was checked by parliament for fear it might provoke Dissenters. It was within this framework that the subject of bishops for America was revived by the bishop of London, Thomas Sherlock, in 1751. At that time the duke of Newcastle, archbishop of Canterbury (Thomas Herring), Lord Hardwicke, and Horatio Walpole devised a policy on the subject that remained in force for the balance of the colonial period, though there was a vigorous effort made in the 1760s to change it. In essence this decision denied bishops for America and urged the subject not be reintroduced.

Part of the loss of influence of the bishops of London in the 1760s and 1770s, however, could not be helped. The short tenure of both Thomas Hayter and Richard Osbaldeston was ended by death. Richard Terrick (1764–77), however, refused to accept the commission for America and there was apparently no attempt to coerce him to assume the traditional role. Due to a lack of consistency of administration on the part of the English hierarchy and particularly the bishops of London toward the colonies, there was less episcopal supervision of the American churches in the sixties than there had been under Bishops Henry Compton (1675–1713) and Edmund Gibson (1723–48).[9] With the decline of episcopal supervision it is little wonder American clergymen with "high church" principles felt more keenly than ever the need for a resident episcopate. Had not Thomas Secker, when he became archbishop of Canterbury in 1758, asserted a supervisory role over the New World churches as primate of the Church of England, the English hierarchy's influence in America would have been even less.[10]

The intransigence of the British government is again evinced by its refusal to accept or sanction proposals that would have provided some episcopal services to the American churches. For example, the possibility of a visiting bishop was proposed several times in the late 1750s and early 1760s, but to no avail.

This suggestion involved sending one of the forty-three bishops in England and Ireland on tour to perform confirmation,
consecration, and ordination. It was argued that it would be
much easier for one bishop to cross the Atlantic than for several ministerial candidates to do so. Moreover, a visiting bishop
would enable the New England clergy who proposed it more
readily to maintain the distinctive features of their church. But
this idea never materialized. Nor did a proposal made after the
Treaty of Paris in 1763 that a bishop be located in Canada to
whom American ministerial candidates could more readily go
and who in time might visit the American colonies.[11] Dr. Johnson was willing in 1769 to accept this plan as an acceptable
alternative to a resident American bishop, but again the proposal did not receive the approval of the government, though
Archbishop Secker backed it.

Perhaps it was the anticipated irreversibility of the British
government on the issue of episcopacy that prompted Dr.
Johnson to share with his successor to the presidency of King's
College, Myles Cooper, a projected scheme whereby the American churches might acquire a bishop. "I have sometimes
thought that when we have tried all reasonable measures to
obtain Bp's from England & are denied, we ought to get a Bp
where we can from Denmark, Sweden, or even *Russia* & to
form an American Chh."[12] Because Dr. Johnson expressed this
view before the meeting of the Elizabeth Town Convention, he
obviously knew that the most formidable obstacle for the proepiscopal forces to overcome was the British government's antiepiscopal policy for America. But the alternative routes to
achieve a resident bishop—Denmark, Sweden, or even Russia,
all of which had state churches with bishops—were far more
intriguing than any scheme that was discussed in convention or
publicly. Dr. Johnson apparently considered the procurement
of a bishop to complete the Anglican church organization so
important that he was willing to entertain the idea of declaring
ecclesiastical independence from England a decade before the

colonies declared formally their political independence. However, no evidence is available to show whether or not Johnson or Cooper ever explored the possibility of pursuing this idea.

In reality, the British government's policy denying even a visiting bishop to the colonies encouraged churchmen to be increasingly innovative and self-reliant. It was the home government's refusal to act positively to the generally recognized need for clerical supervision that partly prompted the clergymen of Connecticut, New York, and New Jersey to meet in Elizabeth Town in 1766 and 1767. Though these interstate conventions did not succeed in changing the British government's policy nor did they manage to allay the fears of Dissenters and many Anglicans about bishops, they did create a workable procedure in the interstate convention concept that proved its great value in the years following independence. If the English government thought it could keep the Americans dependent upon itself by denying the zealous episcopal advocates' request, they were mistaken.

Because the British policy on the issue of an American episcopate was unbending in the third quarter of the eighteenth century does not mean the government was indifferent or uninterested in the status of the Church of England in America. In fact, the ecclesiastical policy of the home government consistently favored the church in the thirteen colonies, but never at the expense of political or economic considerations. This posture is apparent in the 1760s when the Board of Trade and Privy Council recommended the disallowance of colonial laws which in their judgment undermined the church's traditional role. This attitude produced the defeat of George Whitefield's request for a charter authorizing the conversion of Bethesda Orphanage into a College. When Whitefield refused to consent to having an Anglican clergyman serve as president and declined responsibility for the regular use of the Prayer Book, his request stalled and he finally withdrew it.[13] North Carolina's Vestry Acts were consistently disallowed, except the 1765 one, because they delegated the patronage to the vestries.[14] When the government of New York refused to charter Presbyterian churches in the late 1760s, the Privy Council did not recommend a reversal because in its opinion legal incorporation was reserved for the Church of England.[15] Moreover, after 1763 royal governors were reminded of the articles in their instructions requiring them to uphold the worship of God, the Prayer Book, and the sacraments according to Anglican rites.

It was, then, the benign favoritism of the British government toward the Church of England in America that indirectly encouraged parish vestries to consolidate their position. Unless the parishioners took a vital interest in their churches there was no way the English government had to sustain them. Once they became successful either through a colonial establishment or a self-supporting congregation they were no more prepared to bow to a royal governor's claim to the patronage than the assemblies were to obey the imperial stamp agents. Surprisingly, the home government did not retaliate against the growing self-consciousness of the American churches by withholding ministerial licenses to new ordinands or delaying or suspending S.P.G. stipends. At most the Board of Trade and Privy Council had disallowed those measures that appeared to them injurious to the church. In the meantime, the parishioners knew there was little the hierarchy could or was likely to do to interfere with their prerogatives.

EPISCOPACY WITHOUT EPISCOPI

The appearance in print of Chandler's *An Appeal to the Public in Behalf of the Church of England in America* in 1767 provided the fullest and most detailed description of any episcopal plan proposed for America in the eighteenth century. The reasons given for the need of bishops were clearly and vigorously stated. The type bishops (primitive bishops) and their powers of ordination, confirmation, consecration, and visitation were precisely stated. Chandler flatly denied that such bishops would have a title, receive tithes, or conduct church court. Indeed, the argument presented in a forceful and logical style might well have convinced one of the simplicity and justness of the episcopal cause had one been unaware of the variety of complicated factors and conditions which Chandler did not mention. But it was Chandler's tailoring of his argument to win his case that left him exposed on important issues he either minimized or ignored.

One very important question never answered by Chandler was whether he had assurance that the type of bishops he proposed would be permitted by the English government. Because he claimed but produced no written assurance of this implied consent, he never convinced Dissenters and many churchmen that such a scheme was realistic. Nor was Chandler clear on who and how these bishops would be appointed. Since the creation of a diocese required an act of parliament, and the appointment of a bishop was a royal prerogative, it appeared that both king and parliament would have to cooperate to produce an American bishop. But on this question Chandler only vaguely admitted the king would be the appointer.[16] But the questions of how and by whom the candidates would be selected was never answered. Whether or not Chandler and his associates expected to play a role in the selection process was never clarified. In fact, there was no specific provision in the plan to ensure that American Anglicans over whom the bishop(s) would preside would be given any voice in the process of selection. The claim that such bishop(s) would not require tithes or taxes to support them because funds had been bequeathed by interested persons in England sounded good. In reality the fund contained £4000, which would have produced less than £300 interest each year, or a sum less than the smallest sum paid an English bishop.[17]

The Dissenters, of course, were quick to point out these obvious weaknesses in the Johnson-Chandler plan and publicize their opposition. But beyond this, there were statements and references in Chandler's treatment that gave thoughtful people cause to suspect the "primitive type" bishops might be a temporary arrangement and only an opening wedge of what could follow. For example, Chandler admitted he could not say whether the government might not invest these bishops with some degree of civil power. Then when he stated "but notwithstanding, Episcopacy and Monarchy are, in their Frame and constitution, best suited to each other. Episcopacy can never thrive in a Republican Government, nor Republican Principles in an Episcopal Church,"[18] he, in effect, made clear the direction in which he would have favored the church to develop. His claim to the superior position in religious affairs among the colonies for the Church of England did much to counter his argument that the type of bishops sought would be the primitive type.

The general response of the Anglican laity is perhaps best described by William White, who in the early 1770s was assistant to Richard Peters and then Jacob Duché in Christ and St. Peter's churches in Philadelphia. In his *Memoirs* he stated, "from what he then heard and observed, he believed it was impossible to have obtained the concurrence of a respectable number of laymen in any measure for obtaining an American bishop." The reason White noted that produced this attitude was fear a bishop might be made an instrument of civil government and thus become dangerous to future security. The prevalence of this attitude was also recorded and followed by the observation, "Certain it is that no endeavours for lay petitions for episcopacy were made."[19] But in particular instances the laity forcefully opposed the Johnson-Chandler plan. Lord Baltimore and his agents, Governors Sharpe and Eden, virtually blocked discussion of the plan in Maryland. Virginia's House of Burgesses overwhelmingly opposed the efforts of Horrocks and Camm to promote the scheme, primarily because it clashed with their ecclesiastical constitution. The indefatigable defender of Virginia's constitution, Richard Bland, even wrote to Thomas Adams, colonial agent in London, urging him to publish in the public papers there the activities of Horrocks and Camm in an effort to stir up English Dissenters who could help defeat the effort.[20] Though Carolina and Georgia Anglicans did not openly confront the issue, their actions in response to England's interference in their internal affairs left no question about how they would have addressed the episcopal issue had it been forced upon them. For the majority of American Anglicans the decade of the 1760s was the wrong time to raise the issue of a resident episcopate. But the recorded reactions of churchmen did serve as a Gallup-poll-type sampling of opinion to instruct those who in the 1780s reconstructed the Church of England into the Protestant Episcopal Church and managed to include bishops.

WHY THE CONTROVERSY?

In light of the general indifference or resistance among American Anglicans toward the Johnson-Chandler plan and the inflexible British policy on the subject, the fundamental question emerges: why did such a controversy erupt over the issue in the late sixties? Part of the answer has to be that the period from 1765 to 1770 was so charged with resentment toward England that any subject related in any way to the home governemnt would be seen as a threat and reacted to more forcefully than at another time. Under the emotionally charged conditions that existed Dissenters were quick to point out that the Test and Corporation Acts denying their fellow religionists full civil and political rights were still in force in England and a version of them might well be imposed upon the colonies. Indeed, it was recalled that in the Massachusetts Charter revision of 1691 the home government had required Puritans to grant the franchise to Anglicans and permit them to hold office for the first time. Thereafter New England Anglicans realized that an effective way to intimidate the Massachusetts and Connecticut establishments was to threaten petitions requesting a charter review in England. Then too, it was entirely possible that in the tense political environment that existed some Congregationalists sincerely believed a bishop would attempt to substitute the Church of England for their church as the legally established church. Such fear was fostered by references to Archbishop William Laud, who in the 1630s had projected a bishop for New England and actually attempted to impose bishops and Prayer Book upon Scotland by force.

Also the episcopal controversy in several colonies became intertwined with local political issues which increased the dimensions of the argument. For example, Congregationalists in Massachusetts had passed an Indian Missions Act that was disallowed by the Privy Council in 1763, due largely to opposition from Archbishop Secker. It was not a complete surprise, therefore, that an Anglican-sponsored effort to found a college called Queens in the Berkshires was prevented from winning the assembly's approval even though Governor Bernard favored it.[21] Then too, Anglicans in both Massachusetts and Connecticut complained that their governments denied them a portion of the church taxes to which they were entitled whenever their parishes were without a minister. So concerned were the Connecticut and Massachusetts legislatures about the possibility of bishops being introduced that in 1768 and 1771 they instructed their agents in London to be alert to such possibilities. As Samuel Adams, writing for the Massachusetts House of Representatives in 1768, phrased it, "we hope in God such an establishment will never take place in America, and we desire you would strenuously oppose it."[22]

In New York the contest between Anglican episcopal promoters and their Presbyterian opponents was more deeply involved in local issues than the contests in Connecticut and Massachusetts. Here two political factions, "court" and "country," were led by James DeLancey and William Livingston respectively. Because DeLancey was an Anglican and Livingston a Presbyterian, these labels were sometimes used in the political contest of the 1760s. The DeLancey faction tended to dominate the appointive offices of New York's royal government and were more oriented toward mercantile pursuits and disposed to obey British authorities. The Livingston faction was comprised of nonconformists, Presbyterians, and Dutch Reformed religionists. Though the lines between these two groups were drawn after 1760, as early as 1752 Livingston, William Smith, and John Morin Scott with other Presbyterians and lawyers founded a Whig Club which led the fight against Anglican domination of King's College and endeavored to get the Ministry Act of 1693, which provided tax support to Anglicans, repealed. After the Great War for the Empire, the Livingston or "country" faction also opposed the imperial program set forth by the Grenville ministry.[23]

In spite of the outcry against the imperial measures of 1765 and 1767, in the New York elections of 1768 and 1769 the DeLancey or "court" faction increased its hold on the assembly. The Livingston losses in 1768 can be attributed to several factors, but one was the use of religious labels. DeLanceyites were dubbed the Episcopal party and Anglicans who might have voted for the "country" faction voted otherwise. The Dutch Reformed refused cooperation with Livingston and the Presbyterians in the use of such tactics. Then in the election of 1769 religious name calling went beyond labels into broadsides and newspaper articles. The issue of an American episcopate was introduced and DeLancey, who had traveled to England in 1767–68, was accused of having gone to plead for a bishop. However, again the tactic did not work and the "court" faction captured all four assembly seats from New York City and controlled the government. When measures were introduced to repeal the Ministry Act of 1693 and make real estate available to every church and congregation of reformed Protestants in Albany County, the council held them until they died. In this way the DeLancey forces in the assembly simply let the council quietly quash the issue rather than have the assembly perpetuate the quarrel.

Throughout these years, however, the issue of a resident bishop was a subject of sharp partisan political debate. In 1767 John Ewer, bishop of Landaff, preached the annual S.P.G. sermon and in it called for the establishment of an American episcopate. When a printing of this sermon was soon followed by the publication of Chandler's *Appeal*, the New York Dissenters were alarmed. The pamphlet and newspaper warfare that ensued endeavored to paint the specter of "episcopal palaces . . . pontifical revenues . . . spiritual courts, and all the pomp, grandeur, luxury and regalia of an American Lambeth." Moreover, a strong parallel between imperial and church hierarchies was drawn suggesting that Anglicans favored oppression and governmental tyranny at the expense of liberty and Dissenters' rights. Then the attempt was made to associate the episcopal scheme with an "ecclesiastical stamp act."[24]

In the two proprietary colonies of Pennsylvania and Maryland the Johnson-Chandler plan did not become identified with local political issues and thus did not cause near the stir it did in New England and New York. Dr. William Smith of Philadelphia deftly diverted the intended involvement of Pennsylvania's Anglicans in the scheme and Maryland's Governors Sharpe and Eden managed to keep the issue out of Maryland's internal problems. Three Maryland clergymen who tried to promote the scheme found themselves on the receiving end of governmental and public scorn. When Jonathan Boucher insisted on arguing for episcopacy and loyalty to England, his life was threatened and he retired from his parish and by 1775 fled to England. Three of the four royal colonies from Virginia to Georgia escaped entanglement in episcopal conflict; in Virginia, where it did rage for a year, the House of Burgesses on

July 12, 1771, terminated the issue for all practical purposes by authorizing a resolution of public thanks to the clergymen who had opposed the scheme.

Another force that fanned the flames of controversy over the American episcopate issue was the colonial press. One of the most striking facts of the entire revolutionary movement was the extent to which the Whigs, or those favoring home rule and religious toleration as opposed to imperial authority, controlled the press. Of the forty-two newspapers in America by 1775, prior to 1774 not one of them was essentially an organ of pro-British propaganda. One explanation for this was the Stamp Act which hit all printers hard and bound them to the Patriot cause. After the Stamp crisis, even editors with pro-British sympathies were responsive to the Whig or Patriot side. But the result was that all the leading newspapers—*Boston Gazette, New York Gazette, Pennsylvania Journal, Pennsylvania Gazette, Maryland Gazette,* Virginia's two *Gazettes,* and the *South Carolina Gazette*—were strong for the colonial rights and privileges. It is then not surprising that the episcopal controversy was front-page material in New England, New York, Pennsylvania, and Virginia, where the forces against it were most vocal and forceful. Moreover, after 1765 there was a real attempt made by editors to keep their readers informed about events in different colonies.[25]

A careful analysis of the letters in the Virginia *Gazettes* on the episcopal issue reveals a preponderance of opinion that was antiepiscopal and anti-established church. Of twenty-three printed letters, the vast majority contain an attack upon the religious establishment as a threat to political liberty, the sins of the clergy, or the weakness of the claim of apostolic succession. This same study found that Dissenters received a "good press" and the itinerary of George Whitefield was reported with enthusiasm. Again in 1773 a dispute between Samuel Henley, a professor at William and Mary, and the Bruton parish vestry broke into print in a series of twenty-six letters over a fourteen-month period. In this dispute, as in the episcopal one, the same complaints were registered against the established church, its clergy, and apostolic succession. With the wide circulation of Virginia papers and other newspapers, the picture of the Church of England that was being projected to the general public was less than flattering in the years after 1768–69. To claim the least, the Church of England in America came out of the newspaper phase of the ecclesiastical conflict with an image far less acceptable than the one it held a few years earlier.

The attack upon the Johnson-Chandler plan continued even though the key Dissenters who opposed it knew from sources close to the English government there was little chance it would be accepted and implemented. Perhaps the persistence of Dissenter opposition was a safety measure to prevent giving the impression that they were indifferent or not opposed to bishops. Even reports like Thomas Hollis's, the Massachusetts agent in London, in 1763 did not dilute that colony's determination to resist. "You are in no real danger," he wrote, "at present, in respect to the creation of Bishops in America, if I am rightly informed."[26] In 1766, Charles Chauncy confided to Ezra Stiles, "the great men have too little regard for religion in any form, and too much business of more importance in their apprehension of another kind, than to concern themselves about the settlement of bishops in this part of the world."[27] Then in 1768 Ezra Stiles informed Chauncy, "I am told that Mr. Wheeler, just returned from obtaining episcopal orders in London, was several hours alone with Dr. Secker, Archbishop of Canterbury, who told Mr. Wheeler that the ministry were entirely averse to sending bishops to America at present and assigned this reason among others viz., that as America seemed on the point of rebellion and independence, the ministry were determined to retain every hold on America: that by necessitating the American episcopalians to have recourse to England for ordination they would be held in part."[28] As late as 1772 Stiles's information conveyed the same message. Yet the American Dissenting leaders did not relinquish their opposition for fear the home government's policy might be changed.

SUSPICIONS VINDICATED

One of the reasons that prompted Dissenters to remain vigilant toward the proepiscopal leaders was the belief that in a showdown with Great Britain they would remain loyal to England rather than the colonies. Evidence for this suspicion had been provided by Dr. Johnson of Connecticut during the Stamp Act crises and by members of the "court" or Episcopal party in New York. Unfortunately for many Anglicans in this region, they too subsequently became categorized as Loyalists because of the actions of their leaders. In contrast, William Smith and Richard Peters in Philadelphia both supported the colonial contention in the Stamp and Townshend disputes. Smith preached a number of sermons during this period that were clearly supportive of natural rights as well as nationalistic in tone. Though the personal judgments of the majority of Anglican clergy for this period are not ascertainable, the overwhelming response of the identifiable laymen was one of opposition to the imperial measures. Nevertheless, the suspicion that Drs. Johnson, Chandler, Cooper and Messrs. Seabury, Inglis, Boucher, and Camm were desirous of strengthening Britain's hold on her colonies with or without the aid of a resident episcopate was enough to keep the New England Dissenters apprehensive about what the episcopal promoters were engaged in. Time and events proved their suspicions correct.

It was, however, the meeting of the First Continental Congress in Philadelphia in September 1774 that touched off a series of pro-British writings by members of the former proepiscopal group. Chandler contributed three pamphlets to the defense of Britain's actions and the repudiation of America's responses. The first was entitled *A Friendly Address to All Reason-*

able Americans on the Subject of our Political Confusions. . . . The same viewpoint was expressed by Myles Cooper in *The American Querist: or Some Questions Proposed Relative to the present Disputes between Great Britain and her American Colonies*. After Thomas Paine's *Common Sense* appeared in January 1776, Charles Inglis attempted to rebut it with two pamphlets titled *The True Interests of America* . . . and *Plain Truth*. But it was Samuel Seabury who became best known for a series of pamphlets signed A. W. Farmer and known as *Letters of a Westchester Farmer*. With titles like *Free Thoughts on the Proceedings of the Continental Congress* . . . and *What Think Ye of Congress Now?* . . . this series attracted considerable attention and the reputation acquired followed Seabury for the rest of his life.[29] In full agreement with Chandler, Cooper, Inglis, and Seabury, Jonathan Boucher recorded in his *Reminiscences*, "I endeavored in my sermons and in various pieces published in the Gazettes of the country, to check the immense mischief that was impending, but I endeavoured in vain."[30] John Camm, like Boucher, clung to a concept of British authority and was forced to relinquish his parish.

While the best-known members of the proepiscopal coterie became identified as Loyalists, they by no means represented an overview of Anglican reaction to the cause of independence. The American Anglican churches by 1775 had no effective intercolonial or diocesean organization. Thus there could not be a joint decision on the momentous issues churchmen faced. But of the 250–60 clergymen in America at the time, perhaps one-third became Loyalists and the remainder divided between those who supported the Patriot cause and others who attempted to remain neutral by becoming inactive. For each thoughtful clergyman, the decision was difficult because his ordination vows contained an oath of allegiance to the king of England.[31] But of the total clergy at least one-third sided with the Patriots. Of the 122 clergymen in Virginia, 13 were known Tories, 4 traitors, but 44 made public contributions to the American war effort. In twenty of sixty counties, the parsons were elected members of Committees on Safety. There were several instances of parsons and their entire vestries serving as members of Committees on Safety.[32] But one who has studied the *Virginia Gazette* for the period noted that "a reader of the Gazettes might receive a completely distorted impression of the clergy's loyalty . . . from the emphasis placed by the newspaper on Tory clergymen."[33] Of the twenty-three clergymen in South Carolina in 1775, only five were reported loyal to England.[34] Even though the political positions of all the Anglican clergy are not complete, it is abundantly clear they cannot be categorized by the general word Loyalist because of the actions of a few leading members of their church.

It is also important to note that in the crucible experience of the Revolution, large numbers of southern planters who were almost to a man Anglicans made alliance with middle colony and New England Dissenters in the contest for liberty and independence. Their common interests muted their religious differences. Anglicans like Richard Bland, Richard Henry Lee, George Mason, Samuel Chase, William Paca, Charles C. Pinckney, and John Rutledge were joined by fellow churchmen Francis Hopkinson, John Jay, James Duane, Samuel Provoost (who became the first Episcopal bishop in New York), and Alexander Hamilton in the middle states. In fact, it was Alexander Hamilton who rebutted the *Letters of a Westchester Farmer* in his *A Full Vindication of the Measures of Congress* . . . and *The Farmer Refuted*. It is also necessary to note that in Philadelphia where Jacob Duché, Thomas Coombe, and William Smith early supported the colonial cause, they fell short of full commitment and Duché fled to England. But a young member of their number, William White, identified fully with the Revolution and accepted a chaplaincy to Congress. There White must have felt at ease because, of the fifty-five men who signed the Declaration of Independence, two-thirds belonged to the Anglican communion and six of these were either sons or grandsons of Anglican clergymen.[35]

THE DILEMMA

In 1776 the Church of England in America was in a twofold bind. The question of loyalty to the crown was one that each churchman, clergy and laity, had to resolve. But the other problem was created by official separation from England, which severed the churches from their traditional relationship with the mother church. Without a central leader or organization, the churches, either as parishes or establishments in the states from Maryland to Georgia, were thrown completely on their own. For communicants of the Anglican churches the immediate future was bound to be a trying time. Had not the parish-vestry concept developed in the colonial period as extensively as it did, it is probable the churches would have suffered more. The absence of centralized leadership, a growing shortage of ministers, and by 1784 the loss of all state tax support for the former establishments were all severe blows that threatened the church's survival and painted a stark contrast to what the Church of England in America had been in the prosperous decade of the sixties.

The dilemma in which the American Anglican churches found themselves after 1776 was likely to continue indefinitely unless they organized and procured episcopal leadership. Faced with this reality, the next problem was if the British won the war, a resident bishop in America would be doubly resented because then he would also symbolize a victorious power. On the other hand, if the United States won the war, it was not known whether England would alter her laws to permit Americans to be ordained ministers and consecrated bishops without the oath of loyalty to the king. Besides, no one could predict how deep and prolonged the hostilities between America and Britain would go or what wounds would be inflicted upon the body politic. It was, moreover, impossible to tell how American Anglicans would react to a resident bishop in the event one were obtainable in the postwar years. If the prewar reaction to the Johnson-Chandler plan was any indication, the settlement of bishops among former constituents of the Church of England would be a major undertaking. In any event, to thoughtful Anglicans it became clearer and clearer that to survive in the postwar era they would have to reorganize their church structure, accept a new status, and achieve their identity under drastically altered conditions from those they had known in the past.

Charles Inglis, who became rector of Trinity Church, New York City in 1777 upon the death of Samuel Auchmuty, realized the precarious future the Anglican churches in America faced. He expressed the belief that whatever was to be done in regard to bishops for America would have to be done within a reasonable time after the war to be successful. In a pamphlet he wrote, *The State of the Anglo-American Church in 1776,* he expressed a prophetic view. "If fifty years elapse without any episcopate here, there will be no occasion for one afterwards; and to fix one then will be as impracticable as it would be useless. . . . The time indeed, is not yet fully come to move in this affair; but I apprehend it is not very distant, and, therefore, it should be thought of."[36]

II

THE PROTESTANT
EPISCOPAL SOLUTION

1782–1789

*To include in the proposed frame of government a general approbation
of episcopacy, and a declaration of an intention to procure the succession as soon as conveniently may be; but in the mean time to carry the
plan into effect without waiting for the succession.*

William White, *The Case of the Episcopal
Churches in the United States,* 1782

*We think nothing can be more clear than that our Church has ever
believed bishops to have the sole right of ordination and government,
and that this regimen was appointed of Christ himself, and is now, to
use your own words, humbly submitted to consideration, whether such
Episcopalians as consent even to a temporary departure and set aside
this ordinance of Christ for conveniency, can scarcely deserve the name
of Christians.*

The Connecticut Clergy to William White,
March 25, 1783

*Art. 4. The Bishop or Bishops in every State shall be chosen agreeably
to such rules as shall be fixed by the Convention of that State. And
every Bishop of this Church shall confine the exercise of his Episcopal
office to his proper Diocise or District, unless requested to ordain or
confirm, or perform any other act of the Episcopal office, by any Church
destitute of a Bishop.*

The Constitution
of the Protestant Episcopal Church
in the United States of America, 1789

7

The Crucial Years

"The people voted almost unanimously to open the church, omitting the prayers for the King and Parliament."

John Tyler, Norwich, Connecticut
November 27, 1778

The Declaration of Independence officially terminated the traditional connection between the American Anglican churches and the Church of England, and the Revolutionary War ensured that even the reestablishment of a fraternal relation between the two ecclesiastical bodies would not necessarily come easily. For the first time in a century and a half, American churchmen could not look to England for guidance or assistance. During the war the number of Anglican clergymen was reduced by nearly one half, and in 1783 there were no immediate replacements. If ministerial vacancies were filled, the candidates for Holy Orders would have to come from the American churches. Moreover, seven years of war inflicted extensive property damage upon the churches. Prejudice engendered against Great Britain was in turn focused upon the American Anglican churches because of their former ties with England. Then too, the six states in which the Church of England was established by law, all disestablished the church by 1784. No other religious body in America suffered so severely and extensively from the war, nor was any other religious group so suddenly thrown completely on its own. Yet in the six years between the Treaty of Paris in 1783 and the implementation of the Federal Constitution of the United States in 1789, the Episcopal churches successfully reorganized, resupplied their clerical ranks, built new

157

churches, developed a capacity for financial support, and consummated an ecclesiastical revolution in the area of episcopacy.

CLERGYMEN

The Peace of Paris in 1783 brought to an official conclusion the Revolutionary War and recognized the independence of the United States. While the problems that confronted the new nation were immense, those that the former Anglican churches faced were proportionately of comparable size. An episode occurred late in 1783 that accented the type of problem the newly independent but unorganized churches had to resolve. In that year two candidates for Holy Orders, Mason Locke Weems and Edward Gantt, left Maryland for England in the hope of receiving ordination from the bishop of London. However, their applications were denied and three audiences with the archbishop of Canterbury, John Moore, failed to solve the problem. Weems and Gantt were denied ordination because the rite included an oath of loyalty to the king, and since America was independent such an oath was inconsistent for those who planned to serve there. Furthermore, the English bishops believed an act of parliament was necessary to give them permission to omit the loyalty oath, but no one would predict when or if parliament would authorize the modification to accommodate the Americans.[1] In the meantime the shortage of ordained men continued, and the possibility that American churchmen might seek ordination elsewhere or substitute a different type of ordination to temporarily supply their needs increased.[2]

The number of ministerial losses that had occurred over the decade from 1774 to 1785 was large. In 1774 there were 286 clergymen compared with 155 in 1785.[3] The reduction in the total number of Anglican clergymen was due to several factors. Among the clergy in the northern states several were Loyalists, and most of them fled to Nova Scotia or England. A majority of this group who departed were S.P.G. missionaries who preferred to leave rather than remain in America and possibly be pressured into breaking their oath of allegiance to the crown. In addition, most of the Anglican leaders—Henry Caner, Myles Cooper, Mathew Byles, Thomas B. Chandler, Charles Inglis— removed themselves to England. One list identifies thirty-nine of sixty-eight clergymen in the area from New Jersey northward who left the United States.[4] Although five of these men eventually returned to serve parishes, the permanent loss of thirty-four men from one region was a severe blow. From Pennsylvania Thomas Barton, Daniel Batwell, Jacob Duché, Alexander Murry, and Samuel Cooke took leave.[5] South of Pennsylvania, however, the course of action taken by the clergy was different. In Maryland twenty-four rectors resigned their parishes rather than take an oath of loyalty to the state, but not all of them became Loyalists. It is probable that the majority acted like Thomas J. Claggett, who retired to his farm and tried to maintain a neutral position.[6] Of the 105 Anglican clergymen in Virginia, only 14 or 15 were known Loyalists, while 90 took the oath of allegiance to the state.[7] In North Carolina four established ministers were Loyalists and possibly a fifth one too. South Carolina had only five Loyalists among its established clergy, but Georgia lost both its church parsons. At least 25 percent of the Anglican clergymen present in America in 1774 can be identified as Loyalists.

Within the Loyalist group almost all were S.P.G. missionaries, but not all S.P.G. missionaries were Loyalists, for a few sided with the American cause. The fact that the missionaries' primary financial support (or at least part of it) came from England only served to reinforce the royal loyalty oath. Indeed, any suspicion of disloyalty on the part of a missionary usually led to dismissal by the Society. It was on this basis that in 1779 payments to Robert Blackwell, missionary at Gloucester and Waterford, Massachusetts, and Edward Bass at Newburyport, Massachusetts were stopped. Bass was specifically charged with preaching in favor of the rebels and observing the fast and thanksgiving days appointed by the Continental Congress. In December 1782, Blackwell and Bass were officially dismissed from the Society.[8]

Death is the second factor that accounts for the sizable loss of clergymen between 1774 and 1785. At least three and perhaps five of the clergy in Massachusetts died, and in New York the rector of Trinity Church, Samuel Auchmuty, also died. Three of Pennsylvania's clergymen expired during the war, as did eleven of Maryland's parsons. Although the number of ministers claimed by death in Virginia is not definite, there were nineteen present in 1774 who are unaccounted for in 1784. Besides those who "rested from their labors," there were five in Virginia, and one each in New Jersey and Connecticut who collapsed emotionally during the war. A total of thirty-six ministers were lost through death and seven from emotional disorders.[9] These plus the 65 to 70 Loyalists who fled the new republic add up to 113 of the 131 fewer ministers who were in the states in 1785. However, in spite of a major loss in manpower, the former Anglican churches by 1789 were able to rebuild their ministerial ranks to a point that almost equaled their numbers in 1774. Between the years 1785 and 1789, there were ninety-one new deacons ordained and though the record of these who became priests has not survived, presumably all or almost all did within the same time period. This means that within a relatively short time Episcopalians filled 91 of the 131 vacancies.[10] Instead of the church being broken and shattered by the scourge of war, it demonstrated a remarkable degree of resiliency and vitality. In no equivalent time span before the war had the colonial churches, even with British help, come close to equalizing this pace of ministerial recruitment.

It is also noteworthy that of the fifty-one names that appear on one list of ordinands, the places of education for twenty-seven of them are given. All but one of the twenty-seven were trained in American colleges. Fourteen received their training at Yale, four at Harvard, three at Dartmouth, two each at

King's College and Washington College, and one at Princeton. Only one was a graduate of a European college, and that college was Trinity College, Dublin.[11] Although the places of birth of these men are not given, it is natural to assume that they were American-born with perhaps one exception. The trend toward an American-born and educated Anglican ministry evident in the late colonial period became the established pattern for ministerial candidates in the 1780s.

Beyond the successful efforts at ministerial enlistment, many local parishes made use of lay readers to continue worship services after the loss of their minister or to reinstate their worship service at a later time. No composite list of laymen who served as lay readers in the eighteenth-century American churches exists, but judging from the spotty evidence available their numbers were substantial. In 1784, seven or eight lay readers were serving congregations in Massachusetts, and at least two were supplying churches in Rhode Island.[12] By 1787, the Episcopal conventions that had formed in New Jersey, Maryland, and Virginia were urging churches without clergymen to open and appoint "proper persons" to read divine service.[13] In all probability this type of action was taken by other state conventions and local parishes. Moreover, from the lay readers employed under these conditions the denomination subsequently received a number of candidates for ordination.

CHURCHES

The former Anglican communion in the United States was further depressed during the war years by the closing of many of its churches. In 1775, the Continental Congress set July 20th as a day of fasting and prayer for the American cause. Throughout the northern and middle Atlantic states, Anglican churches with few exceptions decided to close rather than cooperate with Congress. In many cases, the churches that did not open on July 20, 1775 remained closed throughout the war as a silent protest against the Revolution. Only two Anglican churches remained open in Massachusetts and one in New Jersey, and in Pennsylvania only the city churches demonstrated their support of congress.[14] After July 20, 1775, it was considered a treasonable act to pray for King George instead of congress. Later, however, some churches such as Christ Church, Norwich, Connecticut, voted to open and omit the prayers for king and parliament. The minister, John Tyler, who stayed at his post throughout the war, was criticized by some of his clerical associates for bowing to the congregation's decision, but by 1779 a number of other congregations had taken similar steps to reopen their churches. At St. John's Church, Providence, Rhode Island, the congregation voted to resume service, omitting the objectionable parts of the prayers. When the minister refused to accept the congregation's action, the vestry employed a lay reader. Later when the minister sought readmission to his post in 1783, the church refused and sponsored the lay reader for ordination.[15]

In 1779 Samuel Seabury expressed concern about the number of churches that were closed in the northern and middle states. He was also probably alarmed by the independent action taken by the Norwich and Providence congregations to modify the liturgy of the church by an elective process. Seabury sought the aid of Dr. Chandler in London and requested him to procure the bishop of London's permission to omit the objectionable prayers. Chandler did consult with Bishop Lowth, but he could only report that "His Lordship thought the matter should be left to the discretion of the clergy themselves, and said that the archbishops and bishops in general agreed with him in this opinion."[16] The problem was, therefore, left to the individual clergyman's conscience or to the increasingly republican-minded congregations. The basic question each minister had to decide was whether his oath to the king was equal to or inherent in his obligation to God and church. In this light, Abraham Beach of New Jersey, Jeremiah Leaming of Connecticut, and Edward Bass of Massachusetts omitted the prayers for the king and served as many congregations as they could in their respective states.

The part of the Anglican ritual including prayers for the king, royal family, and parliament caused no serious problem for the churches in the South. The Virginia legislature in 1776 passed an act requiring the clergy to use an amended version of the prayers that excluded the offensive references. The Maryland state convention in 1776 directed that every mention of the king be omitted from the church services.[17] With these modifications the churches in Maryland and Virginia remained open, provided of course that they were able to retain their ministers. A new constitution adopted in North Carolina disestablished the Church of England, thus freeing the individual churches to modify their order of worship. When South Carolina dropped its state support of the Anglican establishment in 1778, each individual church was free to adopt its own liturgy.[18] By 1778 the clergy who favored England had departed, and those who remained had no difficulty in revising the prayers for worship.

During the military conflict many former Anglican churches, parsonages, and glebes were partly or wholly destroyed. The records of these losses are at best piecemeal, but the incidents reported indicate the seriousness and extent of the problem. In Massachusetts at least four churches were totally or partly destroyed. Connecticut churchmen lost two churches and at least one parsonage. One of the Rhode Island churches was burned. Trinity Church, New York was one of the major churches destroyed. Trinity Church, Newark was burned, and St. Peter's, Perth Amboy was extensively damaged. Both St. Philip's and St. Michael's churches in Charleston were damaged, as was Christ Church, Savannah, Georgia.[19] Added to these losses was the problem of property deterioration, which took a heavy toll especially in churches that were closed and sometimes left unattended.

In the period from 1783 to 1789, Episcopalians did not mount a church building campaign that equaled their accomplishments in the 1760s, but they did demonstrate the ability to rebuild their destroyed churches, repair those that were damaged, and add some new ones. This in itself was a remarkable achievement. Within this six-year period Connecticut built three churches (two were probably replacements), Pennsylvania added three more, New Jersey acquired two, and New York one, for a total of nine. In the decade of the 1790s another eight new houses of worship were constructed.[20] Clearly the description of the Protestant Episcopal Church as being in a state of "suspended animation" between the years 1775 to 1800 is a generalization unsupported by the facts of the church's accomplishments during these crucial years.[21]

Another way to measure the vitality of the Episcopal churches in the years immediately following the Treaty of Paris is to note and compare the number of active parishes by 1789 with those of 1774. In 1789 there were 259 active parishes compared with 318 in 1774. Since these figures for 1789 are based upon the several state convention minutes (several of which are admittedly incomplete), which report the parishes that sent delegates, either clerical or lay or both, to one or more meetings, the total is a conservative one.[22] It is entirely possible that some of the fifty-nine parishes functioning in 1774 were serving in 1789, but they may have been served by a lay reader or may simply have delayed making contact with the emerging state conventions until a later date. Since only clergy represented the parishes of Connecticut to the convocation, it is probable that more than twenty-nine parishes were active in 1789, but the absence of delegates from specific parishes held down the number that were noted in the records. But the verified operation in 1789 of approximately four-fifths of the parishes that had been reported in 1774 is proof positive that the churches on the parish level had weathered the fifteen years of war and uncertainty extremely well.

CONSTITUENTS

In New England and New York, Anglicans were generally associated with crown officials as supporters of the king. This image
of churchmen was largely the result of the pro-British writings
and activities of Thomas B. Chandler, Myles Cooper, Samuel
Seabury, and Charles Inglis. Then too, the proepiscopal campaign these men had led in the late 1760s and 1770s convinced
many that they were interested in strengthening the influence of
the home government by seeking a resident episcopate. Furthermore, more than a majority of the Anglican clergy in New Jersey
and Pennsylvania remained loyal to the crown. Indeed, in the
northern region of the United States it was rumored that Episcopalians provided an intelligence-gathering system for the British
forces.[23] But in Maryland, Virginia, and South Carolina, where
a majority of Anglican ministers did not become Loyalists, the
impression is that only a small number of churchmen left because they preferred their British citizenship. The estimate that
between 60,000 and 80,000 Loyalists departed the thirteen
states between 1775 and 1785 is generally accepted. Of this
number the largest groups apparently migrated from New
York, New Jersey, and Georgia; the fewest numbers to leave
were from Massachusetts, Virginia, and Maryland. Although it
is impossible to determine how many Loyalists were Anglicans, it
is conceded that the church lost a considerable number of its
constituents in this way. One historian reports that by 1784,
35,000 to 40,000 Loyalists took refuge in Nova Scotia and that
almost without exception they were Church of England people.
Of the approximately 7,000 Americans who took refuge in Britain, it appears that a considerable majority were of the Anglican
way.[24]

Although precise statistics on the actual number of churchmen who left the United States between 1775 and 1785 cannot
be had, it is obvious that the former Anglican communion in
America sustained a serious loss. But by no means were all

churchmen in New England, New York, and New Jersey Loyalists. Indeed, there were several who were leaders in their respective states for the American cause. For example, Samuel Livermore of Holderness, New Hampshire was a staunch Revolutionary leader as well as a churchman. In New York, John Jay and James Duane performed outstanding services for the new republic and their state. The vestrymen of Christ and St. Peter's churches in Philadelphia were almost to a man supportive of the American cause.[25] Thus, while a majority of the Anglican clergy and a significant number of the laity in the northeast were Loyalists, a considerable group backed the Patriot side and were determined to make their own church a loyal American institution. The fact that a number of congregations voted to reopen after 1779 and omit prayers for the king, with or without clerical consent, probably means that Episcopalians who favored the American effort for independence were in control of a growing numer of congregations.

Another force that eroded the numberical strength of Episcopalianism, especially in the South, was the success of the evangelical denominations. The Great Awakening had been a major stimulus to Presbyterians, Baptists, and eventually Methodists. In Virginia, Presbyterians made significant advances in and around Hanover County. By the outbreak of the Revolutionary War they were an influential religious body and in the forefront of those demanding the disestablishment of the Anglican Church. Baptists too multiplied rapidly in the 1770s and 1780s in Virginia and North Carolina, and since their polity was more consistent with the democratic concepts of the revolutionary ideology it had a wide appeal. The Methodists, who were theoretically under the Anglicans until they organized separately in 1784, prospered remarkably well in Virginia. Here, Devereux Jarratt, rector of Bath parish, Dinwiddie County, aided the Methodists in becoming a recognized religious force in the greater Virginia-North Carolina region. Then too, Presbyterians were gaining increased numbers from the immigrants who settled along the frontier from Pennsylvania to Georgia. This rise of competitive denominationalism in areas once dominated by the Church of England, along with the concurrent attacks upon the establishment, had a depressing impact upon Episcopalians. The remarkable fact is that the Episcopal churches survived as well as they did the triple tragedies of war, disestablishment, and the loss of constituents.

Another force that all religious denominations had to contend with in the revolutionary generation was religious liberalism. This type of thought was usually expressed in the form of Unitarianism, Universalism, or Deism. Essentially all three of these religious philosophies promoted toleration, but they also raised serious questions about the theological doctrines of traditional Christianity. The confrontation of these forms of liberalism with orthodoxy produced controversy and defections from the recognized churches, including the Episcopal churches. For example, one church, King's Chapel, Boston, was lost to the Unitarians as a result of the controversy in that city. Moreover, presumably a number of churchmen who were described at the time as being indifferent to their faith were to some degree influenced by deistic notions which emphasized reason and individual morality and minimized revelation and the need for corporate worship.

The loss of King's Chapel, Boston, was a shock to Episcopalians because it, like all other Anglican churches in America, was thrown on its own with the separation from England. What happened to King's Chapel could set an example for other churches, and if this experience spread the Episcopal churches would cease to be identifiable by their distinctive form of worship. For example, in 1782 King's Chapel had been reopened by the laity, and James Freeman was invited to serve as lay reader. In a short time, Freeman became known as a liberal thinker. Then, partly under the influence of William Hazlitt, an English Unitarian minister, Freeman altered the church liturgy. Subsequently he accepted the idea that the people or the congregation who chose their minister were the proper ones to ordain him. The result was that on June 19, 1785, King's Chapel adopted a Unitarian liturgy and twenty-five months later ordained Freeman after he had been refused Episcopal ordination because of heretical ideas. This nonclerical ordination by a once-Anglican congregation was a very significant event because it demonstrated how deeply one form of religious liberalism could penetrate a traditional-oriented parish and it clearly showed what could happen to the unorganized Episcopal churches.

During the late colonial period, deistic speculation was less conspicuous in the South than in the North, but the Presbyterians and Baptists were aided in their struggle for the disestablishment of the Church of England by a deistic Thomas Jefferson and a liberal James Madison. Both men were motivated by an anticlericalism that had been growing in Virginia and by their conscientious scruples against using public funds to support religious institutions. In fact, a large number of Virginia's statesmen were either deistic or liberal in their religious views at one time or another. George Washington, George Mason, and Edmund and John Randolph were in this category. It was this type of thinking, coupled with a commitment to the republican ideology of the Revolution, that brought about the disestablishment of the church in Virginia.[26] However, the duration of the process, which lasted from 1775 to 1784, kept the churches of the Old Dominion from rebounding from the impact of the war as quickly as did their sister churches in the northern and middle states.

DISESTABLISHMENT

The loss of Loyalist constituents weakened the Episcopal churches numerically, and the stultifying effects of religious liberalism did nothing to revitalize the churches. But a far more serious blow to the Anglican churches from Maryland to

Georgia was their disestablishment. Between 1776 and 1784 all the Church of England establishments in America were discontinued and therefore would receive no further tax assistance. Moreover, the civil functions that vestries had performed were ended. Although disestablishment worked an immediate hardship upon the parishes, the ability of the vestries and congregations to adapt to their new status and survive was in many cases outstanding. In contrast, the New England Congregational establishments were not overturned, but after 1784 Anglicans and other Dissenters were legally recognized and permitted exemption from taxes for the state church.[27] But in the larger picture, although Episcopalians lost state financial aid and with it prestige, they acquired a new freedom which permitted them to develop and manage their churches to a degree they had not known before.

In 1784 the Connecticut legislature passed a general toleration act which made dissent halfway respectable. Dissenters (including Episcopalians) who presented a certificate declaring their membership in a regular religious society to the county officials were exempted from paying the tithe to the Congregational church. Although the Congregational establishment was retained by the Massachusetts Constitution of 1780, the state Supreme Court in 1789 ruled that any Dissenter who presented a certificate stating that he had paid his share of taxes to his own church would be excused from further church levies.[28] New Hampshire followed the example of Massachusetts and made it possible for Episcopalians to have their church taxes go to the support of their own churches and ministers.[29] In spite of the fact that Episcopalians were still treated as second-class citizens in the northeastern states, they did improve their status by acquiring the use of their ecclesiastical taxes for their own parishes.

When New York State adopted its first constitution in April 1777, it incorporated guarantees for religious liberty and the separation of church and state. These two concepts seem to have been accepted without any serious disagreement although this meant the disestablishment of the Church of England in the four lower counties. John Jay, a devout churchman who participated in the state constitutional convention, like many of his fellow Episcopalians, wanted to see a loyal American Episcopal church arise from the ruins of the former establishment. By 1784, the constitutional provision for religious liberty was supplemented by legislation granting incorporation to formerly Dissenter churches. The charter for King's College was revised so that the board of trustees and professors reflected all shades of opinion, and all religious tests for employment were discontinued. The charter of Trinity Church was revised to ensure that it would have no claim to preeminence in the state. Then the legislature intervened in the internal affairs of Trinity parish to remove Loyalists from positions of control, and it placed the church in the hands of patriotic churchmen.[30] In these ways the issues that had exacerbated tensions between Anglicans and Dissenters in the late colonial period were resolved, and in the process Episcopalians were freed from a legal establishment that had probably cost them more in public esteem and acceptance than it had earned them in financial aid.

Rhode Island, New Jersey, Pennsylvania, and Delaware had no difficulty over the question of disestablishment because no one of these states had had a state church. However, the Episcopal parishes were hit hard by the withdrawal of all S.P.G. support after 1782, and it was a number of years before the constituents were able to provide adequate salaries through voluntary subscriptions. The development of their financial resources apparently worked, because there is no indication that any of the churches in the region failed to recover for want of financial means. The clergy and laity from all four of these states assumed a very active role in the reconstruction of the churches both on their respective state levels and in the national organization.[31]

The region where the Anglican churches were hit hardest by

disestablishment was south of the Mason-Dixon line. Here dis-establishment moved quickly and decisively except in Virginia. In Maryland, there does not appear to have been any radical movement against the church *per se,* but the view of the revolu-tionary government was that an established church was incon-sistent with the basic right of religious freedom. Certainly, the struggles over clerical patronage between vestry and governor in the colonial period and the public response to such conflicts prepared the way for disestablishment. The Declaration of Rights set forth in November 1776 forbade taxation for church support. Provision was made, however, to reserve the property of the Anglican church for its future use.[32] In taking these steps there was no controversy in Maryland, and churchmen seemed willing to have their parishes freed from state control provided the responsibility for operating them was left in their hands. In 1779, this position was granted in the form of a Vestry Act, which provided for the election of vestrymen in each parish who would serve as trustees to administer the local properties. Under this arrangement the laity and clergy alone would determine church polity; however, the role of the laity as trustees of the property had been considerably strengthened.

The immediate problem which the Maryland parishes had to solve was how to provide support for the incumbent rectors. In the first five years after disestablishment thirty-three ministers left their posts, and by 1783 only fifteen clergymen of a prewar total of fifty-four remained in parishes. Although fifteen of those who left were Loyalists, the others probably found it too difficult to serve a parish and earn a living in another type of employment at the same time. But parishes like All Saints and Chester, which managed to institute adequate ministerial com-pensation, had services continuously throughout the war years. The All Saints vestry simply agreed that the rector should use the glebe land to supplement his income, and the faithful pa-rishioners provided subscription offerings. Chester parish made provision for its rector with 600 bushels of wheat per year.[33] While other churches responded similarly, some were tardy in developing creative solutions. Because of delay, two ministers who were originally rectors in Maryland received invitations to parishes outside Maryland, and seven others who discontinued services were not encouraged to reenter active service.

Resentment against the established church in Virginia had been growing for several years, especially among Dissenters, but a climax was reached in 1776. After the adoption of the Declaration of Rights in 1776, Dissenters petitioned for disestablishment of the Church of England. The Presbyterians of Prince Edward, Albemarle, Amherst, and Buckingham counties were resolute opponents of the church, but the Baptists, whose numbers multiplied during the revolutionary generation, were the most obdurate opponents of a state church. Between 1776 and 1780, the committee on religion of the legislature received sixteen petitions favoring disestablishment, the largest one containing 10,000 signatures. In contrast, three parishes of the ninety-five in the state submitted petitions requesting retention of the establishment. The assembly in December 1776 exempted Dissenters from paying church taxes, and in 1779 state financial support of the clergy was terminated. But a number of communities and counties petitioned for a general assessment to support religion and for regulation of the ministers by the state because they believed religion and morality, which the churches and clergy represented, were essential to the welfare of the state.[34] The advocates and opponents of this plan were so evenly divided that a decision was impossible. In 1784, the legislature did provide for the incorporation of the Episcopal churches, but the general assessment bill died in committee, although it had the backing of Patrick Henry, Richard H. Lee, George Washington, and John Marshall. It was primarily James Madison, allied with the Presbyterians and Baptists, who fought first to delay the bill and then to defeat it.[35]

The opponents of the general assessment bill pointed out that with state financing for the clergy, once a vestry accepted a minister it would be virtually impossible to remove him. The state under this system would become the receiving and dispensing agent for ministerial salaries. Furthermore, Madison's "Memorial and Remonstrance Against Religious Assessments," which circulated in at least nine counties, argued that freedom of religious expression was an inalienable right and must be kept free from the pressures of society and the legislature. The debate that resulted from the contest over a general assessment reached such proportions that Washington confessed to George Mason, "As the matter now stands, I wish an assessment had never been agitated, and as it has gone so far, that the bill should die an easy death."[36] In the end, Washington's wish was realized.

The long ordeal through which the Virginia churches were put before achieving disestablishment was detrimental. Local vestries were never sure until 1786 whether they would have to provide full or partial support for the clergy. The act to incorporate the Episcopal churches, passed in 1784, was repealed in 1787, placing the once-established parishes on the same footing with all other denominations. Throughout the contest for disestablishment the press had painted a one-sided picture of the former establishment.[37] By 1787, even those churchmen in the assembly who had previously defended the church seem to have abandoned the cause. But the years of debate and uncertainty had inhibited and retarded the process of ecclesiastical reorganization in Virginia. Had a clearcut decision to disestablish the Church of England been made in 1776, the Virginia Episcopalians would not have been behind their brethren in meeting the pressing problems of the churches. Indeed, it is likely that Virginians would have led in church reorganization, as many of them did in the service of the state and nation.

Official disestablishment of the Church of England in North Carolina came with the adoption of the state constitution in

1776. Article Thirty-four stated, "There shall be no Establishment of any one religious Church or Denomination in this state."[38] In part, this article was the result of Presbyterian and Baptist agitation to achieve religious freedom, but it was also the result of the widely held belief that one's religious practice was a natural right with which the state should not interfere. Tax-supported religion was therefore an encroachment of the state upon the rights of believers and nonbelievers and should be abolished. Presbyterians in particular disliked the Marriage Act of 1741, which gave virtual control of the marriage ceremony to the Anglican clergy. Moreover, many remembered that the British government had disallowed a Presbyterian-backed petition for a charter to establish Queen's College in Charlotte because the home government favored such projects to be under the auspices of the Church of England. Besides, the establishment was never strong in North Carolina. The identification of most of its clergy and some of its laity with the Tory position cost the church dearly. By 1783 there were reportedly only five Episcopal clergymen in the state and but a few hundred constituents.[39]

South Carolina disestablished the Church of England in 1778 when the legislature purposely omitted making financial provision for it in the new state constitution. This action, however, had been a long-sought goal of William Tennent, pastor of the Congregational Church in Charleston. Tennent was a native of New Jersey, educated at Princeton, who was licensed to preach in 1760. He served in Connecticut until 1772, when he accepted a call to the Charleston church, where he served until his death in 1777. During his Carolina pastorate, Tennent became the leading opponent of the Anglican establishment. On January 11, 1777, Tennent made a public plea before the Commons House of Assembly for the free and independent support of each church by its members. Toleration, he argued, was not good enough. He pointed out that even in 1777 the marriage laws of the state required the recipients of a marriage license to use exclusively the services of the established clergy. Moreover, Dissenting churches still could not sue for damages or in defense of their property, yet they had to pay taxes like every citizen. In the area of religion, he contended, Dissenters were in effect doubly taxed because they supported their own churches in addition to paying the state levy for the maintenance of the Episcopal churches. Tennent's efforts carried weight, but a year later when disestablishment was effected, he was not present to enjoy the fruit of his labor, for he died August 11, 1777.[40]

In addition to William Tennent's labor in behalf of disestablishment there appears to have been a carefully and cautiously executed maneuver among some leading churchmen to encourage or at least permit disestablishment. One who conspired in this move was Chief Justice William Henry Drayton, an Episcopalian. He worked indirectly through friends in the upcountry part of the state to encourage Dissenters to seek disestablishment of the state church. In 1777, there were twenty Episcopal churches but seventy-nine of other denominations. Mathematics seemed to argue that Episcopalians were not entitled to a preferred ecclesiastical status. Another factor working toward disestablishment was a rumor that circulated, claiming that those who supported the state church were secret Loyalists in a "left-handed alliance with the enemy."[41] Within this context, it seems fair to assume that many churchmen concluded that a religious establishment was inimical to their revolutionary ideology of self-rule. However, so influential were the Rutledges, Henry Laurens, Ralph Izford, and Thomas Bee, all churchmen, in the government that unless they had at least acquiesced to the disestablishment scheme it would not have passed in 1778.[42] That disestablishment proceeded smoothly and quickly in South Carolina is the best evidence that a number of churchmen were to some degree in sympathy with it.

In 1777 the first state constitution of Georgia granted the free exercise of religion and specified that "no one was to be forced to support any religious teacher other than those of one's own profession."[43] Theoretically, however, it remained possible for one to be taxed for the support of one's own church until 1798, when this provision was removed. In the meantime there was no outcry from Georgia's Dissenters resembling those in Virginia. In contrast with the situation in Virginia and South Carolina, Dissenters in Georgia had always received liberal treatment. Besides, the Church of England had never been strong or the predominant religious body in the state, and at the time of the Revolutionary War only two parishes, Christ in Savannah and St. Paul's in Augusta, were well organized.

The belief by churchmen that an ecclesiastical establishment was inconsistent with their revolutionary ideology and conduct, coupled with opposition from various Dissenter groups, brought the privileged position of the Church of England to an end in the four lower counties of New York and in the states from Maryland to Georgia. Each parish vestry in these states was of necessity thrown upon its own resourcefulness to survive. In addition, the civil services which the vestries once performed—e.g., poor relief, land surveys, and tobacco inspection—were reassigned to state and county government. The vestries of Christ Church, Savannah, and St. Philip's and St. Michael's, Charleston no longer served as municipal governments. Now those who served as vestrymen were elected only by those who were constituents of the Episcopal churches and not by the freeholders, as was true before disestablishment. Much of the prestige in the office of vestryman was lost with the removal of civil status from the position. No longer was election to the vestry the first rung upon the ladder of governmental service. Although several laymen in Virginia still found the vestry a valuable training experience for public service, it no longer served as the nucleus of local government.[44] It was, therefore, the need to come to terms with this new status thrust upon the Episcopal churches that prompted concerned clergy and laity to assume the lead in reorganizing the several churches into state conventions and eventually a national one.

EDUCATIONAL-HUMANITARIAN ACTIVITIES

Anglican influence in higher education was reduced substantially by the impact of the Revolution, but it was by no means eliminated as a force in academic circles. In the colonial period both William and Mary College and King's College had been centers of church activity, and the College of Philadelphia had had a definite Anglican flavor because of Provost William Smith. But by the end of the 1780s a major transition had been completed in all three institutions. For example, William and Mary was reorganized in 1779, and in the process the two schools of divinity were excluded from the new university formed. James Madison, an Episcopal minister, was elected president, but the church influence was diminished by the absence of a divinity faculty and student body. The Episcopal Church in Virginia had no seminary in which to educate clerical candidates for the next forty years. Then in 1784 King's College, New York was renamed Columbia College by its new board of trustees, a name in keeping with the patriotic temper of the time. The newly elected president, William Samuel Johnson, son of the first president Dr. Samuel Johnson, was the first layman to serve as head of the institution, and he was probably the only lay person who was president of an American college at that time. The younger Johnson's disagreement with his father over the episcopal campaign and Stamp Act issues in the 1760s had won him the respect of his fellow Connecticut citizens. Although William Johnson was hesitant to support the American cause in 1776, he nevertheless served in the Confederation Congress from 1784 to 1787 and was a delegate from Connecticut to the Federal Convention of 1787, where he participated in the evolvement of the Connecticut Compromise whereby all states were equally represented in a senate and proportionately represented in a house under the new federal constitution.

The College of Philadelphia also experienced difficulties in the war years because in 1779 the assembly of Pennsylvania confiscated its charter and property. The University of the State of Pennsylvania was established in place of the college, but William Smith was not hired as provost. However, when the College of Philadelphia was restored to its former status in 1789, Smith returned to his former post. But Smith's reinstatement was short-lived because in 1791 the college and university were merged and a new provost, John Ewing, a Presbyterian minister, was selected.[45] The issue that probably brought about Smith's departure from the provostship was related to his hesitancy in supporting American independence in 1776. Smith had been a strong supporter of colonial rights up to the point of separation from England, but at that point he temporarily faltered. In that period he was suspected of having written eight essays entitled *Plain Truth* under the name "Cato" in an effort to answer Thomas Paine's *Common Sense*. Moreover, a statement of Smith's in an oration delivered in 1775, expressing a prayerful petition for the restoration of the former harmony between Great Britain and the colonies, gave offense to many people. Although Smith took the oath of allegiance to the state of Pennsylvania in 1776, he was never able fully to dispel the suspicions that he had been a Loyalist or that he had sided with the American cause for reasons other than personal conviction.

Another dimension of the educational-humanitarian enterprise of the Church of England in America was not only diminished but discontinued when the S.P.G. withdrew all its financial aid after 1782. This action hit all the churches located outside the major cities to some degree in the middle and northern states. This meant an end to the mission among the Iroquois and the catechists for Trinity Church, New York, and Christ and St. Peter's in Philadelphia. Moreover, the Bray Associates had discontinued their work in Providence, New York, Philadelphia, Williamsburg, and Petersburg in 1777. Even in states where a significant number of parsons remained in their parishes—e.g., Virginia, it is doubtful they continued to serve as tutors. Also, the reassignment of welfare cases to overseers of the poor in Virginia probably meant that the half-dozen vocational and training schools once operated by the parishes in which they were located were transferred to county control. Thus, at the parish level, the Revolutionary War and disestablishment seriously curtailed the activities of the Episcopal churches.

In spite of the reverses sustained by the once-dynamic Anglican communion in the colonies, interest in educational and humanitarian enterprises did not die. At the very time the aforementioned setbacks were happening, churchmen were participating in the founding of Washington College in Chestertown, Maryland, and in the organization of St. John's College in Annapolis, Maryland. So successful was Washington College under the presidency of William Smith that two years after its origin there were 140 students enrolled under a faculty of 5. By 1784, two graduates of this institution entered the ranks of the Episcopal clergy. Then, in South Carolina, the College of Charleston opened in 1785 with the rector of St. Philip's parish, Robert Smith, the first president. The Wilmington Academy in Delaware, which had closed in 1777, was reorganized in 1786 and reopened. Philadelphia churchmen, under the leadership of William White, rector of Christ and St. Peter's parish, organized a new school, the Academy of Philadelphia, in 1785. In Connecticut, active interest in education during the 1780s led to the founding of the Episcopal Academy of Connecticut in 1796. It is also possible that among the forty-one academies chartered by the North Carolina legislature between 1777 and 1780, the Episcopal schools in New Bern and Edenton were included. Although the Church of England had had little to do with George Whitefield's Bethesda Orphanage, it did survive the war and continued its mission of mercy.

The variety of ways in which Episcopalians expressed their humane interests were revived in the 1780s and in specific instances advanced beyond what they had been in the colonial era. The Boston Episcopal Charitable Society, for example, was rechartered by the state of Massachusetts in 1784, and it continued its work. At a joint meeting of Episcopalians in Boston on April 13, 1784, a collection produced £44 4S. 7d. to be divided among the city parishes for distribution to the poor.[46] In Philadelphia Christ Church Hospital, opened in 1772, continued to receive and care for those unable to sustain themselves. The Corporation for the Relief of Widows and Children of Clergymen, chartered in Pennsylvania in 1769, was reconvened in 1784 at New Brunswick, New Jersey. William Smith was chosen chairman and with characteristic determination had the charter revised to read "The Corporation for the Relief of Widows and Children of Clergymen of the Protestant Episcopal Church in the United States of America." New subscribers were recruited, and they included Alexander Hamilton, John Jay, Robert and Gouverneur Morris, and Robert R. and Walter Livingston. When the financial records were tallied, the corporation showed a balance of £ 4,051 5S.4 3/4d. or approximately £ 1,400 more than it had in October 1774.[47]

The losses sustained by the Episcopal churches in the United States during the years of war were substantial. The reduction in ministerial members by almost 50 percent was a staggering blow. Financially, the loss of tax funds and S.P.G. stipends put the once-subsidized churches completely on their own resources. If the churches remained open between 1776 and 1783 or reopened during this period after having been closed, it was due more than ever to the commitment and dedication of the parishioners. Then too, the clouds of suspicion and mistrust that hung over the former churches of the Church of England, because of the once-official tie with the British government and the Loyalism of perhaps one-third of the clergy and a significant number of the laity, left Episcopalians in the United States in an awkward position in the minds of their fellow citizens. That these churches resupplied their ministerial ranks, developed financial resources, and added new churches at the same time they were rebuilding and reorganizing demonstrates remarkable vitality and dedication.

8

An Ecclesiastical Confederation

"Sixth. That no powers be delegated to a general ecclesiastical government, except such as cannot conveniently be exercised by the clergy and laity, in their respective congregations."

Fundamental Principles

The successful reorganization of the former Anglican churches in the United States depended upon the willingness of the clergy and laity to achieve it. Both ministers and churches were free from any vestige of control from the bishop of London and the British government. Those parishes and parsons that had been controlled by state legislatures were all freed by 1784. Therefore, if state and national associations were developed, churchmen would have to show initiative and imagination. The unwillingness of a few churches to combine in a movement for unification could frustrate the formation of a state convention or diocese and also delay or disrupt efforts to generate a national church organization. Until such a time as ecclesiastical authority was centralized on the state and national levels, each congregation, vestry, or minister was at liberty to alter the liturgy, redesign local church polity, or even reject the traditions of the Church of England. The inability of English bishops to ordain American clerical candidates until after August 13, 1784, and the inappropriateness of their encouraging an American episcopate highlighted the problems of the Episcopal churches.[1] Indeed, no area of the church's reorganization was more uncertain than that of episcopacy. If a bishop were procured, the request would certainly have to come from the American churchmen, and in the early 1780s there was no sign that a majority of Episcopalians were ready to take this step. Nevertheless, to meet their urgent needs, Episcopalians generally (with the exception of the clergy of Connecticut) followed the organizational plan offered by William White in *The Case of the Protestant Episcopal Churches in the United States Considered*, revived the prewar clerical convention type of meeting but with the addition of laymen, and wrote their ideas about church government into constitutional form.

THE CASE

In the summer of 1782, William White, rector of Christ and St. Peter's churches, Philadelphia, prepared a pamphlet entitled *The Case of the Protestant Episcopal Churches in the United States Considered*. This pamphlet in time proved to be the most important piece of literature on the subject. It was White's first publication (he was thirty-four at the time), and made him the central figure in the postwar reorganization of the church. When *The Case* was published, the United States was still at war with Great Britain. However, a preliminary peace treaty was signed, November 30, 1782, a few months after *The Case* appeared, although the treaty was not made final until September 3, 1783. This rapid change in the political situation was not anticipated by White when he wrote; but, instead, he had expected a prolonged period of uncertainty before a final peace agreement was reached.[2] Whether the sudden change in Anglo-American relations would have altered White's original proposals on reorganization is difficult to ascertain. In any event, White's consistent adherence to his original proposals after the 1783 Treaty of Paris indicates that he was convinced of the value of his plan as offered.

White contended that the former ties binding the churches in America together were broken, and "their future continuance can be provided for only by voluntary associations for union and good government."[3] In essence this meant that each Episcopal church in America was independent and free to decide whether to participate in any plan for organizing on the state and national levels. There was a real possibility that a church or churches might decide not to cooperate with initiatives for unification. In this event there was no coercive action the other churches could take to produce union. The churches themselves were, therefore, the ones to decide whether there would be an organized Episcopal church or whether they would remain individual churches. But, if they decided for union, White's plan offered as a basic tenet that they build their organization from the parish up and not from the diocese down, as had been the case in the development of the Church of England. This proposal of White's, like many others he offered, was in full agreement with the revolutionary idea that in a free government the people's interest and good government are identical, and the best way to ensure this is to allow the people a maximum voice in the formation and operation of government.[4] In this instance White argued that what was good for the formation of the state and national governments was equally valid for the development of ecclesiastical polity.

In order to provide a forum where the problems and solutions involved in reorganization could be fully discussed, White advocated a convention composed of clergy and laymen elected from the local parishes to decide all matters in respect to religion. "In the parent church," he pointed out, "though whatever regards religion may be enacted by the clergy in convocation, it must afterwards have the sanction of all orders of men, comprehended in the parliament. It will be necessary to deviate from this practice (though not from the principles) of that church, by convening the clergy and laity in one body."[5] White proposed that there be no designated differentiation between the power of the clergy and that of the laity in convention. Both groups would meet in one body and vote on all issues.

Moreover, no area of church government was placed beyond the authority of this body, and no one or ones were granted the power of veto. This assembly, White believed, should exercise the authority to elect a "superior order" of ministers. In other words, he was applying the concepts of natural rights and contract theory of government to the practical problem of reorganizing the Episcopal churches. In principle, each Episcopalian had a basic right to participate in the development of his church's government, and this right could be expressed through the parish delegate elected to the state convention. On all these points, White's suggestions were carbon copies of ideas that had been developed and used in the preparation of the several state constitutions and the Articles of Confederation.[6]

It was on the issue of episcopacy, however, that White advanced the most controversial idea of his career. In respect to a bishop in America White was careful to use only terms characterizing the spiritual functions of the office—e.g., "superior order," "overseer," and "president,"—rather than the traditional ecclesiastical titles for episcopacy. He also believed that any clergyman elevated to the office of bishop should continue to serve as a parochial clergyman, confined to a small district. Moreover, White was extremely careful to avoid giving the impression that he favored the English ideas of prestige and authority that were associated with the episcopal office. Except for his powers of ordination and confirmation, he wrote, a clergyman of a "superior order" would serve as every other parish minister. There is no expressed or implied suggestion in *The Case* that a clergyman elected to the "superior order" would be separate or distinct from the clergy and laity when assembled in convention. The authority to decide issues of major concern for the church would still reside with "a majority of the clerical and lay delegates."[7]

White frankly admitted that in colonial America "there cannot be produced an instance of laymen . . . soliciting the introduction of a bishop; it was probably by a great majority of them

thought an hazardous experiment." Furthermore, he believed
the basic reason for the opposition was fear that the king's
authority might be extended over the colonies through the
episcopal office. Therefore, he was very careful not to arouse
former anxieties and prejudice. When Episcopalians decided to
introduce episcopacy, it would be free, he believed, from the
slightest hint of tyranny, temporal or spiritual. Even this moderate gesture in the direction of bishops White counterbalanced
with the assertion that a temporary departure from episcopacy
was justifiable under the conditions that existed in America in
1782. A Presbyterian type of ordination in which three or more
ministers ordained another by the laying on of hands was considered acceptable. This alternative method of ordination was
presented because it was believed that it would be impossible to
obtain ordinations in England for an indefinite period. It was,
therefore, more important to find a substitute method of ordination than to permit the churches to languish for lack of ministers. In time, bishops could be added to the church and episcopal ordination rites reinstated, but in the meantime, White
was convinced that his proposal was in the best interest of the
churches and that he expressed the views of a majority of
churchmen. He was soon to learn, however, that there was a
minority of clergy who were adamant in their opposition to this
section of *The Case*.

In support of this position White asserted, "It will not be
difficult to prove, that a temporary departure from episcopacy
would be warranted by her [Church of England] doctrines, by
her practice, and by the principles on which episcopal government is asserted." First, the work of the noted Anglican apolo-
gist, Richard Hooker's *Ecclesiastical Polity*, was cited. Although
Hooker upheld the essential place of episcopacy in the Scriptures and church tradition, he recognized that some churches
had devised different forms of church government. These deviations from episcopacy were lamentable, but sometimes they
were due to the "necessity of the present hath cast upon

them."[8] In neither case did Hooker label differing forms of polity as apostate, but the implication is clear that churches that wanted to imitate the Scriptures closely would adopt bishops. Moreover, White presented evidence to prove that Archbishops Thomas Cranmer, John Whitgift, and James Ussher, as well as Bishop Benjamin Hoadly, had held similar views.[9]

The point the author of *The Case* was making was illustrated by referring to a temporary departure from the episcopal ordination within the Church of England in the sixteenth century. During the reign of Queen Mary (1553–58), many Protestants fled England and took refuge in Frankfort, Germany, and Geneva, Switzerland. Some English Protestants were ordained in the presbyterian tradition while in Germany and Switzerland, and when they returned to England in the reign of Elizabeth I (1558–1603), they were not required to be reordained by bishops. One outstanding example was William Whittingham, who was ordained in Geneva in 1555 with the encouragement and possibly the participation of John Knox and John Calvin. Whittingham returned to England in 1560, and in 1563 was appointed Dean of Durham. He was offered the archbishopric of York in 1577 but declined the appointment. When a future archibishop of York, Edwin Sandys, tried to discredit Whittingham by pointing out his irregular ordination, the earl of Huntingdon and Matthew Hutton defended him. They pointed out that the "parliament had already passed an act (13 Eliz. c. 12) practically acknowledging the validity of the ordination of ministers whether according to Roman Catholic or the rights of the reformed churches on the continent." Archbishop Sandys' charge was dismissed.[10] In the 1780s, those who rejected White's view of episcopacy expressed in *The Case* did not attempt to refute the primary sources on which he built his argument.

It was too much to expect all former Anglicans to agree to White's plan for reorganization, especially the section on episcopacy. The most violent reaction came, as might be expected, from a Connecticut clergyman who had been a zealous advocate for a colonial episcopate. Abraham Jarvis, one of the pre-war Elizabeth Town coterie, attempted to reprove White for his argument favoring a temporary departure from episcopacy. "Really sir, we think an Episcopal Church without Episcopacy, if it be not a contradiction in terms, would however, be a new thing under the sun. . . . We know it is totally abhorrent from the principles of the church in the northern states, and are fully convinced they will never submit to it."[11] Charles Inglis, who was still in New York City in June 1783, expressed his opposition when he wrote, "In short my good brother, you proposed not what you thought absolutely best and most eligible, but what the supposed necessity of the times compelled you to adopt."[12] But Inglis apparently could not forget White's plan, or perhaps the discussions about *The Case* which he heard among the S.P.G. missionaries waiting in New York for passage to England prompted him to write to White again. In any event, Inglis was sufficiently disturbed by the innovations White proposed to state, "I must be candid in telling you that I can neither see the propriety or the advantage of the scheme you propose."[13] Inglis soon departed for England, and in 1785 he was rewarded for this service to the Church of England and the British government by being consecrated the first bishop of Nova Scotia.

The Case was circulated in England as well as in America, and in England it provoked two Anglican clergymen, formerly S.P.G. missionaries in the colonies, to write the author. Alexander Murry had been a missionary at Reading and Mulatton, Pennsylvania, and Jacob Duché was the former rector of Christ and St. Peter's churches, Philadelphia, under whom White had served. The issue that disturbed both Murry and Duché most, as it did Jarvis and Inglis, was the discussion of a temporary departure from episcopal ordination. Murry advised White to write the English bishops and apply for episcopal ordination, and if that failed there would be time enough to consider an alternate plan. Duché, too, urged that an attempt should be made to secure English episcopal ordinations before any other substitute method was adopted. But neither Murry nor Duché were so hostile in his response to *The Case* as were Jarvis and Inglis. Two others who generally approved White's pamphlet were Abraham Beach and John Stuart, although both questioned the necessity of departing from episcopal ordination.[14]

In contrast with those who disagreed with *The Case* or who took some exception to its proposals, there were many who heartily approved of it. Samuel Provoost, the newly installed rector of Trinity Church, New York City, strongly approved of the pamphlet. James Duane, vestryman of Trinity Church and mayor of New York City, endorsed *The Case*. There were many others in the northeast who accepted White's plan and registered their approval by working for its implementation in the years immediately ahead. There is, moreover, no indication that the laity reacted in any other way than with approval toward *The Case*. The clergy and laity in the states from Pennsylvania southward, except in North Carolina and Georgia where the churches were too weak and the churchmen too disorganized to respond, expressed approval of White's plan either through correspondence with him or in subsequent efforts at organization. South Carolina churchmen, for example, did not express their opinion of *The Case* in 1783, but their subsequent support for the adoption of the measures proposed by White revealed their hearty approval of the plan. But more important than the immediate reactions of Episcopalians to *The Case* was the fact that by the time the Treaty of Paris was signed in September 1783, the former Anglicans in America had the outline of a plan for reorganization. Whether all churchmen would agree with White's proposals, even if modified, was not as important as the opening up of communications among various Church leaders so that the attention of all interested churchmen could be focused upon the needs of the churches.

REORGANIZATION IN MARYLAND

In Maryland, the first efforts to reorganize the former Anglican churches after their disestablishment occurred before White's pamphlet appeared. At Chestertown, Maryland, on November 9, 1780, three clergymen and twenty-four laymen assembled, apparently in response to an invitation by William Smith, the newly installed rector of St. Paul's parish, who had moved from Philadelphia to accept this position. Smith quickly became a dominant figure in Episcopal circles in Maryland, for he founded Washington College in 1780, secured a charter in 1782, and later represented the churches to the national conventions. But in the first meeting of Maryland's churchmen, they prepared a petition to the General Assembly requesting public support for religion. The request was denied, but the Chestertown meeting took another step which had far-reaching results when it adopted the name "Protestant Episcopal Church" to identify the former Anglican churches.[15] Although the name was not used officially in Maryland until 1783, it later became the official title for all the churches in America formerly belonging to the Anglican communion. Another meeting was held in Chestertown in 1781, but no record of the sessions has survived. A third meeting met in Baltimore in 1782, but no significant action was reported. Perhaps it was natural that the Maryland Episcopalians were apparently the first to meet in conventions of clergy and laity after the Declaration of Independence and disestablishment of the Church of England in their state, because throughout the colonial period the clergy had wanted to meet in convention but had been prevented by the proprietor.

At the commencement exercises of Washington College in May 1783, the few ministers present decided to petition the General Assembly for permission to make changes in the liturgy and to authorize provision for the continuation of the ministry. This request was granted, and in order to implement it a convention met in Annapolis the following August. At this meeting, William Smith was elected president, and Thomas Gates, rector of St. Anne, Arundel County, was made secretary. *A Declaration of Certain Fundamental Rights* was adopted, which in four points stated the position of the clergy. First, the clergy claimed the right to possess and use the Protestant Episcopal churches independent of any foreign or local ecclesiastical power. Second, the three orders of ministers—deacon, priest, and bishop—were affirmed, and the requirement of episcopal ordination for ministerial orders was upheld. Third, no other clergy except those episcopally ordained were to be admitted into the churches formerly belonging to the Church of England. The group next claimed the right to meet in synod or convention comprised of clergy and laymen, to reorganize the churches, and to revise or alter the liturgy, prayers, and order of worship. Following the adoption of the *Declaration,* the fifteen clergymen present elected William Smith bishop and prepared testimonials in his behalf to the bishop of London. This convention also formed two committees of three clergymen each to serve, one on the eastern and one on the western shore of the Chesapeake Bay, to interview and examine candidates for ordination and to supply the vacant parishes with lay readers.[16]

The *Declaration* of 1783 expressed concern in articles two and three that no clergymen other than those episcopally ordained be admitted into the Maryland parishes. There is no evidence that clergymen from the nonepiscopal traditions were admitted, but the need for clergy might prompt some local vestries to look upon the clergy of other denominations with interest. In Providence, Rhode Island, the vestry of St. John's Church temporarily employed a Baptist preacher in 1782, and although this was an isolated incident, it illustrated the authority that each independent vestry or congregation had. If this type of action had developed into a pattern in a number of churches, a different reorganization plan from the one attempted in Maryland and proposed in *The Case* would have become necessary. In Maryland, the clergy were obviously determined to control insofar as possible those who entered the clerical ranks. This concern partly explains the haste with which Smith was elected bishop. Another indication of this concern was the appointment of two committees to handle prospective ministers and lay readers. But the exclusion of the laity from the episcopal election and from two important church committees was a bold step which provoked the ire of several powerful laymen.

Of the fifteen clergy present at Annapolis in August 1783, eight had been active during the episcopal campaign of the late 1760s and early 1770s, but not one of them had supported the episcopal scheme then. John Gordon, rector of St. Michael's parish, Talbot county, 1749 to 1790, who had opposed the Johnson-Chandler plan and advised Walter Dulany that many of his colleagues felt as he did, was present. But in 1783, three of the staunchest advocates for a colonial episcopate—Jonathan Boucher, Henry Addison, Bennet Allen—had long ago fled Maryland. The election of William Smith to be bishop probably resulted primarily from his personal powers of persuasion applied at a time when most clergymen were genuinely concerned about the future status of the episcopal ministry. Perhaps, too, there was some fear that White's idea about a temporary departure from episcopal ordinations would become a reality. It is also possible that an alternative type of ecclesiastical authority other than a bishop might have been acceptable to many; therefore, Smith moved quickly in an effort to thwart any such development.[17] By 1783, Smith had altered his prewar position that a commissary was better suited to America than a bishop. Then, too, it is entirely possible that Smith thought he saw an opportunity to fulfill his personal ambition for a pair of lawn sleeves. But the failure of the fifteen clergy who elected Smith to consult the laity was a serious mistake. None of the laity in colonial Maryland had expressed a desire for a bishop, and many had opposed the Johnson-Chandler plan. The assump-

tion made by the clergy that the laity had changed their attitude on this subject or that they would acquiesce to the clergy's
judgment on this matter was unwarranted.

A copy of the *Declaration* was forwarded to Governor William
Paca with a request for legislative approval. The governor reviewed the document and in response expressed an objective
and impartial opinion:

As every denomination of clergy are to be deemed adequate judges of
their own spiritual rights . . . it would be a very partial and unjust
distinction to deny that right to the respectable and learned body of
the Episcopal clergy in this state; and it will give me the highest happiness and satisfaction, if, either in my individual capacity, or in the
public character which I now have the honor to sustain. I can be
instrumental in . . . placing every branch of the Christian Church in
this State, upon the most equal and respectable footing.[18]

If Smith and his associates expected preferential treatment,
they were caught short by Paca's statement. It must have been
difficult for churchmen to accept the fact that the once-established church was now one among equals in the eyes of the
state. After more than seventy years of church-state union, Governor Paca's response was clear evidence of the ecclesiastical
revolution that had taken place.

If Paca's reaction to the request for legislative sanction for
the Protestant Episcopal Church was shocking, his personal
opinion about bishops must have been unnerving to William
Smith. In earlier years, Paca had been a student under Smith at
the College of Philadelphia, but this former relationship did
not affect his opposition to episcopacy. The governor expressed sharp disapproval of the election of Smith as bishop in
a letter to General Joseph Reed of Pennsylvania. He wrote:

As to their proceedings they can be viewed in no other light than the
private opinion and sentiment of so many clergymen of such a
church. . . . As to your first question I answer and say *for myself* the
Episcopalian clergy shall not represent out Episcopal Church independently of the laity. . . . The clergy may assemble and propose but the

laity must adopt or consent. I hope it has not been represented that I have recommended any particular person for *Bishop* or *President.* I can assure you I never did: for I am one of those who think a Bishop unnecessary.[19]

It is evident from Paca's letter that the August 1783 convention and the election of Smith without the expressed approval or participation of the laity had provoked a hornet's nest of opposition. Paca indicated that there were others, presumably laymen, who were convinced that bishops were unnecessary, but he did not reveal who his sympathizers were or how many there were. But a few powerful laymen like the governor could obviously make life difficult for the proepiscopal clergy. In 1771, Paca and Samuel Chase had forcefully opposed their minister, Jonathan Boucher, in his proepiscopal activities. In the years since their encounter with Boucher, both Paca and Chase had been ardent supporters of colonial rights against Great Britain, signers of the Declaration of Independence, and in the 1780s leaders in state government. Moreover, the laymen who had been given the trusteeship of church property by the Vestry Act of 1779 were probably not interested in having a bishop whom they would have to consult on church business. Now that the laity was providing all the financial support the churches received voluntarily, their sense of self-importance was intensified. Paca and his sympathizers (and they were probably many) were not willing to acquiesce to the clerical claim of a superior role in church reorganization.

The next scheduled convention met on June 22, 1784, the day on which the General Assembly reconvened. Presumably this date was agreed upon to give lay delegates who were also representatives to the assembly in Annapolis a better opportunity to attend. When the convention was formed, the lay delegates requested permission to retire and discuss the *Declaration* privately. They approved the *Declaration* as originally written, but they recommended four additional articles. First, any clergyman ordained bishop, priest, or deacon in any foreign state was forbidden to take an oath or obligation to any foreign power, civil or ecclesiastical. Second, a bishop's authority was defined as the right to ordain, confirm, and serve as president of ecclesiastical meetings, and any alteration in this provision required the action of the convention. Third, the training, examination, and recommendation of clergy was left to the clergy, but the acceptance of a minister into a parish was reserved exclusively for the people who supported him. Fourth, it was determined that every parish was entitled to a representation of one clergyman and one layman at all future conventions, and any change in these rules required a two-thirds vote of the convention.[20] The clergy accepted these four additional articles.

If William Smith had hoped to achieve a swift consecration in England, the action of the 1784 convention shattered it. Although the laity did not nullify his election, they did define the episcopal office. The prohibition against any oath or obligation to a foreign power, civil or ecclesiastical, was, however, the stipulation that ruled out an immediate consecration in England. Obviously the Episcopalians in Maryland were not expecting a bishop soon, because they took no action and provided no funds to assist Smith in his search for consecration. The question whether a bishop would serve a parish remained unanswered. Moreover, there is no evidence that the laity added their recommendation to that of the clergy to give Smith another boost toward acceptance by an appropriate ecclesiastical body. The laity left no room for doubt about their attitude toward episcopacy and the way William Smith had been elected.

The actions of the Maryland laity in the 1784 convention in effect checked the hierarchical approach to church reorganization and instead insisted that the convention of laity and clergy which represented all the parishes was the proper body to make all major ecclesiastical decisions. To many the action of the clergy in electing Smith probably appeared to be an aristocratic rather than a popular approach to church government, and this method was definitely out of fashion with those who had accepted the republican implications of the Revolution. Subsequently Maryland's churchmen followed the methods and procedures outlined in White's *The Case*. If proof were needed that William White had perceived and expressed the sentiment of a majority of his fellow religionists, especially from Pennsylvania southward, the experience of the Maryland Episcopalians is ready evidence. William West, rector of St. Paul's, Baltimore, and secretary of the 1784 Annapolis convention, admitted the change in approach to reorganization that resulted from that meeting. To White he wrote: "I conceive it not only prudent, but even necessary that lay members be delegated by the people for the purpose and that they concur with the clergy. As to the usage of the primitive church with respect to the election of Bishops I need not mention to you that it is difficult to speak positively. The approbation of the Laity, tho' desirable, was not I believe necessary. . . . Yet still the approbation of the laity would have its one effect for the encouragement and support of a Bishop."[21]

West seemed relieved by the inclusion of the laity in the convention to participate in decisions on all issues. Nor did he resent their additions to the *Declaration*. He, like his fellow churchmen, had come to realize that the colonial experience had brought an increased number of laymen into the decision-making processes of the church, just as the revolutionary ideology had insisted upon the right of the people to be consulted on issues of government. These forces confirmed the place of the laity in the governmental functions of the church.

PENNSYLVANIA AND MASSACHUSETTS

In Pennsylvania, William White followed his own plan set forth in *The Case*. He took the initiative in promoting reorganization by conferring with his fellow clergyman, Samuel Magraw, rec-

tor of St. Paul's Church, Philadelphia. Next these two ministers
requested their respective vestries to appoint lay representatives to meet with them to discuss the needs of the churches.
This group then informed in writing all the Episcopal congregations in the state of their activities and invited them to send
delegates to a meeting scheduled for May 24, 1784, to be held
in Christ Church. Four clergymen and nineteen laymen attended this first formal meeting. This was the first duly authorized ecclesiastical assembly of Episcopalians in America at
which laymen were officially a part. To symbolize the working
relationship between clerics and laymen, although White was
elected president of the meeting, William Pollard, a layman,
was made clerk. A committee on correspondence was authorized to communicate the activities of Pennsylvania's meeting to
the churches within and beyond the state and to provide a
means of cooperation with others who were interested in developing a general ecclesiastical constitution.

A set of six *Fundamental Principles* was prepared for the Episcopal churches in Pennsylvania. The first article declared the
Episcopal churches in these states free and independent, and
the right to regulate the concerns of the communion was the
prerogative of the churches in each state. The desire was expressed, however, that the churches stay as close as possible to
the Church of England in matters of doctrine and worship.
The three traditional orders of the clergy were reaffirmed, but
the definition of the rights and powers of each was delayed for
a future convention to decide. Moreover, a convention comprised of clergy and laymen was designated as the only body
that could make laws and canons for the churches in Pennsylvania. Lastly, it was specified that no power was to be delegated
to a general ecclesiastical government which a local congregation or vestry could exercise.[22] It is clear that Pennsylvania's
churchmen had no reservations about the importance of the
laity or the fundamental importance of local autonomy as the
cornerstone of ecclesiastical polity. This position advocated by

White in *The Case* and incorporated in the *Fundamental Principles* is evidence that this body of Episcopalians fully recognized that the basic issue between the colonies and Great Britain had been the right of self-determination versus imperial control and the right to decide who should rule in America. That Pennsylvania's churchmen took these steps seems logical when it is noted that a majority of the delegates were active supporters of the Revolution.

The *Declaration* of Maryland and the *Fundamental Principles* of Pennsylvania are essentially the same in their first four articles. The fifth and sixth articles of Pennsylvania, which designate the convention as the authoritative body to safeguard the rights of the local parishes, were added to the Maryland *Declaration* at the insistence of the laymen. Of the Maryland laity who participated in the church conventions, several can be identified as leaders or supporters of the Revolution in their state, and they probably concurred with Governor Paca's insistence on the rights of laymen. Furthermore, the *Declaration* and the *Fundamental Principles* differed on another important issue because the former required episcopal ordination and the latter did not. Whether the Pennsylvanians simply assumed that all their clergy would have episcopal ordinations or whether the subject was purposely left open is not apparent. It is possible that White was being cautious in not raising the subject of episcopacy in any form in order to avoid a premature discussion of the subject. But on this important subject the difference between William Smith's approach to reorganization and William White's was very great. While Smith's precipitous actions antagonized the laity, White's judicious handling of the most sensitive issue won their admiration and eventually their full support.

The results of the 1784 Pennsylvania meeting were forwarded to Samuel Parker (among others), rector of Trinity Church, Boston. Parker had replaced Henry Caner as the leading Anglican clergyman in Massachusetts after Caner's flight to England early in the war. Both Parker and the vestry of Trinity were sympathetic to the American cause, and together they had eliminated objectionable prayers from the liturgy and kept the church open throughout the war. After examining the *Fundamental Principles,* Parker wanted to know whether it was intended as a national or as a state plan. He then added, "Is it meant to carry the Independence so far as to exclude the obtaining a Bishop from England?"[23] Parker detected immediately the absence of expressed concern over an episcopate on the part of Pennsylvanians. It was apparent to him that the plan had merit, but the issue of episcopacy, he felt, needed clarification.

White answered Parker's queries when he responded that the *Fundamental Principles* were intended as guidelines for Pennsylvania and for any state that cared to use them. On the question about episcopacy, White replied that separation from England should not prevent the procurement of a bishop, provided he became a citizen of the United States. The experience of Smith's episcopal election and the lay opposition it generated was not relayed to Parker. In fact, White seems to have tried to postpone further discussion about bishops by saying, "Proper measures for procuring an Episcopate we wish to see taken at the ensuing meeting in New York."[24] The meeting to which White referred was scheduled for October 1784, and it was to be the first attempt to get the several states that had formed conventions to send delegates to a national meeting. By suggesting postponement of the episcopal question until the meeting of delegates for the general church, White was also hinting that the issue was too important to be decided by a few zealous advocates or a number of headstrong opponents. White apparently believed that the best possible approach to this perennial problem could be evolved by a cross-section of church delegates.

The Episcopal clergy of Massachusetts met in conjunction with their colleagues from Rhode Island in Boston on September 8, 1784. Parker was selected president and John Graves secretary. By convention action the *Fundamental Principles* were adopted with only two modifications. Article One was altered to encourage the procurement of a bishop. Article Five was amended to equalize the voting power between the clergy and laity. The new article read, "The laity ought not to exceed or their votes be more in number than those of the clergy." The Massachusetts clergy at this time favored full lay participation, but they clearly did not want a lay-dominated church. However, rather than deprive a church of one lay and one clerical vote at a future convention, it was recommended that churches without ministers confer their clerical vote upon a neighboring minister who would cast it for the church. Moreover, the Massachusetts convention returned White's courtesy to them by sending him a copy of their transactions with a request that he share it with the churches to the south. Then they added, "It is our unanimous opinion that it is beginning at the wrong end to attempt to organize our church before we have obtained a head."[25] Yet the nine Episcopal clergymen who met in Boston did not elect one of their number bishop.

VIRGINIA, NEW YORK, NEW JERSEY, SOUTH CAROLINA

The first Virginia convention to consider the reorganization of the churches met from May 18–25, 1785, in Richmond, with seventy-one laymen and thirty-six clergymen representing sixty-nine of the state's ninety-five parishes. The Reverend James Madison, president of William and Mary College, was elected president of the convention, and Robert Andrews, rector of York Hampton parish, was secretary. Although Madison was president of the convention, Carter Braxton, a layman from St. John parish and a signer of the Declaration of Independence, served as chairman of the convention at least seven times during the sessions. The parliamentary maneuver used to place Braxton in the chair was simple. Since the laymen outnumbered the clergy almost two to one, when a critical issue was before the body, someone would move that the convention resolve itself into a committee of the whole, and the motion would be passed. Then the committee of the whole selected its own chairman, who was Carter Braxton. Thus Madison could exercise the powers of the presidency only when the laity permitted it. Although traditional courtesies were extended to the clergy throughout the convention, it was obvious that the laymen dominated the overall deliberations.

This body devised forty-three *Rules for the Order, Government, and Discipline of the Protestant Episcopal Church in Virginia*. From the minutes of proceedings it is evident that the convention was accepted as the governing body of the church. Article Six stated that in all future conventions all members, ministerial and lay, would have to present signed testimonials from the parish churchwarden or clerk that they were authorized to serve as delegates. The right of parish vestries to continue the long-standing practice of presentation or appointment was guaranteed. Although episcopal ordination was required for all ministers, the vestry retained the right to examine a candidate before it accepted him. Bishops were recognized in the forty-three *Rules,* but their office was defined as being no different from that of any other minister, except for the prerogatives of performing ordination, confirmation, and clerical visitations, and serving as president of ecclesiastical assemblies. Besides, every bishop in Virginia would be required to hold a parish and perform the duties of a parish minister. Six other articles defined even more precisely the episcopal office. For example, a bishop could be elected only in convention. If charged with misconduct, he was subject to the judgment of the convention. Vestries were given the right to initiate complaints against a bishop, but the convention investigated and directed the disposition of the charges. On the other hand, a bishop could reprove or discipline a clergyman, but only the convention could suspend or dismiss.

Virginia Episcopalians did more to ensure the status of the

vestries and define the office of bishop than did any other state convention in the 1783 to 1785 period. Why? First, it was a conditioned response for a state in which the vestries had been the locus of strength for the local churches. The loss of their taxing power and civil functions as a result of disestablishment was a major setback. To maintain a semblance of their former authority it was necessary to guarantee their traditional ecclesiastical authority. Second, the attitude expressed toward episcopacy by churchmen, many of whom had resisted the prewar Johnson-Chandler plan, revealed that their thoughts on that subject had not changed. The office of bishop still symbolized to them a prerogative position related to a foreign or alien power. To guard against the possibility of a future aristocratic type of bishop, they defined the episcopal office in explicit and primitive terms. Moreover, it is possible that part of the attitude toward bishops was expressed because some feared that the other state conventions of the Protestant Episcopal Church would look to Virginia to take the lead in procuring one. Since Virginia had the largest number of churches and clergy of any state in 1785 and potentially the foundation to warrant a bishop, it appeared logical to some that to avoid this title role in reorganization a clear definition of episcopacy was needed.

In 1785 there was therefore no chance that a proepiscopal campaign would be developed in Virginia, and there was little concern expressed over the ministerial shortages that would result in the absence of episcopal ordination. The Virginia vestries, like their Maryland, Massachusetts, and New Jersey counterparts, probably made extensive use of lay readers.[26] Moreover, the proepiscopal leaders of the 1760s and 1770s had long before left Virginia. James Horrocks departed at the height of the episcopal conflict in 1771; William Willie and John Camm, who continued the struggle after Horrock's departure, were themselves forced to retire because of their Loyalism. Besides, the 1785 convention demonstrated its lack of concern over ministerial ordination when it did not respond positively to an

offer from the Danish national church to ordain ministers episcopally. The offer originated as an indirect result of Mason
Locke Weems's and Edward Gantt's efforts to secure ordination in England in 1783. After they shared their problem with
John Adams, American minister to England, he conferred with
M. de St. Saphorin, the Danish minister in England, to find out
if the Danish church would assist the American Episcopalians.
The positive reply was forwarded to Richard Henry Lee and
then to Patrick Henry, governor of Virginia, and thence to the
convention. But the Virginia churchmen merely listened to the
offer read in convention, postponed discussion on it, and eventually referred it to the General Convention scheduled for September 1785.[27] In the meantime, however, William White cour-
teously declined the offer in behalf of his fellow churchmen.

On June 22, 1785, a convention of five clergymen and eleven
laymen assembled in New York. This body was more flexible in
its attitudes toward reorganization than any previous state conventions. Its main business was the selection of three clergymen
and three laymen to serve as delegates to the forthcoming General Convention. The only instruction to the delegates directed
them to cooperate in whatever way possible in the interest of
the church. This delegation, composed of the Reverends Samuel Provoost, Abraham Beach, and Benjamin Moore, and the
laymen James Duane, Daniel Kissam, and John Davis, was well
aware that New York Episcopalians favored the *Fundamental
Principles* of Pennsylvania. Headed by Samuel Provoost and
James Duane, both of whom had served the American cause
during the Revolution, this delegation was concerned to free
the Episcopal church, as Provoost and Duane had freed Trinity
Church, from the stigma of Toryism.[28] Moreover, the actions
of the New York convention give the distinct impression that it
favored the reorganization of the churches first and the acqui-
sition of bishops later. In this attitude it was unlike the Massachusetts convention but very much in step with the actions of
the conventions in Pennsylvania and Virginia.

New Jersey Episcopalians also held their first state convention in 1785, and it was attended by three clergymen and fourteen laymen. Here as in New York, Massachusetts, Pennsylvania, and Virginia, the clergyman elected president had been favorable to the United States during the war. This body was very definitely of the opinion that it was necessary for the churches to organize on both the state and national levels before proceeding to acquire bishops. Thus, no action on the subject of episcopacy was taken in New Jersey by the first convention. The greatest concern expressed was one of preparation for the September 1785 meeting of a General Convention in Philadelphia.

One action of the New Jersey convention was, however, filled with potential controversy. Thomas B. Chandler, the prewar champion of the Johnson-Chandler plan, had returned to his former home and church, St. John's of Elizabeth Town, in June 1785. The convention elected Chandler one of four clerical delegates to represent New Jersey in the General Convention. Chandler had not been present in the state convention, but it is probable that he was chosen because of his twenty-five-year record of service in the prewar colony. If Chandler had accepted the election and attended the General Convention, he certainly would have encountered his prewar antagonist, William Smith. Moreover, the laity who had actively or passively resisted the Johnson-Chandler scheme were now more obviously in a position to approve or disapprove an episcopal plan than they previously had been. Then, too, Chandler's Loyalism and pamphleteering against the Continental Congress most surely would have been remembered had he appeared in Philadelphia.[29] Because a large number of the delegates, ministerial and lay, who represented the Episcopal conventions to the General Convention had been dedicated Patriots, it was the better part of wisdom that Chandler did not appear. Had he attended and the subject of episcopacy arisen, as it did, the divisive memories of the 1760s and 1770s would have been made all too real.

Episcopalians in one other state, South Carolina, assembled and started on the road to reorganization in 1785. Three clergymen and ten laymen met in St. Philip's Church, Charleston, on July 12, 1785, and a layman, Hugh Rutledge, chaired the meeting. The selection of a delegation to attend the General Convention was the main item of business, and Robert Smith, rector of St. Phillip's, and four laymen—Jacob Read, Charles Pinckney, John Bull, and John Kean—were chosen. It was evident from the outset that South Carolina churchmen had no intention of letting the clergy gain the upper hand in their state or in a national convention. Furthermore, hostility toward episcopacy was so strong among this group that Robert Smith had to promise "there was to be no bishop settled in that state" before the delegation was released to go to Philadelphia.[30] The delegation that did represent South Carolina could hardly have been more pro-Patriot than they were. For example, Jacob Read and Hugh Rutledge had been exiled by the British during their occupation of Charleston because they broke parole and communicated with the American leaders. Charles Pinckney had served as aide-de-camp to General Washington and was later captured by the British and held in a prison until the end of the war. Hostility toward Great Britain and that which symbolized foreign authority was probably more intense in Charleston than in any other major American city.

William White attempted to contact the Episcopalians in North Carolina in 1784 to encourage them to undertake a statewide reorganization and to cooperate with them in the formation of a national convention, but his efforts were unproductive. David Griffith, rector of Fairfax parish, Virginia, informed White in July 1784 that none of the Virginia clergy had heard from their North Carolina colleagues.[31] Actually it was June 5, 1790 before a convention was held in North Carolina. At the meeting which was convened in Tawborough, two clergymen and two laymen were present, and Charles Petti-

grew, rector of Edenton parish, was chosen chairman. Six articles closely resembling the *Fundamental Principles* of Pennsylvania were accepted. On November 12, 1790, delegates were selected to attend the next meeting of the General Convention.
Georgia Episcopalians were even later in reviving their
churches, for in 1793 only one church, Christ Church, Savannah, was functioning.[32]

PROGRESS AND ADAPTATION

In the period 1782 to 1785 several significant steps had been
taken in the direction of forming an ecclesiastical confederation. At the very time when the several states were reorganizing, generally along the lines proposed in *The Case* and formalized in the *Fundamental Principles,* a preliminary meeting was
held in New York in October 1784 (discussed in the next
chapter) to prepare for the first meeting of a General Convention to be held in Philadelphia, September 27 to October 7,
1785.[33] By July 1785, it appeared that a continuation of the
"low-pressure" approach to the church's needs would soon produce a national union. But what appeared to be a relatively
orderly transition for approximately 400 independent churches
in 1776 to a nationally organized Protestant Episcopal Church
in 1789 was anything but a simple transformation. A key factor
facilitating this transition was the adaptation of many of the
ideas used by the several states and the nation in the preparation of their constitutions to the reorganization of the churches.
White was the central figure in the utilization of the concepts of
"natural rights," "representation," "equality," "republicanism,"
"elective process," "constitutional convention," and "participation of the people" in the area of church polity.[34] But the fact
that his suggestions caught on or corresponded with those generated by churchmen in other states demonstrates the perva-
siveness of the language expressing the ideology of the American Revolution. Moreover, at an early stage in the Revolution,

White had come to realize that even on the sensitive and essential question of episcopacy the method of selecting bishops could be adapted to conform to contemporary concepts of leadership selection without endangering or impugning the integrity of a basic ecclesiastical office of the church. The progressive acceptance and utilization of these features of White's thinking brought into reality a unified church by 1789.

The period 1776 to 1781 has been described as a period of constitution-making in the United States. Within these years eleven of the thirteen states prepared their constitutions, and the Articles of Confederation, the first constitution of the United States, was ratified. By 1781, the United States had a central government with a legal foundation and prescribed procedures. In this constitutional development, ultimate power remained with the states, and the central government was sharply circumscribed. Even in the distribution of power between the national and local governments, the states held the upper hand. Then in filling the offices created by the new governments, Americans showed their preference for the elective process. The election of governors, who in colonial days bore no responsibility to local opinion, was a marked change. The principle of governmental responsibility to those governed found constitutional expression. The right of virtually all freemen to vote for a representative annually and possibly a senator increasingly brought those who governed in touch with the citizenry. Even the practice of roll-call voting became almost universally practiced in the 1780s to inform the people at home that they were exercising home rule through their elected representatives.

The leaders in the reorganization of the Protestant Episcopal churches realized, as did their compatriots in the state and national governments, that the Revolution involved more than a separation from Great Britain. It included even more than the organization of so-called free institutions as contrasted with monarchical ones. It was one thing for Americans to argue for "natural rights" against England, but it was another proposition to demonstrate that these rights could be translated into viable agencies of government.[35] The churchmen who led in the reorganization of their churches were, for the most part, committed to the realization of the principles of representative government in church polity. By conducting their church affairs within the acceptable ideological and practical methods of the time, these churchmen managed not only to rebuild their church but also to remove much of the stigma that had fallen upon it because of the actions of Anglican Loyalists.

9

Connecticut's
Hierarchical Scheme

"No laymen admitted to the gathering, and it was so secret as to be known only to the clergy."

Woodbury Convention, March, 1783

The reorganization of the Episcopal churches in the states from New York to South Carolina was conducted openly in conventions of clergy and laymen; minutes were kept; and the local parishes were informed of the results. In only one of these states, Maryland, was a plan to procure a bishop devised, but this plan was checked by the laity. Even the Massachusetts Episcopal clergy, who favored procuring a bishop before state conventions were organized, met publicly and shared their ideas with William White and the churchmen to the south. In contrast to the general pattern, the Episcopal clergy of Connecticut met secretly, adopted a plan to obtain a bishop, and informed only a few well-known proepiscopal clergy in New York who were waiting for transportation to England after the war. It was more than a year before the rest of the Episcopalians who were working for an interstate ecclesiastical confederation learned of Connecticut's hierarchical scheme and determined what attitude they would take toward a bishop in Connecticut.

THE WOODBURY CONVENTION

The Episcopal clergymen in Connecticut met in the home of John Rutgers Marshall, rector of St. Paul's Church, Woodbury, on March 25, 1783. Abraham Jarvis, Daniel Fogg, and John R.

Marshall were present, but no list of the other seven participants has survived, nor is it possible to determine which of the
fourteen Episcopal clergymen in Connecticut were absent. The
only known facts are revealed in the correspondence of Fogg,
who broke his obligation of secrecy by informing Samuel
Parker, rector of Trinity Church, Boston, of the meeting in
July 1783.[1] The rest of the Episcopal clergy were not alerted to
the scheme until May 1784.[2] Not even the leading laymen of
the Connecticut churches were informed or consulted about
the scheme for "fear of opposition, and perhaps the fear of not
having the hearty concurrence of their lay brethren."[3] Abraham Jarvis, minister at Middletown and secretary of the meeting, knew that there was passive resistance toward episcopacy
among the laity because he had been active in the proepiscopal
campaign in the 1760s. When Parker objected to the secrecy of
the Connecticut transactions, Fogg defended it by asserting
that there had not been time enough to consult the Episcopal
clergy outside Connecticut.

The ten zealous Connecticut clergy had one objective in
mind on March 25, 1783: a bishop. In their view, the Episcopal
churches could not organize properly until they first had a
bishop, because it was his prerogative to guide the churches.
To procure a bishop after the churches were organized would
minimize his importance and possibly limit his powers. The
first man selected bishop was Jeremiah Leaming, rector of St.
Paul's Church, Norwalk, Connecticut, from 1758 to 1779, and
a refugee in New York in 1783, but he declined the position
because of age and poor health. There are, however, several
reasons why Leaming was the first choice. He was a native of
Connecticut, a convert to Anglicanism under Samuel Johnson,
and an advocate of a colonial episcopate in the 1760s. Although
Leaming had been a Loyalist in the early years of the Revolution, he later showed sympathy for the American cause, deleted
the prayers for the king from the church liturgy, and reopened
his church. Leaming was once jailed for his suspected Loyalism,

and his property was confiscated, but he did not denounce the Revolution or the patriot leaders, nor did he flee America.

The meeting next selected as bishop Samuel Seabury, a refugee in New York. Seabury's fervor in the proepiscopal cause in the 1760s was second only to Chandler's, and his advocacy of the British cause during the war qualified him as the most outspoken Loyalist among the Anglican clergy. Daniel Fogg raised an objection to Seabury's selection as bishop at the 1783 meeting on this very point, but a majority did not agree with him. Instead, the meeting felt that Seabury at fifty-five had the vigor, capacity, and determination to seek episcopal consecration and succeed. The ten clergy hoped Seabury would receive consecration in England, but in case he failed there, he was encouraged to appeal to the Episcopal church in Scotland. In the event a controversy erupted in America, the group hoped Seabury would settle in Halifax, Nova Scotia, from whence he could ordain prospective ministers for the Episcopal churches and perhaps pay an occasional visit to administer confirmation and dedicate new churches.

No doubt Seabury, Leaming, and Jarvis avoided informing their closest friends of the laity because they anticipated opposition. Perhaps they remembered that two leading laymen in prewar Connecticut, Godfrey Malbone and William S. Johnson, had given no support to the episcopal plan. Johnson was still a leading layman who resided in Stratford, but the clergy did not confer with him. This was a bold step, for the clergy must have realized that the S.P.G. would sooner or later have to withdraw their financial stipends, and then they would be completely dependent on the laity for their support. In contrast, the members of the Woodbury meeting the next day informed the clergy in New York City, who had previously favored bishops. All the clergy who were advised of the plan had been proponents of a colonial episcopate, and most of them soon left for England because of their Loyalist convictions. Charles Inglis of Trinity Church, New York, and Henry Addison, formerly of

St. John's parish, Maryland, were the two most prominent members of this group.[4]

Abraham Jarvis expressed the opposition of the Connecticut clergy to White's *The Case* in a letter dated March 25, 1783. He made it perfectly clear that in Connecticut's view "episcopal superiority is an ordinance of Christ"; therefore, it was a most serious infraction of divine truth to depreciate the importance of bishops.[5] Furthermore, the ten clergy who constituted Connecticut's Episcopal organization had no intention of permitting the laity to sit with them in a convention where matters of organization, faith, and practice were decided. Although Jarvis did not admit it until April 1783, White's *The Case* and the fear of its general acceptance prompted the Connecticut Episcopal clergy to act secretly and independently.[6] They believed that unless they acted quickly and decisively, the American Episcopal churches would organize on a basis of state and national conventions, but with no bishop. To head off these innovations the Connecticut clergy acted first. On April 23, 1783, a meeting of Episcopal clergy in New York prepared a letter of application for Seabury's consecration to the archbishop of York, William Markham, who was the leading bishop in England after the death of the archbishop of Canterbury, Frederick Cornwallis, on March 19, 1783. A testimonial of Seabury's character and qualifications was prepared in May 1783 by Charles Inglis, Jeremiah Leaming, and Benjamin Moore. With these credentials in his possession Seabury arrived in England on July 7, 1783.

The main theme of the documents Seabury carried to England emphasized that unless bishops were quickly introduced into America it would become impossible to do so in the future. The basis for this position was the conviction that the American Episcopalians would find a substitute for bishops. "If it [bishops] be now any longer neglected, there is reason to apprehend that a plan of a very extraordinary nature, lately formed and published in Philadelphia, may be carried into execution.

This plan is, in brief, to constitute a nominal Episcopate by the united suffrages of presbyters and laymen. . . . We think it our duty to reject such a spurious substitute for Episcopacy, and, as far as may be in our power, to prevent its taking effect."[7] The Connecticut clergy clearly admitted that White's proposals provoked them to seek a bishop first, but they also gave the impression that they were a minority group. Furthermore, it is surprising that they applied for episcopal consecration in April, because the formal peace between Great Britain and the United States was not achieved until September 1783.

Three clergy in New York—Charles Inglis, Jeremiah Leaming, and Benjamin Moore—made an additional request in the petition for consecration to the archbishop of York. They made a direct plea for financial assistance from the archbishop to support a bishop in America. Their correspondence pointed out that donations had been made for this purpose in earlier years. The S.P.G. records showed £ 4000 designated to support an American bishop, all of which had been donated between 1717 and 1768. Archbishop Secker had made the last contribution in the amount of £ 1000, but his was the only contribution received between 1741 and 1768. It is obvious that the English hierarchy had not been too interested in the question of an American bishop in the 1760s if only one of their number had been willing to contribute toward it. Nevertheless, the three petitioners wanted these funds for Seabury's support, if he was consecrated. The enthusiastic backers of Seabury were looking ahead to find financial resources in case the laity refused to contribute to an episcopal fund. In any event, they were determined to have a bishop, even if they had to settle him in Nova Scotia and find financial support outside the United States.

SEABURY IN ENGLAND

In the eighteen months Seabury spent in England, he encountered considerable discouragement and very little heartening news. After he presented his case to Archbishop Markham, he notified his American supporters to prepare for a public reaction, since there was no longer any way to keep the scheme secret. "You can make the attempt with all the strength you can muster," he counseled, "among the laity: and at the same time I would advise that some persons be sent to try the State of Vermont on this subject."⁸ Seabury obviously expected a negative reaction from the Episcopal laity and the Connecticut state government when they learned of his activities. He naturally worked under tension in England because of his fear of opposition from Connecticut. Had this happened, Seabury would have found himself in an awkward situation. The English government was still negotiating a peace treaty when Seabury made his mission known to Archbishop Markham. An outcry from America over Seabury's activities could have embarrassed the Anglican hierarchy and revived the prewar fear that a bishop consecrated in England and serving in America had to be an agent of the king.

By September 1783, Seabury confessed to his fellow clergy in Connecticut that he saw no hope of completing his mission successfully. "With regard to my success," he admitted, "I not only think it doubtful, but that the probability is against it. Nobody will risk anything for the sake of continuing Episcopal ordination in America."⁹ Seabury personally discovered what Johnson and Chandler had learned in the 1760s—the Church of England hierarchy was not free to act on its own initiative. The bishops were all appointed by the king and subject to political pressures and ministerial guidance. They were amenable to king and parliament for their official and personal conduct. King George III did not hesitate to intervene directly into ecclesiastical appointments when he wanted a favorite appointed. In December 1776, the archbishopric of York was vacant. The king offered it to Richard Terrick of London, who declined it because of ill health, and only after Terrick's refusal was the position offered to William Markham, bishop of

Chester. Richard Hurd, a king's favorite, was advanced to the episcopal bench in 1772 over other possible candidates. In turn, the temporal nobility continued to exert its influence in filling lesser ecclesiastical appointments. It was therefore natural that the appointees looked to the king and nobility whenever an important ecclesiastical decision had to be made. Unless the king and ministry consented, it was extremely difficult for the bishops to act independently.

The Georgian church continued a placid policy in the last quarter of the eighteenth century, as it had in the previous twenty-five years. There were no new parishes established, in spite of the rapid growth of towns and industry, because a separate act of parliament was required for a new parish and vested interests opposed any realignment of the existing parishes. Few of the established clergy were imbued with enough missionary or evangelistic zeal to deviate from their customary ways and extend their ministry to the unchurched. When Richard Watson was elevated to the episcopal bench in 1782, the hope for parish reform was quickened because he had advocated a realignment of parish lines to provide churches and clergy for new communities. Bishop Watson proposed a redistribution of episcopal and capitular revenues to achieve parish reform, but his episcopal colleagues, with the support of the prime minister, Lord Shelburne, frustrated Watson's proposals. There was no other plan put forth to reform the church internally before the end of the century.

On April 26, 1783, John Moore, bishop of Bangor, was selected archbishop of Canterbury, but only after the king's preference, Robert Lowth, bishop of London, declined the archepiscopal appointment. John Moore was sponsored by Lord Blandford, son of the second duke of Marlborough. Archbishop Moore presided at Canterbury from 1783 to 1805, "but his archepiscopate was far from being a notable one."[10] He was a typically pious, even-tempered, businesslike bishop, but he was a joiner in worthy projects rather than an initiator of new

programs. He gave support to the new Sunday School movement and the association for the reformation of manners and
endorsed missionary work in general, but he took the lead in
none of these projects. A man of Moore's temperament was not
likely to advocate an American episcopate until he was absolutely sure that the king and parliament approved.

Seabury reported to his Connecticut associates that the English bishops refused to consecrate him because they were
afraid their actions would be interpreted as interfering in the
affairs of Connecticut. Archbishop Moore pointed out to Seabury that his supporters had no plan for his financial needs,
and unless these were met the office of bishop would be held in
contempt. Moreover, there was no hint in the archbishop's remarks that the American Episcopalians could expect any financial aid from England. It was also noted that Seabury's application for consecration had only the approval of the Connecticut
clergy and not the laity. Finally, the English bishops directed
Seabury to get a statement from the Connecticut legislature
assuring them that a bishop consecrated by them would be
accepted without a controversy resulting. Thus Seabury had to
seek the assistance of a number of people within and without
the Episcopal church to further his cause. Seabury admitted
that he was constantly plagued by the fear that the Congregationalists would discover the scheme and raise a protest to
crush it. Yet, by May of 1784, Seabury was convinced that
unless he received an endorsement from the Connecticut legislature, and presumably the Episcopal laity in the state, his mission in England would end in failure.[11]

One English bishop, Robert Lowth, bishop of London, did
attempt to assist Seabury in 1783 and 1784. In the 1760s Lowth
had been bishop of Oxford and a consistent friend of the
American church. He received Seabury cordially in 1783, approved of the application for consecration, and promised to aid
the measure. When Bishop Lowth discussed Seabury's request
with his fellow bishops, he discovered he was a minority of one

who thought Seabury could be consecrated without passage of an enabling act by parliament. The problem was that the consecration service contained a loyalty oath to the king which Seabury naturally could not assume if he returned to the United States. Bishop Lowth believed a dispensation from the king could exempt Seabury from the oath, but the other bishops insisted that an act of parliament was necessary. Although Lowth was unsuccessful in his efforts to assist Seabury, he did introduce a bill in parliament on August 13, 1784 to permit the ordination of deacons and priests for America without the loyalty oaths. This bill passed, but there was no mention of episcopal consecration. Subsequently Mason Locke Weems and Edward Gnatt, who had sought ordination in England for almost a year, were ordained deacon and priest, but Seabury had to mark time.[12]

The reasons why Seabury was not granted consecration had been expressed earlier by Archbishop Moore. The Connecticut Episcopal clergy had tried to answer the archbishop's request for confirmation that the Connecticut legislature would not object to a bishop. In January 1784, Jeremiah Leaming, Abraham Jarvis, and Bela Hubbard journeyed to New Haven to confer with the state legislators about the settlement of a bishop in Connecticut. They were informed that an act had already been passed to cover their request. It read, "No sect is invested with privileges superior to another. No creed is established, and no test act excludes any person from holding any offices in government. . . . The regulations, therefore, grant to every person, full liberty to adopt such creed as he pleases and secure to every denomination, the power and privilege of worshipping according to the dictates of their conscience."[13] Although the state officials and the Episcopal clergy thought this act should answer the archbishop's question, it apparently did not. Furthermore, the Connecticut clergy's reply made no mention of financial support for Seabury, nor did they indicate whether they had informed and consulted the laity about their episcopal scheme. In view of these circumstances Archbishop Moore did not encourage Seabury to pursue consecration.

Another factor that Seabury believed undermined his position in the judgment of the English hierarchy was reports from Nova Scotia describing the number of Anglican Loyalists who were settling there. Of particular concern to Seabury was a communication in early 1784 which claimed that three Connecticut clergymen and a large proportion of their congregations were expected that summer. Those specifically mentioned by Seabury were Bela Hubbard of New Haven, Samuel Andrews of Wallingford, and James Scoville of Waterbury. Although Hubbard did not remove to Nova Scotia as rumored, Andrews and Scoville did, and they were joined by another colleague, Richard Samuel Clark. Understandably Seabury complained, "This intelligence operates against me. For if these gentlemen cannot, or if they and their congregations do not choose to stay in Connecticut, why should a Bishop go there?"[14]

It is not absolutely clear who made the final decision against Seabury's consecration. Archbishop Moore felt an act of parliament was necessary to permit it, but he did not initiate the legislation to implement it, nor did anyone else. In his *Memoirs* for August 13, 1784, Seabury listed seven reasons why the British ministry objected to his consecration. First, they felt that a bishop should be settled in Nova Scotia. Second and third Connecticut was only one state, and to be sure there would be no adverse reaction in America, Congress should request it. Fourth and fifth, since the laity had not petitioned for Seabury's consecration, it was assumed by the ministry that they opposed it. Sixth, the absence of any organized diocese deprived a bishop of support. Last, "that not having sent Bps. into America while the 13 states were subject to Great Britain, it would have a very suspicious look to do it now, and would probably create, or augment ill will in that country against G. B."[15] Seabury realized the futility of trying to argue with the archbishop and the ministry. It is certain the British ministry was not about to do anything to antagonize America whether the bishops approved it or not. The Connecticut episcopal scheme had come to a dead end in England.

SCOTTISH CONSECRATION

There was, however, a clergyman in the Church of England, George Berkeley, son of the famous philosopher, Bishop Berkeley of Cloyne, who earlier anticipated Seabury's defeat in England. Berkeley, in November 1783, wrote to Bishop John Skinner of the Scottish Episcopal church: "I have this day heard that a respectable Presbyter, well recommended from America, has arrived in London seeking what, it seems, in the present state of affairs, he cannot expect to receive in our church. Surely, dear Sir, the Scotch Prelates, who are not shackled by any Erastian connexion, will not send this suppliant away."[16] Berkeley, unknown to Seabury, opened the door for Seabury's consecration, because Bishop Skinner made a favorable reply. Had Seabury known of this correspondence he could have saved himself a great deal of time, effort, and expense.

As early as May 1784, Seabury advised Abraham Jarvis that it appeared necessary for him to turn to the nonjuror bishops of Scotland and request consecration. He requested confirmation that consecration in Scotland would be acceptable, but he received no reply. Seabury waited until the end of August before he made an overt gesture toward the Scottish bishops. The absence of a reply from America he interpreted to mean consent, for on August 31, 1784, he asked a former associate from America, Myles Cooper, who was senior minister of the New English Chapel in Edinburgh, to acquaint the local nonjuring minister with his request. John Allan relayed Seabury's message to Robert Kilgour, primus of Scotland. A meeting of nonjurors was held and Seabury's request for consecration approved. When Seabury received the news, he replied, "I propose through the favor of God's good providence, to be at Aberdeen by the 10th of November, and shall there wait the convening of the Bishops, who have so humanely taken this matter under their management."[17]

The opening of the way to consecration for Seabury in Scotland probably ended an intense internal struggle for him. Determined as he was to complete his mission, an opportunity to receive consecration from Bishop Cartwright of Shewsbury, "an irregular nonjuror of the Separatist party in England," must have presented at least a momentary appeal to Seabury. But the fact that Cartwright was of an uncanonically consecrated line of bishops, those often consecrated by one bishop instead of the canonical number of three, raised serious questions about its validity, and Seabury declined Bishop Cartwright's offer.[18] Moreover, the idea to seek consecration from the Danish church must have been another possibility Seabury considered. Perhaps Seabury had learned that his mentor, Dr. Johnson, had entertained this possibility as a solution to the episcopal campaign in the 1760s. He probably knew that the Danish bishops had expressed a willingness to ordain deacons and priests for American Episcopalians. Indeed, the grandson of Samuel Seabury, W. J. Seabury, contends that it was Dr. Martin Routh of Magdalen College, Oxford, who dissuaded his grandfather of the validity of the Danish succession and persuaded him not to pursue a Danish consecration as an acceptable alternative.[19]

Thus, the consecration of Dr. Samuel Seabury in Aberdeen, Scotland, on November 14, 1784, by the Right Reverend Robert Kilgour, bishop of Aberdeen and primus of Scotland, the Right Reverend Arthur Petrie, bishop of Ross and Moray, and the Right Reverend John Skinner, coadjutor, was an achievement of great personal and symbolic significance. The responsiveness and cordiality of the Scottish bishops must have overwhelmed Seabury after his months of delay and frustration in England. Years of proepiscopal agitation by a coterie of American Episcopalians in the prewar and postwar decades had finally succeeded. But at the very time Seabury was enjoying his moment of triumph, the basis was laid for a new round in the episcopal controversy among American churchmen. Even before he left Aberdeen on his return to England, the first evidence of the impending struggle appeared.

In November 1784, a letter from one of Aberdeen's native sons, William Smith, reached the nonjurors. In this letter, Smith opposed the consecration of Seabury forcefully and claimed that such an act would be a stroke against episcopacy. He also claimed (with or without firsthand information is not known) that the archbishops of Canterbury and York had not thought Seabury a proper candidate for bishop since he had served against the United States in the Revolution. In the second place, Smith asserted that Seabury's effort to obtain episcopal consecration had come too soon after the war and had the support of too few Episcopalians. Moreover, the secret manner in which the scheme was devised would cause Seabury to be ignored by many church people when he returned. These objections registered by Smith were probably valid, for Seabury's consecration did complicate the episcopal question for most American churchmen. However, it is difficult to explain Smith's attack, since he too had tried to promote a scheme to become a bishop in Maryland in 1783. Possibly Smith reasoned that Seabury's consecration in Scotland would hinder or prevent his own consecration in England at a future date. This was an actual possibility, because the English bishops were prohibited by law from recognizing the nonjurors. If the English bishops ignored the American Episcopal churches because of Seabury's consecration, the main body of American Episcopalians would be cut off from their parent church without ever having had a voice in the matter.

Seabury's consecration in 1784 by the nonjurors did have far-reaching political implications. Episcopacy had been reestablished in Scotland in 1661 by Charles II of the House of Stuart. After the Glorious Revolution in 1689, those bishops in

Samuel Seabury, D.D. (1729–1796). First bishop of Connecticut and Rhode Island, 1784–1796, from the Duché portrait, the gift of George Dudley Seymour, Yale Hon. M.A., 1913. Courtesy of Yale University Art Gallery.

England and Scotland who did not renounce their loyalty to the House of Stuart existed under strict legal regulations. In 1689 the archbishop of Canterbury, William Sancroft, and 400 clergy refused to take the oath of loyalty to William and Mary. By 1691 they were all deprived of their respective positions, but many found refuge in Scotland, where loyalty to the House of Stuart was prevalent. Their number, however, had steadily decreased between 1691 and 1784, for there were only four bishops and forty-two ministers who continued the nonjuring tradition in 1784. The total constituency they served was not over 10,000. Their religious exercises were restricted so that the clergy had to officiate in private homes and to no more than four persons in addition to the resident family. In rural areas, their places of worship had been frequently burnt, demolished, or closed by the military. Although the severe laws against nonjurors were relaxed in 1784, they had not been repealed because their personal political and ecclesiastical loyalty rendered them obnoxious to the English government and the Church of England.[20] Thus Seabury's consecration made it impossible for the English bishops to accept him. As a sign of their disapproval, the Anglican clergy closed all their pulpits to Seabury upon his return from Scotland.

At first Seabury did not seem to be fully aware of the political and ecclesiastical implications of his consecration. In December 1784, he wrote to Jonathan Boucher, a former proepiscopal advocate from Maryland who was serving Epsom parish, England, and advised him of his consecration. Seabury expressed the belief that his relationship with the Church of England was undisturbed. "Upon the whole," he wrote, "I know of nothing, that ought to interrupt my connection with the Church of England."[21] It seems incredible that Seabury had been in England sixteen months without detecting the enmity which existed between the English and Scottish bishops. Perhaps he did know something of the differences between the English and Scottish bishops but discounted it because he felt his mission was far more important than the internal political differences between two episcopal traditions. He was, however, soon made aware that he was in disfavor with the Church of England.

George Horne, dean of Canterbury, corrected Seabury's estimate of his relationship with the Church of England in January 1785. "I am truly sorry," he confessed, "that our cabinet here would not save you the trouble of going to Scotland for it. There is some uneasiness about it, I find, since it is done. It is said you have been precipitate about it."[22] This notice alerted Seabury to his unfortunate plight in the eyes of the English hierarchy, and he subsequently admitted to the Connecticut clergy, "Since my return from Scotland, I have seen none of the Bishops, but I have been informed that the step I have taken has displeased the two Archbishops."[23] The official church policy withheld any recognition from Seabury, and any request for financial aid from England to support an American bishop was out of the question. Seabury and his associates were now dependent on their own resources except for the moral support the Scottish bishops could offer.

POTENTIAL OPPOSITION

By the end of January 1785, Bishop John Skinner, one of Seabury's ordainers, warned him to expect further opposition in America. Skinner was prophetic when he wrote, "I see the difficulties which you will have to struggle with from the loose, incoherent notions of church government which seem to prevail too much, even among those of the Episcopal persuasion in some of the Southern states; . . . and whatever view they may have had of the future establishment of episcopacy in America, I think they could not have contrived more effectually for suppressing the influence and smothering the benefits of it."[24] Bishop Skinner had clearly in mind the actions taken in several states by Episcopalians to organize according to the plan presented in William White's *The Case*. But William Smith in particular was denounced by Skinner as an incompetent leader of the American churches. Skinner classed Smith with Alexander Murry, a former S.P.G. missionary to Reading, Pennsylvania, who disparaged Seabury in London by declaring that Seabury was the choice of only a few missionaries. Thomas B. Chandler, who had been in London for ten years, heard of Smith's opposition to Seabury, and in April 1785, he wrote to Bishop Skinner about Smith. "In my opinion," he told Skinner, "he [Seabury] has more trouble to expect from a certain crooked-grained false brother (of whose character you must have some knowledge), than from any other person. I mean Dr. S-th, late of Philadelphia College, now of Maryland."[25] Chandler knew from his prewar contest with Smith that he was a formidable opponent, but Chandler expressed hope that loyal churchmen would rally around Seabury.

At the time of his consecration, Seabury signed a concordat of seven articles with the Scottish bishops, and one of them was a source of future serious trouble. Article Two read in part, "The chief ministers or Managers of the affairs of this spiritual Society, are those called Bishops, whose Exercise of their sacred office being independent of all Lay powers, it follows of consequence, that their spiritual Authority, and Jurisdiction, cannot be affected by any Lay-Deprivation."[26] Any attempt to separate episcopacy from lay participation was destined for defeat in America. In 1785, Seabury was not sure the Connecticut laity would accept this position. The Episcopal state conventions of 1783, 1784, and 1785 had all received laymen as equals in all church affairs. To reverse this trend would be next to impossible, and to debate the issue would cause division and possible schism. Furthermore, several of the state conventions had expressed the intention of remaining as close to the Church of England in liturgy and worship as circumstances permitted. Thus the third article, which stated that the Connecticut Episcopal church and the Episcopal church of Scotland were in full communion, was also likely to cause friction. Article Five provided that Seabury would attempt to introduce into the American Prayer Book the communion office used by the Church of Scotland. The last two articles merely concluded the concordat and expressed the good intentions of the bishops involved.

Even Dr. Berkeley, who had prepared the way for Seabury's acceptance and consecration at the hands of the Scottish bishops, was troubled by the terms of the concordat that obligated Seabury to attempt to introduce into the American churches certain Scottish liturgical usages. Other criticism came from Granville Sharp, Esq., grandson of an archbishop of York, who had corresponded with the archbishop of Canterbury and received authorization "to assure the Americans, that if they elected unexceptionable persons, and transmitted proper certificates of their morals and conduct, and of their suitable abilities for so important a charge, he would do every thing in his power to promote their good intentions."[27] Sharp regretted that parliament had not provided for the consecration of bishops and speculated that by Seabury's going to Scotland for consecration the issue of episcopacy would be further complicated for the American churches.

Another American in Britain, Jacob Duché, was worried about the reception Seabury would receive in the United States by Episcopal churchmen. Duché wrote to William White on December 1, 1784, and advised him of Seabury's consecration by three nonjuring bishops and added that "the succession of those Bishops is indisputable, of which he brings ample Testimonies." Duché then urged White and the Episcopal clergy to "receive him [Seabury] with open Arms, and thus effectually prevent the growth of Sectaries, from a Division that must necessarily ensure if this Providential Offer is not immediately accepted." Moreover, this letter did stress that Seabury by receiving consecration in Scotland instead of England was of a truly primitive character, unencumbered with any temporal "*Title*," or "Honors" or "Interests," and "perfectly disposed to yield Allegiance to ye Civil Powers in your States." Then there followed a piece of advice to his former assistant, now rector of Christ and St. Peter's churches: "I hope ye will take ye earliest Opportunity to calling together a Convention, or Synod, or Convocation, or some General Ecclesiastical Meeting from the several States, to receive him, and at ye same time to fix upon an Ecclesiastical Constitution for your future Union and Comfort."[28]

In his effort to promote good relations among American Episcopalians, Duché tended to gloss over potential differences that were matters of conviction and practice. He was, however, correct in asserting that the ecclesiastical succession of which Seabury had become a part was a valid, regular, and canonical succession. Moreover, a free, valid, and purely ecclesiastical episcopacy, which Seabury now represented, was the type of bishop the prewar advocates of an American episcopate claimed they wanted. The consecration at the hands of Scottish nonjurors eliminated any possibility that Seabury could be charged with a secret or implied oath of loyalty to the king of England, as most probably would have happened had he been granted episcopal orders in England. Indeed, in many respects it appeared that Seabury personified many of the qualities and characteristics American churchmen preferred in their church leaders. But what Duché did not face squarely was the secret election of Seabury by a small coterie of clergy, the absence of any lay participation in the selection, the pro-British record of the individual, and the fact that a considerable majority of Episcopalians involved in the reorganization of the churches were determined that their churches when united would conform in polity to the ideology and experience of the American Revolution. The Connecticut hierarchical scheme, though sound in its ecclesiastical tradition, was clearly out of step with events and attitudes in the United States. Under these conditions, Seabury and his loyal supporters were in for a difficult period of adjustment before they achieved general acceptance.

William White and the clergy to the south did not learn of the Connecticut scheme until May 11, 1784. At the suggestion of Abraham Beach, rector of Christ Church, New Brunswick, a preliminary meeting of clergy and laymen was held to consider reviving the Corporation for the Relief of Widows and Children of the Clergy, which had been inoperative during the war. There were ten clergy and six laymen representing New York, New Jersey, and Pennsylvania at this first interstate meeting of the Episcopal churches. It was at this meeting that the Connecticut scheme came to light. Since the representatives present were interested in a national church union, they discussed and agreed upon three points. First, a delegation was selected to confer with the Connecticut clergy and solicit their cooperation in a plan for church union. Second, a voluntary meeting of clergy and laymen was scheduled for October 6 and 7, 1784, in New York, to pursue a plan for union. It was unquestionably the activities of the Connecticut clergy in electing Seabury and sending him to seek consecration that prompted the Episcopalians in general to proceed from the proposal stage to the action stage in forming their ecclesiastical confederation.

NEW YORK MEETING

A voluntary meeting of clerical and lay representatives of the Protestant Episcopal churches met in New York as planned. There were sixteen clergymen and eleven laymen in attendance, representing seven state groups. The New York and Pennsylvania delegations numerically dominated the meeting, for they had eight clergy and eight laymen between them, or more than half the votes. In contrast, Virginia had only one unofficial representative, David Griffith, because the Episcopal church in that state was not completely disestablished until December 1784. Maryland had but one delegate, William Smith, while North and South Carolina and Georgia were not represented. Samuel Parker attended, but he served out of a personal concern for church union after a convention of Episcopalians from Massachusetts and Rhode Island rejected an official invitation. John Rutgers Marshall was present from Connecticut, but he did not participate directly because he was committed to await Seabury's return before engaging in any proposed plan of union. Instead, he officially announced to the meeting the actions taken by the Connecticut clergy.[29]

William Smith was selected chairman, and Benjamin Moore, assistant rector of Trinity Church, New York, was made secretary. A preliminary constitution of seven articles was prepared, adopted, and recommended to the several state conventions for consideration. Article One proposed that a General Convention be organized. State representatives to the General Convention were to consist of both clergy and lay delegates, and Article Three provided for joint representation by two or more states. The New York meeting also felt it advisable to remain as close to the Church of England as possible in matters of doctrine and liturgy, consistent with the American Revolution and the constitutions of the respective states. Article Five specified that in every state having a bishop, he would be considered an *ex officio* member of the General Convention. The clergy and laity were to vote separately on all issues, but the concurrence of both was required to pass any measure. The seventh article set the first meeting of the General Convention for September 27, 1785, in Philadelphia, and every state Episcopal convention was invited to send delegates.

William White in his *Memoirs* expressed the belief that it was a significant step to lay a foundation on which the doctrine, discipline, and worship of the Episcopal church was continued and at the same time to accommodate local interests in a way that secured the concurrence of the great body of Episcopalians without any exterior opposition. Indeed, the ability of the meeting to agree on a simple and specific formula for organizing a General Convention when the known differences of opinion on the issues of lay representation, liturgy, episcopacy, and an independent church organization are noted, is remarkable. Moreover, the actions of the New York meeting paralleled closely the proposals of White's *The Case* and the new political practices adopted in several state constitutions. For example, the meeting was held publicly after the churches had been notified and invited. The laity were urged to attend and were treated as equals. The results were published and circulated, but there is no indication that the votes of the representatives on particular issues were recorded, as was becoming the practice in state legislative journals. Moreover, it was clearly decided by this body that a national ecclesiastical legislative body would be formulated first and the episcopal question or executive-type authority was postponed. A representative process was instituted whereby each local church, state convention, and each delegate to the General Convention had an equal vote in all decisions. This republican structure, supported by a majority of Episcopalians and formalized at the New York meeting, was in stark contrast to the hierarchical approach adopted by the Connecticut clergy.

Moreover, the first formal interstate convention of the postwar era used the name "Protestant Episcopal Church" to identify itself.[30] This was an important step toward the eventual official adoption of the title. This name had originated in Maryland in 1780 and was used to identify the former Anglican churches before it was officially adopted in 1783. In the eighteenth century the word Protestant, though originally applied only to Lutherans, had come to be applied to any form of Western Christianity not owing allegiance to the Pope. Since episcopacy was the most conspicuous feature which distinguished the former Anglican churches from other non-Roman Catholic bodies, it was a natural development that produced the title "Protestant Episcopal." Eventually this term was adopted more by usage and consent by the General Convention, and at the time only a few of the Connecticut clergy seem to have objected to the word "Protestant."[31]

The Episcopalians who planned and convened the New York meeting found a precedent for their action in the prewar intercolonial conventions of 1766 and 1767 held in Elizabeth Town, New Jersey. Both the prewar and postwar meetings took place in the same geographical area. Nineteen clergymen had met in 1766 and sixteen in 1784, but the adamant proepiscopal exponents were not present in 1784. Chandler, Seabury, Cooper, and Inglis were all in England, although Chandler and Seabury returned in 1785. But the postwar meeting was also different because it included laymen as an integral part of church government. In the colonial period the laymen had achieved virtual control of the local churches, but it was the Revolution and postwar reorganization that posed the necessity and provided the opportunity for them to augment their influence on the state and national levels of church life. If the laymen had been ignored in October 1784, there would have been another lay uprising as there was in Maryland in 1783. Furthermore, only one reference was made by the 1784 meeting to episcopacy, and this reference defined a bishop as an *ex officio* member of the General Convention. In other words, a bishop, if present, could discuss issues, vote, and serve as any other delegate, but he would not be recognized as chairman by virtue of his ecclesiastical rank. A majority of the meeting could carry any issue regardless of the bishop's opinion. No special rank or prerogatives were reserved for the episcopal office, nor were the state conventions encouraged to seek bishops. It was the plain intention of the New York meeting that a representative convention exercise final authority in church matters and not a convocation of bishops.

But the biggest difference between the prewar and postwar meetings was that in 1784 the Episcopalians were free to decide all church issues for themselves. Both the 1766 and 1767 conventions met in defiance of the wishes of the bishop of London. In the colonies where the church was established, the governors and legislatures had the authority to permit or deny the meeting of Anglican clergy in convention. In New England, the Congregationalists were hostile to Anglicanism and suspicious of their gatherings. Even in the middle colonies where religious tolerance prevailed, the Presbyterians kept close tabs on the Anglicans, especially when they met in convention. But after 1784, the Episcopal churches were free in all thirteen states to make their own decisions. Only the Connecticut clergy resembled the 1766 and 1767 conventions, because they took matters into their own hands without consulting the laity and again tried to persuade the English bishops to provide them with a bishop.

10

Impending Schism

"In ye meanwhile I cannot but lament the Prospect there seems to be of so Early a Schism among you."

Jacob Duché to William White
March 25, 1786

Bishop Samuel Seabury landed at Newport, Rhode Island on June 20, 1785. He preached the next Sunday in Trinity Church, Newport, before setting out for his destination, New London, Connecticut. Nine days after his arrival Seabury alerted Abraham Jarvis to call the Connecticut clergy together as soon as possible. Seabury acted with energy and dispatch; by December 1785 he had held two convocations, ordained twelve priests and several deacons, visited numerous churches, and informed the Episcopalians to the south of Connecticut about his ideas for church union. In the meantime the first General Convention of the Protestant Episcopal Church convened in Philadelphia on September 27, 1785, and officially adopted six of the seven articles proposed by the New York Meeting of 1784, and referred one article (IV) to committee for further study.[1] Thus the two different approaches to church reorganization were formalized in 1785 and continued to exist vis-à-vis for the next three years.

SEABURY'S PROGRAM

The first overt act indicating that the Connecticut clergy were committed to follow Seabury's leadership in church reorganization occurred at the August 2nd convocation held at Middletown, Connecticut. Eleven clergy were present from Connecticut in addition to a representative from Massachusetts, Samuel

Parker, and one from New York, Benjamin Moore. Three Episcopal ministers from Connecticut—James Scoville, Samuel Andrews, and Richard S. Clark—had recently moved to Nova Scotia because of their Loyalist sympathies and the migration of part of their respective congregations. Thus all the Episcopal clergymen in Connecticut were present at Middletown, but no laymen were invited nor were any present. After formal greetings were exchanged between Seabury and the clergy, the bishop delivered a charge to the clergy in which he emphasized the importance of sound theology, proper personal conduct, and the opportunity to revive the rite of confirmation. Then four prospective clergymen—Henry Van Dyke, Philo Shelton, Ashbel Baldwin, and Colin Ferguson—were ordained deacons. The first three ordained expected to remain in Connecticut, but the fourth, Colin Ferguson, was from Maryland.[2] At this stage of his episcopal ministry, Seabury did not hesitate to project his influence beyond Connecticut.

Seabury continued to extend his episcopal functions beyond Connecticut when later in 1785 he ordained Joseph Pilmoor of Pennsylvania and John Lowe of Virginia. There were six more men ordained by Seabury before the end of 1785, so that more clergy were ordained for the American churches in the last six months of 1785 than in the previous ten years.[3] Although parliament had passed an Enabling Act in September 1784 to permit the English bishops to ordain priests and deacons without the loyalty oaths, it was obvious that more young men were resorting to Seabury than were traveling to England for ordination. Once a man was ordained by Seabury it was natural to expect him to feel a sense of obligation and loyalty to the bishop. These ordinations also gave Seabury an opportunity to examine the candidates and to impress upon them his particular view of episcopacy. Later, Seabury was charged by his critics with extracting an oath of obedience from the candidates who were ordained by him, but this charge was not proved.[4]

Invitations to serve churches and confirm members outside Connecticut were readily accepted by Seabury. In his capacity of bishop, he visited Boston and Portsmouth, Massachusetts; Newport, Rhode Island; and Hempstead, Long Island; and ordained, confirmed, and ministered as each church required. Since there was no other Episcopal bishop in America, he believed it was within the scope of his office to exercise the functions of bishop wherever he was accepted. These extended activities naturally excited the clergy and laity in other states. Thomas B. Chandler of Elizabeth Town, New Jersey warned Seabury that resistance was mounting against him because of these activities. "I find that some people have a jealousy," he wrote, "that you are aiming at the rule of the whole continent in ecclesiastical matters; and they blame you for hastening to settle the Constitution of the Church in Connecticut, before the meeting of the Continental Convention."[5] The episcopal controversy shaping up in 1785, unlike the one in the 1760s, was almost exclusively an internal one. After Seabury's arrival in 1785, only one attack on him appeared in the major newspapers. The New England Congregationalists stood on the sideline of the episcopal contest in the 1780s.

Next, Seabury informed William Smith in no uncertain terms what he thought of the seven articles of the proposed General Constitution developed at the October 1784 New York Meeting. "But, my dear sir," he chided,

there are some things which, if I do not much misapprehend, are really wrong.... 1. I think you have done wrong in establishing so many, and so precise, fundamental rules. 2. I think you have too much circumscribed the power of your bishop. 3. But I cannot conceive that the laity can with any propriety be admitted to sit in judgment on bishops and presbyters.... In short, the rights of the Christian Church arise not from nature or compact, but from the institution of Christ ... and permit me to hope that you will at your approaching convention so far recede in the points I have mentioned.[6]

The authoritarian tone of Seabury's remarks was not intended to improve relations between Smith and Seabury. Perhaps Seabury derived some secret satisfaction in lecturing his antagonist on the proper way to reorganize the church. In any event, Seabury left no room to negotiate or compromise the issues with which he disagreed.

Not content with admonishing Smith, Seabury, on August 19, 1785, advised William White of his objections. "I hope you will be induced to reconsider the matters pointed out in my letter," he wrote. "The two points which I am most concerned about are your circumscribing the episcopal power within such narrow bounds, depriving the bishop of all government in the church, except as a presbyter, and your subjecting him and yourselves to be tried before a convention of presbyters and laymen."[7] A prelatical attitude permeates this correspondence, and the inference was clear that unless the General Convention concurred with Seabury's recommendations they could not expect his cooperation.

Chandler came quickly to the aid of his prewar lieutenant, Seabury, and urged White to try to persuade the General Convention to rescind articles five and six of the proposed constitution which made a bishop only an *ex officio* member of the convention and subjected him to the joint control of clergy and laity. Because of poor health Chandler could not attend the General Convention, but he exerted his influence against the inclusion of laymen in ecclesiastical meetings on the same basis with clergy. The Virginia convention of May 1785, in which Carter Braxton frequently presided as chairman, particularly incensed Chandler. In Chandler's opinion the church should obtain bishops before it created a constitution, and for this reason he praised the Connecticut clergy because "in Connecticut the constitution of the church is now completed . . . upon right principles."[8]

The leaders of the Episcopalians in Connecticut were invited to attend the General Convention which met on September 27,

1785, but they did not send a representation. In addition, Samuel Parker advised White that the Massachusetts convention decided against sending a delegation to Philadelphia because of article five of the proposed constitution. Although the Massachusetts Episcopalians did not agree with Seabury on excluding laymen from ecclesiastical meetings, they were unwilling to see him demoted to the status of merely a voting member of the General Convention as stipulated by article five. Seabury and his backers were unwilling to attend the first General Convention and take the risk of not having the bishop invited or elected to serve as chairman of that body. If the bishop from Connecticut with his supporters had attended the convention, one can only speculate about what might have happened. It would have been a miracle if Seabury and Smith had received each other amicably, but sometimes a miracle happens, as it did at a later date.

One week before the convention opened, Chandler made a last plea to White in an effort to persuade him "not to give your [his] consent to robbing episcopacy of its essential rights. I am the more urgent with you on this head, as I hope the time is not far distant when I am to see you vested with the Episcopal character."[9] Chandler apparently thought there was still hope White could be persuaded, but White's subsequent actions indicate that he remained unchanged in his attitudes toward episcopacy and lay participation. This was the last attempt Chandler made to sway White from the principles the latter set forth in *The Case* in 1782. The number of state conventions that sent delegations to the General Convention made it very clear that the majority of Episcopalians were in favor of organizing the churches first on a constitutional basis.

THE GENERAL CONVENTION

The first General Convention of the Protestant Episcopal Church opened on September 27, 1785, in Christ Church,

Philadelphia. There were sixteen clergy and twenty-six laymen from the seven states of New York, New Jersey, Pennsylvania, Delaware, Maryland, Virginia, and South Carolina. William White was chosen president and David Griffith of Virginia secretary. The first item of business was the approving of six of the seven articles proposed at the New York convention and the referring of article four, which dealt with the liturgy, to committee for further study. Next a committee was formed of one clergyman and one layman from each state to draft an ecclesiastical constitution, to reexamine the liturgy, and to prepare a plan for obtaining episcopal consecration for bishops elected by the state conventions. William Smith was selected to head this committee.[10]

Many of the men who were sent to the General Convention had distinguished themselves in the service of America during the war. Two of the clergy had served in the armed forces. David Griffith was ordained in 1771 and served in New Jersey and New York before receiving a call to Shelburne parish, Virginia, in 1774. In Virginia he signed the nonimportation agreement along with twenty-four other Anglican clergymen in 1774. During the war he served as chaplain and surgeon to the Third Virginia Regiment from 1775 to 1779. When he returned to Virginia in 1780, he became rector of Fairfax parish. Henry Purcell, rector of St. Michael's Church, Charleston, served as a chaplain and judge advocate in the military service.[11] William White had served as chaplain to the Continental Congress, and Samuel Provoost of New York was elected chaplain of the New York State convention.[12] None of the clergy present had been ardent Loyalists, and all of them had demonstrated a measure of sympathy toward the cause of independence before the end of the war.

There were several laymen in the first General Convention whose patriotism was well known. John Page of Virginia served as lieutenant governor under Patrick Henry during the Revolution and remained in the assembly until 1789, when he was elected to Congress. James Duane of New York had been a member of the Continental Congress almost continuously until 1783; then he became mayor of New York City from 1784 to 1789. Both Jacob Read and Charles C. Pinckney of South Carolina served America faithfully throughout the war. Pinckney served as aide to General Washington for a time, survived as a prisoner of the British, and finally was released in 1782. Richard Peters of Pennsylvania, nephew of the former rector of Christ and Saint Peter's churches, served the Continental Congress and in 1787 was elected to the Pennsylvania assembly.[13] Indeed, of the thirteen laymen who comprised Pennsylvania's delegation, seven were noted for their active support of the Revolution, and only one is characterized as "a moderate Loyalist." Although the other five cannot be clearly labeled in respect to the cause of independence, Samuel Powell was known as the "Patriot Mayor" of Philadelphia and John Clark as one who "served with great distinction as a Major in the Pennsylvania Line"; and Joseph Swift was a signer of the nonimportation resolutions of 1765 and 1767 who continued to support American interests. Besides, four of the five delegates from Delaware are identifiable as Patriots, and one of their number, Thomas Duff, was remembered for denouncing allegiance to George III and for service at the Battle of Princeton. In 1785, Duff was Speaker of the House for the Delaware legislature.[14] Thus, the General Convention was dominated by men, clergy and laity, who had demonstrated their allegiance to the principles of the American Revolution.

A General Ecclesiastical Constitution of the Protestant Episcopal Church in the United States of America was reported to the convention on Tuesday, October 4th. The eleven articles were based upon the seven proposals of the New York meeting. Article one provided for the meeting of a second General Convention in Philadelphia on June 3, 1786, and every third year thereafter. Article two required a state delegation to the General Convention to include both clergy and laymen, and article three reinforced this position. Article five specified that any state which had a bishop who agreed with these rules could have him admitted as a member *ex officio* of the General Convention. The right of every state to decide whether or not to have a bishop was guaranteed in article six, as well as a directive that every bishop should limit his activity to his proper jurisdiction unless requested to do otherwise. Provision was made for other state conventions to join the general body in the future by compliance with the constitution in article seven. Article eight placed all clergymen—bishops, presbyters, and deacons—under the authority of the state convention to which they belonged in matters of suspension or removal from office. The liturgy was dealt with in two articles, four and nine, and the theological position of the church was succinctly defined in article ten. The eleventh article stipulated that the constitution would become law when ratified by the state conventions.

The General Ecclesiastical Constitution made it abundantly clear that there was no attempt made to come to terms with Seabury. The state and general conventions were reinforced as the appropriate governing bodies in their respective areas. Lay representation was insisted upon as a prerequisite for admission into the General Convention. The sixth article, which restricted the activities of a bishop to his own state unless otherwise requested, was a direct criticism of Seabury. Any hope for cooperation with Seabury was removed by article eight, which made a bishop amenable to his state convention for suspension or removal. As far as the General Convention was concerned, a bishop would ordain and confirm upon request but would serve as a regular priest in every other respect.[15]

An incident occurred in the general committee which expressed the antipathy felt by some of the delegates toward Seabury. Someone made a motion that a bishop, if present in the convention, should preside. White, who relates the incident, does not identify the originator of the motion, but he does record that it was defeated. Then the same person introduced his motion again on the floor of the general session. This action apparently produced the emotional climax of the convention, for White commented that this motion brought on a debate, "which produced more heat than any thing else, that happened during the session."[16] Again the motion was easily defeated. White's personal observation was that "a spirit of hostility to the Bp. of Connecticut was manifested by some of the delegates."[17] Instead of making a place for Seabury in the General Convention, the unnamed author of the amendment to article five unwittingly demonstrated how far apart the two factions were.

The General Convention did, however, adopt a plan for securing bishops in the English line. A lengthy application to the archbishops and bishops in England was drawn up which emphasized the past relationship of the American churchmen with the Church of England. A request was made for the English bishops to confer the episcopal character upon persons duly elected by state conventions and recommended by the General Conventions. The application also included an explanation of the separation of church and state which had taken place in many states so that the state had no direct control over the church. The convention agreed to await word from the English bishops before sending episcopal candidates to England, but in the meantime state conventions were encouraged to elect bishops with the concurrence of the laity and to secure certification from the civil rulers that the application for bishops was in no way contrary to the laws of the state. At this time the convention made it definite that "bishops of this church will not be entitled to any such temporal honors as are due to the Archbishops and Bishops of the parent church . . . : that it be recommended to this church in the states here represented, to provide, that their respective Bishops may be called 'The Right Rev. A. B. Bishop of the Protestant Episcopal Church in C. C.' and as Bishop may have no other title."[18]

One wonders whether the first General Convention would have applied to the English bishops for episcopal consecrations if Seabury had not first succeeded in Scotland. At least one Episcopalian, Samuel Parker, credited Seabury with compelling the General Convention to move for bishops. Unquestionably Seabury's achievement and program forced the convention to face squarely the episcopal issue. It is obvious that the general body of Episcopalians benefited from Seabury's experiences in England, for the General Convention wrote in advance to the English bishops, explained their political situation, and waited for the bishops' reply before sending candidates to England. In addition, they solicited the endorsements of an impressive number of political leaders to support their request.

EPISCOPAL ELECTIONS

Before the second General Convention met on June 20, 1786, three state conventions—New York, Pennsylvania, and Virginia—elected bishops and secured certificates from their respective state governments that their election of bishops in no way conflicted with state law. A convention of New York Episcopalians assembled on May 16, 1786, and selected Samuel Provoost as bishop. The first eight articles and article eleven of the General Ecclesiastical Constitution were ratified, and articles nine and ten, which dealt with the Prayer Book and theology, were referred to committee. Then one important item of instruction was given to the delegates to the next General Convention. They were directed "not to consent to any act that may imply the validity of Dr. Seabury's ordinations."[19] The Pennsylvania state convention met on May 22, 1786, and elected William White bishop. Furthermore, an assessment of £ 350 was apportioned among the churches to cover White's expenses for consecration. Pennsylvania Episcopalians were the first to assume the expenses of a bishop-elect, and they apparently did it without hesitation or controversy.

The second Virginia state convention was held on May 24, 1786, at Richmond, with sixteen ministers and forty-seven laymen in attendance. The proposed General Ecclesiastical Constitution was agreed to. The committee which reported on the first General Convention to the state expressed the request that bishops be elected by the several state bodies, but the committee added its opinion "that with respect to obtaining consecration for a bishop to officiate in their church, they thought it unnecessary for them to take any step of that sort."[20] The discussion which followed this recommendation is not recorded, but it is known that two clergymen, Robert Andrews and John Bracken, and two laymen, John Blair and John Page, who comprised the committee that reported on the first General Convention, did not want a bishop for Virginia. The subject of a bishop does not appear in the convention minutes again until five days later, when David Griffith was elected bishop by thirty-two votes.

An analysis of the voting for bishops in Virginia reveals that Griffith was elected by the narrowest possible margin. There were sixty-three delegates, sixteen clergy and forty-seven laymen, at the convention who were eligible to vote. Since issues were decided by a majority vote, a minimum of thirty-two votes was necessary to elect a bishop. Griffith received just thirty-two votes. John Bracken got ten votes, and Samuel Shield seven. All the votes cast for a bishop totaled only forty-nine, so that fourteen or almost one-fourth of the delegates did not vote. If the total possible representation from the 95 parishes had been present, there was a potential of 190 votes, because a parish without a minister could send two lay delegates in Virginia. In any event, Griffith was chosen, but his supporters were so few in number that it is not surprising that he subsequently failed in his bid for consecration. The prewar resistance to episcopacy was still alive in Virginia in 1786 and destined to show itself again and again.

In all three states where Episcopalians elected bishops in 1786, the state officials granted certificates to prove that there was no conflict between church and state interest. Governors

Patrick Henry of Virginia and George Clinton of New York complied, as well as the governing council of Pennsylvania. Richard Henry Lee, president of Congress, and John Jay, the secretary of state for foreign affairs, supplied a certificate on behalf of the federal government. Furthermore, Lee wrote to John Adams, the American minister in England, and advised him of the episcopal problem and indicated how he might help. "It is imagined that before any thing is done in this business by the Bishops in England," he wrote, "that they will consult the King and Ministry; who it is apprehended, may now, as heretofore, suppose that any step of the kind being taken in England, might be considered here as an officious intermeddling. Should this be the case the Church of England Members in Congress have the greatest reliance on your liberal regard for the religious rights of all men, that you will remove mistaken scruples from the mind of the administration."[21]

Both Richard Henry Lee and John Jay were Episcopalian laymen from Virginia and New York, respectively. Jay was elected a lay delegate for New York to attend the second General Convention. Lee's personal approval of the first General Convention went a long way in aiding that body in its quest for episcopal consecrations in England. The sentiments of Lee were expressed in October 1785 to an unnamed friend. "It is with infinite pleasure," he admitted, "I learn that our church convention at Philadelphia has concluded their business with great concord. It was a circumstance of much advantage that their Council were not disturbed by the mischievous [sic] high church principles that prevail with the nonjuring Episcopalians of these Northern regions, who, with Bishop Seabury at their head, would have been very sufficient to disturb the Moderate Councils of any Whig assembly in the world."[22] It was fortunate for the General Convention that it had not tried to negotiate or compromise with Seabury in 1785, because it might well have lost the support of powerful and influential laymen like Lee and Jay.

John Jay expressed his sentiment about bishops to John Adams in a cover letter he wrote for Richard Henry Lee's correspondence on November 1, 1785. As an active Episcopalian, a vestryman of Trinity Church, New York, and a future member of the General Convention, Jay could and did inform Adams of the internal attitude of his fellow churchmen toward episcopacy. First, he emphasized, "The Convention is not inclined to acknowledge or have any thing to do with Mr. Seabury." The authoritarian attitude of Seabury and his independent actions, in addition to his former political loyalty to England, rendered him unacceptable to the Episcopalians in general. Second, there were others at the convention who did not particularly want bishops at all, but they were willing to accept a moderate or constitutional episcopacy for the sake of harmony within their ranks. Jay identified himself as one of those to whom "bishops are of little importance."[23] But he was willing to accept bishops if they were subject to convention control. Under no circumstances did he approve of the Seabury type of episcopacy. Jay was committed to the principles of representative government, and unless these same principles were applied to episcopacy, he would have opposed it.[24] Furthermore, Jay wanted no part in any scheme that would remind Americans of the former British authority. In his attitudes Jay represented the majority position of the General Convention.

Perhaps John Jay was encouraged in his reservations about bishops by his wife, Sarah Van Brugh Livingston. After graduation from King's College in 1764 and admission to the bar in 1768, Jay married Sarah Livingston, daughter of William Livingston. William Livingston was one of a trio including William Smith and John Morin Scott, all Presbyterians, who opposed vigorously the proepiscopal scheme of Johnson and Chandler in the 1760s in the *New York Gazette*. Whether Sarah shared her father's views about bishops is not known, but if she did, she undoubtedly shared them with her husband. In any event, Jay's influence on the settlement of the episcopal controversy reflects the distaste of the Presbyterians toward episcopacy, although his early Anglican training kept him from arguing the issue. Perhaps the presence of his son-in-law in the Episcopal church councils moderated Livingston's earlier abhorrence of bishops, for "after the revolution, Mr. Livingston made not the smallest opposition to the introduction of bishops."[25] In New York it is probable that the marriage of a loyal churchman into a noted Presbyterian family and his subsequent stand on episcopacy cooled the heated tension that existed between the two religious communions for many years.

John Adams, armed with the correspondence of Lee and Jay, visited the archbishop of Canterbury, John Moore, and presented the request of the General Convention for episcopal consecrations. After he explained that his actions were of a personal and not an official nature, he discussed the problem of episcopacy in America. The one question which Archbishop Moore was most concerned about was whether an Episcopal bishop's consecration in England would be viewed as an act of interfering in American affairs. Adams assured the archbishop that "the people of the United States, in general, were for a liberal and generous toleration." Then Adams showed both the letters of Lee and Jay to the archbishop.[26] The reaction of the archbishop to these letters is not related, but he could obviously see that the American Episcopalians, in general, were very careful and cautious in their attitude toward bishops. The General Convention was not obsessed with the need for bishops, but it was desirous of retaining a measure of its traditional form of polity. Unquestionably the archbishop could see that the convention was determined to control its bishops. With full knowledge of these facts, the archbishop favored the request, and Adams was able to report success in his unofficial ecclesiastical mission.

Not all the Episcopalian state conventions complied with the General Convention's recommendation to elect bishops. Massachusetts Episcopalians decided to accept Seabury's guidance in matters of reorganization on November 15, 1785.[27] South

Carolina held a convention on April 26, 1786, ratified eight of
the articles in the General Ecclesiastical Constitution, referred
two to committee for study, and rejected article six, dealing
with the selection of bishops by the state conventions.[28] South
Carolina felt that this article was stated ambiguously so that it
could be construed to give the General Convention authority to
select a bishop for a state. Thus an amendment was prepared
for the next General Convention, but the state convention rejected the article outright. There was no bishop selected in
South Carolina. Also the New Jersey convention, which sat
from May 16–19, 1786, did not elect a bishop.[29] They did not
record their reasons for not selecting an episcopal candidate,
although they were ready to cooperate in all other matters.

In Maryland there was apparently no state convention in
1785, nor was one held until October 24, 1786, four months
after the second General Convention of June 20, 1786. Naturally the Maryland Episcopalians did nothing to forward
Smith's episcopal candidacy under these conditions. There was
a serious attendance problem even in the 1786 meeting, for
only six clergymen and five laymen attended.[30] The crisis in the
Maryland church was probably due to growing disapproval of
William Smith's personal conduct. Late in 1786 it became
known that two laymen, Thomas Cradock and Samuel Johnston, and two clergy, William West and John Andrews, planned
to prefer charges of misconduct against Smith. The charges
grew out of an alleged incident at the New York convention in
October 1784, where Smith was reportedly intoxicated. Ru-
mors of the impending clash between Smith and his four ac-
cusers possibly prevented a state convention in 1785 and account for the very small convention in 1786. One thing is sure.
Maryland took no action to advance the episcopal scheme of
the General Convention on a state or national level. Although
the charges against Smith were never proved, their existence
was enough to prevent the General Convention from certifying
Smith for episcopal consecration.[31]

It is impossible to tell from this distance whether Smith was guilty of the charges, nor is it possible to determine whether the incident was related to the determination of some Maryland laymen not to have a bishop in their church. It appears that the Maryland opponents of episcopacy could not have found a more effective way to scuttle the episcopal scheme for Maryland, as it was not proper to elect another bishop until Smith was convicted or vindicated, and this determination would take some time. The laity apparently did not press the charges once they were made, nor did they drop them. On the other hand, Smith was never officially cleared of the accusation though he vowed he would be, once brought to trial. The result was simply that the way to procure a bishop for the Maryland Episcopalians was blocked and remained closed until 1792.

REACTIONS TO THE GENERAL CONVENTION

At the very time the General Convention was gaining some support for its episcopal scheme, the adherents to Seabury's cause were growing more denunciatory in their remarks about the General Convention. Edward Bass of Newburyport, Massachusetts deplored the attitude of the General Convention toward Seabury. "I have always been of the opinion," he admitted to Parker, "that we never should coalesce with these gentry, and that it was much more natural for us to endeavour to come to a uniformity in these four Northern States. I could never learn that in any of their meetings and debates they have ever taken the least notice of Bishop Seabury. . . . For my part, I wish to have little to do with them."[32] Jonathan Boucher, in Epsom parish, England, in his characteristic blunt manner, castigated the General Convention with his own choice words. "The alarming symptoms appearing in the Southern States is indeed," he exclaimed, "very affecting, and shows a miserable deficiency in point of knowledge, as well as zeal, as could hardly have been suspected among any who had received regular episcopal ordination."[33]

As early as March, 1786, Jacob Duché in London predicted a schism between the two factions of Protestant Episcopalians. Duché was the first to voice openly his fear that schism was imminent. "I cannot but lament," he wrote to White, "the prospect there seems to be of so early a schism among you. Here we could not recognize Dr. Seabury's episcopal character. But with you there can remain but one point . . . the validity of his consecration. If something of this kind is not done, I fear an unpleasant disunion may take place, and put a stop to the progress of your church."[34] Duché's concern over schism caused him to oversimplify the problem of recognizing Seabury by the General Convention. If the American Episcopalians recognized Seabury, a nonjuror, could the English bishop receive permission from parliament to consecrate other bishops for America? A hasty move to bring about a reconciliation between Seabury and the General Convention could have blocked legally the way to episcopal consecration in England for Provoost, White, and Griffith.

White subsequently confessed that he did not question the validity of Seabury's consecration, but he felt it was inconsistent to acknowledge Seabury on the one hand and on the other ask the assistance of the English bishops who were legally forbidden to recognize all nonjurors. Thus White based his resistance to Seabury primarily on political grounds, but Provoost objected to Seabury's consecration on theological grounds as well. Provoost did not explain his theological objection to Seabury's consecration but openly contended that a nonjuror consecration was not valid. The strongest of Provoost's objections was based on his hatred of Seabury's loyalism during the war. When Provoost heard that Pennsylvania and New Jersey refused to accept men ordained by Seabury into their pulpits, he rejoiced. In his correspondence Provoost used his own cynical synonym "Dr. Cebra" for Seabury to reflect his contempt of him.[35] The intense animosity between these two episcopal leaders continued throughout the period of reorganization and became a major stumbling block to church union.

The growing hostility between the Connecticut clergy, their bishop and supporters, and the General Convention, was evident when the second General Convention convened on June 20, 1786 in Philadelphia. The fourteen clergymen and twelve laymen elected David Griffith president and Francis Hopkinson, a layman, secretary. A motion was made almost immediately to recommend to the churches represented in the General Convention not to receive into their pastoral charges clergymen who were subject to any bishop except one duly settled in a state represented in the convention. This motion was offered by White of Pennsylvania and seconded by Robert Smith of South Carolina. The convention left no doubt about what it thought of Seabury's activities, but when Provoost introduced a motion that the convention do nothing to imply the validity of Seabury's consecration, it was defeated.[36] Thus there was a limit beyond which the majority of Episcopalians were unwilling to go in their resistance to Seabury.

In the second place, the reply of the archbishop of Canterbury to the request for episcopal consecration was presented. The English bishops were favorably disposed to grant the American request, but they had heard about certain alterations which the American churchmen had made in their church government and liturgy, and they wanted their questions answered. A committee was appointed to draft a reply and include a copy of the General Ecclesiastical Constitution and the revised Prayer Book. This committee was also empowered to call a General Convention whenever a majority felt it necessary.

The convention next reviewed the General Ecclesiastical Constitution prepared in 1785 and agreed to six articles with a few minor revisions. Article five was clarified to specify that a bishop would be considered an *ex officio* member of the General Convention. The eighth article was amended so that at the trial of a bishop none but a bishop should pronounce the sentence of deposition or degradation. Articles nine and ten, which dealt with the Prayer Book and theology, were completely rewritten. Article eleven was changed so that a majority of the state conventions ratifying the constitution would put it into effect.

The committee appointed to correspond with the archbishop of Canterbury received a reply on July 4, 1786, which they felt warranted the calling of a General Convention on October 10, 1786, in Wilmington, Delaware. There were only ten clergymen and eleven laymen present, representing five states. Two very important states, Virginia and Maryland, were not represented. In the absence of the president of the last General Convention, David Griffith, the secretary, Francis Hopkinson, convened the meeting. Samuel Provoost was selected to succeed Griffith, and Hopkinson was retained as secretary. White reported the reply of Archbishop John Moore and placed it before the convention. A bill had been introduced into parliament by Archbishop Moore on June 16, 1786 to authorize the English bishops to consecrate bishops without the loyalty oaths, and it was passed. Then the archbishop pointed out a few issues in the Prayer Book and General Constitution with which he disagreed. He particularly objected to article eight, which subjected a bishop to a convention for trial and dismissal.[37]

On the issue of the Prayer Book the convention met the archbishop's objections halfway. The revisers in 1785, in an effort to achieve comprehensiveness, had eliminated the Nicene and Athanasian Creeds and excised the clause "descended into Hell" from the Apostles' Creed. Moreover, omission of the sign of the cross at Baptism was permitted, if desired. The Marriage and Commination Services were shortened and orders for Visitation of Prisoners and Thanksgiving Day were added. In July 1786, the convention did restore the Nicene Creed, placing it as an alternative to the Apostles' Creed, but the Athanasian Creed was not reinstated. By a small majority the previously deleted clause was replaced in the Apostles'

Creed. However, on the question of article eight in the constitution the convention voted unanimously to retain it without change.[38] Here they demonstrated a characteristic resistance to outside pressures in church affairs. The delegates did draft a courteous reply to the English bishops, but they were unwilling to increase the prestige or power of a bishop for America. If the English bishops had made the alteration of article eight a requirement for administering episcopal consecrations, one can only wonder what the American churchmen would have done. The convention delegates then signed the appropriate testimonials for Provoost, White, and Griffith in preparation for their departure to England.[39]

A PARTING OF WAYS

After the Wilmington convention, White and Provoost sailed for England in November 1786, and were consecrated bishops by Archbishops John Moore and William Markham, Charles Moss, bishop of Bath and Wells, and John Hincheliffe, bishop of Peterborough, on February 4, 1787, in Lambeth Palace. On April 7, 1787, Easter Sunday, Provoost and White landed in New York. There was no fanfare or opposition, and the event went unnoticed in the press. There was, however, a cloud of uncertainty hanging over the future of the Protestant Episcopal Church in America. Would the General Convention recognize Seabury now that two bishops of the English line had been secured? If the General Convention did recognize Seabury, would he and his supporters cooperate? Then there was the personal conflict between Provoost and Seabury. Could the two bishops be brought to accept and respect each other?

Before William White left America, he made plans to meet John Wesley, the organizer of Methodism, who had served in Georgia from 1735 to 1738 as a missionary, and discuss the problems of the American churches. In the 1780s, the English Methodists were the evangelical wing of the Church of England

and were active in America as well as England. White was personally friendly toward the Methodists, because in 1784 he with
Samuel Magaw invited Thomas Coke, Wesley's superintendent
of the American Methodists, to preach in St. Paul's Church.
The friendly relationship between many Episcopalians and
Methodists grew out of their common heritage. John Wesley
always urged the members of the Methodist societies to attend
the Church of England and receive its sacraments.[40] Furthermore, he cooperated with many officials and parish clergy of
the Church of England and scheduled his preaching services so
that they did not conflict with the established worship. Methodism reached America in the 1760s, largely by Irish immigrants
who had responded to Wesley. By 1768, Wesley received a call
for preachers to serve the nascent Methodist congregations in
America. In 1769, Richard Boardman and Joseph Pilmoor
were sent, and Francis Asbury and Richard Wright joined them
in 1771. As these itinerants preached from Boston to Savannah, they were frequently aided by the Anglican clergy. Devereux Jarratt in Virginia, Charles Pettigrew in North Carolina,
Thomas J. Claggett in Maryland, and Uzal Ogden in New
Jersey were noted for their Methodist associations.[41]

During the Revolution, all the English Methodist preachers
in America were Loyalists, as was John Wesley, and most of
them returned to England. However, Francis Asbury stayed,
and he, aided by the American converts—William Watters,
Philip Gatch, Daniel Ruff, and Freeborn Garrettson—continued to preach. By 1784, there were forty-two circuits and a
total membership of 14,988. John Wesley had requested the
bishop of London, Robert Lowth, to ordain his preachers for
America, but the bishop replied that they were not academi-
cally qualified. There obviously were other reasons why Bishop
Lowth could not grant Wesley's request in 1780. A war was on,
and any ecclesiastical act involving America was out of the
question without the government's consent. Besides, the
Church of England had never officially sanctioned Wesley's

William White, D.D. (1748–1836). Eighth rector of Christ Church in Philadelphia, first bishop of Pennsylvania, 1787–1836. Courtesy of Independence National Historical Park Collection.

methods, although many churchmen approved his work and aided him. Lowth's refusal was one reason why Wesley decided in 1784 to have his preachers for America ordained by three presbyters of the Church of England. Thus, Wesley, assisted by Thomas Coke and James Creighton, ordained Richard Whatcoat and Thomas Vasey on September 2, 1784.[42] They left for America on September 18th, and Coke was commissioned by Wesley as superintendent of the Methodist societies.

In December 1784, Baltimore, Maryland was the place where the American Methodists first organized. Here they adopted the liturgy and articles of religion from the Church of England as modified by John Wesley. But unlike the Episcopalians, the American Methodists did not admit laymen to their conferences. Furthermore, the clergy were elected by the clergy only, and the superintendent had veto power. Also, the clergy-elect were ordained by their clerical colleagues and not by a bishop as in the Anglican tradition. When Francis Asbury, appointed a superintendent by Wesley, assumed the title of bishop, Wesley's criticism was excoriating, but the American Methodists retained the title.[43] The organization of the Methodist Episcopal church revealed that the members were willing to accept Wesley's guidance as far as they agreed with it, but they were not hesitant to enact their own ideas into the law of the church. Their awareness of the political freedom won by the Revolution was apparent in Methodist organization. With the exception of the appointment of preachers, which the superintendent made, all other matters were decided by a majority vote of the conference.

All the Methodists did not agree that their church should organize without conferring with their Episcopalian friends. Charles Wesley, John's brother, poured out his disapproval in a letter to Thomas B. Chandler. Charles was profoundly vexed by his brother's actions in ordaining ministers, and he preferred that the Americans resort to Seabury for ordination.[44] Thomas Haskins, a native American preacher, thought it disrespectful and improper not to counsel with the Episcopalians. In 1786, he left the active Methodist ministry. Joseph Pilmoor, one of the first missionaries, turned Episcopalian and was ordained by Bishop Seabury, and Thomas Vasey was ordained later by Bishop White. Another itinerant, William Duke of Maryland, was also ordained by Bishop Seabury. Thus, the American Methodists' deliberate separation from the Episcopalians caused serious internal tensions and threatened further alienation. Although Wesley always considered Methodism to be within the Church of England, he apparently did not grasp the independent attitude of his American followers.

White secured a letter of introduction to John Wesley from Joseph Pilmoor before he sailed. Once in England, White was busy preparing for his consecration, and so he delayed trying to meet with Wesley. When he wrote to Wesley on January 24, 1787, Wesley was on his way to Dorking. He simply advised White that they could meet in a week or two for "an hour's conversation" if White was still in England.[45] Wesley was too busy to deviate from his rigorous schedule, and White was too soon gone from England, for he departed London on February 5, 1787. It was extremely unfortunate that White and Wesley never personally met and discussed the relationship of Methodism and Episcopalianism in America. It is too much to imagine that they could have resolved the differences in polity and ordination, but they could have set an example of ecumenicity among church leaders. Perhaps this example would have preserved the cooperation between Episcopalians and Methodists which had developed over a generation. Neither man seemed to suspect that this might be their last opportunity to promote unity between two religious bodies with a common heritage. In 1791, when Thomas Coke revisited America, he proposed the union of the Methodists with the Protestant Episcopal church, but the Methodist conference did not support it, and the Episcopalians after deliberation took no action.[46] When John Wesley died in 1791, the last cord which bound the Methodists to the Church of England and its American progeny was broken.

MOUNTING TENSIONS

The Connecticut clergy had felt the rebuffs of the General Conventions more keenly than the outside world knew. It must have appeared to them that union with their fellow Episcopalians was impossible, for on February 27, 1787, they met in convocation at Wallingford to select one or more candidates to go for episcopal consecration in Scotland. Their reasoning was this: if Seabury died or was incapacitated they would be deprived of episcopal service. They certainly realized that under these conditions the clergy and churches would naturally look to the bishops in the states south of Connecticut and to the General Convention. If the southern states obtained three bishops in the English line, they would be able to perpetuate the episcopal order in America, but the episcopal tradition of Seabury and the nonjurors would die out because they did not have the canonical number of bishops to perpetuate themselves. In 1787, time and events were steadily working in favor of the General Convention and the moderate version of episcopacy it upheld.

The convocation selected first Jeremiah Leaming to journey to Scotland for consecration, but he refused because of ill health. The group next turned to Richard Mansfield, rector of St. James Church, Derby, who also declined. Mansfield was a Congregationalist converted to Anglicanism under Samuel Johnson in the 1740s. It is possible, however, that Mansfield was the quiet, devoted type of clergyman, because he served the same church for seventy-two years until his death in 1820 and never seems to have been involved in controversy. Abraham Jarvis was then approached to accept the position of bishop coadjutor to Seabury, and he accepted.[47] There were also intimations that if Jarvis were successful in his bid for consecration in Scotland a third candidate would follow, probably Samuel Parker of Massachusetts.[48] Since Connecticut claimed the support of the Episcopalians in Massachusetts, New Hampshire, and Rhode Island, she could set up a rival form of episcopacy with three bishops in the three or four northern states.

Bishop John Skinner, upon receiving Seabury's request for Jarvis's consecration, saw that the proposed course of action would provoke further steps leading to schism. Skinner naturally regretted the rejection of Seabury by the General Convention, but he was not interested in any type of direct or implied retaliation. The reply Skinner sent to Seabury must have shocked him thoroughly, for in essence Skinner encouraged Seabury to coalesce with Provoost and White for the purpose of consecrating Jarvis. "We can hardly imagine," he wrote, "that the Bishops of Philadelphia and New York will refuse their brotherly assistance in the measure which you propose to us."[49] Actually Skinner proposed a merger of the English and Scottish traditions of episcopacy for the sake of church unity. This decision on the part of Bishop Skinner forced the Connecticut clergy to realize that sooner or later they would have to negotiate with the General Convention if they expected to perpetuate episcopacy in America.

White and Provoost were probably unaware that Seabury had tried to secure additional bishops from Scotland. Upon their return to America, Seabury invited them to join with him in a discussion of church issues. Provoost ignored the invitation, and White replied that as long as Seabury felt the General Ecclesiastical Constitution wrong in its essential points there was no basis for a meeting.[50] It is entirely possible that Provoost and White missed a golden opportunity to advance the cause of church unity at that time. If Provoost and White had known the attitude of the Scottish bishops, it might have made a difference, but because of political barriers there was no open communication between the English and Scottish bishops. Instead White turned his attention to Virginia, where Bishop-elect Griffith was having a difficult time gaining support for his consecration. Thus the two factions of Episcopalians continued in their opposing positions for almost two more years without any outward sign of improved relations.

David Griffith had been elected bishop of Virginia Episcopalians in 1786, but he had received very little personal or financial support to further his consecration. The convention recommended to the vestries that they collect sums of money for the purpose of raising a fund to send Griffith for consecration, but three years later it was reported in convention that there was only £ 28 S17 d10½ in the account. Griffith interpreted these circumstances to White, "The truth is that some of the friends of the measure wish to prevent, if possible, the introduction of a bishop into the state."[51] Unfortunately, Griffith does not elaborate on the opposition he encountered, but the strain of the conflict got to him, for in May 1788, he attempted to resign but could not because no convention met. Again in May 1789, he presented his resignation, but the convention declined taking action on it and Griffith died a few months later, thus vacating his office of bishop-elect.

G. MacLaren Brydon has attempted to minimize the Virginia opposition to episcopacy by pointing out that the state was in a period of economic recession. This condition can be granted, but the records show that the conventions of 1786, 1787, and 1789 all carried a balance of over £ 100, and they were able to defray the expenses of their delegates to the General Conventions without any difficulty.[52] The state convention secured these funds by an assessment of £ 5 per vestry throughout the state and was apparently successful. When the potential resources of the Virginia Episcopalians are compared with those of any other state convention, Virginia, with ninety-five parishes and fifty-seven clergymen, was far ahead of its nearest rival, Maryland, with forty-seven parishes and thirty clergymen. Yet Pennsylvania and New York, whose combined number of churches and clergy did not equal Maryland's, found the financial resources to sponsor Provoost and White. It seems, therefore, that the Virginia Episcopalians found an easy way to frustrate any episcopal plan while outwardly showing conformity to the tradition of episcopal church government.

The resistance to episcopacy in general and the "pretentious" episcopal claims of Seabury in particular was reflected in several local parishes as well as in state and national conventions. These local conflicts simply furnished added weight to the reasons that seemed to predispose the church to schism. For example, in 1787, two rectors in Maryland, Hatch Dent and Francis Walker, fought a furious battle over the validity of Seabury's consecration and the status of those whom Seabury ordained. Francis Walker, rector of William and Mary parish, vociferously denounced Seabury and those ordained by him. In Walker's view, Seabury was not a bishop, and his consecration was not worth "a fig." Such public criticism naturally evoked a defense in behalf of Seabury from one of those ordained by him. Hatch Dent was rector of Trinity parish in June 1787, and an advocate of Seabury's authority. As far as Dent was concerned, "No human or secular power can invalidate an authority derived from Heaven."[53] This controversy ended with Dent's claiming the power of Heaven for his side, but evidently many parishioners in both parishes and perhaps neighboring ones were upset by this incident. Furthermore, it is highly unlikely that the Walker-Dent encounter was the only event of its kind in Maryland.

The state conventions of Episcopalians in South Carolina in 1785 and 1786 demonstrated their distrust of episcopacy. In 1787, Penuel Bowen, rector of St. John's parish, disclosed how a local parish clergyman felt about Seabury in particular and episcopacy in general. Bowen was a former Congregationalist minister who was converted to Anglicanism. For reasons of health he had moved from Connecticut to South Carolina, but he still maintained contact with friends in Connecticut. In a letter to a friend, Bowen related, "My bishop is Dr. White of Philadelphia (not Mr. Seabury of Connecticut), who, I hold was made out of due time, and from whom I never would have received ordination. . . . The bishops late consecrated for our chh—I take have no higher notions of episcopacy. If they had or have—I hope the good sense, a sense of religious liberty in particular of the laity, will effectually convince them they are mistaken."[54] Bowen died fifteen months after he wrote his opinion about episcopacy, but before that time he had come to know the leaders of the Episcopal church in South Carolina. His attitude was very likely a reflection of the sentiment other churchmen expressed verbally but not in writing.

Charles Pettigrew, who was rector of Edenton parish, North Carolina, maintained contact with a former pupil, James Thomson of Charleston, through the 1780s. Thomson apparently conducted a private school, for he related his academic experiences to Pettigrew. However, he also heard the Episcopalians in Charleston discussing episcopacy. "Among your brethren," he told Pettigrew, "there are some whose hearts are panting after the gown and their heads aching for the mitre, or a more compromising system would have been adopted."[55] Apparently there was considerable discussion in Charleston about an alternative to episcopacy in church government, but the consecration of Seabury and the plan of the General Convention forestalled any attempt in South Carolina to develop an alternate source for ordination and confirmation.

One of the clergy of South Carolina, Henry Purcell, rector of St. Michael's, Charleston, was violently antiepiscopal and anti-Seabury. Purcell was rector of St. Michael's from 1782 until his death in 1802. He was so highly regarded by his congregation that they elected him a member of the vestry and did not bestow this privilege upon another minister for almost a hundred years. The growing debate over episcopacy must have disturbed Purcell deeply. Although he managed to control his opposition in the 1780s, he had published anonymously in 1795 his pamphlet, *Strictures on the Love of Power in the Prelacy.*[56] This pamphlet was the most virulent attack made by anyone in the postwar era upon episcopacy. It is hard to believe Purcell could have written his pamphlet in 1795 unless he had developed much of his rationale in the 1780s. In any case, the 1795 General Convention felt that the *Strictures* was so serious an attack on bishops that it conducted an investigation to find the author. Purcell was brought forward, and he apologized publicly, but there is no record that he recanted or changed his personal views.

The internal conflict over episcopacy in the mid-1780s was not confined to Maryland, Virginia, and South Carolina. Some of the Connecticut clergy had had time enough to give second thought to their scheme which secured the first bishop for the American Episcopal church. Ebenezer Dibblee, rector in Stamford, Connecticut, in June 1787, confided to a former S.P.G. missionary to Connecticut, Samuel Peters, that the clergy of the recent convocation resisted successfully an attempt by the bishop to alter the communion service by "dent of episcopal power."[57] By November 1787, Dibblee, who admitted that he was not one of Seabury's favorites, expected a "falling out" among the clergy. He described Bishop Seabury as one who "feels his own importance, is too impatient of contration [sic], too self-sufficient, and in his manner too overbearing."[58]

The seriousness of the internal strife among the Connecticut clergy was witnessed by two former S.P.G. missionaries, Roger Viets and Scovil Andrews, who had earlier fled to Nova Scotia, and in March 1787 returned to visit friends. While in Connecticut, Viets and Andrews attended a convocation held at Wallingford. Among the issues discussed was one for the suppression of all meetings of Episcopalians for worship without the presence of a clergyman. This proposal was intended to eliminate lay readers, an action which would place the laity further under the control of the clergy. The ensuing discussion was so divided that the convocation could agree on nothing. All was not sweetness and light within Seabury's own camp, and unless the bishop was careful he stood to lose influence among his loyal supporters.[59]

By 1788 there were serious problems within both the Seabury forces and the group supporting the General Convention. Neither faction was able to complete the canonical number of three bishops to perpetuate its episcopal tradition. White tried to persuade Parker of Massachusetts to journey to England for consecration after he realized Griffith's way was blocked. Parker refused and advised a union of the bishops from both sides, but his opinion was rejected. Provoost informed White that he had had no success in trying to persuade the New Jersey Episcopalians to elect Abraham Beach bishop.[60] Since Maryland, Virginia, and South Carolina were not willing to secure a bishop, it was impossible to persuade the state conventions representing far fewer Episcopalians to assume the responsibility. The Protestant Episcopal church in America had reached a stalemate. Unless the episcopal problem was solved, the two factions would continue to move toward a final separation.

11

A Negotiated Settlement

"I have determined to go to Philadelphia, and hope to see you there."
Samuel Seabury to Samuel Parker
August 26, 1789

Just when a schism between the Episcopalians in the northeastern states and those in the rest of the states appeared inevitable, a few devoted churchmen took the initiative to negotiate for union. Jeremiah Leaming, the patriarch of the Connecticut clergy, wrote to William White and advised a meeting of the three bishops. Leaming's attempt to bring the bishops together probably had the informal approval of the Connecticut clergy, since he had been their first choice for bishop in 1783. "To reconcile differences," he observed, "when they are come to full growth, is attended with so many difficulties, that it seldom proves successful."[1] The possibility of a permanent division between the two factions of Episcopalians compelled Leaming to propose constructive action. When his direct appeal to White did not produce a meeting of bishops, Leaming persuaded one of his parishioners, Dr. William S. Johnson, president of Columbia College and a delegate from Connecticut to the Constitutional Convention in Philadelphia in May 1787, to intercede personally with White.

INITIAL STEPS

The Constitutional Convention of 1787 exerted an influence toward union upon the Protestant Episcopal church by its example and success in drawing the states into a closer political union. In September 1786, a convention was held in Annapolis, Maryland, largely at the instigation of James Madison and Alexander Hamilton, to discuss the problems existing under the Articles of Confederation. The outgrowth of the Annapolis Convention was the meeting of the May 25, 1787 Constitutional Convention held in Philadelphia to which twelve states sent fifty-five delegates. Two plans emerged at this convention, the Virginia Plan and the New Jersey Plan. The Virginia Plan emphasized a stronger central government, but the New Jersey Plan resembled the Articles of Confederation. A deadlock resulted between the larger and the smaller states which was finally broken by the Connecticut or Great Compromise, granting equal representation to the states in the Senate and representation based upon population in the House. After a contest for ratification lasting more than a year, the Congress of the Confederation declared the Constitution ratified and arranged for a presidential and congressional election. March 4, 1789 was set as the date for the presidential term to begin.

Sometime during the Constitutional Convention William Johnson, who was a delegate from Connecticut, and William White met and discussed the problem of church union among Episcopalians, but no firsthand account of this meeting has come to light. Leaming, who with Samuel Peters had kept Johnson informed about the activities of the Connecticut clergy after Seabury's return to the United States in 1785, was advised of the meeting by Johnson. He was told that White's sentiments on church union were identical with his. There was a misunderstanding, however, between White and Johnson or Johnson and Leaming, for in August 1787, White notified Parker, "That our Convention, adopting the English Book of Ordination and Consecration, had made it necessary for us to adhere to the canonical number,—that besides this, I should be very cautious of breaking down such a bar against consecrations on surreptitious elections, ... —and that it would be indelicate to the English bishops."[2] At this point White still felt that three bishops in the English line were essential to the continuance of episcopacy, and to unite with Seabury on any other basis was improper. Perhaps the apparent ambiguity in White's position from July to August was due partly to Provoost, who stoutly refused to join Seabury or the Connecticut clergy. In August 1787, there was still hope that David Griffith of Virginia would soon sail to England for episcopal consecration.[3] Perhaps what White really agreed to in his discussion with Johnson was a coalescence with Seabury, once there were three bishops in the English line in America. Nevertheless, the moment of hope sparked by Leaming seemed to vanish as quickly as it had appeared.

By March 1788, the Connecticut clergy as a body were pressing for a merger with the southern Episcopalians. On March 11, 1788, William S. Johnson dined with Bishop Samuel Provoost in New York City, and presumably Johnson tried to persuade the bishop to cooperate with the merger effort. Unfortunately no account of their conversation or notation about it other than a line in Johnson's diary has come to light. Ebenezer Dibblee disclosed this mounting sentiment. "A coalition with the southern states," he admitted, "in religious concerns is wished for by the clergy in general." Dibblee did not enumerate the reasons for this shift in attitude on the part of his colleagues, but it is quite likely that they felt isolated from the majority of their fellow churchmen. Unless they altered their position, they stood to lose the fellowship and support of a united church in any program they undertook. There was also a hint in Dibblee's correspondence that some of the Connecticut clergy regretted having endorsed Seabury's visit to Scotland for consecration. "I am confirmed more and more of the premature proceedings of Bishop Seabury repairing to Scotland for consecration," Dibblee confessed, "but I shall never encourage another tour of Scotland for to perpetuate the succession."[4] Some of the clergy, evidently, believed that their bishop was an obstacle to union. Richard Mansfield, who had been selected to go to Scotland for consecration in February 1787, and had refused, urged the only possible alternative—a merger of the three bishops.

The resistance to bishops in the state conventions of Virginia, Maryland, and South Carolina from 1784 to 1787 was known to the General Convention. The convention had not attempted to pressure any state into selecting a bishop. William White, however, had personally encouraged David Griffith of Virginia and counted heavily on his success. In June 1788, Griffith advised White that it was hopeless to expect Virginia to support a bishop. The reason the state convention of Virginia never met in 1788, in Griffith's opinion, was to avoid taking any action to forward his candidacy.[5] His attempt to resign proved futile, because the few delegates who did assemble in Richmond in May 1788, never even elected a chairman. The stiff resistance Griffith had encountered since his election in 1786 was now evident to the entire denomination.

A month later White received word from William West about the May 1788, Maryland state convention. West emphasized the evident lack of interest in bishops. "Our last convention was the only one," he wrote, "at which I have been present without hearing something of a bishop."[6] Maryland, instead of promoting episcopacy, established two superintending committees of five clergy and five laymen each to supervise the churches on the eastern and western shores of the Chesapeake Bay. These committees also examined candidates and recommended them for ordination. The annual convention decided to elect its president annually by ballot. The thirteen articles adopted by the convention of May 27, 1788 contained no mention of a bishop. The Maryland Episcopalians washed their hands of any episcopal scheme for the immediate future. In reality they acted like Presbyterians, who recognized no prelates above them but reserved all spiritual authority for the assembly of elders, clergy and laity, representing the local congregations. However, the Maryland Episcopalians stopped short of granting their clergy the final authority to ordain other ministers as the Presbyterians did.[7] It is possible that the Maryland Episcopal convention would have assumed complete authority over clerical ordination had not the episcopal controversy been largely settled in 1789.

Shortly after White heard from West of Maryland, he received a scathing letter from Henry Purcell of South Carolina denouncing the legality of the October 1786 Wilmington convention.[8] This convention had completed plans for Provoost, White, and Griffith to journey to England for consecration. Purcell charged that the convention was illegal and unconstitutional because a majority of the state Episcopal conventions were not represented and the delegates who did attend from five states had not been elected for that convention. Robert Smith was singled out for strong criticism because, Purcell claimed, he had selected a minor, unbaptized, John Rutledge, Jr., to represent South Carolina. The vital records are not extant to prove or deny this part of Purcell's challenge. Regardless of Purcell's insinuation about Robert Smith, his charge that the Wilmington convention represented only a minority of American Episcopalians was serious, for it could have undermined the authority of Provoost and White and perhaps provoked further controversy. White did not dispute the issues raised by Purcell; instead he concentrated on promoting union. Apparently Purcell did not gain enough support elsewhere to encourage him to pursue the subject.

The issues raised by Purcell were never formally presented to a General Convention, but the charge that the Wilmington convention was illegal was a very serious statement. The accusation that a majority of the state conventions were not represented was true if Connecticut and Massachusetts were counted in the total number of states that had Episcopal conventions and if South Carolina's delegation was disqualified. But the indictment was not true if only the conventions which had previously cooperated with the General Convention were counted. In the 1785 and 1786 General Conventions, seven states sent delegations each time. Thus a majority representation of states was four, and this situation would cancel the charge that a majority of the states were not represented at Wilmington, to which five states sent delegations. Purcell's charge that the delegates who attended the Wilmington convention were not properly elected did not hold up, because the General Convention had the parliamentary authority to adjourn and reconvene without requiring a new election in the interim.[9] What Purcell did point out, however, was that in 1786 the state conventions representing the largest number of Episcopalians, Maryland and Virginia, sent no delegates and looked passively upon the efforts to procure bishops. It is likely that had the episcopal scheme been frustrated in the period from 1786 to 1788 the majority of Episcopalians would not have been greatly disturbed.

DIPLOMATIC MANEUVERING

By late 1788 White was faced with the real possibility that he might have to coalesce with Seabury to get the canonical number of three bishops to perform episcopal consecrations. His shift in attitude is evident from a letter to Samuel Parker, stating, "If there are any matters in which we do not think exactly alike, you may rely on it that there is an accommodating spirit on our part."[10] Both the tone and the content of the correspondence convey the impression that White and those Episcopalians who thought like him were ready to reconcile their differences with Seabury. This was a cautious and in some ways a precarious move by White, because he could have been misunderstood and suspected of infringing on the authority of the General Convention to handle the issue, but it was the only move he had left. Parker's response was heartening, for he reaffirmed the interest of the Massachusetts Episcopalians in church union. He explicitly stated that their acceptance of Seabury's leadership did not require them to reject other churchmen. A complete merger did not seem likely to Parker, but he added, "Still I conceive we may become so far united as to be one church agreeing in the general principles of discipline and worship."[11]

Two points emphasized by Parker contributed to the process of reconciliation. First, he pointed out that there had been a change in the political allegiance of the Scottish nonjurors. Charles Edward of the House of Stuart had died on January 30, 1788, and the only remaining Stuart was Prince Henry, a cardinal in the Roman Catholic church. Obviously the nonjurors could not continue their loyalty to Henry. A synod was held in Aberdeen on August 24, 1788, at which time the nonjurors voted unanimously to submit to the government of King George III and after May 25, 1789, to pray for the king and his family. A bill was introduced into parliament to remove all penalties against the former nonjurors and, although it passed the House of Commons, it was rejected by the House of Lords. Not until 1792 were the penalties removed. Nevertheless, the political objections to Seabury's consecration were removed, and in both England and America there was a lessening of resistance to him. The second point Parker stressed was the need to adjust the requirement that every state which sent delegates to the General Convention had to send laymen as well as clergymen. "If our brethren in Connecticut are so tenacious of the rights of the clergy, as not to be willing to yield any part of church government to the laity," Parker asked, "why need that be an impediment to an union?"[12] If this requirement were amended, it was likely that Connecticut would send representation to the General Convention. A compromise on this issue would also serve to encourage the Connecticut clergy who were working for union to continue their efforts, and perhaps it might persuade Seabury of the earnest intentions of White and his associates. If the General Convention could be persuaded to alter article two of the constitution to permit a state to be represented with or without laymen, it was possible that Leaming, Mansfield, or Dibblee would attend the next General Convention.

Both Parker and White labored patiently to bring a Connecticut delegation to the next General Convention scheduled for July 28, 1789, in Philadelphia. Not everyone, however, approved of this policy. Provoost protested vigorously to White, "An invitation to the church in that state [Connecticut] I conceive to be neither necessary nor proper . . . because it is publickly known that they have adopted a form of church government which renders them inadmissible as members of the convention or union."[13] Provoost was determined that Connecticut should first alter its practice of excluding laymen from their convocations before inviting them to the General Convention. Unless someone could moderate Provoost's malevolent attitude, it was obvious that he would be a formidable obstacle to any union involving compromise. Even if the General Convention voted for a merger and Connecticut responded favorably, no episcopal consecration could take place without Provoost.

Progress was, nevertheless, being made, for on April 10, 1789, Seabury revealed to Parker that Connecticut was ready to act. "I believe," he wrote, "we shall send two clergymen to the Philadelphia convention, to see whether a union can be effected. If it fail, the point I believe will here be altogether given up."[14] It had been five years since a delegate from Connecticut had appeared at a convention of the middle and southern churches. The last time Connecticut had been represented was October 1784, at the New York meeting. Then John Rutgers Marshall attended as an observer. Five years later Connecticut was taking the step toward merger with the main body of Episcopalians which it once refused to take, largely because it wanted a bishop first. Now there were three bishops in the Episcopal church, but they were not yet in full agreement about the terms for union. Unless the overtures for union expressed by Leaming, Johnson, Dibblee, Parker, Johnson, and White were reproduced and expanded by the General Convention, there still could be schism.

Another hopeful sign appeared on July 23, 1789, when Seabury wrote to William Smith in a conciliatory tone. Seabury and Smith had been ordained deacon and priest together in Fulham Palace in 1753, but they had not remained on amicable terms. They were on opposite sides of the episcopal issue in the 1760s and 1780s. During the Revolution they were on different sides of the political and military contest. On one point they seemed to agree, for both wanted to become bishop. In 1789, however, their personal rivalries of the past three decades had become less intense with the passage of time. The transformation was evident in the affectionate mood of Seabury's letter. "The wish of my heart, and the wish of the clergy and the church people of this state, would certainly have carried me, and some of the clergy, to your General Convention, had we conceived we could have done it with propriety. . . . I have, however, the strongest hope that all difficulties will be removed by your convention."[15] Smith apparently did not have an opportunity to reply to Seabury before the General Convention met on July 28th. Nevertheless, Smith's subsequent conduct in the convention revealed a marked change in his opinion of Seabury.

By the time the General Convention met, it is likely that the majority of Episcopalians shared the feeling of the New Jersey state convention of June 3–5, 1789. The most important item of business was the election of a delegation to the General Convention. A set of instructions was prepared for the delegates. "We are unanimously of opinion, that the union of the Protestant Episcopal Church in the United States of America, and uniformity in its government, are necessary for its prosperity and welfare, and ought to be promoted by all Episcopalians, we do therefore earnestly recommend to you, to move for, and use your endeavors to effect the same."[16] If the General Convention put the welfare of the denomination above the interest of each group represented, the controversy and tension which prevailed over the issue of episcopacy could be diminished, perhaps eliminated.

THE GENERAL CONVENTION OF 1789

There were eighteen clergy and sixteen lay delegates representing seven Episcopal conventions who attended the General Convention which opened on July 28, 1789, in Philadelphia. Bishop White presided in the absence of Bishop Provoost, and Francis Hopkinson was again elected secretary of a General Convention, but because of illness another layman, Tench Coxe, served in his place. After the opening sermon by William Smith, the convention examined the certificates of consecration for White and Provoost. Robert Andrews, a lay delegate from Virginia, reported that David Griffith was in town but that illness prevented his attending the sessions. Then Andrews disclosed that Griffith had resigned his episcopal election for Virginia, and the Virginia convention had not elected a successor. A committee was appointed to express the gratitude of the General Convention to the English bishops for the consecration of White and Provoost. One delegate from each state represented was appointed to a committee to review the General Ecclesiastical Constitution and to recommend any alterations, additions, or amendments thought necessary.[17] This decision opened the door to compromise on the issues which the Connecticut clergy would not accept in the constitution.

Of the eighteen clergymen who attended the General Convention, all had previously participated in the national convention except George Spierin of New Jersey, Joseph G. J. Bend of Pennsylvania, and Thomas J. Claggett and John Bisset of Maryland. Claggett had been ordained in 1767, but Bisset had received ordination from Seabury in 1786 and Bend and Spierin from Provoost in 1787 and 1788 respectively. Among the laity, however, twelve were delegates for the first time. Men like Francis Hopkinson, Samuel Powell, Thomas Duff, and James Sykes had been returned by their state conventions, but the absence of John Jay, James Duane, Jacob Read, and Charles C. Pinckney, all of whom were committed to making the Protestant Episcopal church thoroughly American, is very noticeable. Two of the new lay delegates, Philip Reading of Delaware and Samuel Ogden of New Jersey, were probably sons of Episcopal ministers by the same names and presumably were interested in preserving the integrity of their church tradition. Moses Rogers of New York and Robert Strettel Jones of New Jersey are most noted for their respective careers—merchant and state legislator. Dr. Gerardus Clarkson of Philadelphia was a quiet though firm supporter of the Revolution, while his convention associate, Tench Coxe, adopted the Patriot side only after parole from prison for being a Loyalist. Only one member of this new lay delegation, John Cox of New Jersey, is identifiable for outstanding accomplishment in the revolutionary cause. His military service under Washington and his leadership at the Battle of Trenton were well known.[18] Thus, on the whole, it appears that the clerical members, motivated by a desire for church union, coupled with a more moderate type of lay delegation, were prepared for constructive action.

The Episcopal clergy of Massachusetts and New Hampshire had passed an act requesting the General Convention and the bishops of Connecticut, New York, and Pennsylvania to cooperate in the consecration of Edward Bass for their churches. No immediate action was taken on the request, but a resolution was passed affirming the validity of Seabury's consecration. Thus the General Convention went on record favoring the consecration of Bass, provided the bishops could agree. Six days later a series of five resolutions was passed. These stated that a complete order of bishops existed in the United States and that they were fully competent to consecrate a fourth bishop. The convention also offered to do everything within its power to grant the Massachusetts' clergy request, and Seabury, White, and Provoost were requested to perform the consecration. Furthermore, the convention offered to intercede with the English bishops if White or Provoost believed that their cooperation with Seabury in an act of consecration would violate any expressed or implied oath they assumed to the English bishops not to coalesce with Seabury.[19] William Smith offered this set of resolutions which supported the Massachusetts request and placed the responsibility for a union of bishops on the bishops' doorstep. Apparently the General Convention was not particularly interested in gaining a full set of three bishops in the English tradition if this meant further delay. At this time they were not interested in the fine points of the English or Scottish traditions, for they were writing an interpretation of episcopacy through General Convention action. Perhaps some of the delegates felt that it would be better for the two episcopal traditions to merge, rather than delay so that one tradition with three bishops could ignore or minimize the Scottish tradition at a later date. In any event, the General Convention based its action on practical considerations rather than historical or theological tradition.

The General Convention again demonstrated its intentions toward Seabury by three other actions. In 1786 a resolution was passed in General Convention admonishing the state conventions not to do anything that would imply a recognition of Seabury's episcopal powers. This resolution was aimed at preventing clergymen ordained by Seabury from receiving state endorsement for assignment in a parish or church. This recommendation was negated by the reception of three clergymen ordained by Seabury as delegates to the 1789 General Convention. Joseph Pilmoor of Pennsylvania and Colin Ferguson and John Bisset of Maryland were seated in the convention without incident, and Pilmoor was appointed to a committee to prepare a set of canons. There was no discrimination because of the origin of a clergyman's ordination in August 1789. This was the same type of integration the convention encouraged the bishops to practice.

In a separate decision, article two of the constitution was amended to permit a state convention to send a delegation to the General Convention with or without lay representation or with or without clergy delegates. This liberalization of article

Samuel Provoost, D.D. (1742–1815). Fifth rector of the Parish of Trinity Church in the City of New York, first bishop of New York, 1787–1815. Courtesy of The New-York Historical Society.

two would permit the seating of an all-clergy group from Connecticut, but it also legalized the status of Robert Andrews of Virginia. On August 3rd, David Griffith, who had been ill for a week, died. Therefore, Robert Andrews would have had to retire from the convention, because there was no clerical representative from Virginia, but the amendment to article two permitted Andrews to remain a voting member. If Andrews had been expelled at the same time that provision was made for an all-clergy delegation from Connecticut, it would have created an embarrassing problem. The southern state conventions were always dominated by lay members, and to have one ejected from the General Convention probably would have produced a major upheaval. Lastly, article three was amended to create a house of revision whenever three bishops attended the General Convention. After an act passed the convention, it would be sent to the house of revision for concurrence. If the bishops rejected it, the convention could still pass it by a three-fifths majority. In the event that three bishops did not attend a General Convention, the bishop who did attend would vote with his state's clerical delegation, but he could preside. In neither instance was the house of revision or a presiding bishop granted the power to negate the will of the convention.

A committee of three clergy and three laymen was designated to inform the Massachusetts clergy of the convention's decisions to forward the same information to Seabury and the English bishops, and to call a special meeting of the convention when necessary. An adjourned meeting was set for September 29, 1789, at Philadelphia, and Provoost was requested to preach the opening sermon. In the short time of seven weeks the committee composed of William White, William Smith, Samuel Magaw, Francis Hopkinson, Tench Coxe, and William Burrows had its work cut out for its members.[20] A successful union appeared closer in August 1789 than it had in the previous seven years, but the consummation could come only if this committee acted promptly and interpreted correctly the decisions of the General Convention.

RECONCILIATION

The committee first clarified the amendments of articles two and three of the constitution to Seabury. "The church in each state shall be *entitled* to a representation either of clergy, or laity, or of both." This was good news to the Connecticut clergy, who wanted a union with the General Convention. Also some status was granted to the bishops by creating a house of revision and permitting one to preside in the convention if only one bishop attended. This was a far cry from the *ex officio* status a bishop was allotted previously. Next the committee tried to resolve a misunderstanding in Seabury's mind. Seabury was under the impression that the 1786 General Convention had rejected his consecration as invalid. Although a motion to this effect had been introduced by Provoost, it had been defeated. Thus Seabury was informed, "respecting your own *consecration* and the *Scots Episcopacy,* we are persuaded that you have fallen into some misapprehension. . . . Nothing was ever agitated in this convention concerning the Scots Episcopacy, but the contrary."[21] Perhaps White and Smith forgot the motion presented by Provoost and the heated debate over episcopacy which took place in 1786. At any rate, the time to forget past hostilities and imprudent remarks had arrived.

The English bishops were supplied with copies of the convention proceedings before the committee adjourned. William Smith, however, personally continued efforts to woo Seabury to the adjourned session of the General Convention. Certain members, he told Seabury, of the General Convention were working earnestly for union. He listed William White, Benjamin Moore of New York, and Robert Smith of South Carolina. In 1789, Benjamin Moore was assistant rector of Trinity Church, New York. Moore was ordained in 1774 and shortly thereafter became assistant to Samuel Auchmuty. During the war he was a passive Loyalist, but he was also a native American who remained after the war. The vestry of Trinity Church elected him rector after Charles Inglis fled to England, but a new vestry overturned Moore's election and installed Provoost, largely because of his patriotic record.[22] Because of his experiences Moore could sympathize with Seabury. The one influential member from South Carolina who promoted union must have surprised many. In the 1786 General Convention, Robert

Smith was in the forefront of opposition to Seabury, but in the intervening years he reversed his stand. Why Smith changed so drastically is not known, but his frequent attendance at General Conventions brought him into fellowship with White and his moderate associates. In 1795, Robert Smith was elected bishop of South Carolina, but local opposition to episcopacy was so strong that he could not adminsiter confirmation.[23] Seabury was also assured of William Smith's goodwill by an invitation to reside in the latter's home in Philadelphia with Benjamin Moore during the next session of the convention. On the recommendation of Smith and White the College of Philadelphia granted Doctor of Divinity degrees to Edward Bass and Samuel Parker, and one was promised Jeremiah Leaming if he attended the September session. These overtures of goodwill paid off, for on August 26th Seabury assured Parker, "I have determined to go to Philadelphia, and hope to see you there."[24]

In spite of the progress, there was one influential and determined opponent of the merger. Provoost emphatically told White he would not participate in the merger and argued that the New York delegation had violated its instructions of 1786 by voting for the amendment to article two.[25] Technically Provoost had a point, but the issue he missed was that the overall mood of the Episcopal Church had changed from 1784 to 1789; he had not. He did not fulfill the request of the convention to preach the opening sermon in September and claimed ill health as the reason. He did not attend the convention at all; therefore the consecration of Bass was impossible. Perhaps it was best that Provoost did not appear at the convention because Seabury knew how the former felt toward him. A confrontation between the two bishops, one obstinate and the other self-sufficient, could have produced an unfortunate result and marred the optimistic mood of the convention. Instead Seabury received a genuine welcome and responded by cooperating and concurring in the final decisions.

There were thirty-one deputies representing nine states in

attendance on September 29, 1789, for the session of the General Convention. Bishop Seabury attended, accompanied by Bela Hubbard and Abraham Jarvis from Connecticut and Samuel Parker from Massachusetts. Bishop White presided until the preliminaries were completed. Robert Smith made the first move to demonstrate the desire of the convention, to promote union when he proposed "For the better promotion of an union of this church with the eastern churches, the general Constitution established by the last session of this Convention is yet open to amendments and alterations."[26] After a conference with the Connecticut clergy, a request was made to amend article three to give the bishops the right to originate and propose acts to the convention and to negate any act unless supported by a four-fifths vote of the deputies. The amendment was passed with the stipulation that the House of Bishops must indicate to the House of Clerical and Lay Deputies in writing within three days of their approval or disapproval of a proposal; otherwise it would become law. The Connecticut delegation wanted a full negative for the House of Bishops, but consideration of this request was postponed until 1792. After Connecticut had agreed to these alterations, Hubbard and Jarvis were seated in the convention, while Seabury and White retired to form a House of Bishops.

From October 3–16 the House of Bishops and the House of Clerical and Lay Deputies met separately, revising the liturgy and the Book of Common Prayer, and devising a series of seventeen canons for the Protestant Episcopal church. Both houses initiated proposals, concurred, and raised minor objections, but at no time did the House of Clerical and Lay Deputies override the House of Bishops with a four-fifths vote. A study of the Articles of Religion was postponed to a future convention, and the bishops were authorized to call a special convention when they deemed it necessary. A standing committee was maintained to await the opinion of the English bishops on the request that Seabury, Provoost, and White combine to consecrate Bass. If the reply was favorable, the committee was to make the necessary arrangements for the consecration.[27]

The committee for the reexamination of the Prayer Book recommended a series of alterations which made the book more acceptable to a wide spectrum of Episcopalians. For example, after the inauguration of George Washington as president of the United States on April 30, 1789, it was necessary to substitute in the prayer for civil rulers the clause, "the President of the United States, and all others in authority." Throughout the liturgies the term "Minister" was substituted for "Priest," save at the Absolution, to permit the recitation of the services by deacons and lay readers. The Nicene Creed was retained, but the "hell" clause in the Apostles' Creed, which had been restored in 1786, might be omitted or supplanted by the statement, "He went into the place of departed spirits." Moreover the Sign of the Cross might be omitted at Baptism at the family's request. In short, a greater degree of flexibility was introduced into the 1789 Prayer Book. But the great feature of this book was the inclusion of the Consecration Prayer, accepted with the full concurrence of Bishop Seabury. Seabury had adopted this prayer from the Scottish order of 1764, for use in Connecticut in 1786. In 1789, it became an integral part of the service of Holy Communion with the concurrence of the clergy and laity of the denomination.[28]

Another instrument of worship authorized by the General Convention was the translation of the whole Book of Psalms into metre with hymns. The Hymnal that resulted was the first to contain hymns other than psalms authorized by a church in the Anglican tradition. It contained 150 Metrical Psalms of Tate and Brady (New Version), 6 Metrical Doxologies, and 27 hymns. William Smith chaired the committee that prepared the hymnal, and had he had his way fifty-one hymns instead of twenty-seven would have been included. On the subject of church music, both Bishops White and Seabury were conservative. Nevertheless, the twenty-seven hymns that were retained included "While shepherds watched their flocks by night," "Come, Holy Spirit, heavenly Dove," and "My God, and is thy Table spread."[29] By putting the stamp of approval upon these hymns, the General Convention sanctioned what had appeared as an innovative practice in some Anglican churches in the late colonial period. As it happened, the hymns endorsed in 1789 were harbingers of still greater musical contributions to come.

THE HOUSE OF BISHOPS

The House of Bishops made only three rules to govern their proceedings. First, the senior bishop, based on date of consecration, was president of the house. Second, a majority of the House of Bishops signing a proposal signified their approval. Third, a secretary to the bishops was selected from among the clerical members of the convention. Furthermore, the first bishops started a tradition of attending divine services along with the clerical and lay deputies. The simplicity of these rules was in keeping with the dominant attitude of Episcopalians toward bishops. No attempt was made to develop an archbishop or to wear mitres to distinguish bishop from priest. The participation of the bishops in the general worship services along with the other deputies was obviously meant to illustrate the spiritual equality of all men in the sight of God. The bishops also established the practice of settling proposals among themselves by a majority vote. Nevertheless, in the final analysis the bishops were still responsible to the General Convention and to their respective state conventions.

In 1767 Samuel Johnson and Thomas E. Chandler had proposed a "spiritual" episcopate for the American Anglican churches. By "spiritual" bishop, they meant a bishop who could ordain, confirm, and visit clergy, but could have no state function, title, or support. At the time Johnson and Chandler proposed their episcopal plan, no one was able to persuade their fellow churchmen that a "spiritual" bishop was all they contemplated. Yet the publication and promotion of the idea did serve a purpose, for it fostered the conviction of some that bishops should be only church officials. After the Revolutionary War, this was the only practical solution to the episcopal problem if the Protestant Episcopal church wanted to continue episcopacy as a part of its government. In view of the war and its aftermath, it was fortunate for the Episcopal churches that Johnson and Chandler had failed in their episcopal scheme. If they had procured a bishop in the 1760s, it would have intensified the growing hostility toward Great Britain and convinced many people, within and without the church, that the office of bishop was being used to serve the king's interest. This would have made it much more difficult eventually to solve the episcopal problem. The resistance of a majority of Anglicans to the scheme in the 1760s demonstrated that the members themselves were not interested in furthering any scheme that would interfere with their established practices or tie them in any way more closely to England.

The compromises that produced the union between the Connecticut clergy and the General Convention did not completely satisfy the Connecticut clergy. Bela Hubbard, one of the delegates, reported, "The terms are not altogether pleasing to us here, but they are the best that could be obtained for the present."[30] The particular point that disturbed the Connecticut clergy was the four-fifths rule whereby the General Convention was able to override the House of Bishops. Ebenezer Dibblee, one of Seabury's critics, derived pleasure out of relating that "Bishop Seabury did himself honor, but he returned with the loss of a fifth part of his dignity; as four-fifths of the lower house of convocation, made up of lay delegates, will carry any point against the bench of Bishops."[31] Although the Connecticut clergy tried to secure a full negative for the bishop at the 1792 General Convention, they were unsuccessful. It was 1808 before the House of Bishops acquired the full negative. Instead, the 1792 Connecticut convocation, which had omitted laymen from its meetings, accepted them for the first time; and two were sent to the next General Convention in New York along with the clergy.[32]

The English bishops did not reply directly or immediately to the request of the 1789 General Convention to give their opinion on the propriety of Provoost, White, and Seabury combining to consecrate Edward Bass. Indirectly, however, the English bishops replied when in 1790 they consecrated James Madison of Virginia. On September 19, 1790, the archbishop of Canterbury, John Moore, the bishop of London, Beilby Porteus, and the bishop of Rochester performed the consecration in Lambeth Palace. This action showed that the English bishops had felt all along that there should be three American bishops in the English line before there was a union with Seabury. In 1792, Madison united with Provoost, White, and Seabury to consecrate Thomas J. Claggett the first bishop for Maryland.[33] No objection was registered with the General Convention from the English bishops, and in this case silence meant consent.

The election of James Madison to the episcopate by the Virginia Episcopalians must have come as a shock to the General Convention after the first bishop-elect, David Griffith, had been frustrated in his efforts to achieve consecration. In 1790, Madison was president of William and Mary College. He had accepted the deletion of the divinity school from the college. Jefferson had approved of Madison when he was named president in 1779. Furthermore, Madison, unlike Griffith, was a native Virginian, trained at William and Mary, and well known throughout the state. He, too, had served the patriot cause during the Revolutionary War. If anyone knew the local attitude toward episcopacy in the 1780s Madison did, and he would certainly represent that position. It is also possible that the Virginia Episcopalians had come to the conclusion that it was in their interest to have a bishop and to have him represent them in the House of Bishops. Unless they were represented among the bishops, their influence as the largest single segment of the Protestant Episcopal church would diminish. Thus in May 1790, the treasurer of the state convention reported £ 126, which was quickly augmented to £ 200 by the convention to cover the expense of consecration.[34] There is no explanation in the convention journal as to how or why the money appeared spontaneously, but it was probably evident to every delegate that a bishop was now in the best interest of Virginia.

The consecration of Thomas J. Claggett was the first time an episcopal bishop had been so honored in America. There were two events which made this consecration possible. First, the Massachusetts Episcopalians had withdrawn their request for the consecration of Edward Bass. Bass's first wife died on May 5, 1789, and within six months he remarried. The Episcopalians of Massachusetts, feeling Bass's remarriage came too soon after his first wife's death, withdrew their petition to the General Assembly.[35] Second, William Smith had returned to Philadelphia in 1789, thus vacating his position as bishop-elect from Maryland. In 1790 the Maryland Episcopalians elected Thomas J. Claggett, a native son, and requested his consecration by the American bishops. As it happened, this was the only episcopal consecration in which Seabury participated before he died in 1796.

Behind the ostensible explanation for the withdrawal of the petition for Bass's consecration is an episode which reveals that not all clergy who opposed lay participation in state and national church conventions were in Connecticut. As it happened, Bass had been elected bishop by six colleagues on June 4, 1789, in Salem. Neither the meeting nor the election had been announced, but when Bishops Seabury, Provoost, and White were advised of the election they apparently were not apprised of these circumstances. These six Massachusetts clergy who were eager to promote the union of the church through a coalescence of the three bishops in Bass's consecration were soon overwhelmed by clerical and lay opposition to their actions. On September 18, 1789, William Wheeler and Nathaniel Fisher, the two senior ministers in Massachusetts, complained to Bishop Provoost that they learned of Bass's election only in the newspapers. So incensed were they that they denounced the methods and the election by their brethren.[36] If Provoost had needed a reason to boycott the second session of the General Convention, to which he had been invited to deliver the opening sermon, this was it.

After Tristram Dalton, a prominent vestryman of St. Paul's, Newburyport, Bass's church, learned of the Salem meeting, he and other leading laymen were furious. Dalton, along with Stephen Greenleaf, Benjamin Greene, Thomas Ives, and eight other laymen, had participated in the 1785 state convention in which lay participation in all future conventions was agreed upon. It is not surprising, therefore, that Dalton, who was one of Massachusetts' first two senators to the United States Congress, made "Dr. B. uncomfortable at Newburyport."[37] He was joined by the vestrymen of St. Peter's parish, Salem, who prepared a circular letter protesting that "neither our Minister, nor we ourselves, do yet know when, nor by whom that Election was made."[38] Had not the clergymen involved in the election withdrawn the request for consecration, a major battle over the issue surely would have ensued. What the laity seemed most upset about in the whole affair was the attempt to overturn their right of participation in the significant function of the election of a bishop. To them the principle of home rule and who shoule rule at home applied as much to church polity as it did to civil government.

The one man who stands out throughout the postwar reorganization is William White. Even the editor of Seabury's *Memoirs*, William J. Seabury, adjudged White "the master mind in the whole movement for union."[39] White knew how to take advice as well as give it, how to propose ideas as well as listen. He not only proposed a plan for reorganization; he demonstrated its viability in Pennsylvania. When it came time to negotiate with Seabury, White was wise enough to accept the lead of

Jeremiah Leaming and agree to the compromises proposed by Samuel Parker. Also, White had a sense of timing whereby he never rushed reorganization, but when it was time to act, he was prepared. The impression White made upon the Connecticut delegation to the 1789 General Convention prompted Bela Hubbard to exclaim, "Bp. White grows a better churchman and is a man of much humanity."[40] Throughout the 1780s White maintained a positive and open attitude toward reorganization. He personally communicated with the leaders of the Episcopal churches in every state. There is no record that he spoke one censorious word about any of his opponents or associates. For Seabury, White expressed the highest regard, although he did not agree with his independent actions. Finally, White was extremely careful not to offend the English bishops, even though it delayed for three years the merging of the full House of Bishops in an act of consecration. It was largely because of his efforts that a friendly relationship continued between the Protestant Episcopal church in America and the Anglican church in England.

12

Mitre Without Sceptre

"The power of electing a superior order of ministers ought to be in the clergy and laity together, they being interested in the choice."

William White, *The Case*

The successful negotiations between the delegates from the eastern churches (those east of the Hudson River) and the southern churches (those south of the Hudson River) in 1789 ended for all practical purposes the controversy over bishops within the Protestant Episcopal church. The hostility that existed between the Congregationalists and the Anglicans over episcopacy had ceased in 1775, and it did not recur in the 1780s. Moreover, in the crucial years of the eighties those churchmen who participated in the reconstruction of their church organization incorporated within it an ecclesiastical revolution in respect to episcopacy. For the first time since the Norman Conquest in 1066, the Episcopalians in America made a bishop of a major religious body an elected official of a convention of clergy and laity. Furthermore, the office of bishop in a major denomination was completely separated from the state for the first time since Emperor Constantine officially recognized Christianity in A.D. 313. In many respects, the American churchmen recaptured the "primitive episcopacy" of the early church and thus gained the very type of bishops Drs. Johnson and Chandler had campaigned for in the prewar years.

METAMORPHOSIS OF EPISCOPACY

In England prior to 1066 episcopal "election by the clergy and people of the episcopal city had been the primitive practice. . . .

Hence the generally accepted canonical form was popular election followed by the appropriate confirmations, a framework which could tolerate most political stresses."[1] This procedure could be traced to earlier church practices whereby bishops were made by the process of election and confirmation. There are also indications that the choice of presbyters and deacons, like that of bishops, was subject to the general vote of the church.[2] But in England, once a man became a bishop, he was answerable to those who selected him and was bound to their church for life. Before the eleventh century it was rare for a bishop to be translated from one see to another. However, once the role of church councils was developed, a movement that began at Nicaea in the East in A.D. 325 and appeared in England with the Council of Whitby in A.D. 663, the bishops, under the influence of emperor or king, increasingly became the only participants in major church decisions.[3] Although the right of the lower clergy and the laity to participate in the selection of bishops was continued, their influence upon other issues of the church was significantly diminished.

In the age of Bede (c. 673–735), the state of religion in any part of England depended on the activity of its bishop. The division of a diocese into parishes, each under the charge of its own priest, was still a remote ideal. It was Bede's opinion that preaching was the first duty of a bishop, but to facilitate his work he ordained priests to provide Christian instruction and the sacraments in the districts he could not hope to reach.[4] In the eighth century, a bishop still took part in every stage of the process by which admission was gained into the Christian community. He was, therefore, the principal instructor of candidates for baptism, and he frequently administered the rite. The bishop was the only one who performed the rite of confirmation. Moreover, it was the bishop who exercised responsibility for the discipline, doctrine, and administration of his diocese. The clergy looked to him for subsistence, and because of this relationship they were tightly bound by the bishop's authority. The development of this type of episcopal control was explained and justified by the fact that since the bishop admitted every Christian into the church he was responsible for their continued well-being.[5]

It was, however, during the Anglo-Saxon period that bishops were made members of the Witenagemot, the council of nobles. This was done by the appointment of the king in consultation with the members of the Witan, the king's advisory council. Once the English bishops became members of the king's council the distinction between their church and their state functions was blurred. On the local level, bishops served in the hundred courts and judged cases involving both clergy and laymen. In the everyday workings of society bishops became responsible for the settlement of feuds and conflicts as well as the supervision of the procedures of oath-taking and trial by ordeal. In a sense, they became symbols of legal right in both business and church affairs. As members of the king's council, they were often selected to perform diplomatic services. Although the number of bishops in pre-Conquest England was small (probably never more than seventeen or eighteen at any one time), their functions in the administrative and judicial service of the kings steadily increased, thus fusing their roles as church and civil servants. These developments, which demanded much of the bishops' time, were primarily responsible for the lack of organization and administration on the lower levels of the church. Before 1066, diocesan administrative machinery, where it existed at all, was simple and primitive. The modern concept of the "parish" with its canonical and administrative personnel was unknown.[6]

The status of bishops was revolutionized by the Norman Conquest and King William I (1066–87) who exercised a thoroughgoing control over the church in England. Episcopal selection was retained as a matter of royal prerogative by the Norman kings.[7] Under the Angevin monarchs, it was a rare occurrence when a bishop was elected without first receiving the endorsement of the king.[8] Even after King John signed a charter in 1214 stating that the election of bishops theoretically rested with the cathedral chapters, the king generally managed to get his man elected.[9] The result of this development was that bishops and archbishops, who had become intimately involved in state affairs under the Anglo-Saxon kings, were under the Norman monarchs given specific and additional duties. This situation necessitated the emergence of a group of priests and clerks who assisted the bishops so that they could better serve the sovereign. Within the bishop's staff, therefore, emerged the offices of registrar and vicar general. The first served as the bishop's permanent delegate in judicial affairs, and the second exercised the bishop's powers in all jurisdictional and administrative matters. Later, in some dioceses, the functions of registrar and vicar general were combined in the office of chancellor. But, in the meantime, the bishops were further removed from their sees because of their membership in the Great Council, and when parliament developed in the thirteenth and fourteenth centuries they were included in the House of Lords.[10]

The additional duties exacted from the bishops by the king were an outgrowth of feudalism. With William I all England was organized under the feudal system, and bishops were made his tenants-in-chief. Therefore they were obliged to provide knight-service, and it became rather common for a bishop to fight, and some died, in the service of their lord. But inherent in feudalism was centralization, whereby the bishoprics were located in cities and placed under the closer supervision of the archbishops of Canterbury and York. In the process of redistricting the sees, all bishops were directed by William I to appoint an archdeacon, who would act as their agent in their absence. Furthermore, in 1072 William I authorized bishops' courts, in which ecclesiastical pleas would be heard instead of in the hundred courts.[11] As a result of these acts, bishops were pushed further into the arena of secular responsibilities than ever before. But a consequence of this was that the king considered the bishops to be his servants, and thus he had a right to demand their services. By the second half of the fourteenth century bishops were expected to continue in the king's service, which necessitated their quasi-permanent absence from their dioceses. Against this background it is, therefore, not surprising that in the early sixteenth century, one of the prelates, Cardinal Thomas Wolsey, served as chancellor of England under King Henry VIII.

In the centuries immediately preceding the Reformation in England, diocesan bishops had come to be regarded primarily as secular magnates and officers of the state. The medieval concept of the prelate had become the accepted model of what a bishop was and ought to be. But in this process of episcopal evolution, the bishops' long association with the secular government had caused them to adopt secular modes of conceiving authority. Their spiritual authority became thought of as the right "to rule souls." No longer were the clergy considered in any real sense coadjutors of the bishops, but rather they were viewed as subjects. Bishops were thought of more for their judicial functions than for their preaching. When a bishop was in his diocese, he was probably known to the clergy either at their institution in one of the chapels on his manor or through his visitation. Even in the event of a visitation, it was usually the bishop's commissioners whom the local clergy saw and not the bishop himself.[12] Thus, English bishops, as well as those in other areas of Christendom, had moved far from the "father in God" type of leader who knew all his clergy and went about preaching. It is, therefore, not surprising that the Tudor sovereigns, Henry VIII and Elizabeth I, in the Reformation era treated their successive primates as state officials and instinctively perpetuated the medieval concept of episcopacy.

ENGLISH EPISCOPACY 1557–1689

The makers of the Elizabethan religious settlement found it impossible to get away from the prince-prelate concept of episcopacy. Bishops, therefore, continued to live and serve as befitted the dignity conceded to them by society. Moreover, once Elizabeth pledged herself to the maintenance of the traditional ecclesiastical order there was no turning back. In this period the definition of episcopacy that emerged was that bishops and bishops alone, by divine ordinance and Catholic custom, possessed certain apostolic powers to perpetuate their own ministry. Although presbyters shared with the bishops the power to administer the sacraments and perform various pastoral functions, they were expressly excluded from the authority to constitute in themselves the essential body without which there could be no church.[13] In support of this view the Elizabethan divines cited the example of the primitive church. A consequence of this interpretation of episcopacy was that toward churches of the Reformed tradition Anglicans extended an attitude of general toleration. This attitude, however, was rather vague and broad and was based primarily upon mutual dislike for the pretensions of the Roman church. While the Church of England insisted upon the maintenance of her own historic episcopate, she was not yet sure upon what grounds she could actually condemn the ministry of nonepiscopal bodies as invalid, nor yet if she wanted to do so.[14]

King James I (1603–25) became famous for the divine-right concept of kingship. This doctrine had as its inevitable corollary the divine right of bishops. This corollary was interpreted to mean that the authority of bishops was bound up with the sovereign, whose will in spiritual matters was delegated to the bishops to interpret and execute. Although this was not a purely theological doctrine, it convinced many people, including James I's successor, Charles I, and his archbishop, William Laud, to assert that the episcopal form of church government was divinely ordained and stood or fell with the king. The next logical step was to stress the divine origin of the hierarchy and the essential difference between bishops and presbyters or priests. This emphasis upon the uniqueness of the episcopal office was further accented when Anglicans found it necessary to defend their position against virulent Puritan opposition to it.[15] Although the argument between Anglicans and Puritans over bishops was intertwined with grave political issues, it seems fair to claim that both Archbishop Laud and Charles I, at least in part, were executed respectively in 1645 and 1649 because they insisted on following their divine right of bishops doctrine to its ultimate conclusion.

After the Puritan Interregnum, during which bishops as heads of the church were removed, the Restoration of Charles Stuart in 1660 signaled the reinstatement of episcopacy. In Charles II's reign the divine institution of episcopacy doctrine was reasserted. This was done partly to justify the Church of England's breach with Rome but also to provide a background against which the principles that separated Anglicans from Presbyterians could be clearly defined. The Act of Uniformity in 1662 enforced the Anglican view of bishops, because it required all incumbents in the Church of England to be episcopally ordained or be deprived of their livings. Moreover, the tide of political events in Restoration England was running heavily against any kind of compromise with nonepiscopal groups. Thus, the triumph of episcopacy was due to the support of the crown and the dominant political Tory party. Furthermore, the "high church" view of episcopacy held by the bishops themselves was reinforced by the fact that almost all of them in 1661 had suffered for their faith under the former regime, which had been pledged to extirpate "prelacy." Among the Restoration bishops the concept of the divine right of kings was again an article of faith.

The Restoration settlement in regard to episcopacy was, however, disrupted by the political events of the period 1685 to 1689. Twice in five years, some of the most distinguished members of the episcopal bench found themselves unable to reconcile their consciences to comply with an order of the state. In 1688 seven bishops refused to publish James II's Declaration of

Indulgence granting toleration to religious minorities and were in turn tried in court but acquitted. Then in 1689, five of this group of seven, plus two others, refused to take the oath of loyalty to the new sovereigns, William and Mary. The problem for these bishops was that after the abdication of James II in 1688 they could not bring themselves to accept parliament's claim to sovereignty in place of the king. Because William and Mary were enthroned as a result of parliamentary action these bishops declined taking the oath of allegiance. However, the Tudor-Stuart concept that held the church and state to be two distinct parts of one Christian community under the supremacy of the crown had been superseded by the claim that royal authority was derived from parliament. This claim meant that after 1689 the church as well as the crown was brought under the control of the state, and parliament would determine increasingly the roles of each.[16]

Owing to deprivations and deaths, William III appointed twenty bishops in the thirteen years of his reign. All the new bishops subscribed to the sovereignty of parliament, the salient doctrine of the Whig party, and took the oath of loyalty to William and Mary.[17] In religion the Whigs were Protestant and Latitudinarian, and their governmental policies were fashioned accordingly. The Act of Religious Toleration in 1689 was the result of Whig action. In this measure the concessions offered to nonconformists in an effort to achieve a general religious comprehension policy presented a problem to the bishops. For example, the act threatened Anglican claims to uniqueness in regard to their church and ministry. Under these conditions no member of the episcopal order could avoid defining his attitude toward episcopacy. In this crisis experience many bishops were perhaps more conscious of their political than of their spiritual responsibilities. Because bishops after 1689 were selected more for their political views, family connections, or at best their intellectual attainments, respect for them waned. Throughout the eighteenth century the Erastian status im-

posed upon the Church of England in 1688–89 kept the bishops of the church in line with the policies of parliament and the
several ministries that exercised power.

DIVERGENT VIEWS OF EPISCOPACY

Between 1715 and 1833, there existed in England the widest
possible diversity of opinion among churchmen concerning ecclesiastical polity and the necessity of bishops. In the earlier
part of this period, the orthodox views of Archbishops William
Wake and John Potter were overshadowed by the opinions of
the Latitudinarians and the Erastians and especially Bishops
Hoadly and Watson.[18] While Archbishops Wake and Potter upheld the essentialness of episcopacy, the bishop of Bangor,
Benjamin Hoadly, attracted considerable attention by denying
that Christ had delegated authority to any officers in the
church. In Hoadly's view, the church was simply a number of
men, either small or large, who truly and sincerely subjected
themselves to Jesus Christ alone as their lawgiver and judge.
Thus, the door to unrestrained individualism was open, and
the claims of episcopal authority were subverted. As Regius
Professor of Divinity in Cambridge, Richard Watson, before
becoming bishop of Llandaff, attracted attention by applying
the principles of scientific inquiry to the doctrines of Christianity and disregarding tradition as representing the speculations
of the dark ages. It is, therefore, not surprising that he gave no
emphasis to the value and continuity of the episcopate.[19] Indeed, another clergyman, William Paley, in a sermon entitled
"A Distinction of Orders in the church defended upon principles of Public Utility," acknowledged the practical necessity for
organizing church communities but contended that the New
Testament and the apostolic tradition specified no single ecclesiastical constitution. In England, the three orders of the clergy
were justified because they corresponded to the three orders of
secular society. Also, within the same century, John Wesley,

leader and organizer of the Methodists, became convinced of the validity of presbyterian ordination and put it into practice while professing to be a loyal son of the Church of England.

It was, however, William Law who set forth the classic defense for the "high church" position. In his trenchant style, Law took issue with Bishop Hoadly and charged him with having left Christians with neither priests nor sacraments nor church but only with sincerity. How could Hoadly remain a bishop, confirming and ordaining, if he genuinely believed what he said about episcopacy? For Law, the apostolic succession was a matter of conviction about which he claimed, "We do not say that episcopacy cannot be changed, merely because we have apostolical practise for it; but because such is the nature of the Christian priesthood, that it can only be continued in that method which God has appointed for its continuance. Thus, episcopacy is the only instituted method of continuing the priesthood; therefore episcopacy is unchangeable, not because it is an apostolical practise, but because the nature of the thing requires it."[20]

Because of these varied and contrasting schools of churchmanship in eighteenth-century England, it is difficult to determine where the *via media* on the question of episcopacy was located. The best judgment on this issue is that of the late Professor Norman Sykes, who concluded that the majority of Anglicans probably held a view similar to the one expressed by Jonathan Swift in his *Sentiments of a Church of England Man with respect to Religion and Government.* "A Church of England man," Swift wrote, "hath a true veneration for the scheme established among us of ecclesiastic government and though he will not determine whether Episcopacy be of divine right, he is sure it is most agreeable to primitive institutions, fittest of all others for preserving order and purity, and under its present regulations best calculated for our civil state."[21]

Views about episcopacy among American Anglican churchmen varied as much as they did in England. Drs. Johnson and

Chandler and the contingent of proepiscopal advocates in the prewar and postwar decades held a view of episcopacy that was compatible with the views of Archbishops Wake and Potter and the nonjuror, William Law. In contrast with this position was the one of Richard Bland of Virginia, who bluntly stated, "I profess my self a sincere son of the established church; but I can embrace her doctrines, without approving her hierarchy, which I know to be a relic of the papal encroachment upon the common law."[22] With this expression, Bland would seem to be in perfect agreement with Bishop Watson. Moreover, the opinion about episcopacy which Richard Bland expressed was probably the one held by a majority of the Anglican laymen from Maryland southward. In addition to these two positions, there was a third which probably included most of the clergy and possibly some of the laity from Pennsylvania northward. In this third group were those who did not have strong feelings for or against bishops but were willing to accept them as essential to the episcopal form of church government, provided their office could be separated from the state. In the prewar years such an assurance was never given, and the fear of what an aggressive imperial administration might impose upon an American episcopate, if established, was a major stumbling block in the minds of American churchmen. Although the postwar crucial years witnessed the same three positions in respect to episcopacy, when it was realized that bishops could be secured from England without entangling obligations and that their functions in the church would be completely separate from the respective governments, the Protestant Episcopal church completed its traditional form of church government.

While the Episcopalians decided to complete their church government by the installation of bishops, the method by which they chose them reveals an awareness of primitive Christian practice as well as a conformity to political realities in revolutionary America. For example, an anonymous author wrote an arti-

cle which was published in the *Virginia Gazette* in 1778, demonstrating that he was well aware of the early church practice of
electing bishops by the vote of clergy and laity. After reviewing
the plight of the Episcopal churches in America, he concluded:
"Circumstances unavoidable must soon leave us without proper
or desirable persons for the performance of the duties of the
clergyman. . . . Perhaps we shall be able to prove that episcopacy, as established in England at present, is one of the many
encroachments of this power upon the just rights of the people,
and that a *free election* to that office was not only the most
ancient usage of that country, but also the true apostolic
mode." This author next cited Blackstone as evidence for his
position. "The learned Blackstone, in his commentaries, book I,
chapter 11, informs us, 'that election was, in very early times,
the usual mode of elevation to the episcopal chair throughout
all Christendom, and that (says he) was promiscuously performed by the laity, as well as by the clergy.' " Emperors and
kings, he argued, had overthrown this practice and taken control of the episcopal offices.[23] Therefore, it was proper for the
clergy and laity in republican America to reclaim the former
prerogative of episcopal elections.

In his *Case of the Protestant Episcopal Churches in the United
States Considered,* William White used the same line of reasoning
that had appeared in the anonymously written article printed
in the *Virginia Gazette.* Actually, White was more nearly precise
in his argument. "The power of electing a superior order of
ministers," he wrote, "ought to be in the clergy and laity together, they being interested in the choice. In England, the
bishops are appointed by the civil authority; which was an usurpation of the Crown at the Norman conquest. The primitive
churches were generally supplied by popular elections; even in
the City of Rome, the privilege of electing the bishop continued
with the people to the tenth or eleventh century."[24] Thus there
were a number of Episcopalians in America who were aware or
who were made aware that they were overturning seven hun-

dred years of ecclesiastical tradition and returning to a practice of the early church when clergy and laity joined to elect bishops. Only the Connecticut Episcopal clergy dissented from this practice and made their episcopal election a purely clerical affair, but even they could not uphold the traditional ties between episcopacy and the state. Without the church-state ties even the Congregationalists did not fear Seabury or protest his presence. In their attitude toward episcopal elections the Connecticut clergy were a very small minority, and in time they too altered their views.

The disestablishment of the Anglican churches from Maryland to Georgia made it impossible for an Episcopal bishop to be "clothed with the garments of Caesar." The English bishops, moreover, did not consecrate bishops for America until they were assured that the United States would not consider bishops as a source of irritation. Once they were convinced that bishops would not be viewed in an adverse light by the federal and state governments, they consecrated White and Provoost. In America the church-state relationship which had prevailed in varying degrees since A.D. 313 was broken, and every bishop was strictly an ecclesiastical official for his own denomination with such powers as the denomination allotted to him. In this respect the Protestant Episcopal church broke with almost fifteen hundred years of church-state tradition. In a real sense an Episcopal bishop in the United States was purely a spiritual church leader—a father in God.

Another person who played a role in shaping the process whereby American Episcopal bishops were elected and in assuring the bishops in England that in 1784 and 1785 Americans were ready to accept bishops was Granville Sharpe, Esq. Sharpe was a grandson of an archbishop of York who took a keen interest in procuring an episcopate for the American churches. Sometime in the early 1780s he wrote a "Tract on the Election of Bishops" which was circulated in America. In this treatise Sharpe supported the concept of lay and clerical participation in episcopal elections and gave evidence that this had been not only primitive practice but had actually happened in the selection of the first bishops chosen for Scotland following the Reformation. Benjamin Franklin, for one, considered the electing of bishops as described by Sharpe and approved it. Furthermore, Sharpe corresponded with Dr. Benjamin Rush, a physician and leading Presbyterian layman, and Dr. John Witherspoon, president of the College of New Jersey and the best-known Presbyterian minister in America, and received assurances that they had no objections to the elected primitive style of bishops Sharpe described in his "Tract." In turn, Sharpe communicated this information to the archbishop of Canterbury, John Moore, who was probably cognizant of the fact that both Dr. Rush and Dr. Witherspoon were signers of the Declaration of Independence.[25]

Indeed, a purely spiritual bishop was what Chandler, Johnson, and their associates had claimed they wanted in 1767. They tried in vain to convince the public and their fellow Anglicans that such a bishop would only ordain, confirm, and visit the clergy. The point that could not then be explained was how such a bishop could exist within the existing Anglican church structure. This idea of the 1760s, however, became a necessity in the 1780s if the Protestant Episcopal church was to survive. Unless ordination and confirmation were available, the most basic functions of the church would be neglected, for in the episcopal tradition only a bishop could perform these rites. When the state and national conventions of the Episcopal church had been reorganized, they defined and simplified the office of bishop in terms they could accept. When the process was completed, they had a purely spiritual bishop, elected by the state convention, defined by the General Ecclesiastical Constitution, and amenable to the national and state conventions. A bishop retained the spiritual functions symbolized by the mitre, but the sceptre, which symbolized the authority to rule with the aid of the state, was removed.

THE AMERICAN EPISCOPATE

A comparison of the canons of the Church of England and those of the Protestant Episcopal church will illustrate the changes that were made to render a bishop purely spiritual. The canonical basis for English episcopacy is found in the canons of 1603–04. These 141 canons, with few alterations, furnished the guidelines for the Church of England throughout the seventeenth and eighteenth centuries. Many of these English canons had no direct bearing upon the American church, but others may be directly compared with the nine articles of the constitution and the seventeen canons of the Protestant Episcopal Church. Canons 1–12 of the Church of England dealt with episcopacy and specified that bishops be appointed by the king and subject only to his authority although they were consecrated by bishops. The archbishops automatically presided at convocations and bishops at synods at which only clergy attended. No mention was made of the laity.[26] In America, the constitution allotted three articles to the subject of episcopacy, and three or four of the seventeen canons defined in certain facets the functions of bishops. It was left to each state convention to decide whether it wanted a bishop. If a bishop were present, he served as president. The clergy and laity jointly had to pass on every measure pertaining to episcopacy.

The American attitude toward ecclesiastical courts differed completely from the English. Thirty-six of the English canons defined and described the church's ecclesiastical court system, consisting of archbishop's, bishop's, and archdeacon's courts. These courts were staffed by ecclesiastical officials. Cases involving morals, wills and bequests, and the issuance of marriage licenses were handled by these courts as a part of the church-state relationship. In addition, a special convocation court was provided to handle charges against an archbishop, bishop, suffragan, coadjutor, or assistant bishop. The president of this court was a bishop, and all its members were clergy.[27]

The Protestant Episcopal church did not organize an ecclesiastical court system *per se,* but authorized the state convention to devise a way to try clergymen, including a bishop. The concept of bishops' courts was alien to the American churchmen, for they had never experienced one in colonial America. Instead, the colonial governors had handled most of the responsibilities of the English ecclesiastical courts, and the Episcopalians were happy to leave them with the state in the 1780s. An ecclesiastical court for an American bishop was out of the question. In fact, the constitution delegated to each state convention the authority to try a bishop and to include laymen as well as clergymen in the court.[28]

The authority to make canons, ordinances, or amendments for the Church of England was inherent in the convocation consisting of the Upper and Lower Houses of Clergy but subject to the authority of king and parliament. The archbishop of Canterbury summoned the convocation and presided; the bishops comprised the Upper House; and the deans, archdeacons, and proctors comprised the Lower House. Again there was no place for the laity. In America, on the other hand, alterations in the constitution or canons had to be initiated at the state or general convention. The convention set the time and place of meeting, although after 1789 the bishops could call special meetings. There were two houses: the House of Bishops and the House of Clerical and Lay Deputies. In the House of Deputies the laity were represented equally with the clergy. It normally required the concurrence of both houses to pass an act, but a four-fifths vote of the clerical and lay representatives could override the bishops on any issue.[29]

A bishop in America was restricted in still another way. In England the bishop or his chaplain conducted the examination of prospective clergymen. Apparently the English bishop's word was decisive. In America, however, the canons provided for a committee of laymen and clergy to examine ministerial candidates and recommend them for ordination. Also, a prospective candidate had to have the endorsement of the vestry of the church or parish from whence he came, and this provision gave the laity another opportunity to pass upon their future clergy. The conventions of the 1780s were unwilling to permit bishops to exercise any power they could rightfully retain in a representative committee.

A majority of states in organizing their churches used ecclesiastical terms that were more meaningful to them than consistent with English ecclesiastical tradition. For example, the words "convocation" and "diocese" seldom appear in the documents of the period. Instead the terms "convention" and "district" are more often used.[30] In 1785 Thomas B. Chandler advised the use of the terms "diocese" and "dean" in the Episcopal church in Virginia, but he was completely ignored. Many of the terms of the Church of England denoting ecclesiastical rank were not even mentioned in the 1780s by the American churchmen. There was no place given in the constitution to an archdeacon, proctor, apparitor, or surrogate. The names and titles which represented the various rungs in the ladder of ecclesiastical preferment in the Church of England were rejected in America. The American Episcopalians modified their ecclesiastical terminology to please themselves, and in the process they demonstrated their independence.

American bishops were in every way more democratic than their English counterparts. The bishoprics of Canterbury, Winchester, York, and London were noted for their social and economic prominence. In 1762 Canterbury had a yearly income of £ 7000, Winchester £ 5000, York £ 4500, and London £ 4000.[31] The bishops of these sees were influential at court and also in their archdiocese or diocese, because they worked closely with the king and nobles in the filling of benefices. Unless a parish priest had the support of a recognized patron and the approval of his bishop it was virtually impossible to advance in the church. But in America White, Provoost, and Seabury served a local church as well as ministering as bishops. White proposed this in *The Case* because he knew the episcopal hierarchy of the Church of England was objectionable to most of his associates. He personally remained rector of Christ and Saint Peter's churches until his death in 1836. Bishop Provoost of New York remained rector of Trinity Church, and Bishop Seabury was rector of Saint James Church, New London, Connecticut, where his father, Samuel Seabury, Sr., had served in the 1730s and early 1740s. Virginia Episcopalians also required a bishop in their state to serve a parish. Thus the early American churchmen were determined to make their bishops servants of, and not lords over, the church.

The English bishops were addressed as members of the peerage. Richard Terrick, bishop of London, signed his name "Richard Bp. of London," and Archbishop Secker signed himself "Thomas Archbishop of Canterbury." This style of signature clearly implied that the title or office was more important than the holder's family name. Samuel Seabury was the only early American bishop who imitated the English style. His signature, "Samuel Bp. of Connecticut," provoked Ezra Stiles to criticize him severely for his arrogance.[32] In contrast, White and Provoost used a much simpler style—"Bp. White" or even "Wm. White"—and Provoost did likewise. In neither case was there any adverse criticism.

In the area of episcopal garb only Seabury wore a mitre on some occasions to symbolize his episcopal office. Although the mitre was not used by English bishops in the eighteenth century, it symbolized to many Americans features of episcopacy to which they objected. White and Provoost never wore a mitre during their respective episcopal careers. Seabury was wise enough not to antagonize his Episcopal associates to the south after the merger in 1789 by wearing a mitre in the General Convention. There is no indication that any of the first bishops carried a crozier. Possibly this would have been too much for even the Connecticut Episcopalians to accept.

HIGH OR LOW CHURCH

The position which William White maintained throughout his career can be termed "Low Church"; Samuel Seabury was "High Church." The Constitution and canons of the Protestant Episcopal church in 1789 to some extent were a compromise between these two positions. But by comparison with past precedents and the contemporary English church, the American episcopate was Low Church. This was a natural development when it is remembered that the colonial Anglican churches had taken many steps in the direction of self-sufficiency. The vestries had long been elected bodies, and all the colonial establishments had permitted the vestry or the vestry and congregation to select the parish minister. In every colony from Massachusetts to Georgia there had been a growing trend among Anglicans toward self-determination in church affairs. These developments were aided and abetted by the prolonged neglect of the American churches by the British government. Moreover, these tendencies were encouraged by a growing conviction among Americans that they ought to have home rule and to determine who should rule. Translated into ecclesiastical polity, this quite naturally meant that Episcopalians should control their own churches and decide who their leaders or bishops should be. The resulting transference of authority in ecclesiastical affairs from king, parliament, and hierarchy and placing it in the hands of delegates, clerical and lay, who were designated by their fellow parishioners to represent them, was not only a return to primitive church practice but also an ecclesiastical revolution.

Fortunately for the Protestant Episcopal churches in the crucial years, their leaders were of one mind in seeking union, and they all agreed that bishops were necessary. While Seabury stressed the primacy of bishops and expected to rule the church in Connecticut in an autocratic way through his clergy acting as a council, White knew that any procedure that smacked of the divine-right concept of bishops was objectionable to most Episcopalians. In the 1780s, any semblance on the part of the American bishops to the type of episcopacy representative of the divine right of bishops theory would have been just as objectionable to the American citizenry as was the theory of the divine right of kings. White was determined that the churches should reorganize with due regard to the rights of the people expressed through their representatives. Furthermore, the recognition of the laity as an integral part of the church governmental structure seemed right and proper to most churchmen. From 1607 to 1784 the laity had played a leading role in the churches. In the parishes the laymen had often formed the most permanent element. Thus their inclusion in the conventions of the 1780s was a natural extension of their role. With the presence of at least an equal number of laymen (and sometimes more) in each state and national convention it was certain that the constitution of the reconstituted churches would conform to the ideology of the American Revolution. That the state and general conventions achieved this by 1789 while obtaining and installing bishops as the chief pastors of their respective dioceses is no less than remarkable.

Notes

ABBREVIATIONS

AJT   American Journal of Theology
EHR   English Historical Review
GHQ   Georgia Historical Quarterly
HMPEC   Historical Magazine of the Protestant Episcopal Church
JEH   Journal of Ecclesiastical History
JSH   Journal of Southern History
MHM   Maryland Historical Magazine
NEQ   New England Quarterly
NCHR   North Carolina Historical Review
PMHB   Pennsylvania Magazine of History and Biography
VHM   Virginia Historical Magazine
VMHB   Virginia Magazine of History and Biography
WMQ   William and Mary Quarterly

CHAPTER 1

1. Edward N. West, "The Music of Old Trinity," *HMPEC,* XVI (1947), 102–3; Morgan Dix, *A History of the Parish of Trinity Church in the City of New York* (New York, 1898), I, 222, 301; Edwin Liemohn, *The Organ and Choir in Protestant Worship* (Philadelphia, 1968), 113.

2. Leonard Ellinwood, *The History of American Church Music* (New York, 1953), 47–49. Max Savelle, *Seeds of Liberty: The Genesis of the American Mind* (Seattle, 1948), 525.

3. Henry Wilder Foote, *Three Centuries of American Hymnody* (Cambridge, Mass., 1940), 166; Winfred Douglas, *Church Music in History and Practice* (New York, 1937), 220–23; Edward Lambe Parsons and Bayard Hale Jones, *The American Prayer Book* (New York, 1937) 99, 180–81.

4. James Downey, *The Eighteenth Century Pulpit* (Oxford: The Clarendon Press, 1969), 8–29; F. R. Webber, *A History of Preaching in Britain and America* (Milwaukee, Wis., 1952), 281–320. *The Works of William Smith,* (Philadelphia, 1803), 22.

5. Glenn Weaver, "Anglican-Congregationalist Tensions in Pre-Revolutionary Connecticut," *HMPEC,* XXVI (1957), 281; Gerald J. Goodwin, "The Anglican Reaction to the Great Awakening," *HMPEC,* XXXV (1966), 243–371; for a study on Anglican evangelicalism see Alexander C. Zabriskie, *Anglican Evangelicalism* (Philadelphia, 1943).

6. Borden W. Painter, Jr., The Anglican Vestry in Colonial America (unpubl. Ph.D. diss., Yale University, 1965), 57, 148, 186, 192, 197.

7. George E. DeMille, "One Man Seminary," *HMPEC,* XXXVIII (1969), 373–79; Frederick V. Mills, "Anglican Expansion in Colonial America," HMPEC, XXXIX (1970), 322–23. Joan R. Gunderson, The Anglican Ministry in Virginia 1723–1776: A Study in Social Class (Unpubl. Ph.D. diss., University of Notre Dame, 1972). Gunderson found that from 1760 to 1776 at least one clergyman per year was produced in Virginia: self-taught, Grammar School, or the College of William and Mary.

8. William S. Perry, ed., *Papers of the Church in Maryland, 1694–1775* (Privately Printed, 1878), 345–47; George M. Brydon, *Virginia's Mother Church and the Political Conditions Under Which It Grew,* 2 vols. (Philadelphia: Historical Society, 1952), II, 415; Richard J. Hooker, ed., *The Carolina Backcountry on the Eve of the Revolution: The Journal and Other Writings of Charles Wood-Mason, Anglican Itinerant* (Chapel Hill, 1953), 72; William L. Saunders, ed., *The Colonial Records of North Carolina,* 30 vols. (Raleigh, 1890), IV, 1027; Allen D. Chandler, *The Colonial Records of the State of Georgia,* 19 vols. (Atlanta, 1906), IX, 55, 341.

9. J. Steven Watson, *The Reign of George III* (Oxford, 1960), 336; and Norman Sykes, *Church and State in England in the Eighteenth Century* (Cambridge, 1934), 206.

10. George W. Lamb, comp., "Clergymen Licensed to the American Colonies by the Bishops of London: 1745–1781," *HMPEC,* XIII (1944), 128–43.

11. Edwin S. Gaustad, *Historical Atlas of Religion in America* (New York, 1962), 9, 5, and Appendix B, 167.

12. Gerald Joseph Goodwin, The Anglican Middle Way in Early Eighteenth Century America: Anglican Religious Thought in the American Colonies, 1702–1750(unpubl. Ph.D. diss., University of Wisconsin, 1965), 40; W. G. Andrews, "Parentage of American High Churchmanship" *The Protestant Episcopal Review* (1899), 196–221.

13. Stephen P. Dorsey, *Early English Churches in America 1607–1807* (New York, 1952), 44–47; Harold Wickliffe Rose, *The Colonial Houses of Worship in America* (New York, 1963).

14. Francis L. Hawks and William S. Perry, *Documentary History of the Protestant Episcopal Church in Connecticut 1704–1789* (Hartford, 1959), I, 102.

15. Devereux Jarratt, *The Life of the Reverend Devereux Jarratt* (Baltimore, 1806), 94–95.

16. Hooker, *The Carolina Backcountry*, 200.

17. Brydon, *Virginia's Mother Church*, II, 462.

18. Louis B. Wright, *The Cultural Life of the American Colonies 1607–1763* (New York, 1957), 16, 83–84, 87.

19. Sidney and Beatrice Webb, *English Local Government from the Revolution to the Municipal Corporation Act: The Parish and the County* (London, 1924), 146–269.

20. Painter, The Anglican Vestry in Colonial America, 39–207.

21. Bradford Spangenberg, "Vestrymen in the House of Burgesses; Protection of Local Vestry Autonomy During James Blair's Term as Commissary (1690–1743)," *HMPEC*, XXXII (1963), 77–99; Arthur Pierce Middleton, "The Colonial Virginia Parish," *HMPEC*, XL (1971), 431–46; Edward Ingle, "Local Institutions of Virginia," in *Johns Hopkins University Studies*, 3d Ser., nos. 2 and 3 (1885).

22. Edwin S. Gaustad, *The Great Awakening in New England* (Gloucester, Mass., 1965), 113.

23. G. MacLaren Brydon, "New Light on the Origins of the Method of Electing Bishops Adopted by the American Episcopal Church," *HMPEC*, XIX (1950), 202–13; Brydon, "The Origin of the Rights of the Laity in the American Episcopal Church," *HMPEC*, XII (1943), 313–38.

24. William W. Manross, *A History of the American Episcopal Church* (New York, 1950), 66, 124; John W. Pratt, *Religion, Politics, and Diversity: The Church-State Theme in New York History* (Ithaca, 1967), 68.

25. Louis Franklin Snow, *The College Curriculum in the United States* (New York, 1907), 73; Edward P. Cheyney, *History of the University of Pennsylvania 1740–1940* (Philadelphia, 1940), 71–85.

26. Arthur Ben Chitt, "College of Charleston: Episcopal Claims Questioned, 1785–," HMPEC, XXXVIII (1968), 413–16.

27. G. MacLaren Brydon, "A Venture in Christian Education," *HMPEC*, XV (1946), 30–31; Guy Fred Wells, *Parish Education in Colonial Virginia* (New York, 1923), 20–22, 23, 27, 48, 66, 76.

28. John Calam, *Parsons and Pedagogues: The S.P.G. Adventure in American Education* (New York, 1971) stresses the initiatives of the S.P.G. in education while giving little attention to the efforts of colonial Anglicans, who in many cases continued the work of education after S.P.G. withdrew in 1783. See Bernard Bailyn, *Education in the Forming of American Society* (Chapel Hill, 1960), 70–73. This author suggests areas for further study and points to the need to note that much Anglican educational activity was initiated in the colonies.

29. For a more positive view of Anglican role in Negro education see Frank J. Klingberg, "The African Immigrant in Colonial Pennsylvania and Delaware," *HMPEC*, XI (1942), 126–53.

30. Frank J. Klingberg, "Sir William Johnson and the Society for the Propagation of the Gospel (1749–1774)," *HMPEC*, VIII (1939), 36; Gerald J. Goodwin, "Christianity, Civilization, and the Savage: The Anglican Mission to the American Indian," *HMPEC*, XLII (1973), 93–110, argues that Anglican Indian missions were an extension of old Dissenter vs. Anglican rivalry in the 1760s. This is a rather weak argument because the Anglicans would not have enlarged their Indian missions in the colony of New York at the time had not Sir William Johnson urged their participation. See also Frank J. Klingberg, *Anglican Humanitarianism in Colonial New York* (Philadelphia, 1940).

31. Walter H. Stowe, "The Corporation for the Relief of Widows and Children of Clergymen," *HMPEC*, III (1934), 19–33; William Lawrence, D.D., *An Historical Address at the Two Hundredth Anniversary of the Boston Episcopal Charitable Society* (Boston, 1924); Theodore C. Knauff, *A History of the Society of the Sons of Saint George* (Philadelphia, 1923), 23–24.

32. Thomas B. Chandler, *An Appeal to the Public in Behalf of the Church of England in America* (New York, 1767), 75–77, 174. Charles Chauncy in *An Appeal to the Public Answered* (Boston, 1768), 114, 133–34, estimated 300,000 Anglicans in the thirteen colonies, but as an arch-opponent of episcopacy his figure is probably low. His estimate of 270,000 churchmen in Maryland and Virginia acknowledged only 30,000 Anglicans outside the Chesapeake region. There most certainly were more than 30,000 in South Carolina alone because with an estimated population of 94,074 in 1760 it was considered predominantly Anglican.

33. Arthur L. Cross, *The Anglican Episcopate and the American Colonies* (New York, 1902), 227; Simeon E. Baldwin, "The American Juris-

diction of the Bishop of London in Colonial Times," *Proceedings of the American Antiquitarian Society,* New Ser., XIII (1899), 179–222; J. H. Bennett, "English Bishops and Imperial Jurisdiction," *HMPEC,* XXXII (1963), 175–188; Elizabeth H. Davidson, *The Establishment of the English Church in Continental America* (Durham, 1936), 9.

34. Lawrence L. Brown, "Henry Compton 1632–1713," *HMPEC,* XXV (1956), 55; G. MacLaren Brydon, "James Blair, Commissary," *HMPEC,* XIV (1945), 91.

35. Manross, *A History of the American Episcopal Church,* 72, 162–164, 167; Cross, *The Anglican Episcopate in the American Colonies,* 228–29.

36. Cross, *The Anglican Episcopate and the American Colonies,* 122. Horatio Walpole to Bishop Sherlock, 29 May 1750, Appendix A, 323–25.

37. Sykes, *Church and State,* 36.

38. Norman Sykes, "The Duke of New Castle as Ecclesiastical Minister," *EHR,* LVI (1942), 59–84.

39. Archbishop Secker to Dr. Johnson, 10 Dec. 1761, Harold and Carol Schneider, eds., *Samuel Johnson President of King's College His Career and Writings,* 4 vols. (New York, 1929), III, 261.

40. Archbishop Secker to Dr. Johnson, 30 March 1763, Schneiders, eds., *Samuel Johnson,* III, 269.

41. Charles J. Abbey and John H. Overton, *The English Church in the Eighteenth Century,* 2 vols. (London, 1878), II, 400–401.

42. Archbishop Secker to Dr. Johnson, 22 May 1764, James S. M. Anderson, *The History of the Church of England in the Colonies,* 3 vols. (London, 1856), III, 434.

43. Archbishop Secker to Dr. Johnson, 28 Sept. 1763, Schneiders, eds., *Samuel Johnson,* III, 278.

44. Sir William Johnson to Lords of Trade, 20 Jan. 1764, Hugh Hastings, ed., *Ecclesiastical Records of the State of New York,* 7 vols. (Albany, 1905), VII, 591.

45. East Apthorp, *Considerations on the Charter and Conduct of the Society for the Propagation of the Gospel* (Boston, 1763), 1–24; Cross, *The Anglican Episcopate and the American Colonies,* 146–58.

46. Jonathan Mayhew, *Observations on the Charter* (Boston, 1763), 107.

47. Thomas Hardy, ed., *The Works of Thomas Secker,* 4 vols. (London, 1804), IV, 514.

48. Archbishop Secker to Dr. Johnson, 22 May 1764, Thomas B. Chandler, *Life of Samuel Johnson, D.D.* (London, 1824), 199.

49. Archbishop Secker to Dr. Johnson, 10 Dec. 1761, ibid., 184–85; 200–201.
50. Saunders, ed., *The Colonial Records of North Carolina,* IX, 83–84.
51. William W. Manross, *The Fulham Papers in the Lambeth Palace* (Oxford, 1965). There are no letters of Archbishop Cornwallis listed in this index.

CHAPTER 2

1. Samuel E. Morison et al., *The Growth of the American Republic,* 2 vols. (New York, 1969), I, 140, 143–59, 242. The Stamp Act of 1765 required the payment of a fee for stamps on commercial and legal documents, pamphlets, newspapers, etc. The Townshend Acts of 1767 imposed duties on glass, lead, painters' colors, tea, and imported paper.
2. Bruce E. Steiner, "New England Anglicanism: A Genteel Faith," *WMQ,* 3d Ser., XXVII (1970), 123–35; Nelson R. Burr, *The Story of the Diocese of Connecticut* (Hartford, 1962), 69–70; Goodwin, The Anglican Middle Way in Early Eighteenth Century America, 278.
3. Jacob C. Meyer, *Church and State in Massachusetts 1740 to 1833* (Cleveland, 1930), 14; Richard L. Bushman, *From Puritan to Yankee* (Cambridge, 1967), 168–71; Oscar Zeichner, *Connecticut's Years of Controversy 1750–1776* (Chapel Hill, 1949), 14.
4. Meyer, *Church and State in Massachusetts,* 73; Godfrey Malbone to William S. Johnson, Oct. 1, 1771, William Samuel Johnson Papers, Connecticut Historical Society, Hartford, Conn.
5. Zeichner, *Connecticut's Years of Controversy,* 21; Meyer, *Church and State in Massachusetts,* 14; Bushman, *From Puritan to Yankee,* 168; Robert E. Brown, *Middle-Class Democracy and the Revolution in Massachusetts, 1691–1780* (Ithaca, 1955), 113. This work points out that the Massachusetts government permitted greater privileges to Anglicans than the English government granted to Dissenters.
6. C. C. Goen, *Revivalism and Separatism in New England* (New Haven, 1962), 8–35. The Great Awakening in New England, 102–25, 116–17.
7. Zeichner, *Connecticut's Years of Controversy,* 25–35, 58–59, 69.
8. John Webb Pratt, *Religion, Politics, and Diversity: The Church-State Theme in New York History* (Ithaca, N.Y., 1967), 40–77; Davidson, *The Establishment of the English Church,* 37–46.
9. Leonard Lundin, *Cockpit of the Revolution* (Princeton, 1940), 102; Burr, *The Anglican Church in New Jersey,* 87–115; Donald L. Kemmer, *Path to Freedom: The Struggle for Self-Government in Colonial*

New Jersey 1703–1776 (Princeton, 1940), 315; Richard P. McCormick, *New Jersey from Colony to State* (Princeton, 1964), 86.

10. Minutes of the Standing Committee, 1760–1775 (Library of Congress, microfilm).

11. Manross, *A History of the American Episcopal Church,* 159; Jack M. Sosin, "The Proposal in the Pre-Revolutionary Decade for Establishing Anglican Bishops in the Colonies," *JEH* XIII (1962), 76–84; Cross, *The Anglican Episcopate and the American Colonies,* 255–58.

12. Dr. Johnson to Archbishop Secker, 5 Sept. 1765, Schneiders, eds., *Samuel Johnson,* I, 355.

13. "The Seabury Minutes of the New York Clergy Conventions of 1766 and 1767," *HMPEC,* X (1941), 127; Samuel A. Clark, *The History of St. John's Church, Elizabeth Town, New Jersey* (Philadelphia, 1857), 117–38. Of the two sources "The Seabury Minutes" are the more extensive and reliable. Leonard J. Trinterud, *The Forming of an American Tradition* (Philadelphia, 1949), 238–41, gives the Presbyterian response of these events.

14. "The Seabury Minutes," 127, 132.

15. Letter from Clergy of Convention to Governor Horatio Sharp, 21 May 1767 "The Seabury Minutes," 160.

16. Dr. Johnson to James Camm, 10 April 1767, Schneiders, eds., *Samuel Johnson,* I, 398–99, 433, 435.

17. Sir William Johnson to Dr. Johnson, 2 Dec. 1766, James Sullivan, *The Papers of Sir William Johnson,* 13 vols. (Albany, 1931), V, 440, 837–39.

18. Ibid., V, 837–39; Schneiders, eds., *Samuel Johnson,* I, 399, 433, 435.

19. Schneiders, eds., *Samuel Johnson,* I, 370.

20. Theodore Thayer, *Pennsylvania Politics and the Growth of Democracy, 1740–1776* (Harrisburg, 1953), 91.

21. Penn Correspondence, 10 vols. (Historical Society of Pennsylvania), VIII, 225; IX, 132; Letters to Richard Peters, 8 vols. (Historical Society of Pennsylvania, Bound, 1912), VII, 14.

22. Samuel Auchmuty to Dr. Johnson, 3 Nov. 1766, Schneiders, eds., *Samuel Johnson,* I, 382.

23. Sir William Johnson to Samuel Auchmuty, 22 Sept. 1767, Sullivan, *The Papers of Sir William Johnson,* V, 695–96.

24. William S. Johnson (writing for the ill Dr. Johnson) to Myles Cooper, Feb. 12, 1766, William Samuel Johnson Papers (Connecticut Historical Society, Hartford).

25. William S. Johnson to Myles Cooper, Feb. 12, 1766, William Samuel Johnson Papers.

26. Charles Chauncy, *An Appeal to the Public Answered* (Boston, 1768), 135–36.

27. "The American Whig" No. 1, Parker's *New York Gazette,* March 14, 1768. "The American Whig" series also appeared in the *Boston Gazette* and *Pennsylvania Journal.*

28. Anonymous, "Letter Concerning an American Bishop to T. B. Chandler," 1768, 1–14.

29. Joseph J. Ellis, III, "Anglicans in Connecticut, 1725–1750: The Conversion of the Missionaries," *NEQ* (March 1971), 66–81. Gaustad, *The Great Awakening in New England,* 102–25.

30. Hawks and Perry, *Historical Documents—Connecticut,* 148–58, 179, 185.

31. Bishop Lowth to Dr. Johnson, 3 May 1768, Thomas B. Chandler, *Life of Samuel Johnson, D. D.* (London, 1824), 202–3; William S. Johnson to Dr. Johnson, June 30, 1768, William Samuel Johnson Papers. For other expressions of this view see letters of March 6, 1767; April 4, 1767; July 13, 1767; February 20, 1768.

32. William S. Johnson to Dr. Johnson, March 28, 1770, William Samuel Johnson Papers. Zeichner, *Connecticut's Years of Controversy,* 130. Zeichner believes W. S. Johnson favored an American episcopate in the years 1772 to 1775. If so, it must have been the "purely spiritual" type which Chandler described in his *Appeal,* but the British government refused to countenance. See Burr, *The Story of the Diocese of Connecticut,* 131.

33. Perry, ed., *Historical Collections—Massachusetts,* 531.

34. Ibid., 526–29; Wilson, *The Centennial History—New York,* 203; Vestry Register of Christ and St. Peter's Churches, 1760–1784 (Christ Church, Philadelphia), 55; Brown, *Middle-Class Democracy and the Revolution in Massachusetts,* 104; Perry, ed., *Historical Collections—Massachusetts,* 462.

35. Church official to Solomon Palmer, 21 Feb. 1763; Peter Jay to Dr. Johnson, 1 Dec. 1762, S.P.G. Papers for the American Colonies, 1760–1770 (Library of Congress, microfilm); also S.P.G. Correspondence for New Jersey (Rutgers University Library).

36. Thomas B. Chandler to Dr. Johnson, 9 Sept. 1768, Schneiders, eds., *Samuel Johnson,* I, 446–47.

37. Fulham Papers in Lambeth Palace, 40 vols. (Library of Congress, microfilm), VI, no. 168; Chandler, *Life of Samuel Johnson, D.D.,* 201–3.

38. Dr. Johnson to Archbishop Secker, 10 Nov. 1766, Schneiders, eds., *Samuel Johnson*, I, 378.

CHAPTER 3

1. Sydney G. Fisher, *The Making of Pennsylvania* (Philadelphia, 1896), 209.
2. William S. Perry, ed., *Papers of the Church in Pennsylvania, 1680–1778* (Privately Printed, 1871), 361; J. Wesley Twelves, *A History of the Diocese of Pennsylvania of the Protestant Episcopal Church in the U.S.A. 1784–1968* (Philadelphia, 1969), 100–123.
3. Thomas Penn to Richard Peters, 18 May 1767. Penn Correspondence, 10 vols. (Historical Society of Pennsylvania), IX, 110.
4. Thomas F. Jones, *A Pair of Lawn Sleeves* (Philadelphia, 1972), 18, 32; and Hubertis Cummings, *Richard Peters* (Philadelphia, 1944), 81.
5. Thomas Penn to Thomas Barton, 17 June 1767. Penn Correspondence, HSP, IX, 132.
6. Thomas Penn to Jacob Duché, 29 July 1767. Ibid., IX, n.p.
7. Dr. Burton to Richard Peters, 8 Nov. 1770. Letters of Richard Peters, 8 vols. (HSP, Bound, 1912), VII, 14.
8. Thomas Penn to William Smith 8 March 1765. Penn Correspondence, HSP, VIII, n.p.
9. Perry, ed., *Papers . . . Pennsylvania*, 274, 417–19, 421–22.
10. Albert F. Gegenheimer, *William Smith* (Philadelphia, 1943), 183–91.
11. Vestry Register of Christ's Church and St. Peter's Churches, 1760–1784 (Philadelphia), 184, 208, 249.
12. Theodore Thayer, *Pennsylvania Politics and the Growth of Democracy, 1740–1770* (Harrisburg, 1953), 88; James Hutson, *Pennsylvania Politics* (Princeton, 1972), 47.
13. Hutson, *Pennsylvania Politics*, 48, 152–247.
14. Thayer, *Pennsylvania Politics*, 88, 120; Hutson, *Pennsylvania Politics*, 102, 153.
15. Rothermund, *The Layman's Progress* (Philadelphia, 1961), 100; Hutson, *Pennsylvania Politics*, 208–9.
16. Hutson, *Pennsylvania Politics*, 166, 168, 192–201.
17. Rothermund, *The Layman's Progress*, 45, 47, 48–49, 55–56.
18. Richard Peters to Bishop Terrick, 14 Nov. 1766. Perry, ed., *Papers . . . Pennsylvania*, 410, 415.
19. T. B. Chandler, *Life of Samuel Johnson, D.D.*, 200–201.

20. T. B. Chandler to Dr. Johnson, 19 Oct. 1766. Schneiders, eds., *Samuel Johnson*, I, 370–71.

21. William Smith to Bishop Terrick, 24 Apr. 1768. Horace W. Smith, *Life and Correspondence of the Reverend William Smith, D. D.*, 2 vols. (Philadelphia, 1880), I, 414.

22. Samual Auchmuty to Richard Peters, 11 May 1767. Richard Peters Correspondence, HSP, VI, 49, No. 61, 68.

23. Sir William Johnson to Richard Peters, 8 July 1768. Richard Peters Correspondence, HSP, VII, 55. This is but one of a number of examples that are in the Peters Correspondence and *The Papers of Sir William Johnson*.

24. "Centinel" No. 1, William and Thomas Bradford, *Pennsylvania Journal* (Philadelphia), Mar. 24, 1768. There also appeared a series entitled "Remonstrance" which was in league with "Centinel," and "Anti-Centinel" which was similar in tone to Smith's "Anatomist." Also many of these articles appeared in the *Pennsylvania Gazette* as well as the *Journal*.

25. Ibid., Apr. 28, 1768; June 23, 1768, Apr. 14, 1768.

26. Cross, *The Anglican Episcopate*, 207–10; Bridenbaugh, *Mitre and Sceptre*, 301.

27. "Anatomist," No. 1, *Pa. J*, Sept. 8, 1768.

28. Ibid., Nov. 10, 1768; Jan. 12, 1769.

29. Vestry Register of Christ's Church and St. Peter's Church, 32, 50, 55–56, 82–84.

30. Perry, ed., *Papers . . . Pennsylvania*, 354.

31. Charles H. Maxson, *The Great Awakening in the Middle Colonies* (Chicago, 1920), 110; Albert D. Belden, *George Whitefield, The Awakener* (London, 1931), 100, 207–25. Alan Heimert, *Religion and the American Mind* (Cambridge, 1968), 36, 143, 162–64, 203–6, 432.

32. Vestry Register of Christ's Church and St. Peter's, 112–13, 122, 279–80, 285; Norris S. Barratt, *Outline of the History of Old St. Paul's Church* (Philadelphia, 1917), 34–43.

33. Fulham Papers in Lambeth Palace, Library of Congress, XXIII, Nos. 177, 180; XXII, No. 268; Perry, ed., *Papers . . . Pennsylvania*, 306. It was not unusual for the clergy from Delaware to attend the Pennsylvania conventions.

34. Samuel Seabury to William Smith, 15 Aug. 1785. Eben E. Beardsley, *Life and Correspondence of the Right Reverend Samuel Seabury, D. D.* (Boston, 1881), 230–35.

35. Carl Bridenbaugh, *Cities in Revolt: Urban Life in America, 1743–*

1776 (New York, 1955), 139, 152–54; *Bridenbaugh, Mitre and Sceptre,* 212–14; John C. Miller, *Origins of the American Revolution* (Boston, 1943), 192–97; Heimert, *Religion and the American Mind,* 51, 170–71, 255, 362–64.

36. These data were obtained by taking the names of vestrymen from the Vestry Register of Christ's Church and St. Peter's Church and checking them against the tax records for 1769 and 1774 in *Pennsylvania Archives* (Harrisburg, 1897), 3rd. ser., XIV, 151–220. The category definitions were taken from Jackson T. Main, *The Social Structure of Revolutionary America* (Princeton, 1965), Chapter III and 185–86.

37. Burton A. Konkle, *Thomas Willing and the First American Financial System* (Philadelphia, 1937), 48, 59.

38. These data were gleaned from the tax and will records of the counties in which these parishes were located: Montgomery, Chester (2), and Delaware. Microfilm copies in HSP.

39. Carl and Jessica Bridenbaugh, *Rebels and Gentlemen* (New York, 1965), 16–17, 365, 370.

40. Bridenbaugh, *Rebels and Gentlemen,* 56–59, 103, 139–42, 156.

41. Jones, *A Pair of Lawn Sleeves* 23; Bridenbaugh, *Rebels and Gentlemen,* 167; Max Savelle, *Seeds of Liberty* (Seattle, 1968), 448–51.

42. Glenn Weaver, "Benjamin Franklin and the Pennsylvania Germans," WMQ 3rd ser., 14 (1957), 536–59; Max Savelle, *Seeds of Liberty,* 270–71; Bridenbaugh, *Rebels and Gentlemen,* 52–55.

43. Max Savelle, *Seeds of Liberty,* 529; Bridenbaughs, *Rebels and Gentlemen,* 147.

CHAPTER 4

1. Dr. Johnson to John Camm, 10 Apr. 1767. Schneiders, ed., *Samuel Johnson,* I, 398–99.

2. Nelson W. Rightmyer, *Maryland's Established Church* (Baltimore, 1956), 119; Perry, ed., *Papers . . . Maryland,* 345–47. Brydon, *Virginia's Mother Church,* II, 39, 321, 341.

3. Newton D. Mereness, *Maryland as a Proprietary Province* (New York, 1901), 410, 412, 450, 453, 459; Charles A. Barker, *The Background of the Revolution in Maryland* (New Haven, 1940), 279, 365.

4. Gerald E. Hartdagen, "The Anglican Vestry in Colonial Maryland: Organizational Structure and Problems," *HMPEC,* XXXVIII (1969); John H. Seabrook, "The Establishment of An-

glicanism in Colonial Maryland," *HMPEC*, XXXIX (1970), 287–94; Gerald E. Hartdagen, "The Anglican Vestry in Colonial Maryland: A Study in Corporate Responsibility," *HMPEC*, XL (1971), 315–35; 461–79; Alan L. Clem, "The Vestries and Local Government in Colonial Maryland," *HMPEC* XXXI (1962), 220–29.

5. Arthur P. Middleton, "The Colonial Virginia Parish," *HMPEC* XL (1971), 431–46; William H. Seiler, "The Anglican Parish Vestry in Colonial Virginia," *JSH*, vol. 22 (1956), 310–37; Brydon, *Virginia's Mother Church*, II, 240; James K. Owens, The Virginia Vestry: A Study in the Decline of a Ruling Class (Unpubl. Ph.D. diss., Princeton, 1947), 28, 151.

6. William Nelson to Lord Hillsborough, 17 Apr. 1771. Fulham Papers in Lambeth Palace, Library of Congress, XIV, Virginia, 1761—undated, No. 212.

7. Alan Kenneth Austin, The Role of the Anglican Church and Its Clergy in the Political Life of Colonial Virginia (Unpubl. Ph.D. diss., University of Georgia, 1969), 151, 152.

8. William Robinson to Bishop of London, 17 Aug. 1764. Fulham Papers in Lambeth Palace, Library of Congress, XIV, Virginia, 1761—undated, No. 27.

9. Barker, *The Background of the Revolution in Maryland*, 1, 230–327.

10. Ibid., 366.

11. Lucille Griffith, *The Virginia House of Burgesses 1750–1774* (Montogomery, Ala., 1968). Charles S. Sydnor, *Gentlemen Freeholders* (Chapel Hill, 1952), 91.

12. Jack P. Greene, *The Quest for Power* (New York, 1972), 344, 351.

13. Davidson, *The Establishment of the English Church in Continental American Colonies*, 19; Richard L. Morton, ed., *The Present State of Virginia* (Chapel Hill, 1956), 123.

14. Seiler, "The Anglican Parish Vestry in Colonial Virginia," 310–37.

15. Names of vestrymen were taken from vestry books in the Virginia State Library and compared with lists in *Journals of the House of Burgesses of Virginia*, John P. Kennedy, ed. (Richmond, 1905); 313–14, 163–64.

16. Thad W. Tate, "The Coming of the Revolution in Virginia: Britain's Challenge to Virginia's Ruling Class 1763–1776," *WMQ*, 3rd ser., XIX (1962), 341–43.

17. For descriptions of Virginia's ruling class see Percy S. Flippin, *The Royal Government in Virginia* (New York, 1919) and Jack P. Greene, "Foundations of Political Power in the Virginia House of Burgesses, 1720–1776," *WMQ*, 3rd ser., XVI (1959), 485–506.

18. Albert W. Werline, *Problems of Church and State in Maryland* (South Lancaster, Mass., 1948), 90; Barker, *The Background of the Revolution in Maryland,* 273–89, 363–66.

19. H. J. Eckenrode, *Separation of Church and State in Virginia* (Richmond, 1910), 20–25.

20. Brydon, *Virginia's Mother Church,* II, 297.

21. Eckenrode, *Separation of Church and State in Virginia,* 25–27.

22. James Ogilvie to Thomas Jefferson, 28 Mar. 1770. Julian P. Boyd, ed., *The Papers of Thomas Jefferson,* 19 vols., (Princeton, 1950), I, 38–39, 48, 49.

23. Hugh Hamersley to Governor Sharpe, 11 Nov. 1767. William H. Browne, ed., *Correspondence of Governor Horatio Sharpe,* 3 vols. (Baltimore, 1895), III, 431.

24. Rightmyer, *Maryland's Established Church,* 97–99.

25. Ibid., 281–89.

26. Ibid., 104–9.

27. Bernhard Knollenberg, *Origin of the American Revolution: 1759–1776* (New York, 1965), 57–66; Bernard Bailyn, *Ideological Origins of the American Revolution* (Cambridge, 1968), 252–54.

28. Governor Sharpe to Hugh Hamersley, June 1767. Browne, ed., *Sharpe Correspondence,* III, 395.

29. Governor Sharpe to Lord Baltimore, 11 June 1767. Ibid., 401.

30. Lord Baltimore to Governor Sharpe, 11 Nov. 1767. Ibid., 431.

31. Ibid.

32. Petition to Governor Eden, Sept. 1770. William H. Brown, ed., *Archives of Maryland: Proceedings of the Council of Maryland,* 32 vols. (Baltimore, 1912), XXXII, 379–80.

33. Clergy to Governor Eden, 17 Sept. 1770. Ibid., 386.

34. Jonathan Boucher, *Reminiscences of an American Loyalist* (Boston, 1925), 65–66; J. Boucher, *A View of the Causes and Consequences of the American Revolution* (London, 1792), 94.

35. Anne C. Green and Frederick Green, *Maryland Gazette* (Annapolis), March 8, 1773; March 18, 1773.

36. Jonathan Boucher to Mr. James, 4 Apr. 1771. *MHM,* VIII (1913), 177.

37. John Gordon to Walter Dulany, 11 Oct. 1770. The Dulany Papers, MHS.

38. Boucher, *A View of the Causes and Consequences of the American Revolution,* 94.

39. Brydon, *Virginia's Mother Church,* II, 351; Owens, The Virginia Vestry, 232–36.

40. Purdie's *Virginia Gazette* (Williamsburg), June 6, 1771.
41. Ibid., June 26, 1771.
42. William Nelson to Edward Hunt, 11 May 1771. *WMQ,* V (1897), 150.
43. John P. Kennedy, ed., *Journals of the House of Burgesses in Virginia 1770–1772* (Richmond, 1906), 122.
44. Richard Bland to Thomas Adams, 1 Aug. 1771. "Letters of Richard Bland" *VHM,* VI, 131–32; George W. Pilcher, "The Pamphlet War on the Proposed Virginia Anglican Episcopate, 1767–1775," *HMPEC,* XXX (1961), 266–79; Pilcher, "Virginia Newspapers and the Dispute over the Proposed Colonial Episcopate," *Historian,* XXXIII (1960), 98–113.
45. Richard Bland to Thomas Adams, 1 Aug. 1771. "Letters of Richard Bland," *VHM,* VI, 131–32.
46. John C. Fitzpatrick, ed., *The Diaries of George Washington 1748–1799,* 4 vols. (Boston, 1925), III, 81.
47. Mereness, *Maryland as a Proprietary Province,* 439–51.
48. Rightmyer, *Maryland's Established Church,* 92.
49. Barker, *The Background of the Revolution in Maryland,* 359–62.
50. Richard Bland to Virginia Clergy, 1773. An open letter in the Virginia Historical Society.
51. Charles Inglis to Dr. Johnson, 4 July 1771. John W. Lydekker, ed., *The Life and Letters of Charles Inglis 1759 to 1787* (London, 1936), 134–35.
52. Thomas B. Chandler, *An Address from the Clergy of New York* (New York, 1771), 57.
53. Thomas Gwatkin, *A Letter to the Clergy of New York and New Jersey* (Williamsburg, 1772).

CHAPTER 5

1. William Eddis, *Letters from America 1769 to 1777* (London, 1792), 50–51.
2. Greene, *The Quest for Power,* 3–4, 344.
3. Conkin, "The Church Establishment in North Carolina, 1765–1776," *NCHR,* XXXI (1955), 2–17.
4. William L. Saunders, ed., *The Colonial Records of North Carolina,* 10 vols. (Raleigh, 1890), IV, 1042.
5. Michael T. Malone, "Sketches of the Anglican Clergy Who Served in North Carolina During the Period, 1765–1776," *HMPEC,* XXXIX (1970), 141.

6. Saunders, ed., *The Colonial Records of North Carolina*, VII, 153; Malone, "Sketches of the Anglican Clergy," 348–99.

7. Charles L. Roper, *The Church and Private Schools of North Carolina* (Greensboro, 1898), 24–29.

8. Conkin, "The Church Establishment," 8–9; Harry R. Merrens, *Colonial North Carolina in the Eighteenth Century* (Chapel Hill, 1964), 53.

9. D. D. Wallace, *Constitutional History of South Carolina; 1725 to 1775* (Abbeville, S.C., 1899), 9–10; Frederick Dalcho, *An Historical Account of the Protestant Episcopal Church in South Carolina* (Charleston, 1820), 39; Church Commissioners Book (In State Archives, Columbia, S.C.).

10. M. Eugene Sirmans, *Colonial South Carolina: A Political History 1663–1763* (Chapel Hill, 1966), 97, 250; Church Commissioners Book, 57.

11. Peter Timothy, *South Carolina Gazette* (Charleston, S.C.), June 29, 1769 list members of Commons House. This list was compared with the lists of vestrymen and pewholders in *The Minutes of St. Michael's Church of Charleston, S.C. from 1758–1797* and George S. Holmes, *A Historic Sketch of The Parish Church of St. Michael, in the Province of South Carolina* (Charleston, S.C., 1887).

12. Sirmans, *Colonial South Carolina*, 97, 250; Reba C. Strickland, *Religion and the State in Georgia in the Eighteenth Century* (New York, 1939), 130.

13. Robert L. McCaul, "Whitefield's Bethesda College Projects and Other Major Attempts to Found Colonial Colleges," *GHQ*, 44 (1960), Part II, 383–86.

14. James Johnston's *Georgia Gazette* (Savannah, Ga.), Dec. 6, 1769.

15. Strickland, *Religion and the State*, 85–86; 110, 115; J. J. Zubly to unspecified person, 11 July 1773. *Proceedings of the Massachusetts Historical Society for 1864–65* (Boston, 1866), 214–19.

16. W. W. Abbott, *The Royal Governors of Georgia: 1754–1775* (Chapel Hill, 1959), 7.

17. Greene, *The Quest for Power*, 344–54, 364, 453.

18. Conkin, "The Church Establishment," 22.

19. W. Roy Smith, *South Carolina as a Royal Province, 1719–1776* (New York, 1903), 332–68.

20. Wallace, *Constitutional History of South Carolina*, 62, 64, 88.

21. Smith, *South Carolina*, 392.

22. W. W. Abbot, *The Royal Governors of Georgia*, 102, 108.

23. Ibid., 133, 171–81.

24. Governor Dobbs to S.P.G., 29 Mar. 1764. Saunders, ed., *The Colonial Records of North Carolina,* IV, 1040.

25. Governor Tryon to Dr. Burton, 20 Mar. 1769. Ibid., VIII, 14.

26. John Barnett to Dr. Burton, 11 June 1768. Ibid., VII, 789–90; VII, 495; VIII, 13–14.

27. Bp. of London to Lords of Trade, n.d. Ibid., IX, 82–83.

28. Brydon, "The Origin of the Rights of the Laity in the American Episcopal Church," 313–38; Daniel D. Addison, "The Growth of the Layman's Power in the Episcopal Church," *Papers of American Society of Church History,* III (1912), 65–77.

29. Roper, *North Carolina,* 201–2.

30. Church Commissioners Book, 57.

31. Charles Martyn to Bp. of London, 4 Feb. 1763. Fulham Papers in Lambeth Palace, Library of Congress, X, 158.

32. Martyn to Bp. of London, 20 Oct. 1765. Ibid., X, 160.

33. Richard J. Hooker, ed., *The Carolina Backcountry on the Eve of the Revolution: The Journal and Other Writings of Charles Woodmason, Anglican Itinerant* (Chapel Hill, 1953), 5, 9; Church Commissioners Book.

34. Hooker, ed., *The Carolina Backcountry,* 109; Charles Martyn to Bp. of London, 20 Oct. 1765. Fulham Papers, X, 160. Woodmason and Martyn were close associates, Martyn having recommended Woodmason for Holy Orders.

35. Copy of A Remonstrance Presented to the Commons House of Assembly of South Carolina, by the Upper Inhabitants of the Said Province, November 1767. Fulham Papers, X, 183–85.

36. Strickland, *Religion and the State,* 105–7.

37. Allen D. Chandler, *The Colonial Records of the State of Georgia,* 19 vols. (Atlanta, 1906), XIII, 708.

38. Thomas B. Chandler to Dr. Johnson, 22 Jan. 1768. Schneiders, eds., *Samuel Johnson,* I, 433. See footnote 34.

39. James Johnston's *Georgia Gazette* (Savannah), Dec. 20, 1769.

40. *South Carolina Gazette* (Charleston), Sept. 22, 1766–Oct. 20, 1766.

41. Charles Martyn to Bp. of London, 20 Oct. 1765. Fulham Papers, X, 160.

42. George W. Williams, *St. Michael's Charleston, 1751–1951* (Columbia, 1951), 39.

43. See footnote 39.

44. Franklin B. Dexter, *Extracts from the Itineraries of Ezra Stiles* (New Haven, 1916), 598.

45. J. J. Zubly to anonymous person, 11 July 1773. *Proceedings of the Massachusetts Historical Society for 1864–65* (Boston, 1866), 214–19.

CHAPTER 6

1. Zeichner, *Connecticut's Years of Controversy, 1750–1776*, 69; Don R. Gerlach, *Philip Schuyler and the American Revolution in New York 1733–1777* (University of Nebraska, 1964), 102.

2. Thompson Westcott, *History of Philadelphia 1609–1829*, 32 vols. (Philadelphia, 1913), V, 412.

3. Edward F. Humphrey, *Nationalism and Religion in America 1774–1789* (Boston, 1924), 40.

4. Barker, *The Background of the Revolution in Maryland*, 306.

5. Greene, *The Quest for Power*, 368–69.

6. J.W.C. Wand, *Anglicanism in History and Today* (New York, 1962), Chapter V.

7. Philip V. Frithian, *Journal 1775–1776* (Princeton, 1924), 181, 220, 256; Josiah Quincy, *Memoir of the Life of Josiah Quincy* (New York, 1971), 99, 131; Hooker, *The Journal . . . Charles Woodmason*, 51.

8. Goodwin, The Anglican Middle Way, 134–36.

9. Cross, *The Anglican Episcopate*, 25–30, 52–57.

10. F. L. Cross, ed., *The Oxford Dictionary of the Christian Church* (London, 1957), 1105.

11. Schneiders, eds., *Samuel Johnson*, I, 151, 163; 446–47; III, 253; Perry, ed., *Papers . . . Pennsylvania*, 366.

12. Samuel Johnson to Myles Cooper, 12 Feb. 1766. William Samuel Johnson Papers.

13. Robert L. McCaul, "Whitefield's Bethesda College Projects and Other Major Attempts to Found Colonial Colleges," *GHQ*, 44 (1960), 381–85.

14. Davidson, *The Establishment of the Church of England*, 55–57.

15. Pratt, *Religion, Politics and Diversity*, 74; Dora M. Clark, *British Opinion and the American Revolution* (New Haven, 1930), 184–85.

16. Chandler, *An Appeal*, 54–60, 79, 111.

17. Bernhard Knollenberg, *Origin of the American Revolution 1759–1776* (New York, 1965) 83.

18. Chandler, *An Appeal*, 110, 115, 117.

19. William White, *Memoirs* (Philadelphia, 1820), 69.

20. Richard Bland to Thomas Adams, 1 Aug. 1771. *VMHB*, VI (1898–99), 134.

21. Knollenberg, *Origin of the American Revolution*, 79–80; Bridenbaugh, *Mitre and Sceptre*, 214.

22. Cross, *The Anglican Episcopate*, 235–36.

23. Gerlack, *Philip Schuyler and the American Revolution in New York*, 102, 108.

24. Patricia V. Bonomi, *A Factious People: Politics and Society in Colonial New York* (New York, 1971), 248–54.

25. Philip Davidson, *Propaganda and the American Revolution 1763–1783* (Chapel Hill, 1941), 226–35.

26. Bernhard Knollenberg, ed., "Thomas Hollis and Jonathan Mayhew: Their Correspondence, 1759–1766," *Proceedings of the Massachusetts Historical Society*, LXIX (1956), 142.

27. Charles Chauncy to Ezra Stiles, 5 Nov. 1766. *Itineraries*, 443.

28. Franklin B. Dexter, ed., *Extracts from the Itineraries of Ezra Stiles* (New Haven, 1916), 254.

29. Carl L. Becker, *The History of Political Parties in the Province of New York, 1760–1776* (Madison, Wis., 1909), 278–79; Davidson, *Propaganda and the American Revolution 1763–1783*, 249–57.

30. Jonathan Boucher, *Reminiscences of an American Loyalist* (Boston, 1925), 104.

31. Walter H. Stowe, "A Study in Conscience: Some Aspects of the Relations of the Clergy to the State" *HMPEC*, XIX (1950), 301–23.

32. Compare names in *WMQ*, VII (1898–99), 16–20 with vestrymen of parishes in respective counties.

33. Owens, The Virginia Vestry, 249.

34. Davidson, *Propaganda and the American Revolution 1763–1783*, 42–43, 88, 142.

35. Humphrey, *Nationalism and Religion in America 1774–1789*, 39.

36. Charles Inglis, *State of the Anglo-American Church in 1776*, n.d., n.p.

CHAPTER 7

1. Richard G. Solomon, "British Legislation and American Episcopacy," *HMPEC*, XX (1951), 279.

2. Francis L. Hawks, *Contributions to the Ecclesiastical History of the United States of America*, 2 vols. (New York, 1836), II, 290–91.

3. George W. Lamb, comp., "Clergymen Licensed to the American Colonies by the Bishop of London: 1745–1781," *HMPEC* XIII (1944), 131–43; Walter H. Stowe, "The Clergy of the Episcopal Church in 1785," *HMPEC*, XX (1951), 253. In 1774 the Anglican clergy in Conn. (24), Mass. (14), N.H. (2), R.I. (1), Vt. (0), N.Y. (16), N.J. (11), Pa. (16), Del. (0), Md. (54), Va. (105), N.C. (18), S.C. (23), Ga. (2); in 1785 Conn. (18), Mass. (5), N.H. (1), R.I. (3), Vt. (1), N.Y. (6), N. J. (6), Pa. (9), Del. (2), Md. (30), Va. (56), N.C. (5), S.C. (13), Ga. (0).

4. Arthur W. Eaton, *The Church of England in Nova Scotia* (London, 1892), 155–90.

5. Manross, *A History of the American Episcopal Church,* 182.

6. G. B. Utley, *The Life and Times of Thomas John Claggett* (Chicago, 1913), 29.

7. Brydon, *Virginia's Mother Church,* II, 415.

8. Perry, ed., *Historical Collections . . . Massachusetts,* 602.

9. Kenneth W. Cameron, ed., *Letter-Book of Henry Caner* (Hartford, 1972), 83; see Edmund K. Alden in *DAB,* s. v. "Auchmuty, Samuel"; Perry, ed., *Papers . . . Pennsylvania,* 132; Rightmyer, *Maryland's Established Church,* 118; Brydon, *Virginia's Mother Church,* II, 608–12.

10. ·Bishop Burgess, *List of Persons Ordained Deacons 1785–1857* (Boston, 1874), 3–4.

11. Kenneth W. Cameron, comp., *The Anglican Episcopate in Connecticut 1784–1895* (Hartford, 1970), 234–36.

12. Batchelder, *A History of the Eastern Diocese,* II, 98; see also Walter H. Stowe, *More Lay Readers Than Clergy!* (Lebanon, Pa., 1954), 9–10.

13. *Journals of the Conventions of the Protestant Episcopal Church of the State of New Jersey, 1785–1816* (New York, 1890), 36–42; *Protestant Episcopal Church Conventions in Maryland of 1780, 1781, 1782, 1783,* No date or printer given, 152; *Journals of the Conventions of the Protestant Episcopal Church in Virginia in the Diocese of Virginia from 1785–1787; 1789–1835* (New York, 1836), 22.

14. Clara Loveland, *The Critical Years* (Greenwich, Conn., 1956), 15.

15. Walter H. Stowe, "A Study in Conscience: Some Aspects of the Relations of the Clergy to the State," *HMPEC,* XIX (1950), 306–7, 313.

16. Thomas B. Chandler, *Memorandums 1775–1786,* 66. Typed copy of Mss diary is in General Theological Seminary Library.

17. Brydon, *Virginia's Mother Church,* II, 417. *Maryland Declaration of Rights, November 3, 1776 in Proceedings of the Conventions of the Province of Maryland held at the City of Annapolis in 1774, 1775, 1776* (Baltimore, 1836), 314.

18. Saunders, *The Colonial Records of North Carolina,* X, 1011; George C. Rogers, Jr., *Church and State in Eighteenth Century South Carolina* (Charleston, 1959), 22.

19. Perry, ed., *Historical Collections . . . Massachusetts,* 599–601; Hawks and Perry, *Connecticut,* 203, 205; Manross, *A History of the American Episcopal Church,* 178; Burr, *The Anglican Church in New Jersey,* 393; George W. Williams, *St. Michael's Charleston* (Columbia, 1951), 1.

20. Dorsey, *Early English Churches in America 1607–1807,* 51, 52, 119–20, 165; Dalcho, *An Historical Account of the Protestant Episcopal Church in South Carolina,* 387, 392.

21. This expression was coined by Charles C. Tiffany in *A History of the Protestant Episcopal Church in the United States of America* (New York, 1895) but the idea was earlier expressed by Robert Baird in *Religion in America* (New York, 1856), 207–8 and most recently by Winthrop S. Hudson in *Religion in America* (New York, 1965), 117–18. Frederick V. Mills, Sr., "The Protestant Episcopal Churches in the United States 1783–1789: Suspended Animation or Remarkable Recovery?" *HMPEC,* XLVI (June 1977), 151–53.

22. These minutes are under the state conventions of the Protestant Episcopal church. Some statistics, e.g., North Carolina and Georgia, were taken from secondary sources. The statistics for 1774 were taken from the several histories that deal with the respective colonies, states, or dioceses. In 1789 Conn. (29), Mass.-R.I.-N.H. (18), N.Y. (26), N.J. (19), Pa. (21), Del. (5), Md. (47), Va. (73), N.C. (5), S.C. (15), Ga. (1); in 1774 Conn. (42), Mass.-R.I.-N.H. (18), N.Y. (26), N.J. (21), Pa. (23), Del. (8), Md. (44), Va. (95), N.C. (18), S.C. (20), Ga. (3).

23. Claude H. Van Tyne, *The Loyalists in the American Revolution* (New York, 1902), 4–5, 108–15.

24. Eaton, *The Church of England in Nova Scotia,* 96. Mary B. Norton, *The British-Americans: The Loyalist Exiles in England 1774–1789* (Boston, 1972), 8. For another view of the total number of Loyalists see Paul H. Smith, "The American Loyalists: Notes on Their Organization and Numerical Strength," *WMQ,* 25 (1968), 259–77.

25. Charles B. Kinney, Jr., *Church and State* (New York, 1955), 126; Pratt, *Religion, Politics, and Diversity,* 84–92: The vestry of Christ and St. Peter's parish elected in 1775 served until 1779. Of the 23 names that appear 12 can be identified with definite revolutionary activity; 10 appear to have been quiet supporters of the American cause; one a "moderate Loyalist." This vestry advised Richard Peters that the "sense of the congregation" favored the observance of 20 July 1775 as a Day of Prayer and Fasting; it directed the omission of prayers for king and Great Britain; and it expressed strong approval of William White.

26. G. Adolf Koch, *Republican Religion* (Gloucester, Mass., 1964), 185, 203–8; see also Morais, *Deism in Eighteenth Century America,* 28–30, 112–19.

27. Anson P. Stokes and Leo Pfeffer, *Church and State in the United*

States (New York, 1964), 82; Meyer, *Church and State in Massachusetts 1740–1833*, 134; Richard J. Purcell, *Connecticut in Transition: 1775–1818* (Middletown, Conn., 1963), 11.

28. Meyer, *Church and State in Massachusetts,* 136.
29. Kinney, Jr., *Church and State,* 86, 124.
30. Pratt, *Religion, Politics, and Diversity,* 84, 91, 100.
31. *Journals of the General Conventions of the Protestant Episcopal Church in the United States of America; 1784–1814* (Philadelphia, 1817), 3–111.
32. *Maryland Declaration of Rights,* 314.
33. Rightmyer, *Maryland's Established Church,* 118–20.
34. *Handbook of Legislative Petitions,* in the Virginia State Library, Richmond. See 2–18, 18–23.
35. Eckenrode, *Separation of Church and State in Virginia,* 46, 61, 74–115; Gaillard Hunt, ed., *The Writings of James Madison,* 12 vols. (New York, 1901), II, 183–91.
36. George Washington to George Mason, Oct. 3, 1785. John C. Fitzpatrick (ed.), *The Writings of George Washington* (32 vols.; Washington, 1931), 28, 285.
37. Owens, The Virginia Vestry, 249.
38. Saunders, *The Colonial Records of North Carolina,* X, 1011.
39. Lefler and Newsome, *The History of a Southern State,* 125, 135.
40. David Ramsay, *The History of the Independent or Congregational Church in Charleston, S.C. from Its Origin Till the Year 1814;* With an Appendix: Containing the speech of the Rev. William Tennent, A.M. in the Commons House of Assembly, Charleston, S.C., January 11, 1777, on the Petition of the Dissenters from the church then Established in that State (Philadelphia, 1815), 22.
41. Richard Barry, *Mr. Rutledge of South Carolina* (New York, 1942), 227.
42. Charles G. Singer, *South Carolina in the Confederation* (Philadelphia, 1941), 102. William M. Dabney and Marion Dargan, *William Henry Drayton and the American Revolution* (Albuquerque, N.M., 1962), 142–43.
43. Strickland, *Religion and the State of Georgia in the Eighteenth Century,* 163–67.
44. Of the 159 members of the House of Delegates at least 63 were former or contemporary vestrymen.
45. Albert F. Gehenheimer, *William Smith* (Philadelphia, 1943), 28; Edward P. Cheyney, *History of the University of Pennsylvania* (Philadelphia, 1940), 162.

46. Batchelder, *A History of the Eastern Diocese*, II, 167.
47. Walter H. Stowe, "The Corporation for the Relief of Widows and Children of Clergymen," *HMPEC*, III (1934), 19.

CHAPTER 8

1. Richard G. Salomon, "British Legislation and American Episcopacy," *HMPEC*, XX (1951), 282.
2. Walter H. Stowe, ed., "The Autobiography of Bishop William White," *HMPEC*, XXII (1953), 394; Manross, *A History of the American Episcopal Church*, 190.
3. William White, *The Case of the Episcopal Churches in the United States Considered*, ed. Richard G. Salomon (Philadelphia, 1782), 22–25.
4. Gordon S. Wood, *The Creation of the American Republic 1776–1787* (New York, 1972), 56.
5. White, *The Case*, 22, 23, 26.
6. Andrew C. McLaughlin, *The Confederation and the Constitution 1783–1789* (New York, 1905), 40–49; Morison et al., *The Growth of the American Republic*, I, 227–43.
7. White, *The Case*, 25, 29–33.
8. Ibid., 33; Richard Hooker, *The Laws of Ecclesiastical Polity*, 2 vols. (London, 1954), I, 352–53.
9. White, *The Case*, 39; see also A. J. Mason, *The Church of England and Episcopacy* (Cambridge, 1914), 59, 122, 384; Norman Sykes, *Old Priest and New Presbyter* (Cambridge, 1956), 70–71.
10. See A. F. Pollard in *DNB*, s.v. "Whittingham, William."
11. A. Jarvis to W. White, Mar. 25, 1783. White, *The Case*, 50.
12. C. Inglis to W. White, June 9, 1783. John W. Lydekker, ed., *The Life and Letters of Charles Inglis, 1759 to 1787* (London, 1936), 227.
13. C. Inglis to W. White, Oct. 22, 1783.
14. A. Murry to W. White, 26 July 1783. White, *The Case*, 57; J. Duché to W. White, Aug. 11, 1783. Ibid., 58–59, 64–65.
15. *Protestant Episcopal Church Conventions in Maryland of 1780, 1781, 1782, 1783* (No place or date), 146. For William Smith's role, see Rightmyer, *Maryland's Established Church*, 122–23, 147, 150, 213.
16. William S. Perry, *A Half-Century of Legislation of the American Church*, 3 vols. (Claremont, N.H., 1874), III, 23–24.
17. Francis L. Hawks, *Contributions to the Ecclesiastical History of the United States of America*, 2 vols. (New York, 1836), II, 290–91. There was a rumor that the legislature was about to provide nonepiscopal "ordainers."
18. Perry, *Half-Century of Legislation*, 25–27.

19. W. Paca to J. Reed, 12 Sept. 1783. Walter H. Stowe, "The State or Diocesan Conventions of the War and Post-War Periods," *HMPEC*, VIII (1939), 220–56.

20. *Notices and Journals, and Remains of Journals of the Two Preliminary Conventions of the Clergy, . . . in the Diocese of Maryland* (No publisher or date), 10–11; Perry, *Half-Century of Legislation*, 29.

21. W. West to W. White, 5 July 1784. The Eathan Allen Collection, MHS, Baltimore, Md.

22. *Convention Journals of Pennsylvania 1785–1814* (No publisher or date given), 6.

23. Manross, *A History of the American Episcopal Church*, 176; S. Parker to W. White, 21 June 1784. Perry, *Half-Century of Legislation*, 57–59.

24. W. White to S. Parker, Aug. 10, 1784. Perry, *Half-Century of Legislation*, 61–65.

25. Ibid., 62–65.

26. Hawks, *Contributions*, I, Appendix, 1–11, 22.

27. Ibid., For Benjamin Franklin's idea on the matter of ordination see Salomon, "British Legislation," 282. Also White, *Memoirs*, Appendix, 275.

28. *Proceedings of the Convention of the Protestant Episcopal Church in the State of New York, 1785–1791* (New York, 1791), 3–4; Dix, *A History of the Parish of Trinity Church*, II, 1–20.

29. *Journals of the Conventions of the Protestant Episcopal Church of the State of New Jersey, 1785–1816* (New York, 1890), 3–4.

30. Dalcho, *An Historical Account of the P.E.C. in South Carolina*, 465; Perry, *Half-Century of Legislation*, 52–53.

31. D. Griffith to W. White, July 26, 1784. Perry, *Half-Century of Legislation*, 46.

32. Joseph B. Cheshire, Jr., *The Early Conventions: Held at Tawborough, 1790, 1793, 1794* (Raleigh, 1882), 10–13; Henry T. Malone, *The Episcopal Church in Georgia 1733–1957* (Atlanta, 1960), 53.

33. *Journals of the General Conventions of the Protestant Episcopal Church in the United States of America, 1784–1814* (Philadelphia, 1817), preface, 1–16.

34. White, *The Case*, 23, 24, 25, 26.

35. Merrill Jensen, *The New Nation* (New York, 1950), 25; Main, *The Sovereign States*, 445–51.

CHAPTER 9

1. D. Fogg to S. Parker, Aug. 1, 1783. Eben E. Beardsley, *Life and Correspondence of the Right Reverend Samuel Seabury, D.D.* (Boston, 1881), 78. S. D. McConnell in *History of the American Episcopal*

Church (New York, 1904) and Clara O. Loveland in *The Critical Years* (Greenwich, Conn., 1956) use the terms "federal" and "ecclesiastical" to differentiate the two plans of church reorganization.

2. White, *Memoirs*, 22; William J. Seabury, *Memoirs of Bishop Seabury* (New York, 1908), 185.

3. Beardsley, *Life and Correspondence of the Right Reverend Samuel Seabury*, 78, 105.

4. Groce, *William Samuel Johnson*, 153; John W. Lydekker, ed., *The Life and Letters of Charles Inglis 1759 to 1787* (London, 1936), 219.

5. A. Jarvis to W. White, Mar. 25, 1783. White, *The Case*, 50.

6. A. Jarvis to Archbishop W. Markham, May 24, 1783. Beardsley, *Life and Correspondence of the Right Reverend Samuel Seabury*, 87.

7. A. Jarvis to Archbishop W. Markham, May 24, 1783. Beardsley, *Life and Correspondence of the Right Reverend Samuel Seabury*, 87.

8. S. Seabury to Connecticut clergy, Aug. 10, 1783. Beardsley, *Life and Correspondence of the Right Reverend Samuel Seabury*, 109.

9. Seabury, *Memoirs*, 205; see also Bruce Steiner, *Samuel Seabury: A Study in the High Church Tradition* (University of Ohio Press, 1971), 207.

10. Charles J. Abbey, *The English Church and Its Bishops 1700–1800*, 2 vols. (London, 1887), II, 209.

11. Beardsley, *Life and Correspondence of the Right Reverend Samuel Seabury*, 107, 110–11; Seabury, *Memoirs*, 211.

12. Salomon, "British Legislation and the American Episcopate," 283.

13. Zephaniah Swift, *A System of the Laws of the State of Connecticut*, 2 vols. (Windham, 1795), I, 145; Greene, *The Development of Religious Liberty in Connecticut*, 338–41.

14. E. Edwards Beardsley, *The History of the Episcopal Church in Connecticut* (New York, 1866), 355.

15. Seabury, *Memoirs*, 211.

16. G. Berkeley to Bishop J. Skinner, Nov. 1783. Hawks and Perry, *Connecticut*, 238.

17. Perry, *Half-Century of Legislation*, 231.

18. Beardsley, *Life and Correspondence of the Right Reverend Samuel Seabury*, 134; Walter H. Stowe, "The Scottish Episcopal Succession and the Validity of Bishop Seabury's Orders," *HMPEC*, IX (1940), 322–48.

19. Seabury, *Memoirs*, 224.

20. Walter R. Foster, *Bishop and Presbytery: The Church of Scotland 1661–1668* (London, 1958), 4, 12, 38–40; Carpenter, *Eighteenth Century Church and State*, 60; Beardsley, *Life and Correspondence of the Right Reverend Samuel Seabury*, 147, 171.

21. S. Seabury to J. Boucher, Dec. 3, 1784. Hawks and Perry, *Connecticut,* 253.

22. G. Horne to S. Seabury, Jan. 1785. Seabury, *Memoirs,* 259.

23. S. Seabury to J. Leaming, Jan. 5, 1785. Beardsley, *Life and Correspondence of the Right Reverend Samuel Seabury,* 169.

24. J. Skinner to S. Seabury, Jan. 29, 1785. Perry, *Half-Century of Legislation,* 255.

25. T. B. Chandler to J. Skinner, Apr. 23, 1785. Beardsley, *Life and Correspondence of the Right Reverend Samuel Seabury,* 179.

26. Hawks and Perry, *Connecticut,* 249–50.

27. Prince Hoare, *Memoirs of Granville Sharpe,* Esq. (London, 1820), 214.

28. Loveland, *The Critical Years,* 113–14.

29. *Journals of the General Conventions,* Preface.

30. *Journals of the General Conventions,* Preface, 2–16.

31. Loveland, *The Critical Years,* 205.

CHAPTER 10

1. Seabury, *Memoirs,* 289; *Journals of the General Conventions,* 5.

2. Beardsley, *Life and Correspondence of the Right Reverend Samuel Seabury,* 208; 213.

3. Seabury, *Memoirs,* 289.

4. W. Smith to S. Seabury, July 12, 1786. Hawks and Perry, *Connecticut,* 301.

5. T. B. Chandler to S. Seabury, July 28, 1785. Seabury, *Memoirs,* 288, 289.

6. S. Seabury to W. White, Aug. 15, 1785. Beardsley, *Life and Correspondence of the Right Reverend Samuel Seabury,* 230–35.

7. S. Seabury to W. White, Aug. 19, 1785. Hawks and Perry, *Connecticut,* 281.

8. T. B. Chandler to W. White, Sept. 2, 1785. Perry, *Half-Century of Legislation,* 72–75.

9. T. B. Chandler to W. White, Sept. 20, 1785. Hawks and Perry, *Connecticut,* 283, 285.

10. *Journals of the General Conventions,* 5–6.

11. Manross, *A History of the American Episcopal Church,* 182.

12. See Guy E. Shipler in *DAB,* s.v. "Provoost, Samuel."

13. Maude E. Woodfin in *DAB,* s.v. "Page, John"; Sarah H. J. Simpson in *DAB,* s.v. "Duane, James"; Anne K. Gregorie in *DAB,* s.v. "Pinckney, Charles C"; James H. Pelling in *DAB,* s.v. "Peters, Richard."

14. See William R. Smith in *DAB,* s.v. "Shippen, Edward"; John W.

Jordon, ed., *Colonial Families of Philadelphia,* 2 vols. (New York, 1911), II, 11–112; E. W. Spangler, "Memoirs of Major John Clark, of York County, Pennsylvania," *PMHB,* 20 (1896), 77–86; Thomas W. Balch, *The Swift Family of Philadelphia* (Philadelphia, 1906), 28–29; Henry C. Conrad, *History of the State of Delaware,* 3 vols. (Wilmington, 1908), I, 285; II, 999.

15. *Journals of the General Conventions,* 8–10.
16. Perry, *Half-Century of Legislation,* 210.
17. William S. Perry, ed., *The Life, Times, and Correspondence of William White,* 2 vols. (Privately Printed, 1887), II, 7.
18. *Journals of the General Conventions,* 12–15.
19. *Proceedings of the Convention of the Protestant Episcopal Church in the State of New York.* 7.
20. Hawks, *Ecclesiastical Contributions,* I, Appendix, 13–17.
21. White, *Memoirs,* 325.
22. R. H. Lee to unnamed party, Oct. 10, 1785. James C. Ballagh, ed., *The Letters of Richard Henry Lee,* 2 vols. (New York, 1914), II, 388.
23. J. Jay to J. Adams, Nov. 1, 1785. Charles F. Adams, ed., *The Works of John Adams,* 10 vols. (Boston, 1835), VIII, 334–35, 362.
24. See Samuel F. Bemis in *DAB,* s.v. "Jay, John."
25. Theodore Sedgwick, *A Memoir of the Life of William Livingston* (New York, 1833), 149.
26. J. Adams to J. Jay, Jan. 4, 1786. Adams, ed., *The Works of John Adams,* XIII, 361–62.
27. *Journals of the Conventions-Massachusetts,* 18.
28. Dalcho, *An Historical Account,* Appendix, 469.
29. *Journals of the Conventions—New Jersey,* 5–15.
30. *Notices and Journals—Maryland,* 16–20.
31. Perry, *Half-Century of Legislation,* 338, 341; *Journals of the General Conventions,* 43–44.
32. E. Bass to S. Parker, Jan. 3, 1786. Hawks and Perry, *Connecticut,* 288.
33. J. Boucher to J. Skinner, Jan. 4, 1786. Beardsley, *Life and Correspondence of the Right Reverend Samuel Seabury,* 204.
34. J. Duché to W. White, Mar. 25, 1786. Perry, *Half-Century of Legislation,* 290.
35. S. Provoost to W. White, May 20, 1786. Perry, *Half-Century of Legislation,* 300–301.
36. *Journals of the General Conventions,* 21.
37. Ibid., 19–20, 22–26, 33.
38. Edward L. Parsons and Bayard H. Jones, *The American Prayer Book* (New York, 1937), 47–51.

39. *Journals of the General Conventions,* 42–44.

40. William W. Sweet, *Religion on the American Frontier, 1783–1840;* Vol. IV, *The Methodist* (Chicago, 1946), 18, 7, 9, 11.

41. John Telford, ed., *The Letters of the Rev. John Wesley, A.M.,* 8 vols. (London, 1931), II, 240.

42. Telford, ed., *Letters of John Wesley,* VII, 169, 238.

43. Ibid., VIII, 91.

44. C. Wesley to T. B. Chandler, Apr. 20, 1785. MS letter is in the MHS, Baltimore, Maryland.

45. Telford, ed., *Letters of John Wesley,* VII, 366.

46. Sweet, *Religion on the American Frontier,* 28; White, *Memoirs,* 343.

47. Beardsley, *Life and Correspondence of the Right Reverend Samuel Seabury,* 293–94.

48. Perry, *Half-Century of Legislation,* 343.

49. J. Skinner to S. Seabury, June 20, 1787. Beardsley, *Life and Correspondence of the Right Reverend Samuel Seabury,* 297.

50. W. White to S. Seabury, May 21, 1787. Ibid., 302.

51. D. Griffity to M. White, May 28, 1787. Perry, *Half-Century of Legislation,* 349, 371, 390.

52. Hawks, *Ecclesiastical Contributions,* I, 17, 20, 27.

53. H. Dent to F. Walker, June 26, 1787. The Eathan Allen Collection, MHS, Baltimore, Md.

54. P. Bowen to Mr. Dwight, July 14, 1787. Letter Book of the Rev. Penuel Bowen, SCHS, Charleston, S.C.

55. J. H. Thompson to C. Pettigrew, Feb. 17, 1785. Pettigrew Papers, UNC, Chapel Hill, N.C.

56. Henry Purcell, *Strictures on the Love of Power in the Prelacy* (Charleston, 1795).

57. R. Viets to S. Peters, Oct. 12, 1787. Samuel Peters Correspondence, NYHS, III, No. 45.

58. E. Dibblee to S. Peters, Nov. 16, 1787. Ibid., III, No. 53.

59. Beardsley, *Life and Correspondence of the Right Reverend Samuel Seabury,* 310–11.

60. Perry, *Half-Century of Legislation,* 376.

CHAPTER 11

1. J. Leaming to W. White, July 9, 1787. Beardsley, *Life and Correspondence of the Right Reverend Samuel Seabury,* 306, 318.

2. W. White to S. Parker, Aug. 6, 1787. Hawks and Perry, *Connecticut,* 316.

3. Perry, *Half-Century of Legislation,* 351, 358.

4. E. Dibblee to S. Peters, Mar. 1, 1788. Samuel Peters Correspondence, NYHS, III, No. 73.

5. D. Griffith to W. White, June 12, 1788. David Griffith Papers, 1760–1789, VHS, Richmond, Va.

6. W. West to W.White, July 14, 1788. MHS.

7. Robert E. Thompson, *A History of the Presbyterian Churches in the United States.* (New York, 1895), 226, 185.

8. H. Purcell to W. White, n.d. Perry, *Half-Century of Legislation,* 371.

9. *Journals of the General Conventions,* 3–4, 18, 31, 64.

10. W. White to S. Parker, 1788. Perry, *Half-Century of Legislation,* 376.

11. S. Parker to W. White, Jan. 20, 1789. Hawks and Perry, *Connecticut,* 325.

12. Ibid.

13. S. Provoost to W., White, Feb. 24, 1789. Perry, *Half-Century of Legislation,* 381.

14. S. Seabury to S. Parker, Apr. 10, 1789. Hawks and Perry, *Connecticut,* 327.

15. S. Seabury to W. Smith, July 23, 1789. Hawks and Perry, *Connecticut,* 332–33.

16. *Journals of the Conventions—New Jersey,* 53–54.

17. *Journals of the General Conventions,* 47, 49.

18. Nelson W. Rightmyer, *The Anglican Church in Delaware* (Philadelphia, 1947), 182; Hamilton Schuyler, *A History of Saint Michael's Church* (Princeton, 1926), 103; *The New York Genealogical and Biographical Record,* V. 14–15 (New York, 1883), 157; George M. Hills, *History of the Church in Burlington* (Trenton, 1885), 811; John Hall, ed., *Memoirs of Matthew Clarkson* (Philadelphia, 1890), 46; See Broadus Mitchell in *DAB,* s.v. "Coxe, Tench"; Hamilton Schuyler, *A History of St. Michael's Church,* 91.

19. *Journals of the General Conventions,* 50–54.

20. Ibid., 64.

21. Standing Committee to S. Seabury, Aug. 16, 1789. Hawks and Perry, *Connecticut,* 347–48.

22. See Milton H. Thomas in *DAB,* s.v. "Moore, Benjamin."

23. See J. G. deR. Hamilton in *DAB,* s.v. "Smith, Robert."

24. S. Seabury to S. Parker, Aug. 1789. Hawks and Perry, *Connecticut,* 350.

25. S. Provoost to W. White, Aug. 26, 1789. Ibid., 351, 352.

26. *Journals of the General Conventions,* 68.

27. Ibid., 72–74, 86.

28. Parsons and Jones, *The American Prayer Book,* 112, 231.

29. Charles W. Douglas, "Early Hymnology of the American Episcopal Church," *HMPEC,* X (1941), 202–18.

30. B. Hubbard to S. Peters, July 5, 1790. Samuel Peters Correspondence, NYHS, IV, No. 86.

31. E. Dibblee to S. Peters, Nov. 6, 1789. Ibid.

32. Percy V. Norwood, "Constitutional Developments Since 1789," *HMPEC,* VIII (1939), 285; *Journals of the General Conventions,* 113.

33. Ibid., 127; Hawks, *Ecclesiastical Contributions,* I, 210.

34. Hawks, *Ecclesiastical Contributions,* I, Appendix, 31.

35. See William A. Beardsley in *DAB,* s.v. "Bass, Edward."

36. W. Wheeler and N. Fisher to Bp. Provoost, Sept. 18, 1789. Bass Papers, HSPEC, Boston, Mass.

37. Eben F. Stone, *A Sketch of Tristram Dalton,* Historical Collection of Essex Institute, XXV (Jan.–Mar. 1888), Nos. 1, 2, 3, 1–29.

38. *William Bentley Diary,* 4 vols. (Salem, 1905–14), I, 354.

39. Seabury, *Memoirs,* 312.

40. B. Hubbard to S. Peters, July 5, 1790. Samuel Peters Correspondence, NYHS, IV, No. 86.

CHAPTER 12

1. Frank Barlow, *The English Church 1000–1066* (London, 1963), 99.

2. *The Cambridge Medieval History,* eds. H. M. Gwatkin and J. P. Whitney, (8 vols., New York, 1911), I, 145–46; A. J. Maclean, "The Position of Clergy and Laity in the Early Church in Relation to the Episcopate," in *Episcopacy Ancient and Modern,* eds. Claude Jenkins and K. D. Mackenzie (London, 1930), 52.

3. Dom Gregory Dix, "The Ministry in the Early Church," in *The Apostolic Ministry,* ed. Kenneth E. Kirk (London, 1947), 227–79.

4. F. M. Stenton, *Anglo-Saxon England* (Oxford, 1943), 147.

5. *The Cambridge Medieval History,* VI, 528–29.

6. Dom David Knowles, "Religious Life and Organization," in *Medieval England,* ed. Austin L. Poole, 2 vols. (Oxford, 1958), II, 384–85; H. R. Lyon, *Anglo-Saxon England and the Norman Conquest* (Oxford, 1962), 238.

7. David C. Douglas, *William the Conqueror* (Berkeley, 1964), 317.

8. C. R. Cheney, *From Becket to Langton: English Church Government 1170–1213* (Manchester University Press, 1956), 20.

9. W. A. Pantin, *The English Church in the Fourteenth Century* (Cambridge, 1955), 9.

10. T. M. Parker, "Feudal Episcopacy" in *The Apostolic Ministry,* 377–78.

11. Douglas, *William the Conqueror,* 330–35.
12. E. F. Jacob, *The Fifteenth Century 1399–1485* (Oxford, 1961), 272; T. M. Parker, "Feudal Episcopacy" in *The Apostolic Ministry,* 380–81.
13. B. M. Hamilton Thompson, "The Post-Reformation Episcopate in England," in *The Apostolic Ministry,* 392–406.
14. Ibid., 423; Norman Sykes, *Old Priest and New Presbyter* (Cambridge, 1956), 81.
15. B. M. Hamilton Thompson, "The Post-Reformation Episcopate in England," in *The Apostolic Ministry,* 427–30.
16. Godfrey Davies, *The Early Stuarts 1603–1660* (Oxford, 1959), 191–93; Cecilia M. Ady, "Restoration to the Present Day," in *The Apostolic Ministry,* 433.
17. Ibid., 440; G. V. Bennett, "King William III and The Episcopate," in *Essays in Modern English Church History,* eds. G. V. Bennett and J. D. Walsh (London, 1966), 104.
18. Ady, "Restoration to the Present Day," 444; Norman Sykes, *William Wake,* 2 vols. (Cambridge, 1957), 333–39; Sykes, *Old Priest and New Presbyter,* 167–68.
19. Sykes, *Church and State,* 355; Robbins, *The Eighteenth Century Commonwealthman,* 295–304, 333–34.
20. Sykes, *Old Priest and New Presbyter,* 168–76.
21. Ibid., 175–76.
22. R. Bland to T. Adams, Aug. 1, 1771 "Letters of Richard Bland," *VHM,* VI, 131–32.
23. G. MacLaren Brydon,"New Light on the Origins of the Method of Electing Bishops Adopted by the American Episcopal Church," *HMPEC,* XIX (1950), 207–8.
24. White, *The Case,* 24.
25. Prince Hoare, *Memoirs of Granville Sharpe,* Esq. (London, 1820), 209, 212–14; B. Franklin to G. Sharpe, July 5, 1785, John Bigelow, ed., *The Works of Benjamin Franklin,* 12 vols. (New York, 1904), XI, 77–78, 217, 221, 224.
26. Robert Phillimore, *The Ecclesiastical Law of the Church of England* (2 vols., London, 1895), I, 47–49, 144, 148.
27. Ibid., II, 924–27; I, 65–71, 607, 638–41; II, 832, 972, 1927.
28. *Journals of the General Conventions,* 76.
29. *Journals of the General Conventions,* 75–76.
30. White, *The Case,* 32.
31. Sykes, *Church and State,* 61.
32. Ezra Stiles, *Diary,* III, 173.

Bibliography

PRIMARY SOURCES

MANUSCRIPTS

Bass Papers. MSS are in the Historical Society of the Protestant Episcopal Church in Boston.

Church Commissioners Book, 1717–1742. MS is in the Archives of the State of South Carolina, Columbia.

David Griffith Papers. MSS are in the Virginia Historical Society, Richmond.

Dulany Papers. MSS are in the Maryland Historical Society, Baltimore.

The Eathan Allen Collection, 1754–1799. MSS are in the University of North Carolina Library, Chapel Hill.

Henry Laurens Letter Books. 5 vols. MSS are in the South Carolina Historical Society, Charleston.

John Rutledge Papers, 1766–1819. MSS are in the University of North Carolina Library, Chapel Hill.

Letter Book of the Reverend Penuel Bowen. MS is in the South Carolina Historical Society, Charleston.

Letters of Richard Peters. 8 vols. MSS are in the Historical Society of Pennsylvania, Philadelphia.

The Penn Correspondence. 9 vols. MSS are in the Historical Society of Pennsylvania, Philadelphia.

Pettigrew Papers. MSS are in the University of North Carolina, Chapel Hill.

Vestry Register of Christ Church and St. Peter's Church, 1760–1784. MS is in Christ Church, Philadelphia, Pennsylvania.

William Samuel Johnson Diaries. MS is in the Connecticut Historical Society, Hartford.

William Samuel Johnson Papers. MSS are in the Connecticut Historical Society, Hartford.

Zubly, John J. Journal of the Revd John Joachin Zubly. MS is in the Georgia Historical Society, Savannah.

PRINTED MATERIALS

Adams, Charles F., ed. *The Works of John Adams, Second President of the United States: with a Life of the Author, Notes, and Illustrations.* 10 vols. Boston, 1853., Boston, 1853.

Apthorp, East. *Considerations on the Institution and Conduct of the S.P.G.* Boston, 1763.

Archbishops' Commission on Canon Law. *The Canon Law of the Church of England.* London: S.P.C.K., 1947.

Ballagh, James C., ed. *The Letters of Richard Henry Lee.* 2 vols. New York, 1914.

Beardsley, Eben E. *Life and Correspondence of the Right Reverend Samuel Seabury, D.D.* Boston, 1881.

William Bentley Diary. 4 vols. Salem, 1905–1914.

Bigelow, John, *The Works of Benjamin Franklin.* 12 vols. New York, 1904.

"Letters of Richard Bland," *VMHB*, VI. Richmond: Virginia Historical Society, 1898–99, 120–32.

"Letters of Jonathan Boucher." *Maryland Historical Magazine,* VIII. Baltimore: Maryland Historical Society, 1913, 177–84, 236–38, 295.

Boucher, Jonathan. *Reminiscences of an American Loyalist.* Boston, 1925.

———. *A View of the Causes and Consequences of the American Revolution.* London, 1792.

Boyd, Julian P., ed. *The Papers of Thomas Jefferson.* 19 vols. Princeton, 1950.

Brown, William H., ed. *Archives of Maryland: Proceedings of the Council of Maryland.* 32 vols. Baltimore, 1912.

———,ed. *Correspondence of Governor Horatio Sharpe.* 3 vols. Baltimore, 1895.

Butterfield, L. H., ed. *Diary and Autobiography of John Adams.* 2 vols. Cambridge, 1961.

Cameron, Kenneth W., ed. *Letter-Book of Henry Caner.* Hartford, 1972.

Cameron, Kenneth W., comp. *The Anglican Episcopate in Connecticut 1784–1895.* Hartford, 1970.

Chandler, Allen D. *The Colonial Records of the State of Georgia.* 19 vols. Atlanta, 1906.

Chandler, Thomas B. *A Free Examination of the Critical Commentary on Archbishop Secker's Letter.* New York, 1774.

———. *An Address from the Clergy of New York and New Jersey.* New York, 1771.

———. *The Appeal Defended.* New York, 1769.

————.*An Appeal to the Public in Behalf of the Church of England in America.* New York, 1767.

————. *The Life of Samuel Johnson, D.D.* London: Reprinted for C. and J. Rivington, 1824.

————. *Memorandumus 1775–1786.* New York: General Theological Seminary Library.

Chauncy, Charles. *An Appeal to the Public Answered.* Boston, 1768.

————. *A Reply to Dr. Chandler's Appeal Defended.* Boston, 1770.

Cheshire, Joseph B. *The Early Conventions: Held at Tawborough, 1790, 1793 and 1794.* Raleigh, 1882.

Clark, Samuel A. *The History of St. John's Church, Elizabeth Town, New Jersey.* Philadelphia, 1857.

Convention Journals of Pennsylvania 1785–1814. No date or publisher given.

"Correspondence between the Right Reverend John Skinner, Jr., and the Reverend Jonathan Boucher." *HMPEC,* X (1941), 163–75.

Dalcho, Frederick. *An Historical Account of the Protestant Episcopal Church in South Carolina.* Charleston, 1820.

Dexter, Franklin B., ed. *Extracts from the Itineraries of Ezra Stiles.* New Haven, 1916.

————, ed. *The Literary Diary of Ezra Stiles.* 3 vols New York, 1901.

Eddis, William, *Letters from America 1769 to 1777.* London, 1792.

Fithian, Philip V. *Journal 1775–1776.* Princeton, 1924.

Fitzpatrick, John C., ed. *The Diaries of George Washington 1748–1799.* 4 vols. Boston, 1925.

————. *The Writings of George Washington.* 32 vols. Washington, D.C.: United States Printing Office, 1931.

Fulham Papers in Lambeth Palace. 40 vols. Microfilm copy on thirteen reels are in the Library of Congress, Washington, D.C.

Gwatkin, Thomas. *A Letter to the Clergy of New York and New Jersey.* Williamsburg, 1772.

Hamilton, Stanislaus M., ed. *Letters to Washington and Accompanying Papers.* 3 vols. Boston, 1901.

Handbook of Legislative Petitions. Richmond, Virginia State Library.

Hardy, Thomas, ed. *The Works of Thomas Secker.* 4 vols. London, 1804.

Hartshorne, Albert, ed. *Memoirs of a Royal Chaplain 1729–1763.* London, 1905.

Hastings, Hugh, ed. *Ecclesiastical Records of the State of New York.* 7 vols. Albany, 1905.

Hawks, Francis L. *A Narrative of Events Connected with the Rise and Progress of the Protestant Episcopal Church in Virginia.* New York, 1836.

The appendix contains Journals of the Conventions of the Protestant Episcopal Church in the Diocese of Virginia from 1785–1787; 1789–1835.

Hawks, Francis L., and William S. Perry. *Documentary History of the Protestant Episcopal Church in Connecticut 1704–1789.* Hartford, 1959.

Hoare, Prince. *Memoirs of Granville Sharpe, Esq.* London, 1820.

Hollis, Thomas. *Diary, 1759–1770.* 2 vols. Williamsburg: Institute of Early American History and Culture.

Hooker, Richard. *Of the Laws of Ecclesiastical Polity.* 2 vols. London, 1954.

———. *The Journal and Other Writings of Charles Woodmason, Anglican Itinerant.* Chapel Hill, 1953.

Hunt, Gaillard, ed. *The Writings of James Madison.* 12 vols. New York, 1901.

Inglis, Charles. *Journal of Occurrences 1785 to 1810.* New York: General Theological Seminary Library.

———. *State of the Anglo-American Church in 1776.* n.d.

Jarratt, Devereux, *The Life of the Reverend Devereux Jarratt.* Baltimore, 1806.

Journals of the Conventions of the Protestant Episcopal Church in the Diocese of Massachusetts, 1784–1828. Boston, 1849.

Journals of the Conventions of the Protestant Episcopal Church in the Diocese of Massachusetts, 1784–1816. New York, 1890.

Journals of the Conventions of the Protestant Episcopal Church in Virginia in the Diocese of Virginia from 1785–1787; 1789–1835. New York, 1836.

Journals of the General Conventions of the Protestant Episcopal Church in the United States of America; 1784–1814. Philadelphia, 1817.

"Letters of Dr. William Samuel Johnson." *Collections of the Massachusetts Historical Society.* 5th Series, IX. Boston, 1885. 211–490.

Kennedy, John P., ed. *Journals of the House of Burgesses in Virginia 1770–1772.* Richmond, Va., 1906.

Knollenberg, Bernhard, ed. "Thomas Hollis and Jonathan Mayhew: Their Correspondence, 1759–1766." *The Proceedings of the Massachusetts Historical Society,* LXIX. Boston, 1956.

Lee, Richard H. *Life of Arthur Lee, LL.D.* Boston, 1829.

A Letter Concerning an American Bishop to T. B. Chandler. 1768.

Lydekker, John W., ed. *The Life and Letters of Charles Inglis 1759 to 1787.* London: S.P.G., 1936.

Mayhew, Jonathan. *Observations on the Charter.* Boston, 1763.

"Minutes of Conventions of the Clergy of Connecticut for the Years 1766, 1784, and 1785." *HMPEC,* III. 1934, 55–64.

Minutes of the Standing Committee of the S.P.G., 1760–1775. Microfilm copy in the Library of Congress, Washington, D. C.

"Letters of William Nelson." *William and Mary Quarterly*, V. January 1897, 149–56.

Notices and Journals, and Remains of Journals, of the two Preliminary Conventions of the Clergy, and of the First Five Annual Conventions and Two Adjourned Conventions of the Clergy and Laity of the Protestant Episcopal Church in the Diocese of Maryland, in the years 1783, 1784, 1785, 1786, 1787, 1788. No date or publisher given.

O'Callaghan, E. B., ed. *Documents Relative to the Colonial History of the State of New York.* 11 vols. Albany, 1856.

Perry, William S., *A Half-Century of Legislation of the American Church.* 3 vols. Claremont, N.H., 1874.

———, ed. *Historical Collections Relating to the American Colonial Church-Massachusetts.* Printed Privately, 1873.

——— ed., *Historical Notes and Documents.* 3 vols. Claremont, N. H., 1874.

———. *Journals of General Conventions of the Protestant Episcopal Church.* 3 vols. Claremont, N. H., 1874.

———, ed. *The Life, Times and Correspondence of William White.* 2 vols. Privately Printed, 1887.

———, ed. *Papers of the Church in Maryland 1694–1775.* Privately Printed, 1878.

———, ed. *Papers of the Church in Pennsylvania 1680–1778.* Privately Printed, 1871.

———, ed. *Papers Relating to the History of the Church in Delaware.* Privately Printed, 1875.

Samuel Peters Correspondence. 8 vols. Microfilm copy. New York: New-York Historical Society.

Pleasants, J. Hall, ed. *Archives of Maryland: General Assembly of Maryland.* 32 vols. Baltimore, 1944.

Proceedings of the Conventions of the Protestant Episcopal Church in the State of New York, 1785–1791. New York, 1791.

Proceedings of the Conventions of the Province of Maryland held at the City of Annapolis in 1774, 1775, 1776. Baltimore, 1836.

Proceedings of the Massachusetts Historical Society for 1864–65. Boston, 1866.

Protestant Episcopal Church Conventions in Maryland of 1780, 1781, 1782, 1783. No date or printer given.

Purcell, Henry. *Stricture on the Love of Power in the Prelacy.* Charleston, 1795.

Quincy, Josiah. *Memoir of the Life of Josiah Quincy.* New York, 1971.

Saunders, William L., ed. *The Colonial Records of North Carolina.* 9 vols. Raleigh, 1883.

Schneider, Harold and Carol, eds. *Samuel Johnson President of King's College His Career and Writings.* 4 vols. New York, 1929.

Seabury, William J. *Memoirs of Bishop Seabury.* New York, 1908.

Secker, Thomas. *An Answer to Dr. Mayhew's Observations on the Character and Conduct of The Society for the Propagation of the Gospel in Foreign Parts.* This pamphlet is found in volume 4 of *The Works of Thomas Secker,* Thomas Hardy, ed. London, 1804.

Sedgwick, Theodore. *A Memoir of the Life of William Livingston.* New York, 1833.

Smith, Horace W. *Life and Correspondence of the Reverend William Smith, D.D.* 2 vols. Philadelphia, 1880.

Smith, James J., ed. *The Grenville Papers.* 4 vols. London, 1852.

Smith, William. *Works.* 3 vols. Philadelphia, 1803.

S.P.G. Papers for New Jersey, 1701–1783. Microfilm copies in Rutgers University.

St. Paul Parish Records 1702–1779. Microfilm copy in University of North Carolina Library, Chapel Hill.

Stowe, Walter H., ed. "The Seabury Minutes of the New York Clergy Conventions of 1766 and 1767." *HMPEC,* X. 1941, 125–62.

Sullivan, James, ed. *The Papers of Sir William Johnson.* 13 vols. Albany, 1931.

Swift, Zephaniah. *A System of the Laws of the State of Connecticut.* 2 vols. Windham, 1795.

Telford, John, ed. *The Letters of the Rev. John Wesley,* A.M. 8 vols. London, 1931.

White, William. *Memoirs of the Protestant Episcopal Church.* Philadelphia, 1820.

"Letter of J. J. Zubly." *Proceedings of the Massachusetts Historical Society, 1864–1865.* Boston, 1866, 214–19.

NEWSPAPERS

Boston Gazette, 1765–75.

Georgia Gazette, 1765–70.

Maryland Gazette, 1765–75; 1782–85.

New York Gazette, 1765–75; 1783–86.

Pennsylvania Gazette, 1765–75; 1787–89.

Pennsylvania Journal, 1765–75; 1783–89.

South Carolina Gazette, 1765–75.
Virginia Gazette, 1765–75; 1787–89.

SECONDARY SOURCES

BOOKS

Abbey, Charles J. *The English Church and Its Bishops 1700–1800.* 2 vols. London, 1887.

Abbey, Charles J., and John H. Overton, *The English Church in the Eighteenth Century.* 2 vols. London, 1878.

Abbott, W. W. *The Royal Governors of Georgia 1754–1775.* Chapel Hill: University of North Carolina, 1959.

Anderson, James S.M. *The History of the Church of England in the Colonies.* 3 vols. London, 1856.

Andrews, Matthew P. *History of Maryland: Province and State.* Garden City, N.Y., 1929.

Archbishops' Commission on Canon Law. *The Canon Law of the Church of England.* London: S.P.C.K., 1947.

Archbishops' Commission on Ecclesiastical Courts. *The Ecclesiastical Courts.* London: S.P.C.K., 1945.

Bailyn, Bernard. *Education in the Forming of American Society.* Chapel Hill, 1960.

———. *Ideological Origins of the American Revolution.* Cambridge: Harvard University Press, 1968.

Baker, Charles A. *The Background of the Revolution in Maryland.* New Haven, 1940.

Balch, Thomas W. *The Swift Family of Philadelphia.* Philadelphia, 1906.

Barlow, Frank. *The English Church 1000–1066.* London: Longmans, 1963.

Barratt, Norris S. *Outline of the History of Old St. Paul's Church, Philadelphia, Pennsylvania.* Philadelphia, 1917.

Barry, Richard. *Mr. Rutledge of South Carolina.* New York, 1942.

Batchelder, Calvin R. *A History of the Eastern Diocese.* 3 vols. Boston, 1910.

Becker, Carl L. *The History of Political Parties in the Province of New York, 1760–1776.* Madison, Wis., 1909.

Belden, Albert D. *George Whitefield, The Awakener.* London, 1931.

Bennett, G. V., and J. D. Walsh, eds. *Essays in Modern English Church History.* London, 1966.

Bonomi, Patricia V. *A Factious People: Politics and Society in Colonial New York.* New York, 1971.

Bridenbaugh, Carl. *Mitre and Sceptre.* New York, 1962.

――――, and Jessica Bridenbaugh. *Rebels and Gentlemen.*, New York, 1965.

Brown, Robert E. *Middle-Class Democracy and the Revolution in Massachusetts, 1691–1780.* Ithaca, 1955.

Broxap, Henry. *The Later Non-Jurors.* Cambridge: At the University Press, 1924.

Brydon, G. MacLaren. *Virginia's Mother Church and the Political Conditions Under Which It Grew.* Vol. I, Richmond: Virginia Historical Society, 1947; Vol. II, Philadelphia, 1952.

Burgess, Bishop. *List of Persons Ordained Deacons 1785–1857.* Boston, 1874.

Burr, Nelson R. *The Anglican Church in New Jersey.* Philadelphia, 1954.

――――. *The Story of the Diocese of Connecticut.* Hartford, 1962.

Bushman, Richard L. *From Puritan to Yankee.* Cambridge, 1967.

Calam, John. *Parsons and Pedagogues: the S.P.G. Adventure in American Education.* New York, 1971.

Carpenter, S. C. *Eighteenth Century Church and State.* London, 1959.

Cheney, C. R. *From Becket to Langton 1170–1213.* Manchester University Press, 1956.

Cheyney, Edward P. *History of the University of Pennsylvania.* Philadelphia, 1940.

Clark, Dora M. *British Opinion and the American Revolution.* New Haven, 1930.

Cocke, Charles F. *Parish Lines: Diocese of Southwestern Virginia.* The Virginia State Library: Richmond, 1960.

Conrad, Henry C. *History of the State of Delaware.* 3 vols. Wilmington, 1908.

Cross, Arthur L. *The Anglican Episcopate and the American Colonies.* New York, 1902.

Cross, F. L., ed. *The Oxford Dictionary of the Christian Church.* London, 1957.

Cummings, Hubertis. *Richard Peters.* Philadelphia, 1944.

Dabney, William M., and Marion Dargan. *William Henry Drayton and the American Revolution.* Albuquerque, N. M., 1962.

Davidson, Elizabeth H. *The Establishment of the English Church in Continental America.* Durham, 1936.

Davidson, Philip. *Propaganda and the American Revolution 1763–1783.* Chapel Hill, 1941.

Davies, Godfrey. *The Early Stuarts 1603–1660*. Oxford, 1959.

Dix, Morgan. *A History of the Parish of Trinity Church in the City of New York*. 3 vols. New York, 1898.

Dorsey, Stephen P. *Early English Churches in America 1607–1807*. New York, 1952.

Douglas, David C. *William the Conqueror*. Berkeley, 1964.

Douglas, Winifred. *Church Music in History and Practice*. New York, 1937.

Downey, James. *The Eighteenth Century Pulpit*. Oxford: The Clarendon Press, 1969.

Eaton, Arthur W. *The Church of England in Nova Scotia*. London, 1892.

Eckenrode, H. J. *Separation of Church and State in Virginia*. Richmond, 1910.

Ellenwood, Leonard. *The History of American Church Music*. New York, 1953.

Fisher, Sydney G. *The Making of Pennsylvania*. Philadelphia, 1896.

Flippin, Percy S. *The Royal Government in Virginia*. New York, 1919.

Foote, Henry W. *Three Centuries of American Hymnody*. Cambridge, Mass. 1940.

Foster, Walter R. *Bishop and Presbytery: The Church of Scotland 1661–1688*. London, 1958.

Gaustad, Edwin S. *The Great Awakening in New England*. Gloucester, Mass., 1965.

———. *Historical Atlas of Religion in America*. New York, 1962.

Gehenheimer, Albert F. *William Smith*. Philadelphia, 1943.

Gerlach, Don R. *Philip Schuyler and the American Revolution in New York 1733–1777*. University of Nebraska Press, 1964.

Goen, C. C. *Revivalism and Separatism in New England, 1740–1800*. New Haven, 1962.

Greene, Evarts B. *The Revolutionary Generation 1763–1790*. New York, 1943.

Greene, Jack P. *The Quest for Power*. New York, 1972.

Griffith, Lucille. *The Virginia House of Burgesses 1750–1774*. Montgomery, Ala. 1968.

Groce, Jr., George C. *William Samuel Johnson, A Maker of the Constitution*. New York, 1937.

Gwatkin, H. M., and J. P. Whitney, eds. *The Cambridge Medieval History*. 8 vols. New York, 1911.

Hall, John, ed. *Memoirs of Matthew Clarkson*. Philadelphia, 1890.

Hawks, Francis L. *Contributions to the Ecclesiastical History of the United States of America*. 2 vols. New York, 1836.

Heimert, Alan. *Religion and the American Mind.* Cambridge, 1968.

Hills, George M. *History of the Church in Burlington.* Trenton, 1885.

Holmes, George S. *A Historic Sketch of the Parish Church of St. Michael, in the Province of South Carolina.* Charleston, S. C., 1887.

Hudson, Winthrop S. *Religion in America.* New York, 1965.

Humphrey, Edward F. *Nationalism and Religion in America 1774–1789.* Boston, 1924.

Hutson, James. *Pennsylvania Politics.* Princeton, 1972.

Ingle, Edward. "Local Institutions of Virginia," in *Johns Hopkins University Studies,* 3rd Ser., nos. 2 and 3, 1885.

Jenkins, Claude, and K. D. Mackenzie, eds. *Episcopacy Ancient and Modern.* London, 1930.

Jensen, Merrill. *The New Nation.* New York, 1950.

Jones, Thomas F. *A Pair of Lawn Sleeves.* Philadelphia, 1972.

Jordon, John W., ed. *Colonial Families of Philadelphia.* 2 vols. New York, 1911.

Kemmer, Donald L. *Path to Freedom: The Struggle for Self-Government in Colonial New Jersey 1703–1776.* Princeton, 1940.

Kinney, Charles B. *Church and State.* New York, 1955.

Kirk, Kenneth E., ed. *The Apostolic Ministry.* London, 1947.

Klingberg, Frank J. *Anglican Humanitarianism in Colonial New York.* Philadelphia, 1940.

Knauff, Theodore C. *A History of the Society of the Sons of Saint George.* Philadelphia, 1923.

Knollenberg, Bernhard. *Origin of the American Revolution: 1759–1776.* New York, 1965.

Koch, G. Adolf. *Republican Religion.* Gloucester, Mass., 1964.

Konkle, Burton A. *Thomas Willing and the First American Financial System.* Philadelphia, 1937.

Lawrence, William. *An Historical Address at the Two Hundredth Anniversary of the Boston Episcopal Charitable Society.* Boston, 1924.

Lee, Sidney, ed. *Dictionary of National Biography.* 22 vols. New York, 1898.

Lefler, Hugh T., and Albert R. Newsome. *The History of a Southern State.* Chapel Hill, 1954.

Liemohn, Edwin. *The Organ and Choir in Protestant Worship.* Philadelphia, 1968.

Loveland, Clara. *The Critical Years.* Greenwich, Conn., 1956.

Lundin, Leonard. *Cockpit of the Revolution.* Princeton, 1940.

McCormick, Richard P. *New Jersey from Colony to State.* Princeton, 1964.

McLaughlin, Andrew C. *The Confederation and the Constitution 1783–1789.* New York, 1905.

Main, Jackson T. *The Social Structure of Revolutionary America*. Princeton, 1965.

Main, Jackson T. *Sovereign States*, New York, 1973.

Malone, Dumas, ed. *Dictionary of American Biiography*. 22 vols. New York, 1933.

Malone, Henry T. *The Episcopal Church in Georgia 1733–1957*. Atlanta: The Protestant Episcopal Church in the Diocese of Atlanta, 1960.

Manross, William W. *The Fulham Papers in the Lambeth Palace*. Oxford: The Clarendon Press, 1965.

Manross, William W. *A History of the American Episcopal Church*. New York, 1950.

Mason, A. J. *The Church of England and Episcopacy*. Cambridge, 1914.

Maxson, Charles H. *The Great Awakening in the Middle Colonies*. Chicago, 1920.

Mereness, Newton D. *Maryland as a Proprietary Province*. New York, 1901.

Merrens, Harry R. *Colonial North Carolina in the Eighteenth Century*. Chapel Hill, 1964.

Meyer, Jacob C. *Church and State in Massachusetts 1740 to 1833*. Cleveland, 1930.

Miller, John C. *Origins of the American Revolution*. Boston, 1943.

Morais, Herbert M. *Deism in Eighteenth Century America*. New York, 1934.

Morison, Samuel E. et al. *The Growth of the American Republic*. 2 vols. New York, 1969.

Morton, Richard L., ed. *The Present State of Virginia*. Chapel Hill, 1956.

Norton, Mary B. *The British-Americans: The Loyalist Exiles in England 1774–1789*. Boston, 1972.

Pantin, W. A. *The English Church in the Fourteenth Century*. Cambridge: At the University Press, 1955.

Parsons, E. L. and H. J. Jones, *The American Prayer Book*. New York, 1937.

Perry, William S. *Bishop Seabury and Bishop Provoost*. Privately Printed, 1862.

Phillimore, Robert. *The Ecclesiastical Law of the Church of England*. 2 vols. London, 1895.

Poole, Austin L., ed. *Medieval England* 2 vols.; Oxford, England, 1958.

Pratt, John W. *Religion, Politics, and Diversity: The Church-State Theme in New York History*. Ithaca, 1967.

Purcell, Richard J., *Connecticut in Transition: 1775–1818*. Middletown, Conn., 1963.

Ramsay, David. *The History of the Independent or Congregational Church in Charleston, S.C.* Philadelphia, 1815.

Rightmyer, Nelson, *The Anglican Church in Delaware.* Philadelphia, 1947.

———. *Maryland's Established Church.* Baltimore, 1956.

Robbins, Caroline, *The Eighteenth Century Commonwealthman.* Cambridge, 1959.

Rogers, Jr., George C. *Church and State in Eighteenth Century South Carolina.* Charleston, 1959.

Roper, Charles L. *The Church and Private Schools of North Carolina.* Greensboro, 1898.

Rose, Harold W. *The Colonial Houses of Worship in America.* New York, 1963.

Rothermund, Dietmary. *The Layman's Progress.* Philadelphia, 1961.

Savelle, Max. *Seeds of Liberty: The Genesis of the American Mind.* Seattle, 1948.

Schuyler, Hamilton. *A History of Saint Michael's Church.* Princeton, 1926.

Singer, Charles G. *South Carolina in the Confederation.* Philadelphia, 1941.

Sirmans, M. Eugene. *Colonial South Carolina: A Political History 1663–1763.* Chapel Hill, 1966.

Skeats, Herbert S. *History of the Free Churches of England 1688–1891.* London, 1891.

Smith, W. Roy. *South Carolina as a Royal Province, 1719–1776.* New York, 1903.

Snow, Louis F. *The College Curriculum in the United States.* New York, 1907.

Steiner, Bruce. *Samuel Seabury: A Study in the High Church Tradition.* University of Ohio Press, 1971.

Stokes, Anson P. *Church and State in the United States.* 3 vols. New York, 1950.

Stowe, Walter H. *More Lay Readers Than Clergy!* Lebanon, Pa., 1954.

Strickland, Reba C. *Religion and the State of Georgia in the Eighteenth Century.* New York, 1939.

Sweet, William W. *Religion on the American Frontier, 1783–1840; Vol. IV The Methodist.* Chicago, 1946.

Sydnor, Charles S. *Gentlemen Freeholders.* Chapel Hill, 1952.

Sykes, Norman. *Church and State in England in the Eighteenth Century.* Cambridge: At the University Press, 1934.

———. *From Sheldon to Secker.* Cambridge: At the University Press, 1959.

————. *Old Priest and New Presbyter*. Cambridge: At the University Press, 1956.

Thayer, Theodore, *Pennsylvania Politics and the Growth of Democracy 1740–1776*. Harrisburg, 1953.

Thomas, Albert S. *A Historical Account of the Protestant Episcopal Church in South Carolina*. Columbia, 1957.

Thompson, Robert E. *A History of the Presbyterian Churches in the United States*. New York, 1895.

Tiffany, Charles C. *A History of the Protestant Episcopal Church in the United States of America*. New York, 1895.

Trinterud, Leonard J. *The Forming of an American Tradition*. Philadelphia, 1949.

Twelves, J. Wesley. *A History of the Diocese of Pennsylvania of the Protestant Episcopal Church U.S.A. 1784–1968*. Philadelphia, 1969.

United States Bureau of Census, Historical Statistics of the United States, Colonial Times to 1957. Washington, D. C., 1960.

Utley, G. B. *The Life and Times of Thomas John Claggett*. Chicago, 1913.

Van Tyne, Claude H. *The Loyalists in the American Revolution*. New York, 1902.

Wallace, D. D. *Constitutional History of South Carolina: 1725 to 1775*. Abbeville, S. C., 1899.

Wand, J. W. C. *Anglicanism in History and Today*. New York, 1965.

Watson, J. Steven. *The Reign of George III 1760–1815*. Oxford: The Clarendon Press, 1960.

Webb, Sidney, and Beatrice Webb. *English Local Government from the Revolution to the Municipal Corporation Act: The Parish and the County*. London, 1924.

Webber, F. R. *A History of Preaching in Britain and America*. Milwaukee, Wis., 1952.

Wells, Guy F. *Parish Education in Colonial Virginia*. New York, 1923.

Werline, Albert W. *Problems of Church and State in Maryland*. South Lancaster, Mass., 1948.

Wescott, Thompson. *History of Philadelphia 1609–1829*. 32 vols. Philadelphia, 1913.

Williams, Basil. *The Whig Supremacy*. Oxford: The Clarendon Press, 1939.

Williams, George W. *St. Michael's Charleston, 1751–1951*. Columbia, 1951.

Wilson, James G. *The Centennial History of the Protestant Episcopal Church in the Diocese of New York 1785–1885*. New York, 1886.

Wood, Gordon S. *The Creation of the American Republic 1776–1787*. New York, 1972.

Wright, Louis B. *The Cultural Life of the American Colonies 1607–1763.* New York, 1957.

Zabriskie, Alexander C. *Anglican Evangelicalism.* Philadelphia, 1943.

Zeichner, Oscar. *Connecticut's Years of Controversy 1750–1776.* Chapel Hill, 1949.

ARTICLES AND PERIODICALS

Addison, Daniel D. "The Growth of the Layman's Power in the Episcopal Church." *Papers of American Society of Church History,* III (New York, 1912), 65–77.

Andrews, W. G. "Parentage of American High Churchmanship." *The Protestant Episcopal Review* (1899), 196–221.

Babcock, Mary K. D. "Difficulties and Dangers of Pre-Revolutionary Ordination." *HMPEC,* XII (1943), 225–41.

Baldwin, Simeon E. "The American Jurisdiction of the Bishop of London in Colonial Times." *Proceedings of the American Antiquarian Society,* New Series, XIII (1899), 179–222.

Bennett, J. H. "English Bishops and Imperial Jurisdiction." *HMPEC,* XXXII (1963), 175–88.

Brown, Lawrence L. "Henry Compton 1632–1713." *HMPEC,* XXV (1956), 50–65.

Brydon, G. MacLaren. "David Griffith, 1742–1789, First Bishop-Elect of Virginia." *HMPEC,* IX (1940), 194–230.

———. "James City Parish in Virginia." *HMPEC,* XI (1942), 65–82.

———. "James Blair, Commissary." *HMPEC,* XIV (1945), 85–100.

———. "New Light on the Origins of the Method of Electing Bishops Adopted by the American Episcopal Church." *HMPEC,* XIX (1950), 202–13.

———. "The Origin of the Rights of the Laity in the American Episcopal Church." *HMPEC,* XII (1943), 313–38.

———. "A Venture in Christian Education." *HMPEC,* XV (1946), 30–40.

Clem, Alan L. "The Vestries and Local Government in Colonial Maryland." *HMPEC,* XXXI (1962), 220–29.

Conkin, Paul. "The Church Establishment in North Carolina, 1765–1776." *NCHR,* XXXII (1955), 1–30.

DeMille, George E. "One Man Seminary." *HMPEC,* XXXVIII (1969), 373–79.

Douglas, Charles W. "Early Hymnology of the American Episcopal Church." *HMPEC,* X (1941), 202–218.

Ellis, III, Joseph J. "Anglicans in Connecticut, 1725–1750: The Conversion of the Missionaries." *NEQ* (March 1971), 66–81.

Fryer, C. E. "Numerical Decline of Dissent." *AJT,* XVII (1913), 235–40.

Goodwin, Gerald J. "The Anglican Reaction to the Great Awakening." *HMPEC,* XXXV (1966), 243–71.

Goodwin, Gerald J. "Christianity, Civilization, and the Savage: The Anglican Mission to the American Indian." *HMPEC,* XLII (1973), 93–110.

Greene, Jack P. "Foundations of Political Power in the Virginia House of Burgesses, 1720–1776." *WMQ,* 3d. Ser., XVI (1959), 485–506.

Hartdagen, Gerald E. "The Anglican Vestry in Colonial Maryland: A Study in Corporate Responsibility." *HMPEC,* XL (1971), 315–35; 461–79.

Hartdagen, Gerald E. "The Anglican Vestry in Colonial Maryland: Organizational Structure and Problems." *HMPEC,* XXXVIII (1969), 349–60.

Klingberg, Frank J. "Sir William Johnson and the Society for the Propogation of the Gospel (1749–1774)." *HMPEC,* VIII (1939), 25–40.

Lamb, George W., comp. "Clergymen Licensed to the American Colonies by the Bishops of London: 1745–1781." *HMPEC,* XIII (1944), 128–43.

McCaul, Robert L. "Whitefield's Bethesda College Projects and Other Major Attempts to Found Colonial Colleges." *GHQ,* 44 (1960), Part II, 383–86.

Malone, Michael T. "Sketches of the Anglican Clergy Who Served in North Carolina During the Period, 1765–1776." *HMPEC,* XXXIX (1970), 399–438.

Manross, William W. "The Interstate Meetings and General Conventions of 1784, 1785, and 1789." *HMPEC* (1939), 257–80.

Middleton, Arthur P. "The Colonial Virginia Parish." *HMPEC,* XL (1971), 431–46.

Mills, Sr., Frederick V. "Anglican Expansion in Colonial America." *HMPEC,* XXXIX (1970), 315–24.

————."The Internal Anglican Controversy Over An American Episcopate, 1763–1775." *HMPEC,* XLIV (1975), 257–76.

————. "The Protestant Episcopal Churches in the United States 1783–1789: Suspended Animation or Remarkable Recovery?" *HMPEC,* XLVI (1977), 151–70.

Norwood, Percy V. "Constitutional Developments Since 1789." *HMPEC,* VIII (1939), 281–95.

Pennington, Edgar L. "Colonial Clergy Conventions." *HMPEC,* VIII (1939), 178–218.

Perry, William S. "The Church in Georgia." *The Church Review,* XLVI (1885), 1–15.

Pilcher, George W. "The Pamphlet War on the Proposed Virginia Anglican Episcopate. 1767–1775." *HMPEC,* XXX (1961), 266–79.

Pilcher, George W. "Virginia Newspapers and the Dispute over the Proposed Colonial Episcopate." *Historian,* XXXIII (1960), 98–113.

Rightmyer, Nelson. "The Anglican Church in Maryland: Factors Contributory to the American Revolution." *Church History,* XIX (1950), 187–98.

Salomon, Richard G. "British Legislation and the American Episcopacy." *HMPEC,* XX (1951), 287–94.

Seabrook, John H. "The Establishment of Anglicanism in Colonial Maryland." *HMPEC,* XXXIX (1970), 278–93.

Sosin, Jack M. "The Proposal in the Pre-Revolutionary Decade for Establishing Anglican Bishops in the Colonies." *JEH,* XIII (1962), 76–84.

Spangenberg, Bradford. "Vestrymen in the House of Burgesses; Protection of Local Vestry Autonomy During James Blair's Term as Commissary (1690–1743)." *HMPEC,* XXXII (1963), 77–99.

Spangler, E. W. "Memoirs of Major John Clark, of York County, Pennsylvania." *PMHB,* 20 (1896), 77–86.

Steiner, Bruce E. "New England Anglicanism: A Genteel Faith." *WMQ,* 3d. Ser., XXVII (1970), 123–35.

Stowe, Walter H., ed. "The Autobiography of Bishop William White." *HMPEC,* XXII (1935), 379–432.

Stowe, Walter H., ed. "The Clergy of the Episcopal Church in 1785." *HMPEC,* XX (1951), 243–77.

Stowe, Walter H. "The Corporation for the Relief of Widows and Children of Clergymen." *HMPEC,* III (1934), 19–33.

Stowe, Walter H. "The Scottish Episcopal Succession and the Validity of Bishop Seabury's Orders." *HMPEC,* IX (1940), 322–48.

Stowe, Walter H. "The State or Diocesan Conventions of the War and Post-War Periods." *HMPEC,* VIII (1939), 220–56.

Stowe, Walter H. "A Study in Conscience: Some Aspects of the Relations of the Clergy to the State." *HMPEC,* XIX (1950), 301–23.

Sweet, William W. "The Role of the Anglicans in the American Revolution." *Huntington Library Quarterly,* XI (1947), 50–71.

Sykes, Norman. "The Duke of New Castle as Ecclesiastical Minister." *EHR,* LVI (January), 59–84.

Thomas, A. S. "A Sketch of the History of the Church in South Carolina." *HMPEC*, IV (1935), 1–12.

Weaver, Glenn. "Anglican-Congregationalist Tensions in Pre-Revolutionary Connecticut." *HMPEC*, XXVI (1957), 275–85.

Weaver, Glenn. "Benjamin Franklin and the Pennsylvania Germans." *WMQ*, 3d. Ser., 14 (1957), 536–59.

West, Edward N. "The Music of Old Trinity." *HMPEC*, XVI (1947), 102–3.

DISSERTATIONS

Austin, Alan Kenneth. "The Role of the Anglican Church and Its Clergy in the Political Life of Colonial Virginia." Ph.D. dissertation, University of Georgia, 1969.

Goodwin, Gerald J. "The Anglican Middle Way in Early Eighteenth Century America: Anglican Religious Thought in the American Colonies, 1702–1750." Ph.D. dissertation, University of Wisconsin, 1965.

Gunderson, Joan R. "The Anglican Ministry in Virginia 1723–1776: A Study of Social Class." Ph.D. dissertation, University of Notre Dame, 1972.

Owens, James K. "The Virginia Vestry: A Study in the Decline of a Ruling Class." Ph.D. dissertation, Princeton, 1947.

Painter, Jr., Borden W. "The Anglican Vestry in Colonial America." Ph.D. dissertation, Yale University, 1965.

Index

357